The Visual Basic .NET Coach

Jeff Salvage

DREXEL UNIVERSITY

Boston San Francisco New York
London Toronto Sydney Tokyo Singapore Madrid
Mexico City Munich Paris Cape Town Hong Kong Montreal

Executive Editor	Susan Hartman Sullivan
Executive Marketing Manager	Michael Hirsch
Senior Project Manager	Mary Clare McEwing
Project Editor	Emily Genaway
Production Services	Adriana Lavergne/Argosy Publishing
Composition	Susannah Cahalane
Copyeditor	Laura Gabler
Technical Art	Craig Witte
Proofreader	Kim Cofer
Interior Design	Gina Kolenda and Joyce Cosentino Wells
Cover Design	Night & Day Design and Joyce Cosentino Wells
Design Manager	Gina Kolenda
Prepress and Manufacturing	Caroline Fell

Access the latest information about Addison-Wesley titles from our World Wide Web site:
http://www.aw.com/cs

Many of the designations used by manufacturers and sellers to distinguish their products are claimed as trademarks. Where those designations appear in this book, and Addison-Wesley was aware of a trademark claim, the designations have been printed in initial caps or all caps.

The programs and applications presented in this book have been included for their instructional value. They have been tested with care, but are not guaranteed for any particular purpose. The publisher does not offer any warranties or representations, nor does it accept any liabilities with respect to the programs or applications.

Library of Congress Cataloging-in-Publication Data

Salvage, Jeff.
    The Visual Basic .NET coach / Jeff Salvage.
        p. cm.
    ISBN 0-321-11350-0 (pbk.: alk. paper)
1. Microsoft Visual BASIC. 2. BASIC (Computer program language). I. Title.

QA76.73.B3 S246 2002
005.2'768—dc21
2002071202
CIP

12345678910-WC-040302

This book is dedicated to my very first computer student, my Mom.

PREFACE

The *Visual Basic .NET Coach* builds on an approach that I introduced in *The C++ Coach* and *The Visual Basic Coach*, and applies it to the exciting new world of Visual Basic .NET. The book's premise is the same one that successful coaches have long used: The more you practice a skill, the better your mastery of that skill becomes.

Given the huge installed base of Visual Basic 6.0 developers, Visual Basic .NET is sure to have a large following. This new version of Visual Basic .NET is much more than a minor update; it is a huge departure from the development environment of version 6.0. Object-oriented development inundates every aspect of development with Visual Basic .NET. More than ever, a textbook is needed that targets the student who is learning programming for the first time or wants to learn the Visual Basic .NET language in a friendlier manner.

Target Audience

Although I was trained as a computer science major, I have done most of my consulting in the Information Systems field. While some computer scientists are striving to become hard-core applications developers who will write the latest operating system from Microsoft, many more programmers are studying to become the information systems professionals of tomorrow. A computer science professional most likely will go on to developing operating systems and application programs like Microsoft Word or Excel.

However, information systems professionals may move on to develop database applications or become network administrators or even database administrators.

The "Coach" series of textbooks are designed specifically for Information Systems professionals. Their needs are unique in that they require non-mathematical, non-scientific examples that relate to topics they already know. Therefore, *The Visual Basic .NET Coach* is comprised of business, humorous, and sports examples so that these professionals can easily relate to the problems they are trying to solve.

Whether you intend to program for the rest of your life, are required to take a course in school, or wish to merely gain an appreciation for programming, this book can help you. It is specifically designed to be a standalone volume for students who are not majoring in computer science and learning Visual Basic .NET. It also may function as a bridge between your current level of understanding and more advanced Visual Basic .NET texts.

Author's Approach

Because the audience for *The Visual Basic .NET Coach* is different from that of most programming texts, I have taken a unique approach by applying many techniques learned from coaching athletes to the teaching of computer programming. I have competed as an international athlete representing the United States and currently am coaching Olympic hopefuls in the sport of race walking. In many ways, the teaching of race walking is similar to that of computer programming.

Race walking is a complex sport that requires combining Olympian endurance with a very complicated technique. In order to master it, one must expend a great deal of practice and attention to the details of proper technique. Coaches do not start athletes by sending them into competition on the first day of practice. Instead, they usually require them to repeat drills over and over again until they have mastered the techniques of the sport.

Similarly, instead of beginning with problem solving, this text teaches sound Visual Basic .NET syntactical fundamentals first. While learning the basic building blocks of Visual Basic .NET, you will perform programming drills repeatedly until you understand the fundamentals and subtleties of Visual Basic .NET. These skills will be reinforced with clearly defined problems and solutions that focus on problem solving. First a problem is defined, then the issues of solving the problem are discussed, and finally the solution is provided.

The many object-oriented aspects of Visual Basic .NET are introduced in a carefully built-up presentation. You will first study simple objects like a form, button, or text box, and then become comfortable with their operation before defining your own. As your programming skills increase, you will grapple with more difficult topics, such as advanced object-oriented techniques, thereby allowing you to master the earlier concepts before trying to tackle the idiosyncrasies of inheritance and overloading methods.

This book is not intended to be a complete reference for Visual Basic .NET. The language and object model are far too large to do everything justice. Instead, throughout the text we will present the most important features of Visual Basic .NET, explain their syntax, and present drills that explore the subtleties of the syntax. We supplement these drills with real-world examples of programming problems and build upon the knowledge gained from these drills. Because there are so many options in Visual Basic, topics deemed optional are added at the end of each chapter in a Coach's Corner so that more advanced students can learn them, while students looking for a basic understanding of the language can skip over them. This approach contrasts with that of many other texts, which try to be complete reference manuals instead of instructional textbooks. They introduce too many constructs of Visual Basic .NET before solidifying a mastery of the most required Visual Basic .NET syntax.

While writing the proper programs is important, so is motivating the group and people around you to get the job done. Whether it is breaking up the monotony of a long race walk or the dryness of a computer text with some light humor, the idea is the same. *The Visual Basic .NET Coach* finds different ways to motivate and amuse you as you read through the text.

Scope of Coverage

The Visual Basic .NET Coach covers Visual Basic .NET as if you have never learned a programming language before. Starting with a brief introduction to computer languages and where Visual Basic .NET fits in, I get students rolling immediately with an example that shows why Visual Basic .NET has the word Visual in its title. Students are introduced to the development environment and how to create an application with images and text.

Once a basic understanding of the environment is mastered, a discussion of fundamental programming constructs—variables, operators, conditional statements, functions, objects, and loops—follows. These constructs are used to develop programs that solve relatively simple, but useful problems. Interwoven between the presentation of these constructs is the introduction of many of the basic controls used regularly by Visual Basic .NET developers. Instead of just listing these controls, examples are given that motivate the benefit of one control over the other, based on the goal of the application.

Once students have gained a firm understanding of the basics, we concentrate on additional features of Visual Basic .NET such as arrays, structures, files, and the advanced concepts of object-oriented development like inheritance and polymorphism. While many introductory classes in Visual Basic .NET do not cover extensive advanced topics, we have made it easy to select the ones that you wish to add to your course. Databases are covered in a single chapter explaining how to access data stored in a database using the built-in wizards and given an introduction to SQL. Also included are sections on graphic routines, menus, and multiform applications.

Pedagogy
Drills

We all know that you cannot learn to program by merely reading a textbook in a narrative format. *The Visual Basic .NET Coach* provides about 100 drills that provide students with immediate feedback on their understanding of what they just learned. The drills are presented as questions, and their complete solutions with detailed explanations are included at the end of each chapter.

The following is a sample of a few drills from Chapter 4 on conditional statements. It shows how students can get immediate feedback with slight variations of the same problem, so they can master all aspects of the concept they are learning.

DRILL 4.8

Assume that the code for the previous example was instead coded as follows:

```
Private Sub btnIfElse_Click(...
        Dim sngPurchasePrice As Single

        sngPurchasePrice = Val(txtInput.Text)

        If (sngPurchasePrice > 100) Then
            lblOutput.Text = (sngPurchasePrice * 0.05).ToString()
```

(continues)

DRILL 4.8 (continued)

```
        ElseIf (sngPurchasePrice > 500) Then
            lblOutput.Text = (sngPurchasePrice * 0.1).ToString()
        Else
            lblOutput.Text = "NO DISCOUNT"
        End If
End Sub
```

What do you think would be contained in lblOutput:

1 If the user enters 600.00 in the txtInput text box?
2 If the user enters 250.00 in the txtInput text box?
3 If the user enters 50.00 in the txtInput text box?

The answers are available at the end of each chapter:

Drill 4.8
With 600.00 Entered by the User

When the program is executed and the button is clicked, the If statement is evaluated. If the user enters 600.00, then the If statement evaluates the expression by comparing the value entered to 100. Therefore, the conditional expression will evaluate to True. This causes all the statements until the ElseIf to be executed. Therefore, the purchase price is multiplied by .05 and the result is converted to a String. So the value "30" is placed in the label lblOutput. Since the conditional expression in the If statement evaluated to True, none of the statements after the ElseIf or Else statements and before the End If statement are executed. Note this is not what you wanted to have happen! Because you evaluated the condition comparing the value to 100 first, it will evaluate to True when you really want the expression > 500 to evaluate to True. The order you evaluate your conditions can make a difference.

With 250.00 Entered by the User

When the program is executed and the button is clicked, the If statement is evaluated. If the user enters 250.00, then the If statement evaluates the expression by comparing the value entered to 100. Therefore, the conditional expression will evaluate to True. This causes all the statements until the ElseIf to be executed. Therefore, the purchase price is multiplied by .05 and the result is converted to a String. So the value "12.5" is placed in the label lblOutput. Since the conditional expression in the If statement evaluated to True, none of the statements after the ElseIf or Else statements and before the End If statement are executed.

With 50.00 Entered by the User

Finally, if the user enters a value less than or equal to 100, neither the If or ElseIf conditional expressions evaluate to True. Therefore, the statements after the Else statement and before the End If statement are executed.

So the text "NO DISCOUNT" is placed in the label lblOutput.

Tips

Throughout the chapters, tips highlight key programming issues.

 COACH'S TIP

A Long variable can hold any value that an Integer variable can, but not vice versa.

Warnings

Commonly made mistakes are highlighted with a warning box.

 COACH'S WARNING

When you list a range of numbers for a `Case` statement, you must list the smaller number first.

End-of-chapter Material

Key Terms

At the end of each chapter all new terms introduced within the chapter are listed with a condensed definition of the term.

Case Studies

A case study in each chapter focuses on the skills developed in the chapter in a practical real-world example. Throughout most of the text, our case study focuses on a business owner creating a system that will process payroll for his company. It is simple to follow and clear. We provide the problem statement, discuss its solution, and then present the coded solution. Such immediate reinforcement of the skills learned in the chapter greatly improves retention.

Coach's Corner

At the end of each chapter, optional topics are included to round out the student's knowledge of the topics introduced in each chapter. These topics may be important to the mastery of Visual Basic .NET, but may not be timely in an academic discussion of a topic.

Additional Exercises

Finally, each chapter is followed with a series of short-answer-style questions and programming assignments for students to practice what they have learned in the chapter.

Different Course Options

This book is designed for a one- or two-semester introductory programming sequence for non-computer science majors. In general, each chapter builds on your programming arsenal and is ideally designed to follow sequentially. However, the text was designed with the idea that many topics are optional. Many of these optional topics are presented at the end of each chapter in the Coach's Corners. These topics can be added or removed without adding dependency issues.

The biggest issue with determining the order in which to teach Visual Basic .NET is when to teach objects. The chapters have been carefully designed so that objects can be moved later or the advanced object topics earlier.

- ◆ Chapters 1–4 are fairly mandatory for any programming sequence. You then have the option of continuing in order or moving chapters around.
- ◆ Chapter 5 on subroutines and functions can be moved after objects are introduced in Chapter 6.
- ◆ Chapter 6 on the basic declaration of objects can be moved before Chapter 5 or after Chapter 7.
- ◆ Chapter 7 on repetition can be moved before Chapter 6 and, with a little tweaking, before Chapter 5 as well.

◆ Chapter 8 on arrays, collections, and structures can be moved as late as desired.
◆ Chapter 9 on files can also be moved as late as desired.
◆ Chapter 10 on advanced object-oriented techniques can be moved up right after the basic objects chapter.
◆ Chapter 11 on database concepts can be taught as soon as Chapters 5, 6, and 7 have been covered.
◆ Chapter 12 on advanced Visual Basic .NET topics can be taught as desired. Many of these topics may or may not be covered and can be added to enhance other topics.

Many of the additional chapters can be skipped, based on the preferences of the instructor.

To the Student

So you're taking a computer course. Odds are you'll either love it or hate it. It's the job of this text to help you through it. Regardless of why you are taking the course, you need to learn the material presented by your teacher. If you follow my advice, you will make the process a lot easier. This book is designed to be interactive. DO NOT just read the drills. Try them. You will learn much more that way. While some of the examples are dry and simply there to help with your mastery of the Visual Basic .NET syntax, many more are colorful statements from things I enjoy. The sports theme shows up in many examples, but I have also included many names and quotes from movies. Try to see if you can figure them out. (Hopefully, I am not dating myself too badly.)

Instructor Supplements

The following supplements are available on-line for qualified instructors only. Please contact your Addison-Wesley representative for information.

◆ **Instructor's Manual**—includes complete answers to the exercises.
◆ **Test Bank** in powerful test generator software—includes a wealth of free response, multiple choice, and true/false type questions.
◆ **Lab Manual**—more than 20 labs, each with a complete step-by-step solution including many screen captures, to accompany the topic progression in the text.
◆ **CourseCompass**—A dynamic, interactive online course management tool powered by Blackboard, CourseCompass provides flexible tools and rich content resources that enable instructors to easily and effectively customize online course materials to suit their needs. Now instructors can track and analyze student performance on an array of Internet activities. Please contact your Addison-Wesley representative for more details.

Student Supplements

Please visit www.aw.com/cssupport for the following resources.

◆ **Source Code** to all programs.
◆ **PowerPoint** slides which include programs and art from the text.

Acknowledgments

There are many more people's efforts that go into the creation of a textbook other than the author's. Obvious thanks go to my editors Susan Hartman Sullivan and Mary Clare

McEwing, without whose efforts *The Visual Basic .NET Coach* would not have reached publication; Patty Mahtani, Emily Genaway, Daniel Rausch, and Adriana Lavergne for their assistance in the production cycle of the text; and Michael Hirsch for making sure the world knows about this text. Additional thanks go to Tim Burke, who helped me proof the text, as well as acting as a sounding board for many examples and to Steve Davis, my technical reviewer.

Along the way many people helped with the many stages my manuscript went through. Additional thanks go to my reviewers:

Tammy L. Ashley, *New Hampshire Community Technical College at Manchester*
Paula Baxter, *San Juan College*
Chris Beaumont, *Queens College*
Dana Johnson, *North Dakota State University*
Bruce W. Mielke, *University of Wisconsin, Green Bay*
Larry Press, *California State University, Dominguez Hills*
Steve Robischon
Alfred J. Seita, *Kapiolani Community College*
Richard Southern, *El Paso Community College*
Preston Vander Weyst, *Edmonds Community College*
Edward J. Williams, *University of Michigan*
Jeff Yeley, *Houston Community College*
David Zolzer, *Northwestern State University*

Special thanks go to Jim McKeown, Dakota State University, who helped improve the object chapters.

Special thanks also go to Dr. Nira Herrmann and Pat Henry, who continue to make teaching at Drexel a pleasure.

BRIEF TABLE OF CONTENTS

CONTENTS

CHAPTER 8
Arrays, Collections, and Structures   313

CHAPTER 9
Files   347

CHAPTER 10
Advanced Object-Oriented Programming   377

CHAPTER 11
Introduction to Database Concepts   401

The Visual Basic .NET Coach

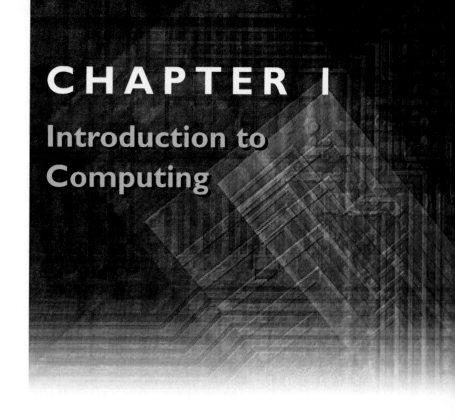

CHAPTER 1
Introduction to Computing

It wasn't that long ago that people thought of computers as tools for the scientist or something out of a science fiction movie. Times have certainly changed. Today our daily lives are inundated with computerized devices wherever we go. We do not feel complete without our cell phone or access to email and an Internet connection, and the list goes on and on.

A scant five years ago, I gave a talk at a non-computer-related conference where I told people that an email address would soon be as commonplace as a fax number. They snickered at the concept. Two years later, at the same conference, almost everyone in the room had one. Technology has changed dramatically and continues to change at an ever-increasing pace that seemingly has no end. All of this technology starts with people writing computer programs. So don't get left behind. Start learning Visual Basic .NET today, because playing "catch-up" is extremely difficult.

1.1 Types of Languages and Why They Are Useful

One can argue about when the first computer was created. Some people consider electronic computers like ENIAC (1940s) as the first computer, while others will point to looms that could be configured to print different patterns as the first form of computer. What all of these early machines had in common was that they required a method of instruction to operate.

Today modern computers get their instructions from **programming languages**. A programming language is an agreed-upon format of symbols that enables a programmer to instruct a computer to perform certain predefined tasks. Symbols are used to communicate a programmer's intent to a computer; how understandable these symbols are determines the level of the programming language.

Some languages are written in an English-style prose that the programmer finds very readable, but the language is more difficult for the computer to understand. These languages are often referred to as **high-level languages**. In contrast, other languages are easy for the computer to understand but very difficult for the programmer to comprehend, test, and debug. These languages are known as **low-level languages**. Just as there are many different computer applications, so are there many different programming languages. What programming language you choose depends largely on the goal of the application you are developing.

The Development of Programming Languages

The earliest computers' programming languages were quite minimal. To instruct these computers to accomplish tasks, early computer programmers entered a series of numbers by manually flipping switches. Programming these machines was also difficult because these numbers were not entered in the common decimal form but in an encoding scheme called binary numbers. Binary numbers are an encoding scheme where values are represented by a series of 1's and 0's. By combining 1's and 0's, different numbers can be represented. These machines were extremely difficult to program and thus were used only to solve simple problems that were repeated over and over again.

It didn't take long for computer scientists to realize that in order for computers to be more useful, they required a programming environment that was a bit more robust than manually flipping switches.

Two major leaps forward were the creation of an **assembly language** and the introduction of **punch cards**. An assembly language utilizes a series of mnemonics to represent commonly used instructions as well as a decimal notation instead of the cryptic binary format previously used. The development of an assembly language allowed computer scientists to focus on solving a problem instead of wasting time encoding their solution into a binary number format.

Another milestone was the creation of punch cards to facilitate the entry and storage of these programs. A punch card was a cardboard card in which a machine popped holes, thereby allowing the representation of an instruction and its operators. These punch cards could be assembled into a program by piling the cards in the proper order and placing them in the card reader to be read in sequence. Once the program was entered into the computer, the punch cards allowed the program to be executed again without having to reenter the entire program.

Although punch cards and the associated assembly language provided a monumental leap forward, they still posed immense problems when dealing with nontrivial programs.

One big issue was that an assembly language program written for one computer system would not work on another computer system. This meant that when your company upgraded its computer system, many of your applications would require rewriting. Time would also be wasted learning the new assembly language required for the new computer system.

The assembly languages available were easy for the computer to understand and better than dealing with the 1's and 0's of a pure machine language. However, they did not map themselves well to real-world problems. Two popular computer languages were developed to combat these problems: **COBOL** and **FORTRAN**. These languages were developed to meet the different needs of computer users. COBOL, which stands for Common Business Oriented Language, was used primarily for business processing. For example, it was used to write programs such as handling a company's payroll or maintaining a company's inventory. In contrast, FORTRAN, which stands for formula translator, was designed primarily to perform mathematical calculations extremely quickly.

These languages were a major improvement over the existing assembly language. They reduced the time required to develop applications and raised the level of the machine to the programmer. By providing built-in commands for commonly used operations, the language allowed programmers to solve their problems by writing less, and more understandable, code.

Aside from reducing the time it would take to solve a problem, another big advantage of these two early languages was that standards were developed so that the language was the same from computer system to computer system. This meant that programs written for one computer system could be run on another computer system without having to be rewritten—an enormous improvement.

Although individuals wrote these programming languages so they were more understandable, they required translation into a language the computer system could understand. As new computer systems were developed, they included a translator for these standard languages that would convert the standard language into a language the computer could understand.

Controversy bubbled up as to whether these languages produced programs that were slower to execute than handwritten assembly language programs. While one camp of computer system developers was trying to improve the efficiency of the machine code generated by these new languages, other camps were developing new and "better" computer languages. The quest for the Holy Grail of computer languages began. Almost with a religious fervor, developers created languages of all sorts to deal with business, mathematical, and artificial intelligence problems. This quest eventually evolved into trying to develop a single universal language that would meet all users' needs.

The quest for a single programming language cycles into popularity from time to time. One of the most ambitious attempts was PL/1. It was IBM's attempt at combining the best of FORTRAN and COBOL. What IBM achieved was a language that many feel was very complex and not as useful as either FORTRAN or COBOL for their respective tasks. This is a lesson that we should all learn from the history of technology. One programming language is not ideal for all situations.

As computer technology, capacity, and speed increased, the need for better and more diverse languages developed. Even teaching languages such as Pascal were developed, which were only intended to teach sound programming principles and not intended for business or scientific applications.

More Recent Programming Languages

While many of these languages addressed the needs of the programmers writing applications, they didn't address the needs of the programmers developing the operating systems of the day. Today we are familiar with operating systems such as Microsoft Windows and UNIX, which are written for more than one type of computer system. For example, when Microsoft wants to develop a version of Windows for another computer platform, Microsoft can translate the operating system by using a program that will compile the operating system on the new computer platform.

The most popular of these languages was **C**. Because of C's popularity, it became much more than a language used for developing operating systems. Programmers quickly started to use C to write applications for many different needs. The programs produced were efficient and rivaled the performance of handwritten assembly language programs. Indeed, with today's efficient compilers and complex computer systems, the C compiler often generates machine code that runs faster than hand-developed assembly language.

As C increased in popularity and a large group of reusable programs were developed, new issues arose. How could programs be reused more effectively?

A new methodology called object-oriented programming was developed for creating reusable programs. The concept was to create an entity that closely wrapped a computer program and the data on which it operated. It would only allow programmers access to the data in ways intended by the original programmer, so that programmers with less knowledge could not damage the data.

Languages like Smalltalk were developed around this approach, but more important, programmers wanted to be able to leverage their existing programs, and therefore, object-oriented extensions to languages that previously existed were developed. Object-oriented Pascal and **C++** were some of these. Because they were not created from scratch, the object-oriented extensions sometimes required kludgey language syntax and led to unnecessarily complicated programs.

Recently, a new language has come on the scene: **Java**. Java is an object-oriented language that is very similar to C++. It has many of the same features as C++ but without the awkwardness of some of the syntax. Additionally, Java is made so that it can be run on any computer without having to recompile your code for that machine. This is a huge advantage when dealing with Internet-based applications, but it has disadvantages as well. Some of the biggest problems with Java are that its performance is much slower than that of C++ and its simpler syntax removes some of the power C++ gives the programmer. It also is inherently slower because the program must be translated into machine language by the computer executing it. This added step is acceptable in small applications that are run from the Web, but for enterprise-wide application development, this presents a performance issue.

1.2   Where Does Visual Basic .NET Fit In?

So where does **Visual Basic .NET** fit into the overabundance of computer languages available? Visual Basic .NET has its roots in the language called **BASIC**. But Visual Basic .NET isn't your mother's BASIC.

BASIC was developed in 1964 by John Kemeny and Thomas Kurtz (at Dartmouth College) as a language for the rest of us. BASIC (Beginner's All-Purpose Symbolic Instruction Code) was a language written to help nonscientists develop computer programs. Indeed, it was the first computer language I learned. However, my experience with it was dramatically different from what your experience with Visual Basic .NET will be.

The original BASIC was a great start but quite limited. Although I was successful in writing small programs in BASIC as a high school student, it proved difficult to write large, integrated systems with BASIC and even more difficult to maintain them. My high school classmates were enthralled with a simple text adventure game I created, which by today's standards of adventure games would be laughable. It allowed a player to navigate by typing simple two-word sentences, to which the program responded with a text display. Today's adventure games allow for interactive 3D graphics and Internet connections to allow multiple-player games. Was it my lack of skill that limited my game? No way! I was a great programmer limited by the constraints of the programming languages of the time. The world of BASIC and other programming languages has changed dramatically to allow games to have capabilities that were not even dreamt of at the beginning of the home computer revolution.

Microsoft got its start writing BASIC compilers. However, the BASIC it developed bears little resemblance to Visual Basic .NET. When the original BASIC compilers were developed, there were no graphical user interfaces (**GUI**) to program, databases to interface with, or objects to develop. So while Visual Basic .NET has BASIC in its name, it is a completely different world from the one I programmed in during high school.

Today's Visual Basic .NET requires understanding many modern-programming concepts. Its use varies greatly from that of C++ and many of the traditional languages. Visual Basic .NET can be used to solve many programming problems, but the most popular uses in the business world are to develop **prototypes** for applications as well as **front ends** for **database** applications.

Both of these uses have arisen because of the strengths and weaknesses inherent in Visual Basic .NET. Visual Basic .NET makes developing GUI very easy. However, this ease comes with the price of performance. The two types of applications that benefit from Visual Basic .NET's strengths are not victims of its weaknesses.

Applications developed to be prototypes are done to show how an application works. If the application works slowly, it is not important since prototypes are discarded with the production application developed in a more efficient language.

Applications that are front ends for databases may perform slightly slower than if they are developed in another language. However, the majority of time that the program uses will involve waiting for information from a database. The requesting of information from a database is not significantly slower in Visual Basic .NET than in other applications. Therefore, the ease in creating the front end and connecting to the database outweigh any performance issues Visual Basic .NET introduces.

Although hard-core programmers have scoffed at previous versions of Visual Basic as not providing a serious development environment, the .NET version will change all of that. Visual Basic .NET is truly object-oriented, containing all of the programming constructs associated with a true object-oriented language. Objects can be designed from scratch, extended from objects already developed, or extended from objects built into Visual Basic .NET.

Visual Basic .NET is actually part of the larger world of the .NET framework. All languages in the .NET framework are developed in the same development environment and contain the same object model. This is a huge advantage to programmers who develop in more than one language. After you master Visual Basic .NET development, you may choose to learn another language, like C++ or C#. Switching between languages in the .NET framework is easy, because the development environment for all languages in the .NET framework is shared.

The similarities between languages aren't only cosmetic. All the objects that come with the Visual Basic .NET development environment are also available to C++ and C#.

Although using the same built-in objects is convenient, a still more powerful feature is that objects developed in any of the .NET languages can be accessed in the others. This allows programmers to develop parts of their applications in the language that best suits their specific needs.

In previous development environments, when a programmer switched languages, it meant switching development environments and learning an entirely new syntax as well as new object models. Visual Basic .NET is simply an amazing step forward.

1.3 What Makes a Quality Program?

What features are embodied in quality programs? Beginning students often argue that since their program functions properly, they should receive an A in their programming class. However, a program that meets the specifications dictated to the programmer meets only the first criterion of a quality program. A quality program should have all of the following characteristics:

- Readability
- Modularity
- Efficiency
- Robustness
- Usability

Let's discuss each in turn.

Readability

In the corporate world, specifications for a program constantly change. After a programmer meets the initial requirements, users often see the value of their new application and desire additional features. This maintenance phase of a computer project can actually be more expensive than the original development process. Therefore, it is imperative that the program be written so that other programmers as well as the original programmer can understand it.

To improve readability, a key method a programmer can employ is to add comments to the program. Comments are statements in a program that explain the program's purpose and any unclear pieces of code along the way. These comments should be written into the code at the time that the code is written, not after the entire program is completed. Sometimes comments within the code are not enough, and it is often necessary to produce external documentation to round out the explanation of a project.

Beginning programmers, as well as some seasoned professionals, will jokingly argue that they do not comment their code to ensure job security. In reality, a programmer who develops readable, reliable code is far more valuable to a company than one who hoards knowledge in cryptic code. Additionally, a programmer who becomes the sole person to understand the code often ends up maintaining that code instead of moving on to more exciting and lucrative projects.

Having a programming standards document is extremely important. In the corporate programming environment, many programmers work together as a team to develop a single program. It is imperative that everyone follows the same conventions. These can include indenting code in a consistent manner, capitalizing the first letter of each word in a variable name, and using the same abbreviations each time a long word is abbreviated.

Modularity

To reduce the cost of maintenance, code must be modularized. This requires that programs be written in an orderly fashion with problems divided into smaller subproblems and then assembled in a logical order. Each piece of code should accomplish one task and be capable of standing on its own.

Efficiency

Should the goal of a programmer be to write compact, super-efficient code or to write clear, readable code that may run a little more slowly and take up slightly more room? Well, that depends on the situation. If the code is being written for an air-to-air combat system, then speed of execution and size are the most important issues. However, Visual Basic .NET is not usually used when high performance is the key design criteria. Therefore, if you are developing in Visual Basic .NET and taking shortcuts to improve the efficiency of your code, you are adding complexity without adding value to the application.

Program size is not usually an issue with Visual Basic .NET applications either. In order to execute a Visual Basic .NET application, many additional files must be installed on a computer that make the size of an individual application not very relevant. Coupled with the fact that computer memory prices have declined significantly, reducing the size of most applications is not the major design consideration.

It is important to realize that the number of characters you write in your program does not necessarily relate to program size. Sometimes small amounts of code require far more space than the remainder of the program.

If you do decide to add lines of code that are cryptic for the purposes of speed or size, then you should do two things. First, explain the intricacies of the code in full detail. Second, if a simpler way exists to implement the code, indicate so in the comments. This will assist future programmers in modifying your code, even if they do not understand your shortcut.

Robustness

If a program is written to accomplish a task, how does it handle cases when the input to the program is not as expected? Does it crash? Does it go into an infinite loop? Or does it display a message indicating the information entered is incorrect and gracefully allow the user to exit or continue? A program should never crash. A programmer should always keep the user in mind when developing applications. A robust program will handle all of these situations in a graceful manner.

Usability

The last issue is probably the most difficult to master. A program must be correct to be useful. Whether the project is an assignment in class or a task given by your boss at work, if the project does not meet the needs of the end user, regardless of the elegance of your solution, it may never be used.

These are all issues that should be considered while programming. Following them will lead to a successful program and will entail a lot less stress in getting there.

1.4   Understanding Algorithms

Although you have been introduced to the concept of different programming languages, you have not been introduced to the concept behind giving instructions to a computer that will perform tasks that you wish.

Instead of jumping right into a programming example, practice by first trying to understand the concept of an **algorithm**. An algorithm is a detailed sequence of steps required to solve a problem. Instead of thinking about algorithms in terms of a computer program, first try to understand an algorithm behind a process that you are already familiar with. It is important to learn how to understand a process completely and then be able to explain it in simple steps before you try to write a program to accomplish a task. This is often easier said than done.

Algorithms can be represented in a graphical format called a **flowchart**.

Flowchart Symbol	Symbol Meaning
Process	Used to represent calculations and data manipulation.
Decision	Used to represent a comparison with either a Yes/True result or a No/False result.
Data	Used to represent the input or output of data.
Terminator	Used to indicate the beginning or ending of a task.
→ — No → — Yes →	These connector lines are used to join the other symbols within the flowchart. The second and third ones are used in conjunction with a Decision Box.

Observe the following algorithm to listen to the radio station 610 WIP on the AM band on your stereo.

Step 1: Turn the stereo on.
Step 2: If the band is set to FM, switch it to AM.
Step 3: If the station is set to a station greater than 610, turn the station to the left until 610 is reached.
Step 4: If the station is set to a station less than 610, turn the station to the right until 610 is reached.
Step 5: Listen to the best sports talk station in the country.

Figure 1.1 shows the algorithm represented as a flowchart.

Figure 1.1
Radio station flowchart

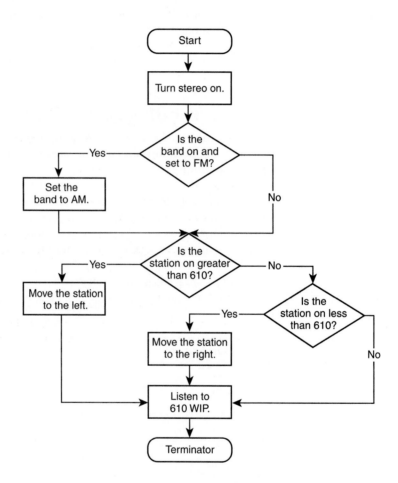

You can see that a simple algorithm can lead to a large flowchart very easily. Even though flowcharts can be large, they are often useful. Flowcharts will be used to graphically represent new programming constructs as they are introduced.

1.5   Top-Down Versus Event-Driven Algorithms

One can classify algorithms into two categories. The first, top-down or **sequential** problems, are usually solved by traditional programming languages. They lend themselves to problems that have a starting point, a predetermined series of steps, and an ending point. The other type of algorithm solves a problem, but not as a straight-line solution.

Algorithms that respond to external stimuli like clicking a mouse or selecting an item from a pull-down menu are considered **event-driven**.

Top-Down or Sequential Algorithm

Consider the steps required to boil an egg.

Step 1:   Open closet door.
Step 2:   Remove pot.
Step 3:   Close closet door.
Step 4:   Place pot under sink faucet.
Step 5:   Turn on the cold water.
Step 6:   Wait until the pot is 3/4 full.
Step 7:   Turn off the cold water.
Step 8:   Place pot on stove burner.
Step 9:   Turn burner on high heat.
Step 10:   Open refrigerator door.
Step 11:   Take out the egg carton.
Step 12:   Open the egg carton.
Step 13:   Remove an egg from the carton.
Step 14:   Close the egg carton.
Step 15:   Place the egg carton back in the refrigerator.
Step 16:   Close refrigerator door.
Step 17:   Open the silverware drawer.
Step 18:   Remove a large spoon.
Step 19:   Close the silverware drawer.
Step 20:   Wait until the water is boiling.
Step 21:   When the water is boiling, use the spoon to place the egg in the pot.
Step 22:   Wait three minutes until the egg is cooked.
Step 23:   Shut off the stove burner.
Step 24:   Remove the egg from the pot.

The previous steps follow a sequential nature. You may not have believed so many steps are required to properly give instructions; however, giving good directions requires including specific details so that ambiguous situations do not occur.

DRILL 1.1

Write down the steps required to describe how you would brush your teeth in the morning.

DRILL 1.2

Write down the steps required to parallel park a car.

Event-Driven Algorithms

Consider the steps required for playing tennis (for simplicity's sake, let's assume that you are the one serving). These steps are not as straightforward as the steps involved in cooking the egg. The key difference is that the sequence of steps required to play tennis cannot be predicted in advance. They must be listed in what-if prose.

Step 1:   Walk up to the serving line.
Step 2:   Toss ball up in the air.

Step 3:   Swing the racket so that you hit the ball to the other player in the opposite box.

Step 4:   Wait for the ball to strike the tennis court.

Step 5A: If the ball lands legally in the box, wait to see if the opponent hits your serve back toward you.

Step 5B: If the ball lands outside the box, you must serve again. Go to Step 1.

Step 6A: If the ball is hit back and it is hit to your right, move toward the right so you are in position to hit it back.

Step 6B: If the ball is hit back and it is hit to your left, move toward the left so you are in position to hit it back.

Step 6C: If the ball is hit back and it is hit directly at you, wait for it to arrive.

Step 7A: If the ball is hit back and it is hit in front of you, move forward.

Step 7B: If the ball is hit back and it is hit behind you, move backward.

Step 8A: If the ball is hit outside the lines, do not hit it but let it pass. Serve again by going to Step 1.

Step 8B: If the ball is hit so that it is a legal shot, hit it to a place the opponent is not. Go to Step 6A.

The answer given for the exercise is obviously incomplete. To document every event that could happen in a game of tennis would take many pages. However, it should be obvious that there is a difference in nature of the algorithm of cooking an egg and the algorithm of playing tennis.

DRILL 1.3

Write down the steps to drive an Audi S4 with an automatic transmission around a block with lights at each corner. Assume that the car is parked on the right side of the street.

1.6   Concept of an Object

You may be wondering if you are ready to talk about **objects** when you haven't even left the first chapter. Don't worry, this won't be a detailed discussion of the intricacies of object-oriented design and all of the implementation problems associated with it. We'll enter into a more detailed discussion as we progress through the text. Instead, you are going to start to think about objects in your life that you are already accustomed to using and try to document their properties and behavior. This exercise is based on the fact that programming with Visual Basic .NET quite often entails using objects with properties and behaviors associated specifically with them. To create an application that solves a problem or mimics a real-world object, you must first understand how to describe such an object. Therefore, you are going to practice documenting the properties and behaviors of a few real-world objects.

DRILL 1.4

Describe in detail the properties of a simple household phone and the actions that can be performed upon it. Assume that the person reading your document has never seen a phone before. If your answers are slightly different from the ones in the back of the chapter, please realize that not all phones will be identical.

DRILL 1.5

Describe in detail the properties of a simple digital alarm clock and the actions that can be performed upon it. Assume that the person reading your document has never seen an alarm clock before.

1.7   Interpreters, Compilers, and JITs

Languages like Visual Basic .NET must be converted into a language the machine understands before it can execute it. There are three main methods for accomplishing this task: interpreting, compiling to native code, and just-in-time (**JIT**) compiling.

An **interpreter** is a program that converts the language written by a developer to a language the computer understands at the time the application is executed. As each line of source code written by the developer is executed, the line of source code is converted on the fly. Although this is convenient, it leads to slow executing applications.

A **compiler**, on the other hand, will perform all of the translations at once. The results are stored in a file called an **executable**. By performing all of the translations ahead of time, the executable will run faster than the application would if it were run on an interpreter. However, this speed does come at a cost. A compiler must produce an executable designed for a specific computer chip known as the central processing unit (CPU). Some computer chips are compatible with others. All of the Intel CPUs are compatible; however, the older chips do not contain all of the features of the new ones. What happens when we attempt to run a program compiled for a Macintosh on an IBM-compatible? It simply doesn't work.

As an answer to this dilemma, some languages compile their source code into an intermediate language. This intermediate language is then translated just in time to be executed by the computer. Java and Visual Basic .NET use this method.

JIT compilers have a huge advantage in that code can be distributed in an intermediate language and then translated to native code. This enables a developer to ship only one version of its code and have it run on multiple platforms. The advantages of JIT compilation are readily apparent on the Internet. When it's unknown what type of computer will download an application, an intermediate language is a must.

You might wonder if JIT compiling has an advantage when you know that you will be compiling only for IBM-compatible machines. Well, there is a great one. Often applications developed in C/C++ and similar languages are compiled to a version of Intel chip. This means that if you have a new CPU version, you cannot take advantage of the new features of that chip. Now with JIT compilation, the intermediate language can be translated to machine code that will take advantage of the new advances in chip design.

Key Words and Key Terms

Algorithm
   The steps required to solve a problem.

Assembly Language
   A low-level programming language utilizing a series of mnemonics to represent commonly used instructions.

BASIC
   An early beginning programming language developed to be easy to program.

C
   A computer language created to develop operating systems like UNIX.

C++
   A computer language that evolved from C to include object-oriented extensions.

COBOL

One of the early computer languages developed for business transactions.

Compiler

A program that converts at once all of the source code of a programming language to a language the computer understands.

Database

A computer system designed to optimize the storing and accessing of large amounts of data.

Event-Driven Algorithm

An algorithm that responds to external stimuli.

Executable

A program produced by a compiler that was translated from a programming language into a language the computer can understand.

Flowchart

A graphical representation of an algorithm.

FORTRAN

One of the early computer languages developed for mathematical calculations.

Front End

A computer program that acts as an interface to display information coming from another computer system.

GUI

A graphical user interface.

High-Level Language

A language written in an English-style prose that is very readable by the programmer but more difficult for the computer to understand.

Interpreter

A program that converts a single line of source code at a time into a language that the computer understands.

Java

A new computer language that is object-oriented and portable to run on any machine.

JIT

Just-in-time compilation will translate an intermediate language to native machine code.

Low-Level Language

A language that is easy for the computer to understand but very difficult for the programmer to comprehend.

Object

An object in computer terms is a programming construct that encompasses both the data and procedures that act upon that data in one unit.

Programming Language

A standardized format of symbols that allows a programmer to instruct a computer to perform certain predefined tasks.

Prototype

A program designed to test a concept and show a user how a program will be developed in another more efficient language.

Punch Cards

A mechanism to enter a program into a computer that stores the program on cardboard cards with holes punched out to represent the program.

Sequential Algorithm

    An algorithm that follows a series of steps in its execution.

Visual Basic .NET

    Microsoft's modern version of the BASIC computer language.

Answers to Chapter's Drills

Drill 1.1

In giving instructions for brushing teeth, you should assume that the person receiving the instructions will take nothing for granted. This is the way a computer operates. A computer does exactly what you tell it, not what you meant to tell it. The following is our teeth-brushing solution—my dentist would be so proud!

Step 1:   Assuming you are still in bed, remove your blanket and swing your legs over the edge of the bed.

Step 2:   Stand up and walk toward the bathroom.

Step 3:   If the door is closed, open it.

Step 4:   Walk into the bathroom.

Step 5:   Turn on the light.

Step 6:   Walk toward the sink.

Step 7:   Turn on the cold-water faucet.

Step 8:   Pick up a cup and fill it with water.

Step 9:   Place the cup down on the counter.

Step 10:   Pick up the toothpaste.

Step 11:   Unscrew the cap.

Step 12:   Pick up the toothbrush.

Step 13:   Place the head of the toothbrush under the running water.

Step 14:   Remove the toothbrush from the water.

Step 15:   Point the toothpaste, open end down, toward the head of the toothbrush.

Step 16:   Squeeze the tube lightly so that a little of the paste is squeezed onto the toothbrush.

Step 17:   Stop squeezing the toothpaste.

Step 18:   Put the toothpaste down.

Step 19:   Bring the toothbrush up to your mouth.

Step 20:   Move the toothbrush back and forth across your teeth.

Step 21:   Repeat until all teeth are well cleaned.

Step 22:   Pick up the cup of water.

Step 23:   Pour some of the water in your mouth.

Step 24:   Place the cup down.

Step 25:   Swoosh the water around in your mouth.

Step 26:   Spit the water out.

Step 27:   Repeat if necessary until all the toothpaste is out of your mouth.

Step 28:   Rinse the toothbrush off.

Step 29:   Place the toothbrush back where you got it.

Step 30:   Put the cap back on the toothpaste.

Step 31:   Shut the water off.

Step 32:   Shut the light off.

Step 33:   Exit the bathroom.

Step 34:   Close the door behind you.

    If you dissect this solution, you will see that I have not left much to chance. When programming a computer, such thoroughness is essential. You will also see that steps like Step 3 involve decisions to make. Most computer programs will make decisions along the way as to whether or not to take additional steps. In Step 21 you can see another concept of programming, the concept of looping. Often it is required to repeat a step a number of times before moving to the next step.

A final issue to notice is that I did not end the algorithm with the completion of the brushing of my teeth, but with the returning of the bathroom to its initial condition. It will be important when you program to make sure that you do not leave resources that you use unreturned to the computer when your programs finish executing.

Drill 1.2

There is no easy answer to this drill. The question was asked to stress an important point: Make sure that you get complete instructions about what you are supposed to be solving.

If you were asked to write instructions to parallel park a car, you should immediately think of other questions to ask before attempting to solve the problem, such as: Is the car an automatic or manual transmission? If it is a manual transmission, where is reverse?

Only by fully specifying a problem may programmers be sure that they are solving the right problem. All too often programmers develop applications that, although they function without error, do not solve the problem they were intended for.

Drill 1.3

In order to solve this problem, we needed to specify exactly the type of car that we were going to use. If we did not, it would be impossible to specify steps on how to drive. Imagine if we did not specify that it was an automatic transmission. Would you have specified that the steps were for an automatic transmission or manual? Obviously a manual transmission would require many more steps.

Step 1:   Unlock the car door.
Step 2:   Open the driver's side door.
Step 3:   Sit down in the driver's seat.
Step 4:   Close the car door.
Step 5:   Put on the safety belt.
Step 6:   Put the key in the ignition.
Step 7:   Turn the key.
Step 8:   Place foot on the brake.
Step 9:   Release the emergency brake.
Step 10:   Put the car in drive.
Step 11:   Place the left turn signal on.
Step 12:   Look to see if any cars are coming.
Step 13:   If a car is coming, wait.
Step 14:   When no cars are coming, turn the steering wheel to the left and release your foot from the brake and gently press the gas pedal.
Step 15:   When the car has pulled out, turn the steering wheel to straighten out the car.
Step 16:   Continue driving down the street.
Step 17:   If a car in front of you slows down, press the brake gently so that you are not too close to it.
Step 18:   If a car to your left has a turn signal on, slow down and let the car pass.
Step 19:   As you approach the light, turn on your right turn signal.
Step 20A: If you reach the light and it is red, come to a complete stop.
Step 20B: If you reach the light and it is yellow, slow down and come to a complete stop.
Step 20C: If you reach the light and it is green, slow down and turn to the right.
Step 21:   If you stopped at the light, and there is no sign stating you cannot turn on red, make a right turn; otherwise, you must wait until the light turns green.

This process would continue around the block and conclude when the car reaches the original starting point.

Drill 1.4

The documentation can be divided into two sections: properties and behaviors. The properties will describe the physical makeup of the phone, while the behaviors will describe what actions can be performed using the phone.

A phone is used by entering a series of numbers called a phone number into the phone on its buttons. The phone number must be obtained from an external source and must be valid in order for the phone call to go through. A phone number is either seven or 10 digits. With 10 digits, phone numbers must be preceded with a 1 before entering the 10 digits. Each digit should be entered by briefly pressing the button corresponding to the digit and waiting a short time before the next digit is entered. When all the digits have been entered, a connection is made to the party you dialed.

Properties:

- Button with the number 1 on it.
- Button with the number 2 and the letters ABC on it.
- Button with the number 3 and the letters DEF on it.
- Button with the number 4 and the letters GHI on it.
- Button with the number 5 and the letters JKL on it.
- Button with the number 6 and the letters MNO on it.
- Button with the number 7 and the letters PQRS on it.
- Button with the number 8 and the letters TUV on it.
- Button with the number 9 and the letters WXYZ on it.
- Button with the number 0 on it.
- Button with an * on it.
- Button with a # on it.
- Button with the word REDIAL on it.
- Large button with no wording on it.

Behaviors:

1. Button 1: If pushed, it enters the 1 digit of a phone number.
2. Button 2: If pushed, it enters the 2 digit of a phone number.
3. Button 3: If pushed, it enters the 3 digit of a phone number.
4. Button 4: If pushed, it enters the 4 digit of a phone number.
5. Button 5: If pushed, it enters the 5 digit of a phone number.
6. Button 6: If pushed, it enters the 6 digit of a phone number.
7. Button 7: If pushed, it enters the 7 digit of a phone number.
8. Button 8: If pushed, it enters the 8 digit of a phone number.
9. Button 9: If pushed, it enters the 9 digit of a phone number.
10. Button 0: If pushed, it enters the 0 digit of a phone number.
11. Button *: Used to interact with computer systems that the phone may connect to.
12. Button #: Used to interact with computer systems that the phone may connect to.
13. REDIAL Button: If pushed, it dials the last phone number entered into the phone.
14. Large Button: This hangs up the phone, which ends the phone call and resets the phone.

Drill 1.5

The documentation can be divided into two sections: properties and behaviors. The properties will describe the physical makeup of the alarm clock, while the behaviors will describe what actions the digital alarm clock can perform.

An alarm clock is used to tell the time of day. It also can be set to sound an alarm at a given time of day. The time of day may be set, or the time the alarm will sound can be set. Both are set in the same way. Exact times are not punched in; instead, the time is moved forward at a quick or slow pace until the time desired is displayed.

Properties:

◆ Hour Display: An LCD output to display the hour of the time being displayed. It can be a number from 1 to 12.

◆ Minute Display: An LCD output to display the current minute of the time being displayed. It can be a number from 0 to 59.

◆ Second Display: An LCD output to display the current second of the time being displayed. It can be a number from 0 to 59.

◆ A.M./P.M. Display: An LCD output to display an indicator of whether the current time is in the A.M. or P.M. for the time being displayed.

◆ Current Hour: The hour of the current time. It can be a number from 1 to 12.

◆ Current Minute: The minute of the current time. It can be a number from 0 to 59.

◆ Current Second: The second of the current time. It can be a number from 0 to 59.

◆ Current A.M./P.M.: An indicator of whether the current time is in the A.M. or P.M.

◆ Alarm Hour: The hour of the time the alarm will go off if it is set to go off. It can be a number from 1 to 12.

◆ Alarm Minute: The minute of the time the alarm will go off if it is set to go off. It can be a number from 0 to 59.

◆ Alarm Second: The second of the time the alarm will go off if it is set to go off. It can be a number from 0 to 59.

◆ Alarm A.M./P.M.: An indicator of whether the alarm will go off in the A.M. or P.M., if the alarm is set.

Behaviors:

◆ Set Alarm: Set the hour, minute, and A.M./P.M. of the alarm.

◆ Set Time: Set the hour, minute, and A.M./P.M. of the actual time.

◆ Fast Button: If the switch is in either Set Alarm or Set Time position, increment the Alarm Time or Actual Time at a fast pace. As long as the button is depressed, the time will continue to increment.

◆ Slow Button: If the switch is in either Set Alarm or Set Time position, increment the Alarm Time or Actual Time at a slow pace. As long as the button is depressed, the time will continue to increment.

◆ Activate Alarm: If the button is pressed, the alarm is set to go off at the time indicated by the Alarm Time.

◆ Deactivate Alarm: If the button is pressed and the alarm is on, shut it off.

◆ Increment Time: The clock will automatically increment the time by a second every second and display it. If the new time is equal to the Alarm Time and the alarm is set to go on, then the alarm will sound.

INTERVIEW

Interview with John Cunningham

John Cunningham is a Project Manager for the Pep Boys of Philadelphia, PA, an automotive retail and service company with centers nationwide. He manages a team of developers which specializes in the engineering of enterprise merchandising applications. The primary development tools of the group are Visual Basic, COBOL, and DB2.

What brought you to Pep Boys?

I was attracted by the opportunity to build and manage a team of bright, young, aggressive technicians while at the same time delivering applications that help the business achieve its goals. Pep Boys was particularly appealing to me because I grew up with "the boys." (My grandfather would take me there to repair my bicycle back in the '60s.)

What kinds of projects are you currently working on?

Currently, my team and I are working toward the delivery of a planogram distribution system and are contributing heavily toward the revamping of our point of customer system. We have recently delivered applications for our pricing and electronic catalog departments. All have utilized Visual Basic 6.0 for presentation and business logic and DB2 as the database server.

How do you like working with VB?

I love the versatility of VB. It can be used as a rapid application development tool in order to quickly solve stand-alone desktop problems but can also be used to develop n-tiered enterprise applications which can service large organizations.

In my case, having done programming in "C," it was a fairly easy transition to VB. The constructs were similar and you didn't have to deal with those messy pointer issues.

How will VB.NET make your job of developing software easier?

I am looking forward to the introduction of inheritance to VB. The advantage to inheritance, of course, is code reuse. Any time you can reuse existing code, it reduces the time it takes to develop the application. As a project manager, this increases the opportunity to deliver a project on time and within budget. I also like the fact that the common language runtime eliminates the need to register components and detects incompatible software versions. These two issues have caused a great deal of lost project time for me over the years.

What advice do you have for students entering the computer field using VB.NET?

I'd tell them to go in with an understanding that VB.NET is not just a new language; it is a new framework that will require a new mindset. Since it requires that programming be done in an object-oriented style, a good start would be for the student to make sure that he or she has built a solid foundation of object-oriented concepts, design, and programming.

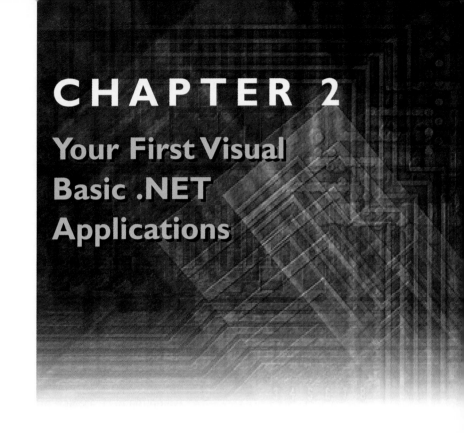

CHAPTER 2
Your First Visual Basic .NET Applications

CHAPTER
OBJECTIVES

- ◆ Discuss the integrated development environment
- ◆ Create your first Visual Basic .NET application
- ◆ Understand the simplest controls
- ◆ Explore basic event handling

This chapter will introduce the integrated development environment (IDE) and show you how to create your first Visual Basic .NET application. While this application is more fun than a real-world example, it will demonstrate Visual Basic .NET's versatility in creating applications with text, graphics, and user interaction.

You will be introduced to development standards from the very first application and continue to use them throughout the text. It is important to follow these standards, because they will improve the readability of your application and reduce the effort it takes to maintain them.

There's an old expression that a book is often judged by its cover. This holds true for the applications you develop as well. In the first few seconds users view your application, they will develop an initial evaluation of its quality. Therefore, the aesthetic nature of your application is important. You will spend a good portion of this chapter familiarizing yourself with the tools Visual Basic .NET provides to assist you in developing aesthetically pleasing applications. It only takes a few more minutes to make your applications look professional. It's time well spent.

2.1 Becoming Familiar with the Integrated Development Environment

Unlike older computer languages that forced programmers to develop their applications in a completely disjointed manner, Visual Basic .NET provides a complete environment to assist developers in creating their applications.

This environment may vary slightly from computer to computer. However, the majority of the key items are essentially the same. Variation in the environment may happen because your computer's display may be smaller or larger than the one used to develop the examples in the text, or it may be that someone may have modified the environment before you used it. You get the idea.

The first step in creating an application with Visual Basic .NET is to familiarize yourself with the main components of the new integrated development environment.

Step 1: When Visual Basic .NET is started, the "Get Started" window for Visual Studio .NET, similar to a home page of a Web site on the Internet, appears.

The Visual Basic .NET "Start Page" (as seen in Figure 2.1) gives you access to the following:

- ◆ Recently used projects
- ◆ The ability to open projects not listed in the recent projects
- ◆ An option to create new projects
- ◆ Links to other resources

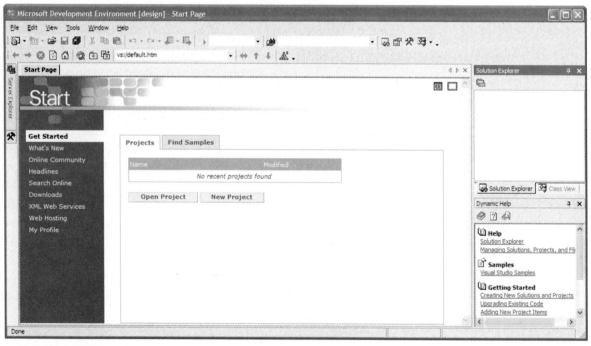

Figure 2.1 The Get Started page

Step 2: The very first time that you run Visual Basic .NET, you will be presented with the My Profile screen like that shown in Figure 2.2. This window will allow you to personalize the settings of Visual Studio .NET. Since the same IDE is used for more than one language, you will want to set the profile to Visual Basic as shown.

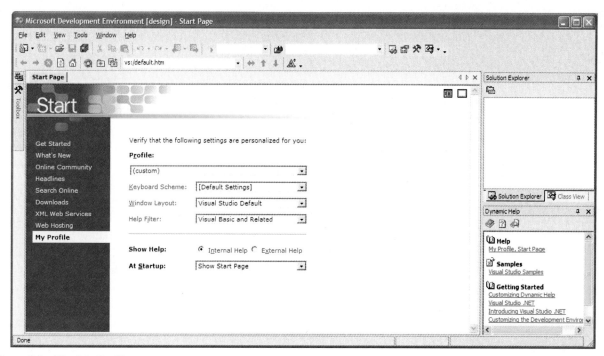

Figure 2.2   The My Profile page

Once these features are set, this screen will no longer appear. If you need to revisit it, you can select My Profile from the VS Start Page and change any of these values.

Step 3: If you select New Project from the VS Start Page, the **New Project window**, as shown in Figure 2.3, will appear. While you have the option to create a great variety of projects, for now, stick to a Windows application. To create a new Windows application for Visual Basic .NET, make sure Visual Basic Projects is selected from the Project Types and Windows Application is selected from the Templates.

With these options selected, all that remains is to specify a name and place to store your new project. A directory for your files, with the name of your application, will be created for you.

Figure 2.3
New Project window

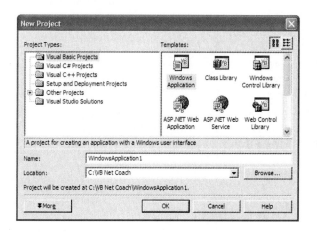

Once the application has been created, you will get your first look at the IDE. (See Figure 2.4.)

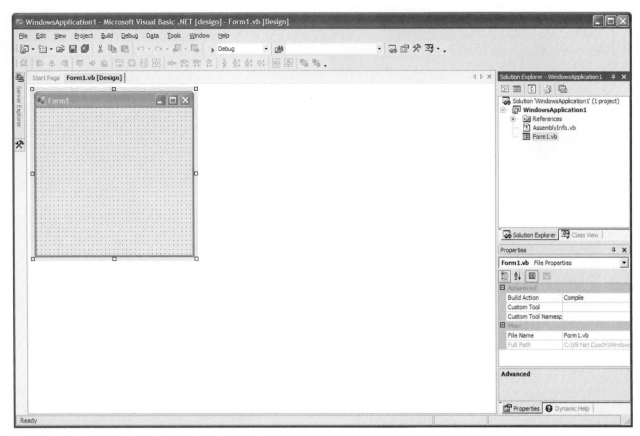

Figure 2.4   Integrated development environment

Form Window

You can imagine the **Form window** like a painter's canvas. It is where you will lay out the design of a form for your application. It is where you will place the components of a form, and it will be the interface for placing the code associated with the components.

The Form window uses a tabbed interface to allow you access to the different information pertaining to your form. Figure 2.5 shows the Form window with the Design tab highlighted. By clicking on the Form1.vb* tab, you can access the code associated with the form. Similarly, by clicking on the Start Page tab, you can access the start page of Visual Basic .NET. This tabbed interface allows you to switch back and forth between different views without having to close windows.

COACH'S TIP

The Form1.vb* tab may not appear until you have entered code, so do not be alarmed if your application does not show this yet. When you are ready to enter code we will explain how to access the tab if it does not automatically appear.

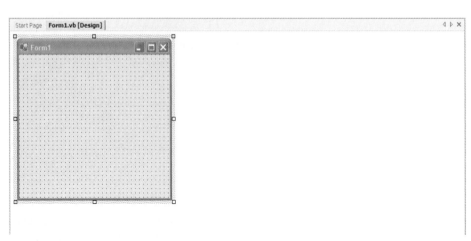

Figure 2.5   Form window

Solution Explorer

The **Solution Explorer window** wraps all of the components of an application into one interface. Here you can access all of the forms, projects, and other modules that are combined to build your application. Currently, you have only a single form included in your project. Later when you create projects with multiple forms, you will learn how to select which form you wish to work on. You can even break your solution up into multiple projects and reference them all from the Solution Explorer. (See Figure 2.6.)

Figure 2.6   Solution Explorer

Standard Toolbar

Just as Microsoft Word has a main toolbar as well as additional formatting toolbars, Visual Basic .NET has a main or **Standard toolbar** as well as additional toolbars to give the developer easy access to commonly used operations. (See Figure 2.7.)

Figure 2.7
Standard toolbar

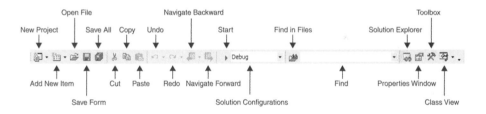

Toolbox Window

Visual Basic .NET's **Toolbox** window can be thought of as a painter's palette, but instead of paint it contains objects called controls that assist you in creating your application. (See Figure 2.8.)

Each control listed contains the icon for the control and the name of the control to the right of it. There are a great many controls, so for ease of access, they are broken into sections. By default the Windows Forms controls are shown.

Along with the form controls are controls with other functionality. These additional controls are grouped and can be selected by clicking on their group name. When the number of controls is greater than can be displayed in the Toolbox, an arrow appears so that you can scroll down the list.

Figure 2.8
Toolbox

Allows you to see the
rest of the controls

To access the Toolbox, click on the Toolbox icon in the Standard toolbar.

COACH'S TIP

You might have noticed that the controls in the Toolbox are not in alphabetical order. They are listed in the order most developers access the controls. If you would like to order the controls alphabetically, right-click on the mouse when the mouse pointer is over the Toolbox and click on the `Sort Items Alphabetically` option from the pop-up menu.

Properties Window

Components of Visual Basic .NET have many properties associated with them. A property is a way of customizing the appearance and behavior of a control in Visual Basic .NET. Among other properties, the **Properties window** (Figure 2.9) allows the developer to control the color, font, and size of Visual Basic .NET constructs. The Properties window is an interface to these properties; it allows developers to click on the property that they wish to set and provides an interface to allow the value for the property to be specified.

Figure 2.9
Properties window

The control pull-down menu indicates the control for the Properties window. Its properties are displayed in the window. This is selected by single-clicking on a control on the Form window. You can also select the control by clicking on the pull-down menu and selecting the control that you wish to work with.

The current property selected is highlighted, and additional information explaining the purpose of that property is displayed at the bottom of the window.

To simplify the organization of the many properties an object may have, properties are sometimes grouped together. Observe Figure 2.10, which shows the `Font` property. A `Font` is composed of a `Name`, `Size`, `Unit`, `Bold`, and so on. All of these individual components cannot be set all at once. By clicking on the ⊞ next to the `Font` property, the Properties window expands to show all of the components making up a `Font` (Figure 2.11).

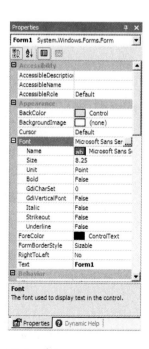

Figure 2.10   Font property selected   **Figure 2.11**   Font property expanded

Menu Bar

The Visual Basic .NET **menu bar** (Figure 2.12) is located just below the title bar. It contains shortcuts to commonly used commands.

Figure 2.12
Menu bar

2.2 Creating Your First Application

Visual Basic .NET applications start with a basic form. You can add controls that come with Visual Basic .NET and code to make the controls work in the way that you wish.

Problem Description

For your first application, you are going to create a form that acts out the classic tale of "The Lady or the Tiger" by Frank R. Stockton. If you are unfamiliar with this tale, blame your English teachers. A brief synopsis of the story is:

> In ancient times there was a semibarbaric king who would not allow anyone but royalty to love his daughter. However, as fate would have it, a peasant from the village fell in love with the princess and the princess fell in love with him. When the king discovered this, he subjected the peasant to a trial of guilt or innocence. The peasant was placed in front of two doors. Behind one door was a tiger; behind the other was a beautiful young maiden. If the peasant picked the door with the tiger behind it, then he was obviously guilty and would be eaten by the tiger. If he picked the door with the young maiden, he would be assumed innocent and would get to marry the young maiden.
>
> When the time came to pick the door, the peasant looked up at the princess and asked which door. The princess replied that it was the right door. The question is, is the princess telling the truth? If she is, would she not be jealous that her love would marry another? Would she lie? We do not answer the question, but we can create an application to simulate it.

When the application is complete, it will appear as in Figures 2.13 through 2.15.

Figure 2.13
Sketch of the application

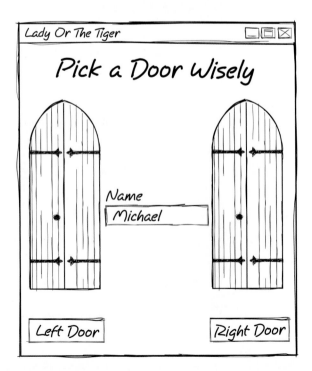

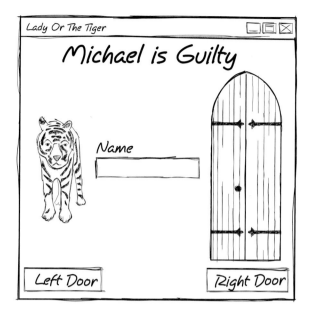

Figure 2.14 Sketch of left door selected

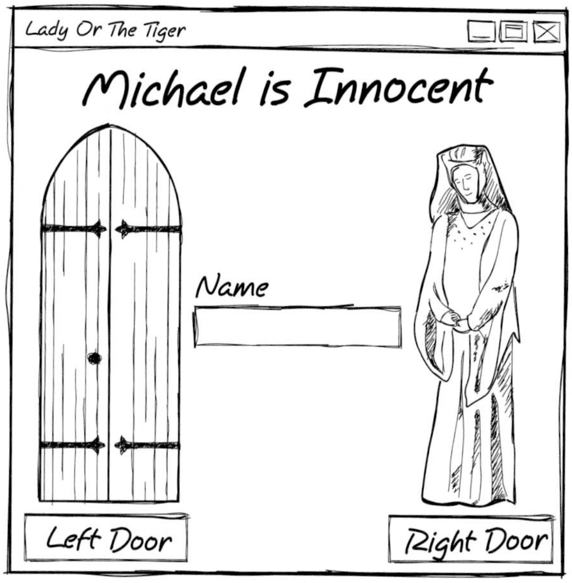

Figure 2.15 Sketch of right door selected

> **COACH'S TIP**
>
> When developing an application, it is always a good idea to sketch how the application looks before you begin to code it.

Problem Discussion

Because you are probably unfamiliar with the process of developing a Visual Basic .NET application, you will develop this application in a stepwise fashion. Start by creating a project and ensuring that it is named properly. You will then add the different controls that will be used to build your application. These include labels, picture boxes, text boxes, and buttons.

After your application looks like it has all the necessary components, you will add functionality to the application by coding a simple event that will be triggered if the user clicks on either the left or right buttons.

Problem Solution

Setting the Project and Form Name The first step in coding any application is to specify the name and location for the application. There are many different types of projects that can be created. You will create the default, a Windows application.

Step 1: From the Start window, click on New Project. The New Project window will appear. (See Figure 2.16.)

Figure 2.16
New Project window

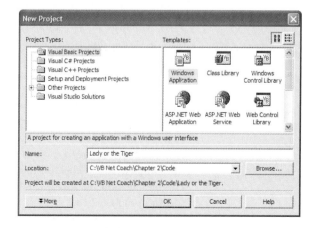

COACH'S TIP

A directory for `Lady` or `the Tiger` will be created automatically.

Step 2: Specify the name of the application as `"Lady or the Tiger"`.
Step 3: Specify the location as `"C:\VB Net Coach\Chapter 2\Code\"`.
Step 4: Click on the OK button and the development environment as shown in Figure 2.17 will appear.

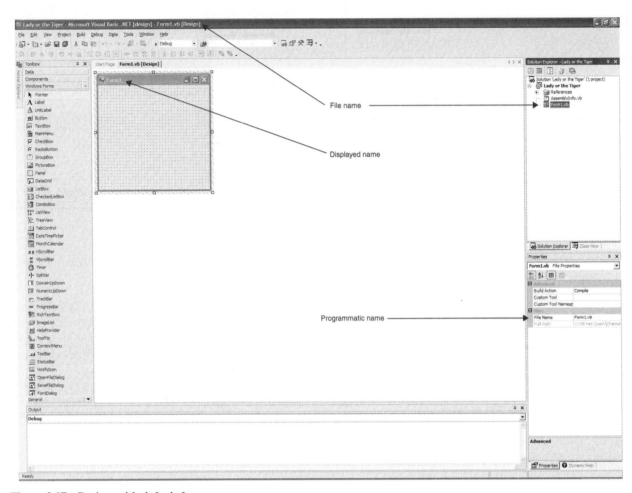

Figure 2.17   Project with default form

Step 5: You should also rename the default form of the application. The default name for a form is `Form1`. It is good practice to rename the form to one that is more meaningful.

When changing the name of a form, it is easy to get confused. Visual Basic .NET will allow you to set a value to display as the name for the form, to set the name you refer to the form from within your program, and to set the actual file name of the form. You will learn how to set all three.

You can see the default name in the title bar of the Form window as well as in the Properties window for the form. You need to rename the form to a name that represents the actions that will occur on the form. However, when naming forms in Visual Basic, your name should follow Microsoft's naming convention. The prefix identifies what type of object you are naming. In this case, you use the prefix `frm` to indicate that your name is associated with a form object. Single-click on the form in the `Form` window.

Step 6: Double-click on the `Name` window containing the name `Form1` to highlight, as shown in Figure 2.18.

COACH'S WARNING

Depending on your computer setup, the directories given may or may not work for you. You may have to consult your instructor to explain the correct file path.

Figure 2.18
Highlighted name in
Properties window

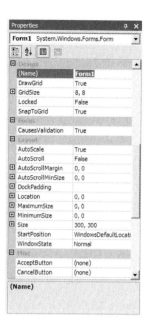

Step 7: Now you can type the new name, `frmLadyOrTiger`, in the Properties window, as shown in Figure 2.19.

Figure 2.19
New name in
Properties window

Notice that once the name has been changed to `frmLadyOrTiger`, the new
name appears in the Properties window; however, the file name still remains as
`Form1.vb`.

Step 8: You can rename the file by right-clicking on the file name in the Solution
Explorer. A pop-up window will appear that will allow you to select Rename.
(See Figure 2.20.)

While it is possible to
use spaces in file
names, you may want
to consider skipping
them. You do not know
where you may run
your application in the
future—some systems
may not be compatible
with spaces in file
names. While this is
not very common in
modern-day computing,
it is a consideration.

Figure 2.20 Renaming the file name for your form

Step 9:   Enter the file name for the form, `frmLadyOrTiger.vb`.

Step 10: The last step is to set the display name for the form. This is done by setting
the `Text` property of the form. (See Figure 2.21.) For your application,
change the displayed name to `Lady or the Tiger`.

Figure 2.21
Setting the `Text` property

The displayed name of
a form can and should
have spaces in between
the words.

Placing a Label Control on the Form   You are now ready to build your application
by adding controls to the form. Your first step is to add a **label control** to the form. A
label control allows you to add **static text** to a form. Static text is text that typically will
not change during the running of your application. The text that you wish to place on
the form is `"Pick a Door Wisely"`.

You need to place a label control on this form so that you can add the text you want
onto the form.

Figure 2.22 Select label control

Step 1: Select the label control by clicking on the **icon** for the label control in the tool-box. This can be seen in Figure 2.22.

Step 2: Place the label in the desired position on the form. The text should appear across the top of the form, so point the mouse near the upper-left corner of the form. While holding the mouse button down, move the mouse pointer to the right end of the form and a little lower than the previous clicked location. This can be seen in Figure 2.23.

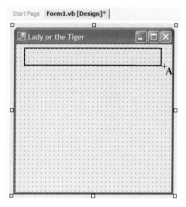

Figure 2.23 Place label control

Step 3: Release the mouse button, thereby completely specifying the location, width, and height of the text box. You can see the outline of the label control in Figure 2.24.

Figure 2.24
Label control placed on form

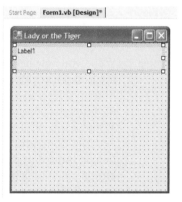

COACH'S TIP

You can add a control to the form by double-clicking on the control in the Toolbox window.

Step 4: Make sure that your label control is roughly the same size as shown. If it is not, there are two ways you can modify your control so that it matches the one shown.

The first method is to adjust it visually. You can point to any of the small outline boxes that define the border of your control, and by clicking on a box and holding the mouse button down, you can stretch the control in whatever direction you wish. When the control is the size that you want, release the mouse button and the label control resizes. You can repeat this process for any of the sizing handles until the label control is the size that you wish.

The second method is more precise. By modifying the properties of the label control, you can set the `Size` property to the exact values of the label in

Figure 2.24. Notice that the `Size` property is not a single value but is composed of both a `Width` and a `Height`. Set yours to `248, 40`, respectively.

To set the properties, make sure the label control is selected. This is accomplished by clicking once on the control. When the control is selected, you will see the outline boxes appear around the border of the label control. You will also see the label control's name appear in the Properties window. Currently, the name is `Label1`.

Although there are many other properties, only set the two that were mentioned. To set each one, select the property by clicking on it in the Properties window and type the new value in it.

Step 5: Although not required, it is a good practice to name your controls. Therefore, set the `Name` property of the label to `lblTitle`.

Step 6: Set the label to display the text value you wish it to display for the title. This is extremely easy to do. Click on the `Text` property and type `"Pick A Door Wisely"`. (See Figure 2.25.)

COACH'S TIP

The prefix for a label is `lbl`.

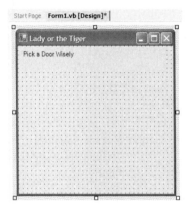

Figure 2.25   Label control with `Text` property set

Step 7: While you now have the desired text displayed, you may notice that the text is not as large as you might like. This can easily be remedied by changing the `Font` property to a larger font style. However, a font is not made up of a simple numerical property. A font is composed of a type face, size, and style. Visual Basic .NET allows you to specify all of these with a single screen.

The `Font` property can be changed by either clicking on the button containing three dots or clicking on the ⊞ button (Figure 2.26). Clicking on the button containing three dots will allow you to make changes to the `Font` property in a separate window (Figure 2.27), while clicking on the ⊞ button will allow you to make changes to the `Font` properties within the Properties window itself (Figure 2.28).

By setting the `Font.Style` to `Bold` and the `Size` to `18` and then clicking on the OK button, you will see the changes to the form as shown in Figure 2.29.

Step 8: The final step is to align the text so that it is centered in the form. There are two ways of doing this. The first is to try to align it visually using the mouse pointer. By clicking on it and dragging it from side to side, you can align the text as desired. However, if the label control is already centered within the form, it is often easier to set the alignment of the text for the label control to `MiddleCenter` and the text will automatically be centered within the label control and the form. Clicking on the `TextAlign` property and selecting `MiddleCenter` from the pull-down menu can do this. The effect is shown in Figure 2.30.

Click to change font

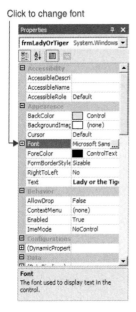

Figure 2.26 Font property selected

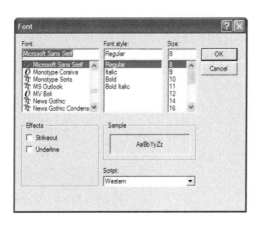

Figure 2.27 Font window

Figure 2.28 Font property expanded

COACH'S TIP

When you first set the size of a control, it is not always the correct size. In this case it was, but if the original size for the label control is not sufficient, you could increase the size of the label by either setting the `Height` and `Width` properties of the label or by pulling the lower-right corner of the form to the size you desire.

Figure 2.29 Label control with reset font

Figure 2.30 Label control with text centered within it

2.3 Picture Box Control

Visual Basic .NET allows you to add pictures to your form easily. In your case, you wish to add a picture of a door twice. To display a picture, you will use the **picture box control**.

Step 1: Start by clicking on the picture box control in the Control toolbox. This is shown in Figure 2.31.

Step 2: Now you want to place the picture box control in a similar manner as you did with the label control. Click just below and to the left of the text in the label control you previously placed. Hold the mouse button down and release it with the mouse pointer near the bottom of the form and aligned in between the o's of the word "Door" in the label control. This is shown in Figure 2.32.

Figure 2.31 Select picture box control

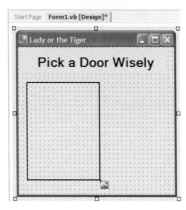

Figure 2.32 Outline when selecting picture box

Step 3: Set the `Name` property of the picture box to `picLeftDoor`.

Step 4: Next you need to select the picture that you wish to display within the box. You must click on the `Image` property. Once clicked, the `Image` property will display a button with three dots. When you click on the button, a dialog box will appear to select the graphic file to display within the picture box control. This is shown in Figure 2.33.

Figure 2.33 Load picture dialog box

When you try this step, your graphic files will be located on the Addison-Wesley Web site (www.aw.com/cssupport). You can navigate through the code and find them in Chapter 2's directory.

Once you select the file that you want and click on the Open button, the graphic file is displayed in the picture box control. This is shown in Figure 2.34.

Figure 2.34 Picture box control with picture displayed

COACH'S WARNING

Depending upon the settings on your computer, the file name extensions may or may not be displayed in the file name window.

Step 5: You should immediately notice that the entire picture is not displayed. This is because you did not make the picture box control large enough. You have a problem—but not for long—in that the form is not large enough to hold a larger picture box control. To solve this dilemma, you can simply increase the size of the form and the picture box.

To increase the size of the form, you need to modify the `Size` property of the form. This can be done by clicking anywhere on the form a control is not already placed. When the form is selected, its name will appear in the Properties window. By clicking on the ⊞ button of the `Size` property, you can access the `Width` and `Height` properties of the form. Since you need to make room for two doors, two buttons, and a text box, you need to increase the size to `Width` and `Height` of `624, 424`, respectively.

Similarly, you need to set the `Size` property of `picLeftDoor` to `100, 248`. Figure 2.35 shows the resized form and picture box.

Figure 2.35
Resized form and
picture box

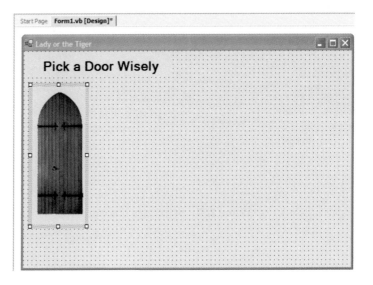

Step 6: The last step is to repeat the process (Steps 2–5) and create another picture box, `picRightDoor`, with the same picture. Since there is now more room on the form, so you may also wish to recenter your label and previous picture box controls. Your form should now look as it does in Figure 2.36.

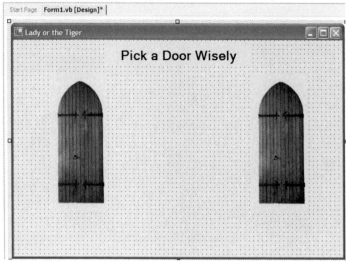

Figure 2.36   Additional picture box and recentered form

2.4   Text Box Control

Often you will require a method to gather text from the user. By using a **text box control** you can place an area on the form where users of the application may enter any text they wish. Anyone who has filled out a form on the Internet is already familiar with this type of control. Conceptually, there is no difference between the text box that you use in a Web page and one that is placed on a Visual Basic .NET form. You are now going to add a text box to your application so the peasant can enter his name.

Step 1: Select the text box control from the Control toolbox. (See Figure 2.37.)

Figure 2.37   Select text box control

Step 2: Once the text box control is selected, place a text box on the form in the same manner as the other controls. See Figure 2.38, where a text box is placed in between the two picture box controls.

Figure 2.38
Text box added to form

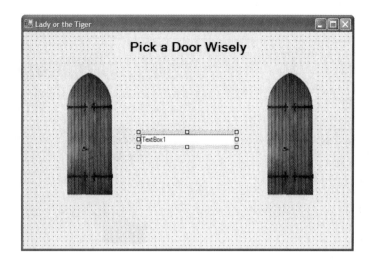

Step 3: Set the Name property of the text box to txtName.

COACH'S TIP

The prefix for a text box is txt.

Step 4: You can see that Visual Basic .NET automatically inserts the default text TextBox1. Usually, you do not wish this default text to be the value initially displayed. As with almost every control, Visual Basic .NET provides a property that allows you to change the default characteristics. You can even set it to nothing at all as in Figure 2.39. You can do this by clicking on the Text property and erasing TextBox1. This is shown in Figure 2.40.

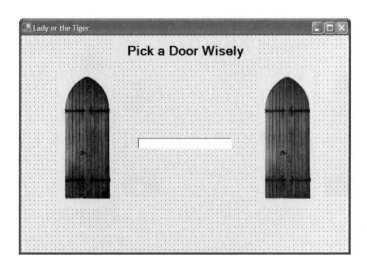

Figure 2.39   Text box with text empty

Figure 2.40   Text box Properties window

COACH'S TIP

Students often confuse a text box and a label control. The label control is primarily used to display text, while a text box allows the user to enter text that can be processed by the application.

Step 5:   While you know the text box is used to enter the peasant's name, the user of the application might not, so add a label control above the text box to indicate the peasant's name. The label should be created in a manner similar to that of the previous label. You need to set the `Name` of the label to `lblName`, the `Font Bold` property to `True`, and the `Text` property to `Name`. This is shown in Figure 2.41.

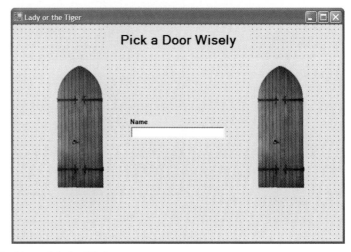

Figure 2.41   Name label added

2.5   Button Control

Until now, there has been very little interactivity in your form. This situation is about to change with the addition of the **button control**. If you have filled out a form on the Internet, you are already familiar with buttons. When you are done filling out a form on a Web page, you must click on a button to submit the form to the Web site for processing. A button in Visual Basic .NET is no different conceptually.

Step 1:   Select the button control from the Control toolbox. (See Figure 2.42.)

Step 2:   Once the button control is selected, place a button on the form in the same manner as the other controls. See Figure 2.43, where it has been placed directly under the picture box control.

Figure 2.42   Select button control

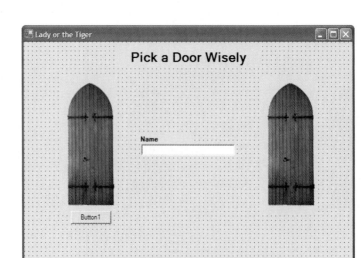

Figure 2.43   Form with button control added

Step 3: Set the `Name` property of the button to `btnLeftDoor`.

COACH'S TIP

The prefix for a button is `btn`.

Step 4: You can see that Visual Basic .NET automatically inserts the default text `Button1` on the button control. As with the text box control, you usually do not wish this default text to be displayed. It is a better practice to identify a button control by setting the `Text` property to indicate what its function will be. So far I haven't discussed what the function of the button is, so I'll give you a little insight. You will program it so it will change the form to display either the Lady or the Tiger picture.

For now, let's just change the button control so that it displays the text `"Left Door"`. This is done by clicking on the `Text` property and typing `"Left Door"`. This is shown in Figure 2.44.

Figure 2.44
Form with button that has the proper `Text` property

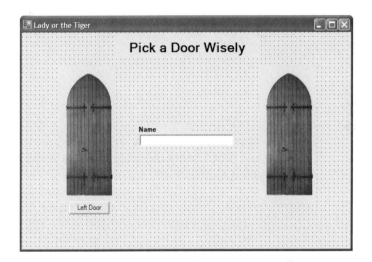

Step 5: The last step is to repeat the process and create another button, `btnRightDoor`. Your form should now look like the one in Figure 2.45.

Figure 2.45
Form with Right Door button added

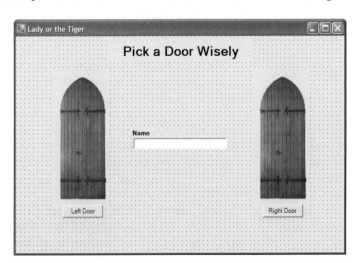

If you ran the application and clicked on the button, you would see that the button depresses and comes back up, but no action is executed. In the next section, you will add the ability to cause actions when a button is depressed.

2.6 Basic Event Handling

You will now add functionality so that clicking on your button will cause the form to display either a young maiden or a tiger. Also, if the young maiden is displayed, the label should change to the person's name and the words " is Innocent". However, if the tiger appears, then the label should change to the person's name and " is Guilty". You will also notice that whatever text is in the text box is erased. This involves your first real coding. In this case, your coding will be triggered by an event. Visual Basic .NET makes it easy to code for events. Built into controls are predefined events that have no action attached to them.

If you double-click on the `btnLeftDoor` button when the application is not running, the code snippet as shown in Figure 2.46 is displayed.

Figure 2.46 Empty code for `Click` event

Events in Visual Basic .NET are coded within the boundaries of the text shown. It may look a little cryptic, but once you recognize the pattern, it is easy to understand.

The first few lines define the object you are working in. In this example you are creating a form called `frmLadyOrTiger`. The first two words, `Public Class`, indicate that you are creating a template for an object that can be accessed by any object in the project. Notice that these words are colored blue. This is because they are **keywords**. Keywords are predefined words in the Visual Basic .NET language that have a special meaning and cannot be used for other purposes.

These two keywords are followed by the name of the class, `frmLadyOrTiger`. While a class can be defined on its own, Visual Basic .NET helps you out by automatically creating this class from another one, the basic Form class. This is why the second line appears with the keyword `Inherits` and the object to inherit from, `System.Windows.Forms.Form`. The concepts behind these details of object creation will be explored later in the text. For now, just ignore these two lines and the one that follows.

COACH'S TIP

Notice that keywords appear in blue while the rest of the code appears in black. This helps differentiate the keywords from the rest of your code.

The code you are concerned with starts with the words `Private Sub`, indicating that the event that you are coding is private (only available in the current form) and a subroutine (a small piece of code that accomplishes a given task). The next text, `btnLeftDoor_Click`, indicates that this code is attached to the `btnLeftDoor` button and will be executed when a `Click` event occurs. The remainder of the text on the line can also be ignored for now.

The final text, `End Sub`, indicates the ending of the event.

Your code belongs in between these two lines. It will be executed whenever the button `btnLeftDoor` is clicked.

First, remove any text that is placed in the `txtName` text box.

In order to change the text box programmatically, you need to indicate that you want to change the `Text` property of the `txtName` text box control. Visual Basic .NET is "smart" in the way it allows you to type information in a code snippet. If you type a control name like `txtName` and then type a period, it will display all of the available properties that you may access. By typing a "T" for `Text`, the pull-down menu displays and the first property starting with the letter "T" is displayed. You have the option of typing out the word `Text` or scrolling down to the `Text` property. When the `Text` property is selected, press the spacebar for the code `txtName.Text` to be displayed. This is shown in Figures 2.47 and 2.48.

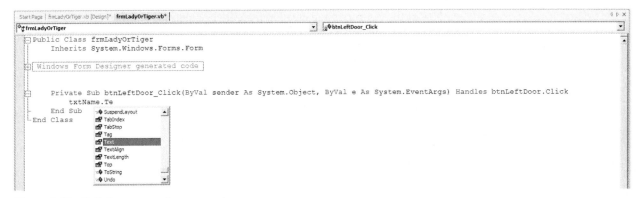

Figure 2.47   Pull-down menu for properties

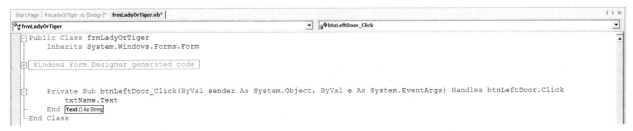

Figure 2.48   Filled-in property text

COACH'S TIP

If you type a period and a drop-down menu does not appear, you have probably incorrectly typed the name of the control.

To cause a text box's `Text` property to change, type an equals sign followed by the new value you want to display in quotation marks. This is shown in Figure 2.49.

Figure 2.49   Code to change label's `Text` property

See what happens when you run the application. Click on the Start button, , in the Standard toolbar to run the application.

COACH'S WARNING

You may need to specify to Visual Basic .NET that you wish the form `frmLadyOrTiger` to be the first form run when you start your application. When you hit the Start button, if you get an error, do not continue. The error will appear in a window at the bottom of the development environment. If you double-click on the error a window will appear. Simply click on your form in the window. Now you can run the application and it will work properly.

Type a name into the text box like `"Michael"`. Click on the button `btnLeftDoor`, and the text in the text box will be removed. This is shown in Figures 2.50 and 2.51.

Figure 2.50
Before `btnLeftButton`
is clicked

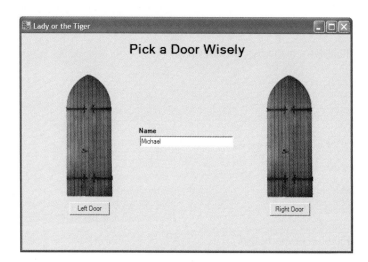

Figure 2.51
After `btnLeftButton`
is clicked

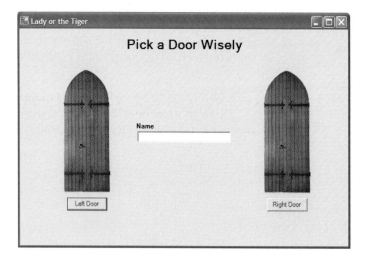

To change a picture, you must programmatically change properties that you previously changed interactively. You need to set the `Image` property in `picLeftDoor` to the new graphic. However, because a picture is a little more complicated than a text message, you must type `Image.FromFile`("Picture name and path goes here") to the right of the equals sign. In your case the picture name and path are `"Tiger.gif"`. This can be seen in Figure 2.52 along with the changing the `Text` property of the label control `lblTitle` to `"Michael is Guilty"`.

```
Start Page | frmLadyOrTiger.vb [Design]*  frmLadyOrTiger.vb*
frmLadyOrTiger                                              btnLeftDoor_Click
Public Class frmLadyOrTiger
    Inherits System.Windows.Forms.Form

    Windows Form Designer generated code

    Private Sub btnLeftDoor_Click(ByVal sender As System.Object, ByVal e As System.EventArgs) Handles btnLeftDoor.Click
        picLeftDoor.Image = Image.FromFile("Tiger.gif")
        lblTitle.Text = txtName.Text & " is Guilty"
        txtName.Text() = ""
    End Sub
End Class
```

Figure 2.52 Complete code

In order to combine the name stored in the `txtName` text box and the text `" is Guilty"`, you must use a concatenation operator. The `&` in between `txtName.Text` and `" is Guilty"` will combine the text contained in the text box with `" is Guilty"`. Much more will be explained about this type of operation in Chapter 3.

Figure 2.53
After `btnLeftDoor` button
is clicked

Figure 2.53 shows the final result of pressing the `btnLeftDoor` button.

Finally, you need to set the code for the `btnRightDoor` button in a similar fashion. The code is shown in Figure 2.54.

```
Start Page | frmLadyOrTiger.vb [Design]  frmLadyOrTiger.vb
frmLadyOrTiger                                              btnRightDoor_Click
Public Class frmLadyOrTiger
    Inherits System.Windows.Forms.Form

    Windows Form Designer generated code

    Private Sub btnLeftDoor_Click(ByVal sender As System.Object, ByVal e As System.EventArgs) Handles btnLeftDoor.Click
        picLeftDoor.Image = Image.FromFile("Tiger.gif")
        lblTitle.Text = txtName.Text & " is Guilty"
        txtName.Text() = ""
    End Sub

    Private Sub btnRightDoor_Click(ByVal sender As System.Object, ByVal e As System.EventArgs) Handles btnRightDoor.Click
        picRightDoor.Image = Image.FromFile("Lady.gif")
        lblTitle.Text = txtName.Text & " is Innocent"
        txtName.Text() = ""
    End Sub
End Class
```

Figure 2.54 Complete code

Figure 2.55 shows the final result of pressing the `btnRightDoor` button.

Figure 2.55
After `btnRightDoor`
button is clicked

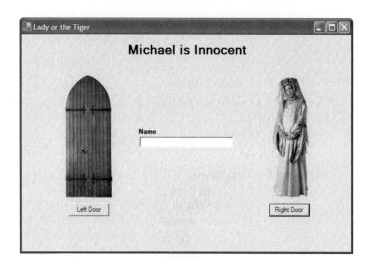

COACH'S TIP

It is possible to assign most of a control's properties programmatically. Observe how you can set the text box `txtName`'s properties in the following code:

```
txtName.Font.Bold = True
txtName.FontSize = 20
```

The code sets the text box `txtName` to be displayed with a bold font and a size of 20.

You can save your project by either clicking on the Save icon in the Standard toolbar or by selecting File and Save from the menu bar.

2.7 Use of Color

COACH'S TIP

True artistic style is sometimes beyond the grasp of some programmers. If this is you, get assistance from someone with a little style to help spruce up your application.

You've now learned how to create a "neat" looking form; however, you have not learned how to use color within the form. Your applications had color, but only in the sense that you used a color photograph. All of the controls were black with a gray background.

Visual Basic .NET gives you the ability to set the color of almost every control. However, how you use color should follow some rhyme or reason. When programmers are given the ability to use color, often they set controls to different colors just because they can. The appropriate use of color must have meaning. Color should be used with some form of artistic style. Certain color schemes go well together, and others do not. This book is not meant to teach you artistic style—it's meant to teach you the techniques to develop applications and give you basic guidelines to style. Always keep in mind that your use of color should be conservative, consistent, and logical.

While the Lady or the Tiger application was an excellent first application, there is little need for adding color to it. Instead, imagine if you developed a travel application. The application would be very simple, since you have not learned much of Visual Basic .NET's power yet. Your application will display a picture box, label, text box, and button. The application will show two possible vacations for a travel company. One location will be Ireland, the other Egypt. To enhance the application, you will set the color scheme of the application slightly differently for each location. For Ireland you will use a green color scheme, while the Egyptian scheme will be set to gold.

For demonstration purposes, step-by-step directions to create this application will not be shown. Instead, just focus on the use of color.

So where should you add color? The question is how much green or gold should be displayed. There is no right answer to this question. Observe the pictures in Figures 2.56 through 2.58.

Figure 2.56   Label in green

Figure 2.57   Label and text box in green

Figure 2.58   Label, text box, and background in green

COACH'S WARNING

Clearly, the third choice looks poorest. I showed it because it is common to change the foreground color of a label but not the background color. The background color, if not set, remains to the default. In this case, it's set to gray.

COACH'S WARNING

You wouldn't want to do all this work and not have your project saved! It is important to save your work regularly. A good habit is to save your work periodically as you make changes.

Which application looks the best is a matter of preference. Personally, I like the second one the best.

The two properties used in the previous applications were `ForeColor` and `BackColor`. Each can be set interactively or programmatically.

To set the color interactively, perform the following steps:

Step 1:   Click on the control that you wish to change the color of.
Step 2:   Click on the property you wish to change (`ForeColor` or `BackColor`).
Step 3:   Click on the drop-down arrow to get the Palette window to appear.
Step 4:   Click on the Custom tab of the pop-up window.
Step 5:   Click on the color you wish to select.

The Palette pop-up window can be seen in Figure 2.59.

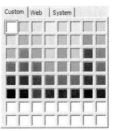

Figure 2.59   Palette pop-up window

To change the color of a control programmatically, you can use any of the predefined Visual Basic .NET colors. The list of predefined colors is long and may be confusing to memorize. If you type `Color` and then a period, a list of the predefined colors will appear.

To change the green colors in the application to gold, you will use the `Color.Gold` value and the code as shown in Figure 2.60.

```
Start Page | frmTravel.vb [Design]  frmTravel.vb |                                                        ◁ ▷ ✕

frmTravel                                              ▼   (Declarations)                                    ▼

Public Class frmTravel
    Inherits System.Windows.Forms.Form

    Windows Form Designer generated code

    Private Sub btnChangeDestination_Click(ByVal sender As System.Object, ByVal e As System.EventArgs) Handles btnChangeDestination.Clic
        lblTitle.Text = "Egypt is the place to be!"
        picPhoto.Image = Image.FromFile("Egypt.jpg")
        txtName.Text = "Egypt"
        txtName.ForeColor = Color.Gold
        lblTitle.ForeColor = Color.Gold
    End Sub
End Class
```

Figure 2.60   Code for button

After the Change Destination button is clicked, the application will now appear as in Figure 2.61.

Figure 2.61
Application after button
is clicked

◆ 2.8   Case Study

Problem Description

A company that sells products on the Internet, Walking Promotions, wants to develop an application to track its financial data. Create an application that allows the entry of the names of the employees, how many hours they work in a week, and a place to display their payment for the week as well as a total cost of payroll. In addition, beautify the form by adding the company's logo as well as a title.

Problem Discussion

While you do not know enough to create an application that will actually process the payroll, you can at least set up the user interface of the application. It will require using text boxes, picture boxes, and label controls.

In order to make programming easier in the future, it is a good idea to name all of the controls something a little more specific than the default values. This will make them more discernible later.

Problem Solution

The project requires a single form and a graphic file containing the logo. The graphic file will be called "WalkingPromotionsLogo.jpg". While you have many options in how to lay out your solution, you will want to come up with a simple, intuitive solution. Your completed application should look something like Figure 2.62.

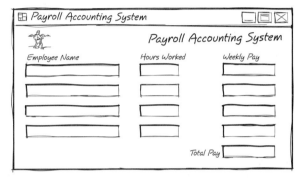

Figure 2.62   Sketch of application

You may add the controls to your form in any order that you wish. However, I recommend that you follow the order given in the solution.

Adding the Logo

To add the Walking Promotions logo to a blank form, follow the steps that you used when adding a picture box control in Section 2.3.

Step 1: Select the picture box control from the toolbox.
Step 2: Place the mouse pointer over the area of the form where you wish to place the upper-left corner of the logo.
Step 3: Hold the mouse button down and drag the pointer to the lower-right corner where the logo will be placed.
Step 4: Release the mouse button and the picture box control will be placed on the form.
Step 5: Click on the `Image` property in the Properties window and click on the "WalkingPromotionsLogo.jpg" to select the appropriate graphic.
Step 6: Click on the `Name` property and change the `Name` property to `picLogo`.

Adding the Labels

You need to add a total of five labels to the form. However, it makes sense to add the first four now and then after you add the text box controls to come back and add the last one so that they line up appropriately.

To add a label control, follow the steps that you did in Section 2.2. You can follow the same steps for each label, and the properties of each label are shown.

Step 1: Select the label control from the toolbox.

Step 2: Place the mouse pointer over the area of the form where you wish to place the upper-left corner of the label control.

Step 3: Hold the mouse button down and drag the pointer to the lower-right corner where the label control will be placed.

Step 4: Release the mouse button and the label control will be placed on the form.

Step 5: Click on the `Text` property in the Properties window and type `"Payroll Account System"`.

Step 6: Click on the `Font` property in the Properties window and set the `Size` property to `14` and the `Bold` property to `True`.

Step 7: Click on the `Name` property and change the `Name` property to `lblTitle`.

Name: lblEmployeeName	**Name:** lblHoursWorked	**Name:** lblWeeklyPay
Text: Employee Name	**Text:** Hours Worked	**Text:** Weekly Pay
Font: Size = 11, Bold = True	**Font:** Size = 11, Bold = True	**Font:** Size = 11, Bold = True
Size: Width = 128, Height = 23	**Size:** Width = 112, Height = 23	**Size:** Width = 104, Height = 23
Location: X = 16, Y = 112	**Location:** X = 240, Y = 112	**Location:** X = 376, Y = 112

In addition, you must place three more label controls on the form. The following are the properties to each control that must be placed:

Adding the Text Boxes

You need to add a total of 13 text box controls on the form. You can place them in any order that you wish, but remember that they all need to be lined up when you are finished.

The following steps are required to place the first text box control on the form:

Step 1: Select the text box control from the toolbox.

Step 2: Place the mouse pointer over the area of the form where you wish to place the upper-left corner of the text box control.

Step 3: Hold the mouse button down and drag the pointer to the lower-right corner where the text box control will be placed.

Step 4: Release the mouse button and the text box control will be placed on the form.

Step 5: Click on the `Name` property in the Properties window and type `"txtEmployee1"`.

Step 6: Click on the `Text` property in the Properties window and clear the default text so that nothing is displayed in the text box when you run the application.

The remaining text boxes are placed the same way, but with the following properties:

Name: txtEmployee2	Name: txtEmployee3	Name: txtEmployee4
Text:	Text:	Text:
Size: Width = 192, Height = 20	Size: Width = 192, Height = 20	Size: Width = 192, Height = 20
Location: X = 16, Y = 168	Location: X = 16, Y = 200	Location: X = 16, Y = 232
Name: txtHours1	Name: txtHours2	Name: txtHours3
Text:	Text:	Text:
Size: Width = 80, Height = 20	Size: Width = 80, Height = 20	Size: Width = 80, Height = 20
Location: X = 240, Y = 136	Location: X = 240, Y = 168	Location: X = 240, Y = 200
Name: txtHours4	Name: txtWeeklyPay1	Name: txtWeeklyPay2
Text:	Text:	Text:
Size: Width = 80, Height = 20	Size: Width = 112, Height = 20	Size: Width = 112, Height = 20
Location: X = 240, Y = 232	Location: X = 376, Y = 136	Location: X = 376, Y = 168
Name: txtWeeklyPay3	Name: txtWeeklyPay4	Name: txtTotalPay
Text:	Text:	Text:
Size: Width = 112, Height = 20	Size: Width = 112, Height = 20	Size: Width = 112, Height = 20
Location: X = 376, Y = 200	Location: X = 376, Y = 232	Location: X = 376, Y = 264

 COACH'S TIP

To save time, after you create the first row of text boxes, you can copy them to the clipboard and paste them back onto the form. You will still have to rename the text boxes, but they will be created as the exact size that you desire as well as the proper spacing in between each text box.

Adding the Final Label

There is no difference in adding the last label. The reason this label is added at the end is so that you can determine the proper location to place it. Here are the properties for the last label:

Name: lblTotalPay
Caption: Total Pay
Font: Size = 11, Bold = True
Size: Width = 296, Height = 264
Location: X = 72, Y = 23

The final application will look like that shown in Figure 2.63.

Figure 2.63
Final application

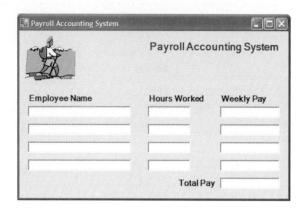

CORNER

Welcome to the Coach's Corner. At the end of each of the remaining chapters, you will find a Coach's Corner explaining some of the subtleties of Visual Basic .NET that are important to the Visual Basic .NET applications programmer but may not be timely in an academic study of the language. These tips can be skipped, but reading them will allow you to create more professional applications.

Tab Index

When you create applications, you often add controls in the order you think about them, not necessarily in the order the user wishes to enter data. When you place controls on a form, they receive a default **TabIndex** that follows the order they are added to the form.

Create a form using the following instructions exactly in the same order that they are listed:

Step 1:   Create a button at the bottom of the form.
Step 2:   Create a text box in the lower-right side of the form, but above the button.
Step 3:   Create a text box directly above the text box created in Step 2.
Step 4:   Create a text box to the left of the text box created in Step 2.
Step 5:   Create a text box to the left of the text box created in Step 3.

Observe that Figure 2.64 shows how you should create your form. Notice that the text boxes have their default text values displayed. It should clarify which text boxes were created first.

Figure 2.64
Form with text boxes

Step 6:   Run the application. Notice the focus of the application is on the button.
Step 7:   Hit the `<TAB>` key. Notice the focus changes to the text box with "TextBox1" showing.

Step 8:   Hit the <TAB> key. Notice the focus changes to the text box with
"TextBox2" showing.

Step 9:   Hit the <TAB> key. Notice the focus changes to the text box with
"TextBox3" showing.

Step 10:   Hit the <TAB> key. Notice the focus changes to the text box with
"TextBox4" showing.

Step 11:   Exit the application.

A well-designed program should start with the focus in the upper-left corner. When
the <TAB> key is pressed, you should move to the next logical control. This may be to
the right or just below the current one. Which order is not as important as that the order
you choose makes logical sense in your application and is consistent throughout your
application.

Fortunately, Visual Basic .NET allows you to control the TabIndex of the application. One of the properties of every control is the TabIndex property.

Observe the TabIndex of the text box in the upper-left corner of the form. It is set
to 4. By setting it to 0, you can make it the first control in the tab order of the application. Then you can set the remaining controls to 1, 2, 3, and 4, so that the application's
tab order behaves in an intuitive manner.

Tab Stop

Often you do not wish a control to be in the tab order at all. Label controls function this
way. If you run an application that contains labels, observe that they do not get focus as
you repeatedly hit the <TAB> key.

Visual Basic .NET provides us with a property, **TabStop**, to control this behavior
for other controls. In your Lady or the Tiger application, you have no reason to tab over
to the picture box control. Therefore, you should set the TabStop property of the picture box to False. A False setting will remove the control from the tab loop. A True
setting will place it in the tab loop. Most controls will have this property.

COACH'S TIP

Be aware that not all
controls have a
TabIndex and a
TabStop.

Key Words and Key Terms

Button Control

A control that acts as an action button. When depressed, the attached code will
execute.

Font

Sets the various typeface and style properties for the font of the control.

Form Window

A window that allows a programmer to create an application's form by attaching
code and controls.

Icon

A small graphic that represents a larger purpose.

Keyword

A special word that is predefined by Visual Basic .NET with a special meaning.

Label Control

A control that displays static text. This text can be changed programmatically.

Location (Property)

Controls the horizontal and vertical placement of a control.

Menu Bar

A series of text shortcuts to commonly used routines in the development of an
application.

Name

Sets the name by which the control can be referenced programmatically.

New Project Window

A window that displays the options for creating a new project.

Picture Box Control

A control that displays a picture.

Properties Window

A window that allows the programmer to change the properties of a control.

`Size`

Controls the horizontal and vertical size of a control.

Solution Explorer Window

A window that shows the major components of a project(s).

Standard Toolbar

A shortcut to commonly used actions that affect the project. The actions are represented by small icons associated with actions.

Static Text

Text that cannot be changed by the user of the application.

`TabIndex`

Sets the order the control as the user tabs from control to control.

`TabStop`

Determines whether or not a control will be in the tab order.

`Text`

Sets the name that will be displayed for a control when the program is executed.

Text Box Control

A control that allows text to be entered into it.

Toolbox

A window with icons that link to commonly used controls that may be added to the form by the programmer.

Additional Exercises

1. The `Name` of a form is a(n) _____.
   a. `Control`   b. `Event`   c. `Property`   d. `Picture`

2. `Click` is a(n) _____ on a button.
   a. `Control`   b. `Event`   c. `Property`   d. `Picture`

3. A text box is a(n) _____.
   a. `Control`   b. `Event`   c. `Property`   d. `Picture`

4. A `Text` is a(n) _____ on a button.
   a. `Control`   b. `Event`   c. `Property`   d. `Picture`

5. Explain when you would use a text box, label, picture box, and button control.

6. Explain the difference between the `Text` property and the `Name` property.

Assume for the next five questions that a button `btnButton1`, a label `lblLabel1`, and a text box `txtText1` are on a form `frmForm1`.

7. Is there an error in the following code? If so, correct it.

```
Private Sub btnButton1_Click(...
    txtText1.Text = 'Will This Work?'
End Sub
```

8. Is there an error in the following code? If so, correct it.

```
Private Sub btnButton1_Click(...
    txtText1.Txt = "Will This Work?"
End Sub
```

9. Is there an error in the following code? If so, correct it.

```
Private Sub btnButton1_Click(...
    lblLabel1.txtText1 = "Will This Work?"
End Sub
```

10. Is there an error in the following code? If so, correct it.

```
Private Sub btnButton1_Click(...
    txtText1.BackColor = LightBlue
End Sub
```

11. Is there an error in the following code? If so, correct it.

```
Private Sub btnButton1_Click(...
    txtText1.BackColor = LighterBlue
End Sub
```

12. Does changing the `TabIndex` of a control change the way the control is displayed in any manner? If so, indicate how.

13. Will the following code change the `Image` property of the picture box `pctPicture` so that it will display the photo stored in the file `"Example-Picture.jpg"`? Assume the photo file is located in the same directory the application is executed.

```
pctPicture.Image = Image.FromFile("ExamplePicture.jpg")
```

14. When you developed your Lady or the Tiger application, you changed the `Text` of the `lblTitle` label so that it displayed `" is Guilty"`. However, you did not change the `Text` of the form to reflect the change. Add the code to the application to do so.

15. Create an application that contains ten buttons and one label. The buttons should be labeled from 1 to 10. If button 1 is pressed, display 1 in the label. If button 2 is pressed, display 2 in the label, and so on.

16. Modify the case study to include a label and text boxes for department.

17. Create an application that contains three buttons and a picture box. When each button is pushed, a different picture should be displayed. You can use any picture files you like. However, it works best if you make all three about the same size. I took three .jpg files of my niece when creating the solution.

18. Create an application that will contain a button, a picture box, and a text box. When the button is pressed, display the picture that is typed into the text box.

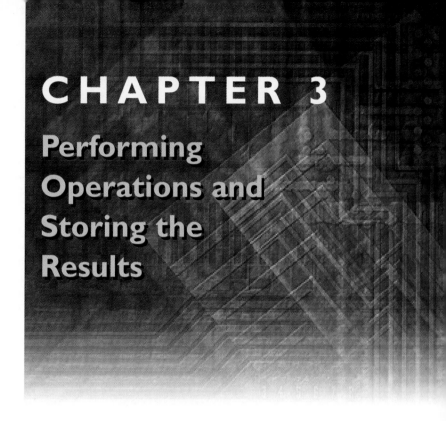

CHAPTER 3

Performing Operations and Storing the Results

So far you have learned how to enter and display values in forms. In this chapter, you will learn how to perform operations on these values and store them in the computer's memory. You will also learn when it is important to set values so they cannot be modified. Finally, you will learn how to inspect a program to see where possible errors may occur.

3.1 Variables

In Chapter 2, you saw that you could store values in controls such as a text box. If all values were stored in robust objects like text boxes, your application would waste valuable resources. It is quite common to require the storage of values in a more efficient manner. Visual Basic .NET allows you to store values in a **variable**.

Variables and objects share similar properties, although you create them differently. To create an object, you select it from a toolbox and drag it onto a form. This gives it a default name and data type. Dragging and dropping cannot create a variable, but creating a variable requires the same specifications as creating an object. In order to use a variable, you must allocate the appropriate amount of space and associate a name and data type for it. You must give the variable a valid **variable name** so that you may reference the stored value throughout the program. Additionally, you must select from a list of **variable data types** indicating to Visual Basic .NET how much space to allocate and how to process and display the variable when it is used within the program.

Variables of different data types exist so that you can store different types of values. One data type is the **Integer**. An integer is a whole number. Typically you would represent integers as a number following this pattern:

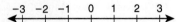

You can see that positive numbers, negative numbers, and the number 0 are all numbers included. Visual Basic .NET provides the variable data type `Integer` to allow the creation of a variable to store only integer values.

Selecting the Proper Data Type

However, selection of `Integer` as a variable's data type requires some thought. The maximum and minimum size of a variable must be taken into account. Does the program you are writing require storing a grade on an exam with a maximum value of 100 and a minimum value of 0? Does the program you are writing require storing the total number of people in the United States? That number would be upwards of 280 million people.

Visual Basic .NET provides three data types that store integers. Which data type is chosen depends on the range of values required by the integer variable you are declaring. If you require an integer that will always remain between –32,768 and 32,767, then you can use the **Short** data type. However, if your variable must store an integer of greater or less than the extremes indicated, then you must use the `Integer` data type. An `Integer` variable can store a value from –2,147,483,648 to 2,147,483,647. Finally, if you need to store really large values, you can use the **Long** data type. A `Long` variable can store an integer with a range of –9,223,372,036,854,775,808 to 9,223,372,036,854,775,807.

What happens if you use the wrong data type? Well, that depends on which data type you choose. Beginning programmers might decide to use the `Long` data type in all cases because it would safeguard against guessing wrong. However, while it will not cause an error in the execution of the program (commonly known as a **run-time error**), it will waste memory. A `Long` variable takes twice the space of an `Integer` variable.

If, on the other hand, you choose a variable to be a `Short` and then set it to a value out of the range of the variable, then you will get an execution error. Observe the following code and the error message you receive when you execute it.

COACH'S TIP

A `Long` variable can hold any value that an `Integer` variable can, but not vice versa. Similarly, an `Integer` variable can hold any value that a `Short` variable can, but not vice versa.

```
Private Sub btnCalculate_Click(...
    Dim shtVariable As Short

    shtVariable = 32767
    shtVariable = shtVariable + 1
End Sub
```

If you ignore the statement with the `Dim` keyword that declares the variable for now, you can see how you can set the variable `shtVariable` to 32767. This is a valid statement since 32767 is a value within the range of acceptable values for a `Short` variable. However, when you execute the next line, the variable should contain the value 32768. Since a `Short` cannot store a value that large, you will get an execution error. The error message is as shown in Figure 3.1.

Figure 3.1
Overflow error

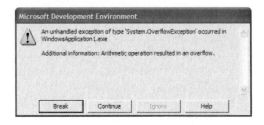

Overflow is the term used to describe when you try to store a value in a variable that is too big. When you learn a bit more of the Visual Basic .NET language, you will learn ways of preventing this type of error.

Other Variable Data Types   Not all values you store will be whole numbers. Often you will need to store decimal numbers. As with integers, Visual Basic .NET provides multiple options for selecting the data type of the variable to use when storing decimal numbers. Each data type for numerical values has different precisions and storage requirements. A programmer can select from **Single**, **Double**, or **Decimal** when creating a decimal variable. They are listed in increasing order of precision and storage requirements.

Another simple data type is a **String**. Visual Basic .NET provides the String data type to allow the storage of characters. A String stores a series of characters together. It is very versatile in that you do not need to define how much space is required. A String's storage requirement is directly related to the length of the string that you wish to store.

You may remember that you have already used Strings in your earlier applications when you changed the text displayed in the label of the Lady or the Tiger application. A String is specified as a double quote ("), a series of characters, and another double quote.

Rounding out the simple data types is the **Date** data type. Although you could store a date as a String, storing it as a Date data type will give you additional functionality, which will be explained shortly. In order to store a Date you need to enclose the date in # signs. The following example assigns the date February 3, 2002.

```
Dim dteSuperBowl As Date
dteSuperBowl = #2/03/2002#
```

There are many other data types, but they will be introduced in later chapters, as they are required.

DRILL 3.1

In each real-world situation that follows, list the variable data type that would be most appropriate.

1 A variable to store an hourly wage of an employee.
2 A variable to store the average score on an exam that has the lowest possible grade of 0 and highest grade of 100.
3 A variable to store the sum of 50 test scores on an exam that has the lowest possible grade of 0 and highest grade of 100.
4 A variable to store the sum of 500 test scores on an exam that has the lowest possible grade of 0 and highest grade of 100.
5 A variable to store the sum of 5,000 test scores on an exam that has the lowest possible grade of 0 and highest grade of 100.
6 A variable to store the total number of products ordered. Up to 1 billion orders can be placed, and each order can contain up to three products.
7 A variable to store the expression "The 76ers are looking great this year!"
8 A variable to store tomorrow's date.

DRILL 3.2

If the following code were executed, would an overflow occur? If so, why?

```
Private Sub btnCalculate_Click(...
    Dim shtVariable As Short

    shtVariable = -32768
    shtVariable = shtVariable + 1
End Sub
```

DRILL 3.3

If the following code were executed, would an overflow occur? If so, why?

```
Private Sub btnCalculate_Click(...
    Dim shtVariable As Short

    shtVariable = 10000
    shtVariable = shtVariable * 3
End Sub
```

DRILL 3.4

If the following code were executed, would an overflow occur? If so, why?

```
Private Sub btnCalculate_Click(...
    Dim shtVariable As Short

    shtVariable = 32767
    shtVariable = shtVariable - 5
    shtVariable = shtVariable + 5
    shtVariable = shtVariable + 1
End Sub
```

Chart Summarizing Data Types		
Data Type	**Description**	**Range**
Boolean	Logical data	True or False
Date	Date and time data	January 1, 0100, to December 31, 9999
Decimal	Large floating point numbers	Varies in size depending on the value stored; can hold values much larger or more precise than a Double
Double	Large or high precision floating point numbers	Floating point number with up to 14 digits of accuracy
Integer	Large integer numbers	–2,147,483,648 to 2,147,483,647
Long	Really large integer numbers	–9,223,372,036,854,775,808 to 9,223,372,036,854,775,807
Short	Small integer numbers	–32,768 to 32,767
Single	Small floating point numbers	Floating point number with up to 6 digits of accuracy
String	Character data	Varies based on the number of characters

Variable Names

A variable name in Visual Basic .NET begins with a letter and may be followed by any combination of letters, underscores, or digits. A variable name can be as small as one letter or as large as 255 letters, underscores, and digits combined. However, when you are picking a variable name, it should be representative of the value that you are storing. Try to stay away from variable names like X. If the represented value is the number of students in a class, a good variable name might be NumberStudents. As your programs get larger, more readable variable names will make the program easier to follow.

Letters used in variable names can be either lowercase or uppercase. Visual Basic .NET will use the capitalization of the variable when it is declared as the proper capitalization. This means that if you refer to the variable with a different capitalization later in the program, it will convert the capitalization to the one used earlier in the program. For example, if you declare a variable as NUMBERstudents and then refer to it in the program as numberSTUDENTS, Visual Basic .NET will automatically convert the variable name back to the way it was initially declared, as NUMBERstudents.

Visual Basic .NET does not differentiate between two variable names that are identical except for the case (i.e., uppercase or lowercase) of the letters in their names. If a language does, it is considered **case sensitive**. Therefore, Visual Basic .NET is not case sensitive with regard to variable names.

A variable name cannot be a keyword already used by Visual Basic .NET. Therefore, variable names like Private, Dim, or Integer are illegal.

Visual Basic .NET will immediately provide feedback if you have violated the rules of declaring a variable. When you write code that violates the rules of the Visual Basic .NET grammar, an underline will appear under the violating text. If you then move the mouse pointer over the underlined text, a pop-up message will appear with an explanation of the error. Figure 3.2 offers an example of a message that you will receive when you declare a variable name improperly.

COACH'S TIP

Variable names may contain a keyword as part of the name of a variable. For example, intDimVariable is an acceptable variable name even though it contains the keyword Dim.

Figure 3.2 Illegal use of keyword

DRILL 3.5

Determine which of the following variable names are valid:

```
1  Maura
2  Ben
3  Maura&Ben
4  Maura_Ben
5  _MauraBen
6  IsThisLegal
7  HowAboutThis?
8  PrivateDancerWasTheNameOfASong
9  Private
```

Declaring a Variable

In order to use a variable in Visual Basic .NET, you must tell the compiler that the variable exists before you actually access it. This is called declaring a variable. Declaring or allocating a variable means that you are indicating to the computer the type of variable that you wish to use as well as the name that you will use to reference it from within the program.

By default, Visual Basic .NET will not allow you to use a variable that you have not declared. While you can set your environment up to allow using undeclared variables, you should not.

Additionally, by adding the code `Option Strict On` to the beginning of your module, you can prevent the accidental conversion of one variable data type to another. Observe Figure 3.3, which demonstrates where `Option Strict On` should be placed and the message that appears when you incorrectly try to assign a floating point number to an `Integer` variable.

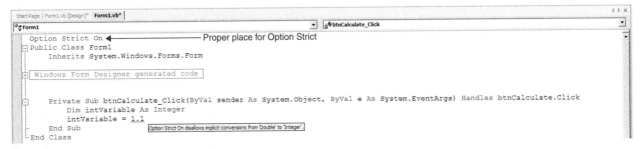

Figure 3.3 Improper conversion of data types

The Dim and Public Keywords

There are two statements that you can use to declare a variable. Which you choose depends on whether you wish the variable to be used solely within the code you declared it in or by other areas of code throughout your application. The degree of visibility that other areas of code can see a variable is known as the **scope** of a variable. The complete concept of scope will be explained after you have had some practice with variable usage.

The **Public** keyword is used when you create applications with multiple forms. You can ignore it for now and stick to using the **Dim** keyword when declaring a variable. To actually declare the variable, you need to first type the word Dim, followed by a space, followed by the variable name, followed by the word As, followed by the data type of variable. The syntax for declaring a variable using the Dim keyword is shown in the following code:

```
Dim VariableName As Data type
```

The code shown in Figure 3.4 is an example of declaring three variables—`intStudentGrade`, `sngStudentAverage`, and `decStudentWage`—in a button's `Click` event code. They are declared as the data types `Integer`, `Single`, and `Decimal`, respectively.

```
Start Page | Form1.vb [Design]* | Form1.vb* |
Form1                                                    btnStudentVariables_Click
    Option Strict On
    Public Class Form1
        Inherits System.Windows.Forms.Form

        Windows Form Designer generated code

        Private Sub btnStudentVariables_Click(ByVal sender As System.Object, ByVal e As System.EventArgs) Handles btnStudentVariables.(
            Dim intStudentGrade As Integer
            Dim sngStudentAverage As Single
            Dim decStudentWage As Decimal
        End Sub
    End Class
```

Figure 3.4 Code for declaring variables

Adding a Comment It is always a good idea to add a comment on the same line indicating the purpose of the variable. You add a comment to a line by typing a single quote and then the comment that you wish to make. Comments are not part of the actual code but a way of documenting the code so that it is more understandable.

Figure 3.5 demonstrates how to document the code from Figure 3.4.

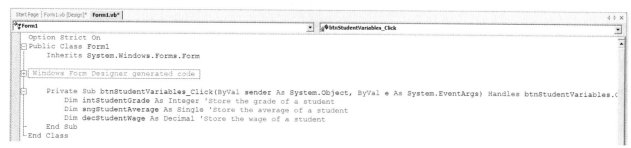

Figure 3.5 Comments added to code

Many beginning programmers may wish to use a dash in a variable name. There is a very good reason why Visual Basic .NET does not allow you to do so. Can you guess what it is? Maybe the bit of code shown in Figure 3.6 will help illustrate the problem with using a dash.

Figure 3.6 Illegal use of dash

If Visual Basic .NET allowed you to declare a variable called `intFirstVariable-intSecondVariable`, then it couldn't distinguish between the operation `intFirstVariable` minus `intSecondVariable` and the variable `intFirstVariable-intSecondVariable`. It is important when writing computer programs that you do not create ambiguous conditions. If there is no clear indication of what you intend the computer to accomplish, then the computer will not be able to guess what you intend.

Naming Conventions

Although not a rule imposed by the Visual Basic .NET language, it is a good practice to use a naming convention when declaring variables.

You should follow a simple standard used throughout the industry for Visual Basic .NET applications. All variable names start with a three-letter abbreviation indicating the variable's data type. You may have noticed that you have already been doing this.

After the three-letter abbreviation, a variable should be described in enough detail so that its purpose is self-explanatory. Another good standard is to capitalize the first letter of each word used in the variable name. It allows the reader of the code to easily differentiate the words in a variable name.

A final convention that will improve your code's readability is to be consistent with any abbreviations that you might use repeatedly throughout your code. For instance, if you wish to abbreviate the word "Number," you could abbreviate it as Num or Nbr. It really doesn't matter which you choose, as long as you use the same one throughout your code.

Chart Summarizing Data Type Prefixes	
Data Type	**Prefix**
Boolean	bln
Date	dte
Decimal	dec
Double	dbl
Integer	int
Long	lng
Short	sht
Single	sng
String	str

DRILL 3.6

What would happen if you tried to write code as follows?

```
Private Sub btnDrill_Click(...
    strDrillValue = "Initial Value"
    Dim strDrillValue As String
    strDrillValue = "What will be the output?"
    MsgBox(strDrillValue)
End Sub
```

COACH'S TIP

A simple way to output values to the user is to use a message box. A message box is called by placing a value in-between parentheses and after the word MsgBox. This will be explained in detail at the end of the chapter.

3.2 Simple Operators

If computers could only allow the entry, storage, and display of values, our society would not be so heavily dependent on them. A programmer begins to tap a computer's power by writing simple programs that perform calculations.

Visual Basic .NET allows you to perform all the numerical operations you are familiar with. A computer uses symbols called **operators** to indicate that an operation is to be performed. You are already familiar with the operator for assignment, the equals sign (=). Addition, subtraction, multiplication, and division are all supported, using operators that you are already familiar with as well. They are +, −, *, and / operators, respectively. The values that operators perform their actions upon are known as **operands**. One other operator you will use that you may not be familiar with is the exponent operator, ^. The exponent operator is used when you wish to raise a number to a power. For example, if you want to raise the number 3 to the fourth power, you can use the code 3*3*3*3, but a much better way to compute the value is to use the code 3^4.

Visual Basic .NET can use these operators in many ways; however, the only way that you have been taught so far is in the button `Click` event. Follow this simple example to see how operators can be used. Start by creating a form with a label `lblTotal` and a button `btnAdd`. In the button's `Click` event, declare a variable `intTotal`, add 1 plus 1 together, and store the result in `intTotal`. Finally, copy the value to the text box for output in the form.

Create Form

Step 1: Create a new project.
Step 2: Set the `Name` property of the form to `frmAdd`.
Step 3: Set the `Text` property to `Addition Operator`.

Add Output Label

Step 1: Place a label control in the middle of the form.
Step 2: Set the `Name` property to `lblTotal`.
Step 3: Clear the default text from the `Text` property.

Add Button

Step 1: Place a button control below the `lblTotal` label.
Step 2: Set the `Name` property to `btnAdd`.
Step 3: Set the `Text` property to `Add`.
Step 4: Double-click on the `btnAdd` button and add the code shown in Figure 3.7.

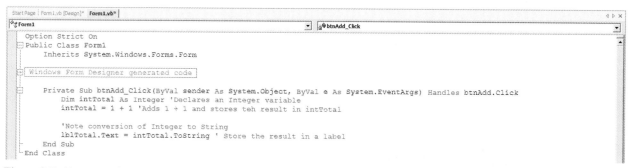

Figure 3.7 Button code

The code within the event `btnAdd_Click` introduces two operators, both of which you are already familiar with and which operate in the manner you would expect. The + operator takes two values and adds them together. The result, 2, is then assigned using the equals operator, =, to the `lblTotal` label. This is shown in Figure 3.8.

Figure 3.8
Application after
button is clicked

Expressions may contain more than just values and operators. They may also contain parentheses. Parentheses tell the computer to calculate the operations inside the parentheses before performing the rest of the calculations. The order in which the operations are performed is referred to as the **order of precedence** of the operations. So far, the operations learned follow the same precedence learned in elementary school mathematics. Therefore, when reading from left to right, you perform all the operations in the parentheses first, then the exponentiations, then all the multiplications and divisions, and finally all the additions and subtractions.

Review of Arithmetic Operators Listed by Order of Precedence	
Operators	**Operations**
( )	Parentheses
^	Exponentiation
* /	Multiplication and Division
+ −	Addition and Subtraction

Converting Data Types

The previous code required assigning a numerical value to the `Text` property of a text box. A text box's `Text` property requires a `String` value. Visual Basic .NET allows you to convert numerical values using a special routine, `ToString`, to convert a numerical value to a `String` data type. While it is possible to set the options in Visual Basic .NET not to require the conversion, it is a bad practice to do so. The routine `ToString` is called a method. Methods and additional features of object-oriented programming will be covered in Chapter 6.

DRILL 3.7

The following code snippets are designed to test your order of precedence knowledge. Try working out each example first; then type in the snippet and execute it. Compare your results to the answers found at the end of the chapter.

```
Private Sub btnDrill_Click(...
    lblOutput.Text = (4 + 5 * 6 - 3 / 3 + 6).ToString
End Sub

Private Sub btnDrill_Click(...
    lblOutput.Text = ((4 + 5) * 6 - (3 / 3 + 6)).ToString
End Sub

Private Sub btnDrill_Click(...
    lblOutput.Text = ((4 + 5) / (1 + 2)).ToString
End Sub

Private Sub btnDrill_Click(...
    lblOutput.Text = (4 * 5 * (3 + 3)).ToString
End Sub

Private Sub btnDrill_Click(...
    lblOutput.Text = (2 - 2 / 2 + 2 * 2 - 3).ToString
End Sub

Private Sub btnDrill_Click(...
    lblOutput.Text = (2 + 2 * 2 ^ 3 - 3).ToString
End Sub
```

The examples in Figure 3.7 and Drill 3.7 were selected with one thing in common. All the calculations produce results that are whole numbers.

Using the same application, you can change the operation from 1 + 1 to 1 / 3. What do you think the result would be? If you were familiar with Visual Basic .NET, you would know the answer is 0.333333333333333. However, programmers already familiar with other languages might not be so quick to guess that. Visual Basic .NET is not as strict in enforcing the use of proper data types as some other languages are. Other languages do not produce results of one data type when the calculation is performed on operands of another data type. In this example, the operands are `Integers` while the result is a `Decimal`.

Example: Counter Application

You now know enough to create an application that acts as a counter. A counter should start at 0 and increment by 1 each time a button is pressed. It is also useful to have an additional button that will reset the counter to 0. The application will look as shown in Figure 3.9.

Figure 3.9
Simple counter application

You can attach code to the button for the counter, `btnCounter`, to add 1 to your counter. The counter will be stored in an `Integer` variable, `intCounter`, and displayed as the `Text` in the label `lblCounter`. You can then attach similar code to the button `btnReset` to set the variable and label to reset the counter back to 0.

To develop this application, start with a blank form and perform the following steps:

Create Form

Step 1: Create a new project.
Step 2: Set the `Name` property of the form to `frmCounter`.
Step 3: Set the `Text` property to `Simple Counter Application`.
Step 4: Right-click on `Form1.vb` in the Solution Explorer and rename the form to `frmCounter.vb`.

You need a variable to store the current value of the counter. Because this variable will be accessed from multiple controls' `Click` events, you need to declare it in the `Declarations` section.

Add intCounter Variable

Step 1: Right-click on the form.
Step 2: Click on the `View Code` item of the pop-up menu.
Step 3: Your code should default to the `Declarations` section. The pull-downs of your code should look like those shown in Figure 3.10.

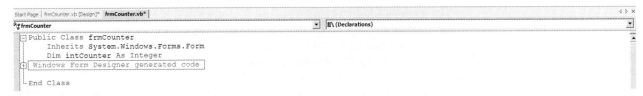

Figure 3.10 `Declarations` section

Step 4: Type `Dim intCounter As Integer`.

For the remaining steps, you must switch back to the object view of the application. Remember, you can switch to the object view by clicking on the `frmCounter.vb [Design]*` tab.

Add Title Label

Step 1: Place a label control in the middle of the form.
Step 2: Set the `Name` to `lblTitle`.
Step 3: Set the `Text` to `Simple Counter Application`.
Step 4: Set the `Font Size` property to `14` and the `Font Bold` property to `True`.
Step 5: Set the `TextAlign` property to `MiddleCenter`. (See Figure 3.11.)

Figure 3.11
Application with
title label placed

Add Counter Label

Step 1: Place a label control in the middle of the form.
Step 2: Set the `Name` property to `lblCounter`.
Step 3: Set the `Text` property to `0`.
Step 4: Set the `Font Size` property to `24` and the `Font Bold` property to `True`.
Step 5: Set the `TextAlign` property to `MiddleCenter`. (See Figure 3.12.)

Figure 3.12
Application with counter
label added

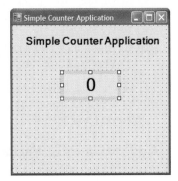

Add Counter Button

Step 1: Place a button control in the lower-left side of the form.

Step 2: Set the Name property to btnCounter.

Step 3: Set the Text property to Counter.

Step 4: Double-click on the button.

Step 5: Attach the code to add 1 to the counter. First you must add 1 to the counter variable, intCounter, and store the results in intCounter. Then update the label, lblCount, with the new value. (See Figures 3.13 and 3.14.)

Figure 3.13
Application with
btnCounter button placed

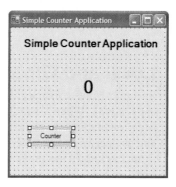

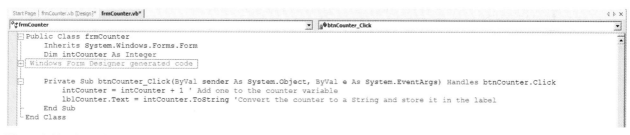

Figure 3.14   Code for btnCounter button

COACH'S TIP

A variable should always be initialized to a value before it is used.

Add Reset Button

Step 1: Place a button control in the lower-right side of the form.

Step 2: Set the Name property to btnReset.

Step 3: Set the Text property to Reset.

Step 4: Double-click on the button.

Step 5: Attach the code to reset the counter to 0. First you must set the counter variable, intCounter, to 0 and store the results in intCounter. Then update the label, lblCounter, with the new value. (See Figures 3.15 and 3.16.)

Figure 3.15
Application with btnReset
button added

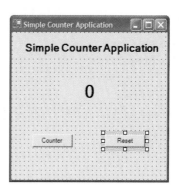

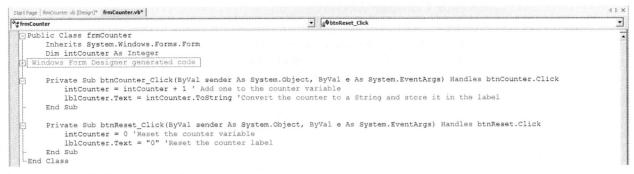

Figure 3.16   Code for `btnReset` button

3.3   Local and Global Variables

In the previous examples, you saw variables declared in different locations within the applications. When a variable is declared within an event, it is only visible within the code for that event. Variables of this nature are known as local in scope. When a variable is declared within the `Declarations` section of a form, it is visible to the entire form and known as global in scope.

Scope Drills

For the following three drills, assume that a form has been created with three buttons: `btnInitialize`, `btnAdd`, and `btnOutput`.

DRILL 3.8

If the following three `Click` events are coded, what would the output be if the buttons were clicked in the following order: `btnInitialize`, `btnAdd`, and `btnOutput`?

```
Public Class frmDrills
    Inherits System.Windows.Forms.Form

    Private Sub btnInitialize_Click(...
        Dim intDrillValue As Integer
        intDrillValue = 10
    End Sub

    Private Sub btnAdd_Click(...
        intDrillValue = intDrillValue + 10
    End Sub

    Private Sub btnOutput_Click(...
        MsgBox(intDrillValue.ToString())
    End Sub
End Class
```

DRILL 3.9

If the following three `Click` events are coded, and the variable `intDrillValue` is declared in each of the events, what would the output be if the buttons were clicked in the following order: `btnInitialize`, `btnAdd`, and `btnOutput`?

```
Public Class frmDrills
    Inherits System.Windows.Forms.Form

    Dim intDrillValue As Integer

    Private Sub btnInitialize_Click(...
        intDrillValue = 10

    End Sub

    Private Sub btnAdd_Click(...
        intDrillValue = intDrillValue + 10
    End Sub

    Private Sub btnOutput_Click(...
        MsgBox(intDrillValue.ToString())
    End Sub
End Class
```

DRILL 3.10

If the following three `Click` events are coded, and the variable `intDrillValue` is declared in the `Declarations` section, what would the output be if the buttons were clicked in the following order: `btnInitialize`, `btnAdd`, and `btnOutput`?

```
Public Class frmDrills
    Inherits System.Windows.Forms.Form

    Dim intDrillValue As Integer

    Private Sub btnInitialize_Click(...
        Dim intDrillValue As Integer
        intDrillValue = 10

    End Sub

    Private Sub btnAdd_Click(...
        intDrillValue = intDrillValue + 10
    End Sub

    Private Sub btnOutput_Click(...
        MsgBox(intDrillValue.ToString())
    End Sub
End Class
```

3.4   **Constants**

Often in programming you will want to represent values that will not change during the execution of the program. These values are called **constants**. They are added to the program for two purposes.

First, by adding a name to associate with the value, your program will become more readable. Imagine if you wrote a program that computed sales tax. While you could type the tax amount directly into the equations using it, a person reading the program would not immediately understand the purpose of the value 0.06 without reading a comment. If you add a constant called `SalesTax` and set it to 0.06, your code is more understandable.

In addition, another benefit occurs if the value 0.06 appears in the program many times. If the sales tax is increased, let's say to pay for a new football stadium, you will have to change it in many places, thus increasing your risk of introducing an error to the program. With the use of constants, you only have to change the value in a single place.

You may be wondering why you just do not use a variable instead of coming up with a new way to define a constant. Simple—a variable has the ability to change within the program. You wouldn't want to risk the chance that you could inadvertently change a value that shouldn't be changed. With a constant, there is no way to change it.

In order to declare a constant, you type the keyword `Const`, a space, followed by the name of the constant, followed by a space, followed by an equals sign, followed by the value to set the constant to. This can be seen in the following code that illustrates the syntax of assigning a constant:

```
Const ConstantName = Value
```

For example, the following code defines a constant called `TaxRate` as 0.06:

```
Const TaxRate = 0.06
```

In addition to the format given, you may include a data type for the constant. You may also use an expression instead of the value shown previously.

Here is a more descriptive way of assigning a constant:

```
Const ConstantName As Data type = Value
```

For example, the following code defines a constant called `sngTaxRate` as `Single` with a value of 0.06:

```
Const sngtaxRate As Single = 0.06
```

> **COACH'S TIP**
>
> The rules for naming a constant are the same as those for naming a variable.

Example: Sales Tax Calculation

Let's create a very simple application to calculate the sales tax for a purchase. It will use a constant in order to indicate the sales tax percentage. In a program this small, you might not think a constant is worthwhile; however, it is good practice, especially if your program may grow in size.

Create Form

Step 1: Create a new project called Sales Tax Calculation.
Step 2: Set the `Name` property of the form to `frmSalesTax`.
Step 3: Set the `Text` property to `Sales Tax Calculation`.
Step 4: Right-click on `Form1.vb` in the Solution Explorer and rename the form to `frmSalesTax.vb`.

Add Title Label

Step 1: Click on the label control in the Control toolbox.

Step 2: Draw a label control on the form.

Step 3: Set the `Name` property of the label to `lblTitle`.

Step 4: Change the `Text` property to `"Sales Tax Calculation"`.

Step 5: Change the `Font Size` property to 14 and the `Font Bold` property to `True`.

Step 6: Change the `TextAlign` property to `MiddleCenter`. (See Figure 3.17.)

Figure 3.17
Label added to application

Next, add three more labels: `"Purchase Price"`, `"Sales Tax"`, and `"Final Price"`.

Add Purchase Price Label

Step 1: Place a label control on the form.

Step 2: Change the `Name` property to `lblPurchasePrice`.

Step 3: Change the `Text` property to `Purchase Price`.

Step 4: Change the `Font Size` property to 14 and the `Font Bold` property to `True`.

Add Sales Tax Label

Step 1: Place a label control on the form.

Step 2: Change the `Name` property to `lblSalesTax`.

Step 3: Change the `Text` property to `Sales Tax`.

Step 4: Change the `Font Size` property to 14 and the `Font Bold` property to `True`.

Add Final Price Label

Step 1: Place a label control on the form.

Step 2: Change the `Name` property to `lblFinalPrice`.

Step 3: Change the `Text` property to `Final Price`.

Step 4: Change the `Font Size` property to 14 and the `Font Bold` property to `True`. (See Figure 3.18.)

Figure 3.18
Additional labels added
to application

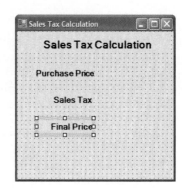

Next, add three text boxes: `txtPurchasePrice`, `txtSalesTax`, and `txtFinalPrice`.

Add Purchase Price Text Box

Step 1: Place a text box control on the form.
Step 2: Set the `Name` property of the control to `txtPurchasePrice`.
Step 3: Erase the value in the `Text` property.

Add Sales Tax Text Box

Step 1: Place a text box control on the form.
Step 2: Set the `Name` property of the control to `txtSalesTax`.
Step 3: Erase the value in the `Text` property.

Add Final Price Text Box

Step 1: Place a text box control on the form.
Step 2: Set the `Name` property of the control to `txtFinalPrice`.
Step 3: Erase the value in `Text` property. (See Figure 3.19.)

Figure 3.19
Text boxes added
to application

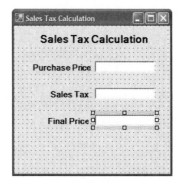

Next you must add a button to perform the calculation.

Add Calculation Button

Step 1: Place a button control on the form.
Step 2: Set the `Name` property of the control to `btnCalculate`.
Step 3: Change the `Text` property to `Calculate`. (See Figure 3.20.)

The final step is to add the code to perform the calculations.

Figure 3.20
Calculate button added
to application

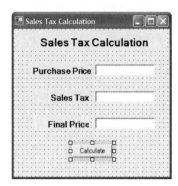

Add Code to the Button

Step 1: Double-click on the `btnCalculate` button.

Step 2: Type the declaration to define a constant called `decSalesTaxRate` as a `Decimal` data type and set it equal to `0.06`.

Step 3: Declare three variables: `decSalesTaxAmount`, `decFinalPrice`, and `decPurchasePrice`.

Step 4: Convert the value stored in the `txtPurchasePrice` text box to a numerical value and store it in the `decPurchasePrice` variable.

Step 5: Calculate the `decSalesTaxAmount` by multiplying the `decSalesTaxRate` by `decPurchasePrice`.

Step 6: Calculate the `decFinalPrice` by adding the amount stored in the `decPurchasePrice` and `decSalesTaxAmount`.

Step 7: Store the `decSalesTaxAmount` in the `txtSalesTax` text box.

Step 8: Store the `decFinalPrice` in the `txtFinalPrice` text box. (See Figure 3.21.)

Figure 3.21 Code for button

3.5 Complex Operators

Visual Basic .NET has introduced a few operators, which, although not earth-shattering in their impact, are a really nice addition.

You will find that you will often wish to perform such mathematical operations as adding a number to, subtracting a number from, or multiplying a number by an existing variable and store the result back in the same variable. It was always frustrating to me that previous versions of Visual Basic did not have these shortcut operators. However, my frustration ended with the addition of several operators to Visual Basic .NET. The following chart shows many of the new operators. If you choose to ignore a new feature, the old method will work fine.

Operation	Long Way of Writing the Statement	Short Way of Writing the Statement
Addition	intVar = intVar + 1	intVar += 1
Subtraction	intVar = intVar - 1	intVar -= 1
Division	intVar = intVar / 1	intVar /= 1
Multiplication	intVar = intVar * 1	intVar *= 1
String concatenation	strVar = strVar & "New Text"	strVar &= "New Text"

DRILL 3.11

What is the output if the btnOperators' Click event is executed?

```
Private Sub btnOperators_Click(...
    Dim intDrillValue As Integer

    intDrillValue = 10
    intDrillValue += 5

    MsgBox(intDrillValue.ToString)
End Sub
```

DRILL 3.12

What is the output if the btnOperators' Click event is executed?

```
Private Sub btnOperators_Click(...
    Dim intDrillValue As Integer

    intDrillValue = 1
    intDrillValue *= 5
    intDrillValue += 5

    MsgBox(intDrillValue.ToString)
End Sub
```

DRILL 3.13

What is the output if the btnOperators' Click event is executed?

```
Private Sub btnOperators_Click(...
    Dim strDrillValue As String

    strDrillValue = "This "
    strDrillValue &= "and "
    strDrillValue &= "that"

    MsgBox(strDrillValue)
End Sub
```

DRILL 3.14

What is the output if the btnOperators' Click event is executed?

```
Private Sub btnOperators_Click(...
    Dim strDrillValue As String

    strDrillValue = "This "
    strDrillValue = "and "
    strDrillValue = "that"

    MsgBox(strDrillValue)
End Sub
```

3.6 Using the Debugger

So far the programs you have written have been simple enough that if you did not write them correctly the first time and an error occurred, it was easy enough to figure out the error's source.

However, as your programs become more complex, you will need more sophisticated ways of determining the source of errors. Therefore, you must learn how to use a tool in Visual Basic .NET called the **Debugger**.

As more features of the Visual Basic .NET language are introduced, so will more features of the Visual Basic .NET Debugger. The goal for now is to introduce the Debugger and show how you can step through the execution of your program while watching how objects and variables change.

To demonstrate this, you will use the previous example and step through its execution. Since you do not wish to step through the code Visual Basic .NET created for you, you will set a **breakpoint** at the start of the code you wrote. A breakpoint is a signal to the Debugger to stop the execution of the application and wait for further instructions on how to continue executing the application.

Step 1: A breakpoint is set by clicking to the left of the code you wish to be set as the breakpoint. Observe Figure 3.22, where you set the breakpoint to the beginning of the Click event code for the btnCalculate button.

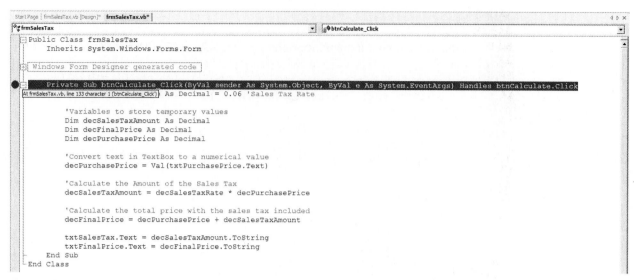

```
Start Page | frmSalesTax.vb [Design]* | frmSalesTax.vb*                                                          4 ▷ ×
frmSalesTax                                                    ▼  btnCalculate_Click                              ▼
┌─ Public Class frmSalesTax
│      Inherits System.Windows.Forms.Form
│
│   ⊞  Windows Form Designer generated code
│
●──┌─    Private Sub btnCalculate_Click(ByVal sender As System.Object, ByVal e As System.EventArgs) Handles btnCalculate.Click
   [At frmSalesTax.vb, line 133 character 1 (btnCalculate_Click')]  As Decimal = 0.06 'Sales Tax Rate
│
│              'Variables to store temporary values
│              Dim decSalesTaxAmount As Decimal
│              Dim decFinalPrice As Decimal
│              Dim decPurchasePrice As Decimal
│
│              'Convert text in TextBox to a numerical value
│              decPurchasePrice = Val(txtPurchasePrice.Text)
│
│              'Calculate the Amount of the Sales Tax
│              decSalesTaxAmount = decSalesTaxRate * decPurchasePrice
│
│              'Calculate the total price with the sales tax included
│              decFinalPrice = decPurchasePrice + decSalesTaxAmount
│
│              txtSalesTax.Text = decSalesTaxAmount.ToString
│              txtFinalPrice.Text = decFinalPrice.ToString
│      └─  End Sub
└─ End Class
```

Figure 3.22 Starting the Debugger

Step 2: Start running the application in the normal manner by clicking on the Start button or hitting the <F5> key.

Step 3: Next, enter a value for the purchase price. In this example, you will enter 49.95. Notice that you do not have to enter the dollar sign. (See Figure 3.23.)

Figure 3.23
Application executing with
purchase price entered

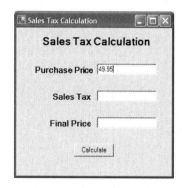

COACH'S TIP

The idea of finding and removing errors in your application is known as debugging. You may be wondering how the process got such a nontechnical name. In the early days of computers, a problem developed with one computer's execution. It turned out that an insect had flown into the computer and broken it. Thus the term debugging was born.

Step 4: Then click on the btnCalculate button. Notice that instead of executing the code, the actual code is displayed. You are now in the Visual Basic .NET Debugger. The yellow highlighting indicates what line you are about to execute. As you can see from Figure 3.24, you are about to enter the code to execute the btnCalculate button.

Figure 3.24 Code being stepped into

You can step through the `Click` event line by line by clicking on the `Debug` menu item and then clicking on `Step Into` or you can press the `<F11>` key.

Step 5: Unlike in Step 4, to move to the next line of code, you may wish to use the `<F10>` instead of the `<F11>` key. While there is only a subtle difference, the `<F10>` key will step over code instead of stepping into it. By stepping over code you will prevent the accidental entry into additional code that may complicate the tracing of the application.

Press the `<F10>` key once. Notice how the yellow bar skips over the declarations and is over the first line of code to be executed. (See Figure 3.25.) You cannot trace the declaration of variables.

Figure 3.25 First line of code about to be executed

Step 6: The Visual Basic .NET Debugger allows you to do much more than just step through the code. If you move the mouse pointer over objects and variables and then pause, the object's or variable's value will be displayed in a mini pop-up window. Figure 3.26 shows how, as you move your mouse pointer over the decPurchasePrice variable, you can see the value, 0, contained within. It contains the value 0 because the line of code hasn't been executed yet. Notice the D next to the value. This is because the number is being displayed in a decimal format. Other formats exist, but do not worry about them for now.

Figure 3.26 Mouse pointer over variable shows initial value

Step 7: Press the <F10> key one more time. The yellow highlighting is now over the next line of code that is about to be executed.

Step 8: Place your mouse pointer over the variable decPurchasePrice again. Notice this time the value has been set to 49.95. (See Figure 3.27.)

Figure 3.27 Mouse pointer over variable shows value after assignment

Notice that the values do not appear as currency values as you would like. You need to round the result to two decimal places. There are a few ways of doing this that will be shown in Chapter 5.

Step 9: You can either press the <F5> key once or press <F10> a few more times and the rest of the code is executed. You will arrive at the final screen of the application. (See Figure 3.28.)

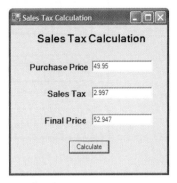

Figure 3.28 Final view of the application

◆ 3.7 Case Study

Problem Description

This case study will modify the one from Chapter 2 and add the computational functionality that was missing. Now, instead of only allowing the entry of a person's name, hours worked, and weekly pay, you need to add a btnCalculate button that will automatically calculate a person's weekly pay as well as the total payroll cost. A person's weekly pay is calculated by multiplying the number of hours a person worked by a fixed hourly rate of $9.50/hour. After all of the employees' weekly pay is calculated, then you must calculate the total payroll.

Figure 3.29 demonstrates what the input to your application may look like.

Figure 3.29
Sketch of application

Payroll Accounting System

Payroll Accounting System

Employee Name	Hours Worked	Weekly Pay
Jeff Salvage	60	
John Nunn	40	
John Cunningham	30	
Tim Burke	50	
Calculate		Total Pay

After the btnCalculate button is clicked, Figure 3.30 would be sample output for the input shown in Figure 3.29.

Figure 3.30
Sketch of application and
how it will work

Payroll Accounting System

Payroll Accounting System

Employee Name	Hours Worked	Weekly Pay
Jeff Salvage	60	570
John Nunn	40	380
John Cunningham	30	285
Tim Burke	50	475

Calculate   Total Pay 1710

Problem Discussion

The solution to the problem will entail two basic steps. You must compute the values for weekly and total pay, and then you must assign those values to the text box controls for display. Both of these functions can be performed from within the code to process a `Click` event from the `btnCalculate` button.

Problem Solution

Fortunately, almost all of the controls for your application were placed on the form in Chapter 2's case study. You need only add a button control, `btnCalculate`. This control will perform the calculations necessary for the application.

Although it is not required, the use of a constant in this solution is desirable. You should code a constant to indicate the pay rate. This way you can change the pay rate once and have it affect the entire application.

To set the constant, perform the following steps:

Step 1: Right-click the mouse and click on `View Code` in the pop-up menu.
Step 2: Type `"Const sngPayRate As Single = 9.5"`.

Your code should look like that shown in Figure 3.31. Notice that the two pulldowns indicate `frmPayroll` and `Declarations`:

Figure 3.31 Code to set the constant

To place a button, perform the following steps:

Step 1: Click on the `frmPayroll.vb [Design]` tab.
Step 2: Click on the button control in the toolbox.
Step 3: Draw a button control on the form.
Step 4: Change the `Name` property to `btnCalculate`.
Step 5: Change the `Text` property to `Calculate`.
Step 6: Add the code for the button.

The button's code must calculate each employee's weekly pay. It computes weekly pay by multiplying the number of hours worked in a week by a pay rate of $9.50. Note that the code does not reference the value $9.50 directly; instead, it uses the constant that you defined `sngPayRate`.

Once the weekly pay is computed, it is converted to a `String` and output in the person's weekly pay text box.

Additionally, you must track the total pay of all four employees. When the first employee's weekly pay is computed, you assign the computed value to the total pay variable, because this is the initialization of the variable. For the second, third, and fourth employees, you add their weekly pay to the total of the previously computed employee pay.

Finally, the grand total is copied to the text box control for display (see Figure 3.32). The code follows:

```
Private Sub btnButton_Click(...
    'Temporary Variables to Store Calculations
    Dim decTotalPay As Decimal
    Dim decWeeklyPay As Decimal


    'First Person's Calculations
    'Compute weekly pay of 1st person
    decWeeklyPay = Val(txtHours1.Text) * sngPayRate
    'Convert weekly pay to String and output
    txtWeeklyPay1.Text = decWeeklyPay.ToString
    'Initialize total pay to first person's weekly pay
    decTotalPay = decWeeklyPay


    'Second Person's Calculations
    'Compute weekly pay of 2nd person
    decWeeklyPay = Val(txtHours2.Text) * sngPayRate
    'Convert weekly pay to String and output
    txtWeeklyPay2.Text = decWeeklyPay.ToString
    'Add to total pay 2nd person's pay
    decTotalPay += decWeeklyPay


    'Third Person's Calculations
    'Compute weekly pay of 3rd person
    decWeeklyPay = Val(txtHours3.Text) * sngPayRate
    'Convert weekly pay to String and output
    txtWeeklyPay3.Text = decWeeklyPay.ToString
    'Add to total pay 3rd person's pay
    decTotalPay += decWeeklyPay


    'Fourth Person's Calculations
    'Compute weekly pay of fourth person
    decWeeklyPay = Val(txtHours4.Text) * sngPayRate
    'Convert weekly pay to String and output
    txtWeeklyPay4.Text = decWeeklyPay.ToString
    'Add to total pay 4th person's pay
    decTotalPay += decWeeklyPay


    'Convert Total Pay to a string and copy to TextBox
    txtTotalPay.Text = decTotalPay.ToString
    End Sub
```

Figure 3.32
Final application

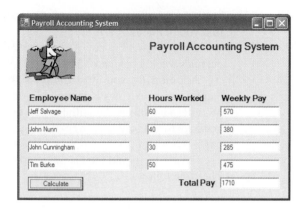

Converting Data Types

The code for your solution presents two new problems. When the values for the number of hours each employee works are entered, they are stored in a text box. When a value is stored in a text box, it is stored as a `String`. However, in order to perform mathematical calculations, you need to convert it to a numerical value. This is accomplished with a built-in function called `Val`. When you place `Val` in your code, it will return the numerical value for the `String` placed within the parentheses.

The second problem is that once you have calculated the weekly and total pays, you need to store them back in the `Text` property of the text boxes. Therefore, you use the `ToString` method to convert a numerical value to a `String` data type. While a text box will allow a numerical value to be assigned to its `Text` property, it is good programming practice to convert the type directly.

You will learn more about methods in Chapter 6.

CORNER

COACH'S

Throughout this and the previous chapter, you have seen that you can display information in a text box control. However, often you may wish to display information to the user of the application but not take up space on your form for it. A message box is an excellent way to solve this dilemma.

The following code illustrates the syntax of a simple call to a message box:

```
MsgBox ("Message")
```

`MsgBox` is the function that indicates to Visual Basic .NET that you wish a message to be displayed in a small window. Small windows like the one used for a message box are commonly referred to as a dialog box. To display a message, place any text you want displayed within a series of double quotes.

Follow these simple steps to create your first message box.

Step 1: Add a button to a blank form.
Step 2: Change the `Name` property of the button to `btnMessage`.
Step 3: Change the `Text` property of the button to `Message`.

The application and the associated code should look like Figure 3.33.

Figure 3.33
Application demonstrating a message box

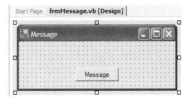

Step 4: Assign the code `MsgBox("Don't Forget To Pay Your Taxes")` to the button. (See Figure 3.34.)

Figure 3.34 Code demonstrating a message box

Step 5: Run the application.
Step 6: Click on the button.
Step 7: The message box appears, as shown in Figure 3.35.

Figure 3.35 Message box being displayed from the application

This message box is the simplest of the ones provided by Visual Basic .NET. You may have noticed that when you typed `MsgBox` and then a space, additional information appeared. (See Figure 3.36.) This information serves as a guide for you to provide additional options to the `MsgBox` command. The first option is for the `Prompt`. The `Prompt` is the value that you typed to be displayed. The other items are optional ways of further modifying the message box displayed.

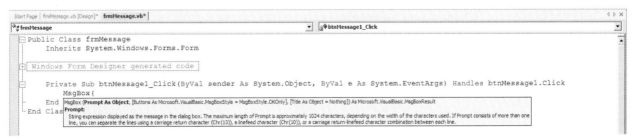

Figure 3.36 Message box prompt

Items listed with square brackets ([]) around them are optional, while items like `Prompt` are mandatory because they are listed without square brackets surrounding them.

There are too many options to list here, but by selecting different values, you can change the way your message box is displayed.

For instance, imagine if someone entered data that would cause a number to be divided by 0. Since computers cannot divide by 0, a good developer would check to see if this was about to occur. If it was, then a good procedure is to indicate that a critical error has occurred in the execution of the application. This is preferable to actually attempting the illegal operation and getting an error message that is native to Visual Basic .NET. You could use the following code:

```
MsgBox("Division By Zero Occurred", MsgBoxStyle.Critical)
```

The message box shown in Figure 3.37 would be displayed.

Figure 3.37
Critical message box displaying division by zero message

Another option is to display a message box with an exclamation point in the window. If you use the following code:

```
MsgBox("You Had Better Pay Your Taxes Now", MsgBoxStyle.Exclamation)
```

the message box shown in Figure 3.38 would be displayed.

Notice that the message box automatically adjusts its size so that it holds the entire message. That is just another useful feature Visual Basic .NET has built in for you.

Figure 3.38   Exclamation message box displaying a tax message

These are just a few of the examples. You should explore more options by checking the help system or by exploring the type ahead feature. Notice that if you have typed your commands up to and including the comma after the prompt, a list appears that you may choose from. (See Figure 3.39.) Try them out and see what happens. Most are self-explanatory.

Figure 3.39   Message box type ahead showing different types of message boxes

COACH'S TIP

If you want your message to appear on more than one line, use the constant `vbNewLine` in your message. By adding the constant at the appropriate places, you will be able to control where one line begins and another ends (see Figure 3.40). This is demonstrated in the following code:

```
MsgBox("This is the first line." & vbNewLine & "This is the second line.")
```

Figure 3.40
Message box with
`vbNewLine`

Adding a Title to the Message Box

You may not have noticed, but the previous message boxes had a title of `MessageBox` in the window's title bar. This is poor application development. By adding an additional parameter to the `MsgBox` statement, you can specify a title for the title bar of the message box so that the message box does not use the title of the project as the title of the window. Observe the following code, which will place the title `"Tax Message"` in your message box, as shown in Figure 3.41.

```
MsgBox("Don't Forget To Pay Your Taxes", MsgBoxStyle.OKOnly, "Tax Message")
```

Figure 3.41
Message box with title

Key Words and Key Terms

Breakpoint
  A signal to the Debugger to stop the execution of the application and wait for further instructions on how to continue executing the application.

Case Sensitive
  A language that considers variables spelled with different capitalization as separate variables.

Constant
  A value that does not and cannot change during the execution of the program.

Date
  A variable data type that stores a date.

Debugger
  A utility in Visual Basic .NET that allows programmers to step through their program and determine the source of an error.

Decimal
  A variable data type that allows the storing of a floating point number with an accuracy greater than a `Double` variable.

Dim
  Defines a variable with a scope local to the code it's declared within.

Double

A variable data type that allows the storing of a decimal value with up to 14 digits of accuracy.

Integer

A variable data type that allows the storing of an integer value between –2,147,483,648 and 2,147,483,647.

Long

A variable data type that allows the storing of an integer value between –9,223,372,036,854,775,808 and 9,223,372,036,854,775,807.

Operand

An entity upon which operators will perform their action.

Operator

A representation of an action that will be performed upon whatever operands are placed next to it.

Order of Precedence

The order in which the operations are performed when evaluating an expression.

Overflow

A run-time error that occurs when a value is attempted to be assigned to a variable that is outside of the acceptable range for that variable data type.

Public

Defines a variable that is visible throughout the entire application.

Run-Time Error

An error caused by the execution of the application.

Scope

The extent a variable or an object is visible to the rest of the application.

Short

A variable data type that allows the storing of an integer value between –32,768 and 32,767.

Single

The smallest variable data type that allows the storing of a decimal value with up to 6 digits of accuracy.

String

A variable data type that allows the storing of a series of characters.

Variable

A way the computer stores a value in memory.

Variable Data Type

The classification of a variable so that Visual Basic .NET knows how much space to allocate and how to operate upon it.

Variable Name

The name to which a variable is referred from within the source code of the program.

Answers to Chapter's Drills

Drill 3.1

1. The most appropriate variable data type to store an hourly wage of an employee is a `Decimal`. `Decimal` variables are designed to store floating point values needed to store the dollars and cents of an hourly wage.

2. The most appropriate variable data type to store an exam that has the lowest possible grade of 0 and highest grade of 100 would be a `Short`. A `Short`'s range is

from –32,768 to 32,767. All the values between 0 and 100 are within the range of a `Short` without being so large that it would waste memory.

3. In order to figure out the answer for this, you need to calculate the range of values the sum may be. The lowest possible sum would be if everyone got a 0. Therefore, the lower bound is 0. The highest possible sum is if everyone got a 100. Therefore, the upper bound is 5,000. Since all the values between 0 and 5,000 are within the range of a `Short`, a `Short` can be used to store this value.

4. In order to figure out the answer for this, you need to calculate the range of values the sum may be. The lowest possible sum would be if everyone got a 0. Therefore, the lower bound is 0. The highest possible sum is if everyone got a 100. Therefore, the upper bound is 50,000. Since all the values between 0 and 50,000 are not within the range of a `Short`, a `Short` cannot be used to store this value. However, an `Integer` can be used, since its range is from –2,147,483,648 to 2,147,483,647.

5. In order to figure out the answer for this, you need to calculate the range of values the sum may be. The lowest possible sum would be if everyone got a 0. Therefore, the lower bound is 0. The highest possible sum is if everyone got a 100. Therefore, the upper bound is 500,000. Since all the values between 0 and 500,000 are not within the range of a `Short`, a `Short` cannot be used to store this value. However, an `Integer` can be used, since its range is from –2,147,483,648 to 2,147,483,647.

6. In order to figure out the answer for this, you need to calculate the range of values the sum may be. The lowest possible sum would be if there were no orders. Therefore, the lower bound is 0. The highest possible sum is if 1 billion orders were filled and each order contained three products. Therefore, the upper bound is 3,000,000,000. Since all the values between 0 and 3,000,000,000 are not within the range of a `Short`, a `Short` cannot be used to store this value. Additionally, the range of values cannot be represented by an `Integer`, since its range is from –2,147,483,648 to 2,147,483,647. Therefore, you must use a `Long` variable, the range of which is from –9,223,372,036,854,775,808 to 9,223,372,036,854,775,807.

7. The expression you wish to store is nonnumeric. It is a series of characters. Therefore, you would use a `String` variable.

8. Any date can be stored in a `Date` variable.

Drill 3.2

The code indicated would execute without an overflow error. The range of a `Short` is from –32,768 to 32,767. When you add 1 to –32,768, you get –32,767, which is within the range.

Drill 3.3

The code indicated would execute without an overflow error. The range of a `Short` is from –32,768 to 32,767. The value you store in `shtVariable` is 30,000, which is within the bounds of a `Short`.

Drill 3.4

The code indicated would produce an overflow error on the last assignment to `shtVariable`. You can add and subtract from a `Short` as many times as you like as long as you do not exceed the lower or upper bounds of a `Short`.

The initial value of the `Short` is 32,767. This is a valid value. Then you subtract 5, so the value assigned is 32,762. This is valid, so you continue. You then add 5 to get back to the original value. It's as if the two lines of code were never executed.

However, when you add 1 in the last line of code, you attempt to set the value to 32,768. This is out of range, so you get an overflow error.

Drill 3.5

1. `Maura` is a valid variable name. It starts with a letter and is followed by letters.

2. `Ben` is a valid variable name. It starts with a letter and is followed by letters.

3. `Maura&Ben` is not a valid variable name. It contains the `&` character, which is not allowed in variable names.

4. `Maura_Ben` is a valid variable name. It starts with a letter and is followed by a combination of letters and underscores.

5. `_MauraBen` is not a valid variable name. It starts with an underscore, which is not allowed at the beginning of variable names.

6. `IsThisLegal` is a valid variable name. It starts with a letter and is followed by letters.

7. `HowAboutThis?` is not a valid variable name. It contains a question mark, which is not allowed in variable names.

8. `PrivateDancerWasTheNameOfASong` is a valid variable name. It contains only characters, and although it is long, it does not contain more than 255 characters. Remember it is okay to use a keyword as part of a larger variable name.

9. `Private` is not a valid variable name. Although it contains only letters, it is one of the keywords defined in Visual Basic .NET and may not be used as a variable name.

Drill 3.6

When Visual Basic .NET is left to the default settings, you would have received an error indicating that a reference to `strDrillValue` existed before the declaration of the variable.

Drill 3.7

4 + 5 * 6 – 3 / 3 + 6

The first calculation is **4 + 5 * 6 – 3 / 3 + 6**. Reading from left to right, the first calculation you compute is 5 * 6, because there are no parentheses and it is the first multiplication or division.

By replacing the 5 * 6 with 30, you rewrite the expression as **4 + 30 – 3 / 3 + 6**. Since there are no parentheses, you evaluate the next multiplication or division that you see when reading from left to right, 3 / 3.

By replacing 3 / 3 with 1, you rewrite the expression as **4 + 30 – 1 + 6**. Since no parentheses, multiplications, or divisions remain, the solution to the problem is a simple matter of adding and subtracting the numbers from left to right until you get the answer of 39.

(4 + 5) * 6 – (3 / 3 + 6)

The second calculation is **(4 + 5) * 6 – (3 / 3 + 6)**. Reading from left to right, the first calculation you compute is (4 + 5), because 4 + 5 is in the first set of parentheses found.

By replacing (4 + 5) with 9, you rewrite the initial expression as **9 * 6 – (3 / 3 + 6)**. Reading from left to right, you must continue to compute the values in the remaining parentheses. Therefore, you must compute the entire expression (3 / 3 + 6) before you evaluate 9 * 6 –. You start by computing 3 / 3, since it is the first multiplication or division inside the parentheses. Then you can rewrite the expression inside the parentheses as (1 + 6). Adding the 1 to the 6 you get 7.

By replacing (3 / 3 + 6) with 7, you rewrite the initial expression as **9 * 6 – 7**. Since no more parentheses exist, you continue with the evaluation by computing the first multiplication or division found when reading from left to right. Therefore, the next calculation evaluated is 9 * 6.

By replacing (9 * 6) with 54, you rewrite the expression as **54 – 7**. The final answer is then calculated with a result of 47.

(4 + 5) / (I + 2)

The third calculation is **(4 + 5) / (1 + 2)**. Reading from left to right, you must compute the values in the parentheses first. The first expression evaluated is (4 + 5).

By replacing (4 + 5) with 9, you rewrite the expression as **9 / (1 + 2)**. Since there still exists a set of parentheses, you must compute the expression inside the remaining parentheses, (1 + 2).

By replacing the (1 + 2) with 3, you rewrite the initial expression as **9 / 3**. This leaves you with a simple division to calculate the final answer, 3.

4 * 5 * (3 + 3)

The fourth calculation is **4 * 5 * (3 + 3)**. Reading from left to right, you must compute the values in the parentheses first. You compute (3 + 3).

By replacing (3 + 3) with 6, you rewrite the initial expression as **4 * 5 * 6**. This is a simple series of multiplications that can be computed to get a final answer of 120.

2 − 2 / 2 + 2 * 2 − 3

The fifth calculation is **2 − 2 / 2 + 2 * 2 − 3**. Reading from left to right, since there are no parentheses, you compute the first multiplication or division you see. This would be 2 / 2.

By replacing 2 / 2 with 1, you rewrite the initial expression as **2 − 1 + 2 * 2 − 3**. You continue evaluating the expression by finding the next multiplication or division. This would be 2 * 2.

By replacing 2 * 2 with 4, you rewrite the initial expression as **2 − 1 + 4 − 3**. The remaining problem is a simple series of additions and subtractions to reach the final answer of 2.

2 + 2 * 2 ^ 3 − 3

The sixth calculation is **2 + 2 * 2 ^ 3 − 3**. Reading from left to right, since there are no parentheses, you compute the first exponent you see. This would be 2 ^ 3.

By replacing 2 ^ 3 with 8, you rewrite the initial expression as **2 + 2 * 8 − 3**. The next calculation would be the multiplication. Therefore, 2 * 8 would be replaced with 16 in the equation. You would be left with **2 + 16 − 3** as the equation.

The answer is then a simple series of additions and subtractions. The final answer is 15.

Drill 3.8

With Visual Basic .NET left to the default settings, you would have received an error indicating that a reference to `intDrillValue` existed before the declaration of the variable.

Although `intDrillValue` is declared in the `Click` event of the button `btnInitialize`, it is declared to be local to that event. Therefore, the other events treat the variable `intDrillValue` as being undeclared. You will get a build error stating that `intDrillValue` is not declared, and you won't be able to run the program.

Drill 3.9

Unlike Drill 3.8, this drill declares `intDrillValue` so that it is visible to all events within the form. When `btnInitialize` is clicked, the value of `intDrillValue` is set to 10. This value is still 10 when `btnAdd` is clicked. 10 is added to `intDrillValue` and stored back in `intDrillValue`. The value of `intDrillValue` is then 20. When `btnOutput` is clicked, the value of `intDrillValue`, still 20, is displayed.

Drill 3.10

This drill declares the variable `intDrillValue` so that it is visible to all events within the form; however, it also redeclares it within the `Click` event of the button `btnInitialize`. This is acceptable, but the variable seen by the `Click` event of the button `btnInitialize` is a local copy to that routine and does not affect the previously declared variable. So although the `Click` event of the button `btnInitialize` initializes the variable `intDrillValue` to 10, when you reach the `Click` event of the button `btnAdd`, the value of `intDrillValue` is not 10, but the original value `intDrillValue` was initialized originally. The problem is that you did not initialize `intDrillValue` to a specific value. Therefore, the default initialization for `Integers`, 0, is used. The output then would be 10.

Drill 3.11

In this drill the variable `intDrillValue` is initialized to 10. Then 5 is added to `intDrillValue` and stored back in `intDrillValue`. Therefore, the value of `intDrillValue` is 15 and is output in the message box.

Drill 3.12

In this drill the variable `intDrillValue` is initialized to 1. Then 1 is multiplied by 5 and stored back in `intDrillValue`. Therefore, after the second statement, the value of `intDrillValue` is 5. When the third statement is executed, 5 is added to `intDrillValue` and stored back in `intDrillValue`. Now equal to 10, it is output in the message box.

Drill 3.13

In this drill the variable `strDrillValue` is initialized to `"This "`. Then `"and "` is appended to it, and `"This and "` is stored in `strDrillValue`. Next, `"that"` is appended to `"This and "`, and `"This and that"` is stored in `strDrillValue`. Therefore, `"This and that"` is output in the message box.

Drill 3.14

In this drill the variable `strDrillValue` is initialized to `"This "`. Since an = operator is used instead of an `&=` operator, the `"and "` is not appended to `strDrillValue` but is assigned to it. Therefore, after the second statement executes, `strDrillValue` contains `"and "`. The third statement also has an = operator, so `"that"` is assigned to `strDrillValue`. Therefore, `"that"` is output in the message box.

Additional Exercises

1. Which of the following are valid variable names?
    a. IsThisValid?
    b. IfNotThisMustBeValid
    c. Go_Sixers!
    d. 123456
    e. Dim
    f. HOW_ABOUT_ALL_CAPS
    g. Dimension

2. Indicate whether each of the following is true or false.
    a. A variable is considered an operand.
    b. Basic operations in Visual Basic .NET follow a different precedence than traditional mathematics.
    c. The user of the application can change a constant if extreme circumstances exist.
    d. A variable called `COOLNESS` and a variable called `coolness` are considered different variables due to the rules of case sensitivity in Visual Basic .NET.
    e. A variable can be set to different values at different times in the running of an application.
    f. A `Short` data type can store the value 0.

g. A `Short` data type can store the value `50000`.

h. A `Short` data type can store the value `-1.1`.

i. An `Integer` data type can store the value `0`.

j. An `Integer` data type can store the value `50000`.

k. An `Integer` data type can store the value `-1.1`.

l. A `Long` data type can store the value `0`.

m. A `Long` data type can store the value `50000`.

n. A `Long` data type can store the value `-1.1`.

o. A `Decimal` data type can store the value `0`.

p. A `Decimal` data type can store the value `50000`.

q. A `Decimal` data type can store the value `-1.1`.

r. The value `1234` is the same thing as the value `"1234"`.

3. What is the value of the following expressions:

a. `(1 + 8 / 2 + ((1 * 4) + (5 * 4)) / 4)`

b. `((1 + 1 + 1 + 1) / 2 + (1 + 1 + 1) / 3)`

c. `(5 * 5 + 5 / 5 + 6)`

d. `(((3 + 4) + (4 * 7)) / 5)`

e. `((3 * 6 * 7 * 2) + 12 / 2)`

4. Are the following expressions valid?

a. `(3 + 4)`

b. `(3 + 4) * 1`

c. `4 (5 + 6)`

d. `(5) * (5) * ((10))`

e. `)(1 + 1)(`

f. `(5)(5)`

5. Which of the following data types will allow the storing of the number `40000`? List all the data types that apply.

a. `Integer`   b. `Long`   c. `Single`   d. `Decimal`   e. `Date`

6. Indicate whether the following statement is true or false. By using `Option Strict`, Visual Basic .NET will enforce the industry standard naming conventions mentioned in this chapter. (If false, explain why.)

7. Declaring a variable with the _____ keyword will allow the entire application to use it and should be avoided.

a. `Dim`   b. `Public`   c. `Variable`   d. `Constant`

8. A _____ is a useful tool to determine what is wrong with your application.

a. Control   b. Debugger   c. Toolbox   d. Window

9. Is there a difference between the value #1/5/01# and "#1/5/01#". If so, what is it?

10. Write an application that will contain one text box, three labels, and a button. The text box will allow the initial investment to be entered by the user. When the button is clicked, have the application calculate the value of the investment after five years, assuming a 12% return on investment per year, and place it in one of the labels. The remaining label controls should indicate the purpose of the text box and a label to store the result.

For example, if a person invests $1,000, after five years the investment will be worth $1,762.34.

11. Write an application that will calculate a person's interest payment for a year. The application should contain three text boxes and a button. The first text box should accept the amount of a person's debt. The second should accept the interest rate.

When the button is clicked, the third text box should output the amount of interest the person will pay in a year, assuming the interest is compounded annually.

For example, if a person owes $1,000 and is paying 8% interest a year, the person will owe $80 in interest at the end of the year.

12. Write an application that will compute the volume of a pool. Include three text boxes to enter the height, width, and length of the pool. Include a button that will compute the volume and store the result in a fourth text box. Finally, label all of the text boxes. Volume is computed by multiplying the height, width, and length together.

For example, if a pool has a height of 7 feet, a width of 20 feet, and a length of 40 feet, the volume of the pool will be 5,600 square feet.

13. Write an application that will compute the square footage of a home by allowing the user to enter the length and width of up to 10 rooms. Create a text box for each length and width to be entered. Also add labels so that the user of the application understands what the text boxes are to be used for. Finally, add a button that will calculate the square footage of each room and then add the results together to get the total square footage. This result should be displayed in another text box.

For example, if the length and width of the 10 rooms are as follows:

Length	Width
10	10
12	9
7	6
14	7
10	9
12	10
9	9
7	8
10	8
8	9

then the total square footage will be 847.

14. Write an application that calculates a student's GPA for a semester. The application should store grades for up to five classes (each having the same number of credits), each in a separate text box. A grade can be a 0, 1, 2, 3, or 4. Output the student's overall average. Make sure that the program remembers decimal places in its calculation.

For example, if a student receives grades of 4, 3, 4, 2, and 4, the GPA should calculate as 3.4.

15. Write an application that calculates the discount amount for a store's products. The application should accept five sale prices and five retail prices for products a store carries. Create a text box for each price. Also create a text box for each set of prices to store the percentage discount of each product. Finally, create a button that when clicked computes the discount of each item and places the result in the appropriate text box.

Sale Price	Retail Price	Discount
$9.95	$12.95	23.17%
$10.50	$11.00	4.55%
$12.00	$12.00	0
$7.50	$10.00	25%
$14.50	$15.00	3.33%

16. Modify the counter application in this chapter so that it has an additional button, `btnDecrement`. When clicked, `btnDecrement` should reduce the value of the counter by 1.

17. Modify the counter application developed in assignment 17 so that it has an additional text box, `txtValue`. When one of the buttons is clicked, instead of incrementing or decrementing by 1, have it increment or decrement by the value stored in `txtValue`.

18. Write an application that displays the standings of a sports team and all of the statistics that are associated with it. The application should have text boxes for five teams. Each team should have a text box for the following: Team's Name, Number of Wins, Number of Losses, and Winning Percentage. The first-place team should have a text box for the Magic Number, while the remaining teams should have a text box for Games Back. Also include a button to compute the necessary values.

The application should allow the user to enter the Team's Name, Wins, and Losses. They should enter the first-place team first, the second-place team second, and so on. When the user clicks on the button, it should compute the Winning Percentage, Games Back, and Magic Number.

The Winning Percentage value is computed by dividing the number of wins by the total number of games played.

The Games Back value is computed by subtracting the current team's wins from the first-place team's wins and multiplying it by 0.5. Then subtract the number of losses of the first-place team from the current team and multiply the result by 0.5. Add both results together to get the Games Back value.

The Magic Number is the number of victories by the first-place team or losses by the second-place team required for the first-place team to clinch the playoffs. In order to perform the calculation, you must establish the total number of games. This should be a constant declared at the beginning of your application. In professional basketball, for instance, it's 82 games. You can compute the Magic Number by subtracting the number of Games Back of the second-place team from the number of games remaining for the first-place team.

Following is a sample of what the calculations might be:

Team	Wins	Losses	Winning Pct		
76ers	31	10	0.756	36	Magic Number
Knicks	26	15	0.634	5	Games Back
Heat	25	16	0.609	6	Games Back
Magic	22	18	0.55	8.5	Games Back
Hawks	20	20	0.5	10.5	Games Back

INTERVIEW

An Interview with Jeff Hunsaker

Jeff Hunsaker is a Microsoft Certified Solutions Developer and an Engagement Manager for Clarity Consulting, a company that focuses on custom application development using enterprise Microsoft tools. Among other projects, Jeff managed the team of consultants that upgraded Art.com's Web site, a unique online frame shop that allows its customers to select a print, then preview it on-screen in a variety of frames. He also served as Webmaster and DBA while Art.com grew its staff and infrastructure.

With what challenge did Art.com present your company and was it met?

Art.com challenged my firm to build an e-commerce Web site with the ability to scale to the number of visitors and orders required to support their business plan. We met this goal, scaling to millions of page views and hundreds of orders per day.

Our solution consisted of an IIS5 NLB Web farm of 10 servers hosting ASP pages and VB6 components. These components interacted with our six SQL Server 2000 read-only searching database cluster and single transactional database storing visitor, member, and order information. Our solution also used Commerce Server to push Web site orders onto the manufacturing floor. Finally, the VB6 components integrated with Art.com's Great Plains package to provide order billing and fulfillment.

How has VB.NET made your job of software development easier?

VB.NET and the .NET Framework provide all of the tools we need to create a scalable and successful Web site. Nearly all of the tedious, mundane tasks associated with most projects now come for free with the development tool. With the introduction of true object-oriented features in VB.NET, we're able to create much more fluid, understandable, and elegant code. VB.NET finally levels the playing field with languages like Java and even C++. Developers no longer require workarounds for overloading, inheriting, and separation of interface from implementation—it's all built in.

What are some of the pitfalls to avoid when using VB.NET?

Because VB.NET is a complete re-write and has added so many new features, it's difficult to choose the right design pattern. It's also easy to fall back on past development practices and choose a less-than-optimal solution. When first starting with VB.NET, a developer must allot time to experiment and research options and approaches to problems. Don't just use the first thing you get to work; look around in depth. Scour MSDN Help. Talk to other developers. Immerse yourself in reading materials and online resources. Finally, always use Application Center Test (formerly WAST/Homer but supported now) to test the scalability of your proposed implementation.

What kinds of VB.NET projects are you working on now?

I'm working on a project upgrading a VB6, ASP application framework and content management product to VB.NET, ASP.NET. The rich feature set in ASP.NET and the elimination of many legacy workarounds causing performance issues compelled the company to choose .NET.

How will VB.NET affect your work?

It's making development fun again. VB.NET and the .NET platform eliminates a lot of the tedious, repetitive, error-prone coding required to construct a solution. With .NET, I get a lot of features for free without needing to write code.

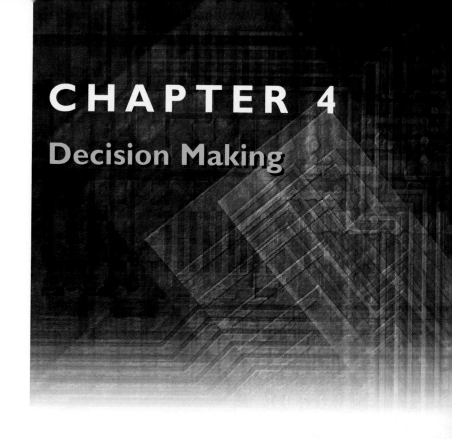

CHAPTER 4
Decision Making

Currently, your computer consists of a glorified calculator with simple input and output operations. A useful computer requires the ability to make decisions. The key to programming the computer to make correct decisions is making sure you understand how to represent and evaluate the expression representing the decision properly. First, you will evaluate the truthfulness of many expressions presented in non-real-world drills designed to reinforce the syntax of their evaluation. Then real-world applications will be demonstrated to show the usefulness of conditional statements. Mastery of the evaluation of conditional expressions will also pay dividends when you study looping statements in future chapters, so your time will be well spent.

4.1 If Statements

You are already familiar with the concept of making a decision. When driving a car, you have to make decisions all the time. When you drive up to a light, you decide to stop the car if the light is red.

Graphically, your decision would look like the diagram shown in Figure 4.1.

Figure 4.1
Graphical representation of
driving a car

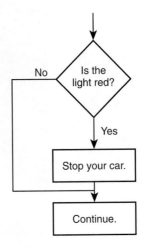

Visual Basic .NET offers more than one way for decisions to be made. Each has its purpose in modeling the way a decision is made. The simplest, which matches the idea of a single decision to a single result, is the **If** statement.

You can program an `If` statement by using the following code illustrating its syntax:

```
If (Expression) Then
    Program statements to execute if expression evaluates to True
End If
```

An `If` statement consists of an expression that determines whether a program statement or statements execute. An expression can be the comparison of two values. To compare values you may use any of the following operators:

<	less than
>	greater than
<=	less than or equal to
>=	greater than or equal to
=	equal to
<>	not equal to

With either a variable or a constant value placed on both sides of the operator, an expression can be evaluated to either **True** or **False**. Here are some sample expressions that evaluate to **True**:

```
1 = 1
2 >= 1
2 >= 2
1 <= 2
1 < 2
1 <> 2
"a" <> "c"
"A" <> "a"
"D" = "D"
```

Here are some sample expressions that evaluate to `False`:

1 = 2
2 <= 1
2 < 2
3 > 4
1 >= 2
1 <> 1
"a" = "A"
"D" <> "D"

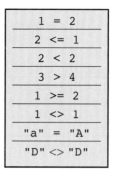

DRILL 4.1

Indicate whether each expression evaluates to `True` or `False`.

1 (5 >= 4)
2 (-3 < -4)
3 (5 = 4)
4 (5 <> 4)
5 (4 >= 4)
6 (4 <= 4)

When the condition in an `If` statement evaluates to `True`, the statements immediately following it are executed until an **End If** statement is reached. If the `If` statement evaluates to `False`, the statements immediately after it, until the End If, are not executed.

Simple If Statement

So far the programs that you have written did not require a decision to be made. Now you will write a program that will output a message if the user enters the word `"Yes"` in a text box. By using an `If` statement, you can determine if the value that is entered in a text box is equal to the value you desire. See the following code as an example that compares the text box contents to the `String "Yes"`. The code assumes that a `btnIf` button has been created to place the code and a `txtInput` text box and a `lblOutput` label (both with their `Text` property empty) have been created to hold the input and output. The code follows:

```
Private Sub btnIf_Click(...
    If (txtInput.Text = "Yes") Then
        lblOutput.Text = "This will output, because the user entered Yes"
    End If
End Sub
```

What do you think would be contained in `lblOutput`:

1 If the user enters `"Yes"` in the `txtInput` text box?
2 If the user enters `"No"` in the `txtInput` text box?

With "Yes" Entered in txtInput   When the program is executed and the button is clicked, the `If` statement is evaluated. If the user enters `"Yes"`, the `If` statement evaluates the expression by comparing `"Yes"` to `"Yes"`, and the conditional expression will evaluate to `True`. Therefore, all the statements until the `End If` are executed. So the text `"This will output, because the user entered Yes"` is placed in the `lblOutput` label.

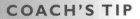

COACH'S TIP

Remember that
`lblOutput.Text &=
" and this is
here as well"` is
the equivalent to
`lblOutput.Text =
lblOutput.Text &
" and this is
here as well"`.

With "No" Entered in txtInput   When the program is executed and the button is clicked, the `If` statement is evaluated. If the user enters `"No"`, the `If` statement evaluates the expression by comparing `"No"` to `"Yes"`, and the conditional expression will evaluate to `False`. Therefore, none of the statements before the `End If` are executed. So no action is taken by the application and the `txtOutput` text box remains empty. It is important to note that any value other than `"Yes"` will produce no output in the `lblOutput` label.

Simple If Statement with Code Following It

Sometimes you will write programs that will have some statements that will execute based on a decision and some that will execute regardless of the evaluation of the condition. Following is an application that will behave in this manner. You can write this application by modifying the previous one. The only change that you must make is to add a concatenation statement after the `If` statement. The code follows:

```
Private Sub btnIf_Click(...
    If (txtInput.Text = "Yes") Then
        lblOutput.Text = "This will output, because the user entered Yes"
    End If

    lblOutput.Text &= " and this is here as well"
End Sub
```

What do you think would be contained in `lblOutput`:

1 If the user enters `"Yes"` in the `txtInput` text box?
2 If the user enters `"No"` in the `txtInput` text box?

With "Yes" Entered in txtInput   If the user enters a `"Yes"` in the `txtInput` text box, the output would be as follows:

```
This will output, because the user entered Yes and this is here as well
```

Both expressions are concatenated because the statement within the `If` statement is executed, since `(txtInput.Text = "Yes")` evaluates to `True` as before, and the second statement is executed because it is not in the `If` statement and therefore always executes.

With "No" Entered in txtInput   However, if the user enters a value other than `"Yes"` in the `txtInput` text box, the output would be as follows:

```
and this is here as well
```

When the value stored in `txtInput` is anything other than `"Yes"`, then `(txtInput.Text = "Yes")` evaluates to `False` and the first assignment to the `lblOutput` label is not performed. However, since the second statement has nothing to do with the `If` statement, it is executed as before.

Drills 4.2, 4.3, 4.4, and 4.5 use the sample application from the previous example.

DRILL 4.2

Given the following code:

```
Private Sub btnIf_Click(...
    Dim intUserValue As Integer

    intUserValue = Val(txtInput.Text)

    If (intUserValue > 2) Then
        lblOutput.Text = "The first statement prints"
    End If
    lblOutput.Text = lblOutput.Text & " and the second statement prints"
End Sub
```

What do you think would be contained in `lblOutput`:

1 If the user enters 1 in the `txtInput` text box?
2 If the user enters 2 in the `txtInput` text box?
3 If the user enters 3 in the `txtInput` text box?

COACH'S TIP

`Val` is used to convert a `String` value to a numerical value.

DRILL 4.3

Given the following code:

```
Private Sub btnIf_Click(...
    Dim intUserValue As Integer

    intUserValue = Val(txtInput.Text)

    If (intUserValue < 2) Then
        lblOutput.Text = "The first statement prints"
    End If
    lblOutput.Text &= " and the second statement prints"
End Sub
```

What do you think would be contained in `lblOutput`:

1 If the user enters 1 in the `txtInput` text box?
2 If the user enters 2 in the `txtInput` text box?
3 If the user enters 3 in the `txtInput` text box?

DRILL 4.4

Given the following code:

```
Private Sub btnIf_Click(...
    Dim intUserValue As Integer

    intUserValue = Val(txtInput.Text)

    If (intUserValue >= 2) Then
        lblOutput.Text = "The first statement prints"
    End If
    lblOutput.Text &= " and the second statement prints"
End Sub
```

What do you think would be contained in `lblOutput`:

1 If the user enters 1 in the `txtInput` text box?
2 If the user enters 2 in the `txtInput` text box?
3 If the user enters 3 in the `txtInput` text box?

DRILL 4.5

Given the following code:

```
Private Sub btnIf_Click(...
    Dim intUserValue As Integer

    intUserValue = Val(txtInput.Text)

    If (intUserValue <= 2) Then
        lblOutput.Text = "The first statement prints"
    End If
    lblOutput.Text &= " and the second statement prints"
End Sub
```

What do you think would be contained in `lblOutput`:

1 If the user enters 1 in the `txtInput` text box?
2 If the user enters 2 in the `txtInput` text box?
3 If the user enters 3 in the `txtInput` text box?

Example: In Stock?
Problem Description

Now that you understand the basic operations of `If` statements, you will write your first relevant application where a decision is required. The application will ask the user to enter the amount of a product a company has on hand. If the number is greater than `0`, then the program outputs that the `"Product is in Stock"`. Otherwise, it outputs that the `"Product is Sold Out"`.

Problem Discussion

It will require creating a form with a `txtStockAmount` text box to store the amount of a product a company has in stock, a `lblAmount` label with the `Text` property set to `"Amount in Stock"`, another label, `lblInStock`, to hold a message, and a button with the `Text` property set to `"Calculate"`.

    This can be seen in Figure 4.2.

Figure 4.2
Sketch of In Stock
application

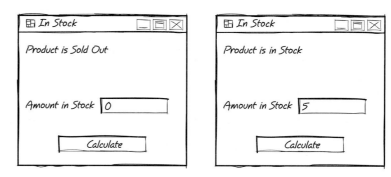

The code of the program compares the number entered by the user to 0. If the number entered by the user is greater than 0, then the message `"Product is in Stock"` is displayed. Then the value is compared to see if it is less than or equal to 0. If so, then the message `"Product is Sold Out"` is displayed.

Problem Solution
Create Project and Form

Step 1: From the Start window, click on New Project. The New Project window will appear.

Step 2: Specify the name of the application as `InStock`.

Step 3: Specify the location as `"C:\VB Net Coach\Chapter 4\Code\ "`.

Step 4: Click on the OK button.

Step 5: Rename the form to `frmInStock`.

Step 6: Rename the file by right-clicking on the file name in the Solution Explorer and setting the name to `frmInStock.vb`.

Step 7: Set the `Text` property of the form to `In Stock`.

Add the Result Label

Step 1: Place a label control across the top of the form.

Step 2: Set the `Name` property to `lblInStock`.

Step 3: Clear the `Text` property.

Add the Amount In Stock Label

Step 1: Place a label control to the right and about halfway down the form.

Step 2: Set the `Name` property to `lblAmount`.

Step 3: Set the `Text` property to `Amount in Stock`.

Step 4: Set the `Font Bold` property to `True`.

Add the Stock Amount Text Box

Step 1: Place a text box control below the in stock label.

Step 2: Set the `Name` property to `txtStockAmount`.

Step 3: Clear out the default value from the `Text` property.

Add the Calculate Button

Step 1: Place a button control in the left side of the form, below the text box.

Step 2: Set the `Name` property to `btnCalculate`.

Step 3: Set the `Text` property to `Calculate`.

Step 4: Double-click on the button.

Step 5: Attach the code to output a message as to whether an item is in stock.

The code for the `btnCalculate` button's `Click` event is shown in Figure 4.3.

```
frmInStock.vb [Design]  frmInStock.vb
frmInStock                                                          btnCalculate_Click
Public Class frmInStock
    Inherits System.Windows.Forms.Form

    Windows Form Designer generated code

    Private Sub btnCalculate_Click(ByVal sender As System.Object, ByVal e As System.EventArgs) Handles btnCalculate.Click
        If (Val(txtStockAmount.Text) > 0) Then
            lblInStock.Text = "Product is in Stock"
        End If

        If (Val(txtStockAmount.Text) <= 0) Then
            lblInStock.Text = "Product is Sold Out"
        End If
    End Sub
End Class
```

Figure 4.3   Code for In Stock application

Figures 4.4 and 4.5 show the two possible outputs.

Figure 4.4   Sold out output

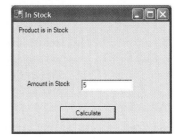

Figure 4.5   In stock output

Example: Expenses?
Problem Description

Write a program that outputs the difference between the amount of your income versus the amount of your expenses, as well as printing a message that indicates whether you are spending more than you are making.

Problem Discussion

First, you must create a form that has two text boxes: `txtIncome` and `txtExpenses`. Each should have a label above it indicating what is stored in the text box: income and expenses, respectively. Additionally, you need two labels to store the difference between the income and expenses and one to hold your output message. Finally, you need a button to calculate the difference and output the message. This can be seen in the form shown in Figure 4.6.

Figure 4.6
Income/expenses form

The code is straightforward. First you declare the local variables that you will need. Then you initialize the variables to the values from the text boxes. Finally, you will perform a simple calculation.

The values in the local variables are evaluated using three conditional statements. Each is used to check a specific condition.

The first condition checks whether the income entered is a larger number than the expenses entered. If so, the `lblResult` label is set to the value `"You did a good job!"`

Whether the first condition is evaluated to `True` or `False`, the second condition is now checked. It checks to see if the income entered is a smaller number than the expenses entered. If so, the `lblResult` label is set to the value `"You need to be more frugal"`.

Regardless of the results of the first two `If` statements, the third condition is checked. It checks to see if the income entered is equal to the expenses entered. If so, the `lblResult` label is set to the value `"You balanced your spending!"`

Finally, the difference is converted to a `String` and copied to the `txtDifference` text box.

Problem Solution
Create Project and Form

Step 1: From the Start window, click on New Project. The New Project window will appear.

Step 2: Specify the name of the application as `IncomeAndExpense`.

Step 3: Specify the location as `"C:\VB Net Coach\Chapter 4\Code\ "`.

Step 4: Click on the OK button.

Step 5: Rename the form to `frmIncomeExpenses`.

Step 6: Rename the file by right-clicking on the file name in the Solution Explorer and setting the name to `frmIncomeExpenses.vb`.

Add the Result Label

Step 1: Place a label control across the top of the form.

Step 2: Set the `Name` property to `lblResult`.

Step 3: Remove the default value from the `Text` property.

Add the Income Label

Step 1: Place a label control a little below the `lblResult` label.

Step 2: Set the `Name` property to `lblIncome`.

Step 3: Set the `Text` property to `Income`.

Step 4: Set the `Font Bold` property to `True`.

Add the Income Text Box

Step 1: Place a text box control below the lblIncome label.
Step 2: Set the Name property to txtIncome.
Step 3: Remove the default value from the Text property.

Add the Expense Label

Step 1: Place a label control to the right of the income label.
Step 2: Set the Name property to lblExpenses.
Step 3: Set the Text property to Expenses.
Step 4: Set the Font Bold property to True.

Add the Expenses Text Box

Step 1: Place a text box control below the expenses label.
Step 2: Set the Name property to txtExpenses.
Step 3: Remove the default value from the Text property.

Add the Difference Title Label

Step 1: Place a label control below the income text box.
Step 2: Set the Name property to lblDifferenceTitle.
Step 3: Set the Text property to Difference.
Step 4: Set the Font Bold property to True.

Add the Difference Label

Step 1: Place a label control below the difference title label.
Step 2: Set the Name property to lblDifference.
Step 3: Remove the default value from the Text property.

Add the Calculate Button

Step 1: Place a button control on the bottom of the form, below the text box.
Step 2: Set the Name property to btnCalculate.
Step 3: Set the Text property to Calculate.
Step 4: Double-click on the button.
Step 5: Attach the code to determine the difference and output a message.

The code for the btnCalculate button is as shown in Figure 4.7. The code could also have been written by comparing the difference of the income and expenses to 0. This can be seen in the code shown in Figure 4.8. It illustrates the fact that there are many different ways to solve the same problem.

Example: Voting Booth Application
Problem Description

With all the commotion surrounding the 2000 presidential election, a better voting booth is needed. Throughout the next few chapters you will develop a number of Voting Booth applications. You will see how, as you learn more commands and controls in the Visual Basic .NET language, you will be able to improve the accuracy of the voting booth. Maybe you can sell it in Florida!

Problem Discussion

Your first application will allow voters to enter the name of the person they wish to vote for, thereby adding 1 for each vote to that person's counter. You will have one counter for Bush, Gore, and Nader. You will create a text box that will accept the name of the person to vote for and a button to process the actual vote. Additionally, you will add a

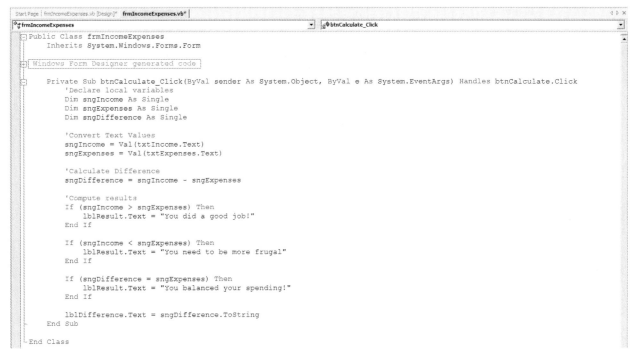

Figure 4.7 Code for `btnCalculate` button

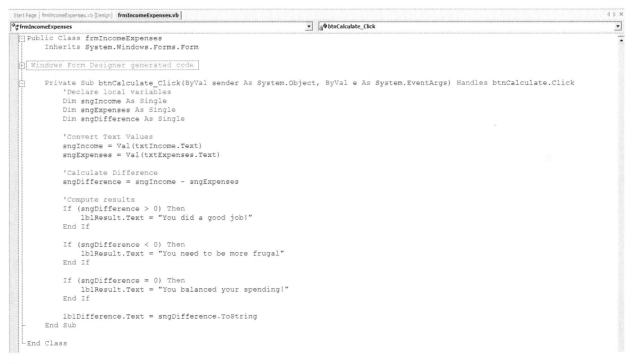

Figure 4.8 Alternative code for button

results button that will display the final results of the election. Just think, no hand counts!

Figure 4.9 shows what your application should look like.

Figure 4.9
Sketch of application

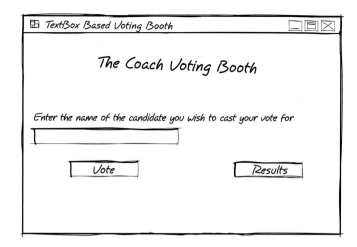

In order to store the number of votes for each candidate, you will require a variable for each candidate. Since the number of votes a candidate can have is a whole number, an `Integer` data type variable will be used. These variables will need to be accessed from both the Vote and Results buttons' `Click` events. Therefore, the variables will need to be declared in the `Declarations` section of the form. Remember, when variables are declared in the `Declarations` section of a form, they can be accessed from any of the events of the form.

One other issue you will have to deal with is to initialize these variables. Technically, you do not have to because the default value for an `Integer` is 0, but it is always a good habit to initialize them. The problem is, where do you want to initialize variables that will be used by a form? Forms, like all objects, have a special routine called a constructor. A constructor is called before the actual object is completely created. This is the appropriate place for initialization of variable in a form. You will learn a great deal about constructors and objects in Chapter 6. For now, just place the code shown in the solution in the appropriate location.

Problem Solution
Create Project and Form

Step 1: From the Start window, click on New Project. The New Project window will appear.

Step 2: Specify the name of the application as `Voting Booth 1`.

Step 3: Specify the location as `"C:\VB Net Coach\Chapter 4\Code\ "`.

Step 4: Click on the OK button.

Step 5: Rename the form to `frmVotingBooth`.

Step 6: Rename the file by right-clicking on the file name in the Solution Explorer and setting the name to `frmVotingBooth.vb`.

Step 7: Set the `Text` property of the form to `TextBox Based Voting Booth`.

Add Variable Declarations and Initialization

Step 1: Insert the code shown in Figure 4.10 to the `Declarations` section of the form.

Figure 4.10   Declarations of variables for application

In order to add code to the constructor, you must first make it visible. If you view the forms code before you have added any other code than the variable declarations, it will look as that shown in Figure 4.11.

Click here to expand

```
Start Page  frmVotingBooth.vb [Design]*  frmVotingBooth.vb*                                    ◁ ▷ ×
frmVotingBooth                                          ▼    (Declarations)                      ▼
⊟Public Class frmVotingBooth                                                                     ▲
     Inherits System.Windows.Forms.Form
     Dim intBushCount As Integer
     Dim intGoreCount As Integer
     Dim intNaderCount As Integer
 ⊞  Windows Form Designer generated code

   └End Class
```

Figure 4.11   Initialized variables

If you click on the ⊞ next to the Windows Form Designer generated code box, the code will expand as shown in Figure 4.12.

```
Start Page  frmVotingBooth.vb [Design]*  frmVotingBooth.vb*                                    ◁ ▷ ×
frmVotingBooth                                          ▼    New                                 ▼
⊟Public Class frmVotingBooth                                                                     ▲
     Inherits System.Windows.Forms.Form
     Dim intBushCount As Integer
     Dim intGoreCount As Integer
     Dim intNaderCount As Integer
⊟#Region " Windows Form Designer generated code "

⊟    Public Sub New()
         MyBase.New()

         'This call is required by the Windows Form Designer.
         InitializeComponent()

         'Add any initialization after the InitializeComponent() call

     End Sub
```

Figure 4.12   Expanded code with only variables declared

Step 2: Add the code shown in Figure 4.13 to the form's constructor so that the variables are initialized.

Your code to initialize the variables should go directly after the comment `'Add any initialization after the InitializeComponent() call` as shown in Figure 4.13.

Click to shrink displayed code

```
Start Page  frmVotingBooth.vb [Design]*  frmVotingBooth.vb*                                    ◁ ▷ ×
frmVotingBooth                                          ▼    New                                 ▼
⊟Public Class frmVotingBooth                                                                     ▲
     Inherits System.Windows.Forms.Form
     Dim intBushCount As Integer
     Dim intGoreCount As Integer
     Dim intNaderCount As Integer
⊟#Region " Windows Form Designer generated code "

⊟    Public Sub New()
         MyBase.New()

         'This call is required by the Windows Form Designer.
         InitializeComponent()

         'Add any initialization after the InitializeComponent() call
         intBushCount = 0
         intGoreCount = 0     ◀──── New code
         intNaderCount = 0
     End Sub
```

Figure 4.13   Expanded code with initialization of variables added

Once you have finished adding code to this section, you may close it by clicking on the minus sign next to the #Region code.

Add Title Label

Step 1: Place a label control across the top of the form.
Step 2: Set the Name property to lblTitle.
Step 3: Set the Text property to The Coach Voting Booth.
Step 4: Set the Font Bold property to True.
Step 5: Set the Font Size property to 18.
Step 6: Set the TextAlign property to Center. (See Figure 4.14.)

Figure 4.14
Form with initial label on it

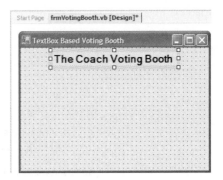

Add Instructions Label

Step 1: Place a label control below the previous one.
Step 2: Set the Name property to lblDirections.
Step 3: Set the Text property to "Enter the name of the candidate you wish to cast your vote for". (See Figure 4.15.)

Figure 4.15
Form with instructions on it

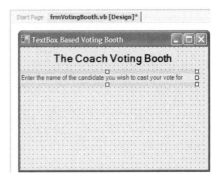

Add Results Label

Step 1: Place a label control at the bottom of the form. Make sure it is large enough to display the election results.
Step 2: Set the Name property to lblResults.
Step 3: Remove the default value from the Text property. (See Figure 4.16.)

Figure 4.16
Form with result label
added to it

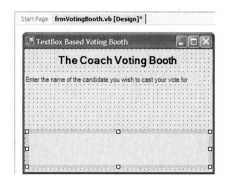

Figure 4.16
Form with result label
added to it

Add Voting Text Box

Step 1: Place a text box control below the instructions label.
Step 2: Set the `Name` property to `txtVote`.
Step 3: Clear out the default value from the `Text` property. (See Figure 4.17.)

Figure 4.17
Form with text box
added to it

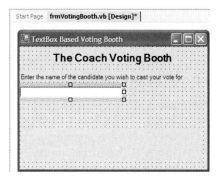

Add Vote Button

Step 1: Place a button control in the left side of the form, below the text box.
Step 2: Set the `Name` property to `btnVote`.
Step 3: Set the `Text` property to `Vote`. (See Figure 4.18.)

Figure 4.18
Form with the `btnVote`
button added

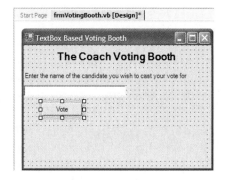

Step 4: Double-click on the button.
Step 5: Attach the code to process the vote. It must add 1 to the appropriate variable
         that stores the number of votes for each person.

The code in the `btnVote` button checks the value entered in the `txtVote` text box against the three valid choices for a vote. If it finds one of the valid choices, it adds 1 to the appropriate total variable. Then it clears the `txtVote` text box so that the next voter does not know who the previous vote was cast for. (See Figure 4.19.)

Figure 4.19
Code for the `btnVote` button

```
Private Sub btnVote_Click(...
    If (txtVote.Text = "Bush") Then
        intBushCount = intBushCount + 1
    End If
    If (txtVote.Text = "Gore") Then
        intGoreCount = intGoreCount + 1
    End If
    If (txtVote.Text = "Nader") Then
        intNaderCount = intNaderCount + 1
    End If
    'Erase the vote
    txtVote.Text = ""
End Sub
```

Add Results Button

Step 1: Place a button control to the right of the other button.
Step 2: Set the `Name` property to `btnResults`.
Step 3: Set the `Text` property to `Results`.
Step 4: Double-click on the button.
Step 5: Attach the code to display the results of the election in the `lblResults` label control. (See Figure 4.20.)

Figure 4.20
Form with the `btnResults` button added

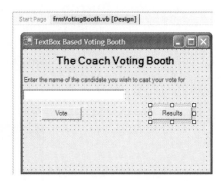

The code for the `btnResults` button formats the results of the election using the `'&'` operator. The `'&'` operator concatenates strings and other variables into one string. It is then set to the `lblResults` label for display. See Figure 4.21.

```
Private Sub btnResults_Click(...
    lblResults.Text = "Bush had " & Str(intBushCount) & _
    " Votes, Gore had " & intGoreCount & _
    " Votes, and Nader had " & intNaderCount & " Votes"
End Sub
```

Figure 4.21 Code for the `btnResults` button

COACH'S TIP

When a line of code is too long to fit on a single line, you can place an underscore character at the end of the line and continue your code on the next line. Be aware that the underscore should have a space in front of it. Also be aware that this tip will not work with comments that extend to more than one line.

What's Wrong with Your Application?　The voting system you have developed is problematic for a number of reasons. First, it allows only three options to vote for. No way exists to enter choices other than the three. Second, if the name is entered in any variation of a proper spelling of the name other than the one in the `If` statement, then it will be ignored. Finally, the program is inefficient because if the vote is for Bush, it still checks the other options. You will develop future versions of the Voting Booth application that deal with each of these issues.

4.2　Else and ElseIf Statements

The previous examples were chosen because they did not require something to be performed when the condition in the `If` statement evaluated to `False`. One could get around this by skillfully crafting additional `If` statements that have the opposite condition listed. However, that would not only add unneeded complexity, but it would also slow the execution of the code.

　　In the real world, situations are much more complex than just checking if a condition evaluates to `True` and then responding with the appropriate action. For instance, if you are driving a car and you approach a light, if it is red, you stop. Otherwise, if it is yellow, you prepare to stop. If it is not red or yellow, you keep going.

　　Graphically, it would look like the flowchart shown in Figure 4.22.

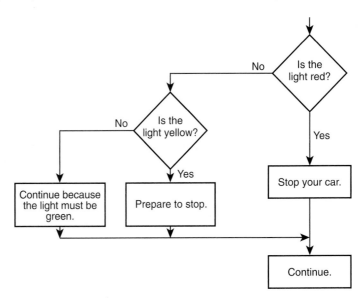

Figure 4.22　`Else/ElseIf` flowchart

This type of situation occurs quite frequently in programming. You already saw in the Voting Booth application that the use of repetitive `If` statements can be inefficient. Therefore, Visual Basic .NET provides the **Else** and **ElseIf** keywords to handle these cases.

When an `If` statement's expression evaluates to `False`, the next `ElseIf` condition is evaluated. If it evaluates to `True`, then the statements directly after it are executed. Otherwise, any additional `ElseIf` statements are evaluated in the same fashion. After all `ElseIf` statements are evaluated, if they all evaluate to `False` and an `Else` statement is included, then the statements directly following the `Else` keyword will be executed.

```
If (Condition) Then
    Do Something
ElseIf (Condition 2) Then
    Do Something Else
ElseIf (Condition 3) Then
    Do Something Else
...
Else
    Do Something Else
End If
```

Simple If/Else Statement

Write an application similar to the earlier one that output a message if the user entered `"Yes"`. However, this time if the user enters anything but `"Yes"`, then you will output a message indicating that `"Yes"` was not entered. The application must compare the input by the user to the `String` `"Yes"`. If the user enters `"Yes"`, then the code will set the `lblOutput` to a `String` indicating so; otherwise, another `String` will be assigned to the label. The code assumes that a `btnIfElse` button has been created to place the code and that `txtInput` text boxes and a `lblOutput` label (both with their `Text` property empty) were created to hold the input and output.

```
Private Sub btnIfElse_Click(...
    If (txtInput.Text = "Yes") Then
        lblOutput.Text = "The user answered the question with a Yes"
    Else
        lblOutput.Text = "The user did not answer the question with a Yes"
    End If
End Sub
```

When the program is executed and the button is clicked, the `If` statement is evaluated. If the user enters `"Yes"`, the `If` statement evaluates the expression by comparing `"Yes"` to `"Yes"`, and the conditional expression will evaluate to `True`. Therefore, all the statements until the `Else` are executed. Therefore, the text `"The user answered the question with a Yes"` is placed in the text box. Since the conditional expression in the `If` statement evaluated to `True`, none of the statements after the `Else` statement are executed.

If the user does not enter `"Yes"`, then the conditional expression will evaluate to `False`. Therefore, all the statements until the `Else` are not executed. Instead, the statements after the `Else` statement and before the `End If` statement are executed. Therefore, the text `"The user did not answer the question with a Yes"` is placed in the text box.

Another Simple If/Else Statement Example

Write an application that will output a message if a discount will be applied. For this application, a discount will be applied if the purchase price is more than $100. The application will have to compute whether or not a discount should be applied to a purchase. If the purchase price is more than $100, then the code will place "DISCOUNT" in lblOutput. Otherwise, the code will place "FULL PRICE" in the text box. The code assumes that a btnIfElse button has been created to place the code and that a text box, txtInput, and a label, lblOutput (both with their Text property empty), were created to hold the input and output, respectively.

```
Private Sub btnIfElse_Click(...
    Dim sngPurchasePrice As Single

    sngPurchasePrice = Val(txtInput.Text)

    If (sngPurchasePrice > 100) Then
        lblOutput.Text = "DISCOUNT"
    Else
        lblOutput.Text = "FULL PRICE"
    End If
End Sub
```

What do you think would be contained in lblOutput:

1 If the user enters 199.95 in the txtInput text box?
2 If the user enters 99.95 in the txtInput text box?

With 199.95 Entered in txtInput   When the program is executed and the button is clicked, the If statement is evaluated. If the user enters any value greater than 100, the If statement evaluates the expression by comparing the value entered to 100, and the conditional expression will evaluate to True. Therefore, the statements until the Else would be executed. Since the user entered 199.95, the condition evaluates to True and the text "DISCOUNT" is placed in the text box. Additionally, none of the statements after the Else statement are executed.

With 99.95 Entered in txtInput   If the user enters a value less than or equal to 100, then the conditional expression will evaluate to False. Therefore, all the statements until the Else are not executed. Instead, the statements after the Else statement and before the End If statement are executed. Since the user entered 99.95, the text "FULL PRICE" is placed in the text box.

DRILL 4.6

Using the same application, but changing the code in the button as follows, what do you think the output would be if the value entered by the user is 0, 1, and then 2, respectively?

```
Private Sub btnIfElse_Click(...
    Dim intDrillValue As Integer

    intDrillValue = Val(txtInput.Text)

    If (intDrillValue <= 1) Then
        lblOutput.Text = "This will output, because intDrillValue <= 1"
    Else
        lblOutput.Text = "Instead this outputs, because intDrillValue > 1"
    End If
    lblOutput.Text &= " and this is here as well"
End Sub
```

DRILL 4.7

Using the same application, but changing the code in the button as follows, what do you think the output would be if the value entered by the user is 0, 1, and then 2, respectively?

```
Private Sub btnIfElse_Click(...
 Dim intDrillValue As Integer

 intDrillValue = Val(txtInput.Text)

 If (intDrillValue < 1) Then
     lblOutput.Text = "This will output, because intDrillValue < 1"
 Else
     lblOutput.Text = "Instead this outputs, because intDrillValue >= 1"
 End If
 lblOutput.Text &= " and this is here as well"
End Sub
```

Simple If/ElseIf/Else Statement

Imagine if instead of writing an application that displayed whether or not a discount would be applied, you wrote one that applied a varied discount based on the total purchase price. The application should compute how much of a discount should be applied to a purchase. If the purchase price is more than $100, then the discount should be 5%. However, if the purchase price is more than $500, then the discount should be 10%. The application will require a `txtInput` text box and a `lblOutput` label (both with their `Text` property empty) to hold the input and output, respectively. A `btnIfElse` button is required to place the code to calculate the discount amount. The code should place the amount of the discount in the `lblOutput` label. If no discount is applied, then place the `String` `"NO DISCOUNT"` in the label.

```
Private Sub btnIfElse_Click(...
    Dim sngPurchasePrice As Single

    sngPurchasePrice = Val(txtInput.Text)

    If (sngPurchasePrice > 500) Then
        lblOutput.Text = (sngPurchasePrice * 0.1).ToString()
    ElseIf (sngPurchasePrice > 100) Then
        lblOutput.Text = (sngPurchasePrice * 0.05).ToString()
    Else
        lblOutput.Text = "NO DISCOUNT"
    End If
End Sub
```

What do you think would be contained in `lblOutput`:

1 If the user enters `600.00` in the `txtInput` text box?
2 If the user enters `250.00` in the `txtInput` text box?
3 If the user enters `50.00` in the `txtInput` text box?

With 600.00 Entered by the User When the program is executed and the button is clicked, the If statement is evaluated. If the user enters 600.00, then the If statement evaluates the expression by comparing the value entered to 500. Therefore, the conditional expression will evaluate to True. This causes all the statements until the ElseIf to be executed. Therefore, the purchase price is multiplied by .10 and the result is converted to a String. So the value "60" is placed in the label. Since the conditional expression in the If statement evaluated to True, none of the statements after the ElseIf or Else statements and before the End If are executed.

With 250.00 Entered by the User If the user enters a value that is less than or equal to 500, then the initial conditional expression will evaluate to False. Therefore, the second condition will be evaluated in the ElseIf statement. The ElseIf condition compares 250.00 to 100, and the conditional expression evaluates to True. This causes all the statements until the Else to be executed. Therefore, the purchase price is multiplied by .05 and the result is converted to a String. So the value "12.5" is placed in the label. Since the conditional expression in the If statement evaluated to True, none of the statements after the ElseIf or Else statements and before the End If are executed.

With 50.00 Entered by the User Finally, if the user enters a value less than or equal to 100, neither the If or ElseIf conditional expressions evaluates to True. Therefore, the statements after the Else statement and before the End If statement are executed. So the text "NO DISCOUNT" is placed in the label.

DRILL 4.8

Assume that the code for the previous example was instead coded as follows:

```
Private Sub btnIfElse_Click(...
        Dim sngPurchasePrice As Single

        sngPurchasePrice = Val(txtInput.Text)

        If (sngPurchasePrice > 100) Then
            lblOutput.Text = (sngPurchasePrice * 0.05).ToString()
        ElseIf (sngPurchasePrice > 500) Then
            lblOutput.Text = (sngPurchasePrice * 0.1).ToString()
        Else
            lblOutput.Text = "NO DISCOUNT"
        End If
End Sub
```

What do you think would be contained in lblOutput:

1 If the user enters 600.00 in the txtInput text box?
2 If the user enters 250.00 in the txtInput text box?
3 If the user enters 50.00 in the txtInput text box?

DRILL 4.9

The code assumes that a `btnIfElse` button has been created to place the code and that a `txtInput` text box and a `lblOutput` label (both with their `Text` property empty) were created to hold the input and output, respectively.

```
Private Sub btnIfElse_Click(...
    Dim intDrillValue As Integer

    intDrillValue = Val(txtInput.Text)

    If (intDrillValue > 0) Then
        lblOutput.Text = "The number is positive"
    ElseIf (intDrillValue < 0) Then
        lblOutput.Text = "The number is negative"
    Else
        lblOutput.Text = "I got a big zero"
    End If
End Sub
```

What do you think would be contained in `lblOutput`:

1 If the user enters –1 in the `txtInput` text box?
2 If the user enters 0 in the `txtInput` text box?
3 If the user enters 1 in the `txtInput` text box?

Example: Letter Grade Program
Problem Description

Write a program that will display a letter grade based on a number grade entered. The program should assign an A if the grade is greater than or equal to 90, a B if the grade is between an 80 and an 89, a C if the grade is between a 70 and a 79, and a D if the grade is between a 60 and a 69. Otherwise, the program assigns an F.

   The application should look like that shown in Figure 4.23.

Figure 4.23
Sketch of application

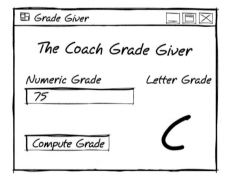

Problem Discussion

The application will require a text box to accept the numerical grade and a label to output the result. The actual computation of the letter grade will be performed in the

Click event of a button. The letter grade can be determined using an If statement with a few ElseIf statements checking the range of each possible letter grade. Using an If statement with ElseIf statements is preferred over using a series of If statements because once a letter grade has been determined, it would be wasteful to check the remaining If statement.

Problem Solution
Create Project and Form

Step 1: From the Start window, click on New Project. The New Project window will appear.
Step 2: Specify the name of the application as GradeGiver.
Step 3: Specify the location as "C:\VB Net Coach\Chapter 4\Code\ ".
Step 4: Click on the OK button.
Step 5: Set the Name property of the form to frmGradeGiver.
Step 6: Rename the file by right-clicking on the file name in the Solution Explorer and setting the name to frmGradeGiver.vb.
Step 7: Set the Text property of the form to Grade Giver.

Add Title Label

Step 1: Place a label control across the top of the form.
Step 2: Set the Name property to lblTitle.
Step 3: Set the Text property to The Coach Grade Giver.
Step 4: Set the Font Size property to 18.
Step 5: Set the Font Bold property to True.
Step 6: Set the TextAlign property to MiddleCenter. (See Figure 4.24.)

Figure 4.24
Form with title label
added to it

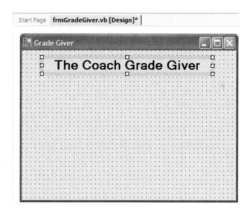

Add Numeric Grade Label

Step 1: Place a label control near the left side of the form.
Step 2: Set the Name property to lblNumericGradeTitle.
Step 3: Set the Text property to Numeric Grade.
Step 4: Set the Font Size property to 12.
Step 5: Set the Font Bold property to True. (See Figure 4.25.)

Figure 4.25
Form with Numeric Grade
label added to it

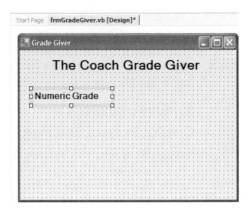

Add Numeric Grade Text Box

Step 1:   Place a text box control below the Numeric Grade label.

Step 2:   Set the `Name` property to `txtNumericGrade`.

Step 3:   Clear out the default value from the `Text` property. (See Figure 4.26.)

Figure 4.26
Form with `txtGrade` text
box added to it

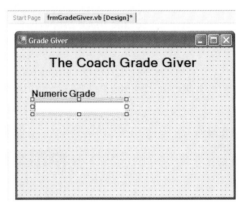

Add Letter Grade Label

Step 1:   Place a label control near the right side of the form.

Step 2:   Set the `Name` property to `lblLetterGradeTitle`.

Step 3:   Set the `Text` property to `"Letter Grade"`.

Step 4:   Set the `Font  Size` property to `12`.

Step 5:   Set the `Font  Bold` property to `True`. (See Figure 4.27.)

Figure 4.27
Form with Letter Grade
label added to it

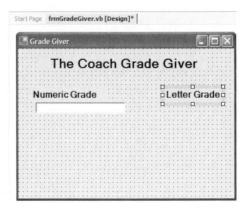

Add lblGrade Label

Step 1: Place a label control near the right side of the form.
Step 2: Set the `Name` property to `lblLetterGrade`.
Step 3: Clear the `Text` property.
Step 4: Set the `Font Size` property to `48`.
Step 5: Set the `Font Bold` property to `True`.
Step 6: Set the `TextAlign` property to `MiddleCenter`. (See Figure 4.28.)

Figure 4.28
Form with the `lblGrade`
label added

Add Compute Grade Button

Step 1: Place a button control in the bottom left side of the form.
Step 2: Set the `Text` property to `Compute Grade`.
Step 3: Set the `Name` property to `btnCompute`.
Step 4: Double-click on the button.
Step 5: Attach the code to display the results of the grade calculation in the `lblLetterGrade` label control. (See Figure 4.29.)

Figure 4.29
Form with `btnCompute`
button added to it

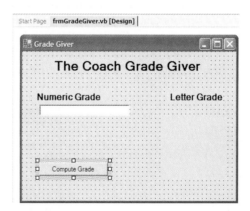

Note that in this example, without the `ElseIf` it would be difficult, given what you know so far, to construct a simple `If` statement program that printed the desired letter grade for a numerical grade.

The code in the button is simple. It converts the user's input to an `Integer`. The converted grade is then compared to `90`. Any grade greater than or equal to `90` causes the letter `"A"` to be assigned to the `lblLetterGrade` label control. The rest of the conditions are not checked. If the grade is not greater than or equal to `90`, it must be less than `90`. Therefore, when you have a grade in the 80s, the first `ElseIf` statement is enough to check for a `"B"`. Similarly, you check for a `"C"` and `"D"`. Finally, if the grade is not greater than or equal to a `60`, you output an `"F"`. (See Figure 4.30.)

```
Start Page | frmGradeGiver .vb [Design]  frmGradeGiver.vb |                                        ◁ ▷ ×
frmGradeGiver                                          ▼  btnCompute_Click                            ▼
Public Class frmGradeGiver
    Inherits System.Windows.Forms.Form

 Windows Form Designer generated code

    Private Sub btnCompute_Click(ByVal sender As System.Object, ByVal e As System.EventArgs) Handles btnCompute.Click
        Dim intGrade As Integer 'Declare tempory variable

        intGrade = Val(txtNumericGrade.Text) 'Convert user input to an Integer

        'Compute Grade
        If (intGrade >= 90) Then
            lblLetterGrade.Text = "A"
        ElseIf (intGrade >= 80) Then
            lblLetterGrade.Text = "B"
        ElseIf (intGrade >= 70) Then
            lblLetterGrade.Text = "C"
        ElseIf (intGrade >= 60) Then
            lblLetterGrade.Text = "D"
        Else
            lblLetterGrade.Text = "F"
        End If
    End Sub
End Class
```

Figure 4.30   Code for `btnCompute` button

Example: Improved Voting Booth
Problem Description

Previously, your Voting Booth application did not keep track of the number of errors in voting. Remember the 10,000 supposed undervotes in Florida? Well, now you can track them by adding that functionality to your application.

Aside from curiosity's sake, there is an important reason to track these errors. A good voting machine should prevent mistakes from ever being entered. Therefore, one way to judge the relative worth of a voting booth would be to calculate the number of errors that are produced when using it.

The application will look relatively the same. The only visible difference will be the addition of the display of the number of improper votes being cast. This can be seen in Figure 4.31.

Figure 4.31
Voting Booth application
with results

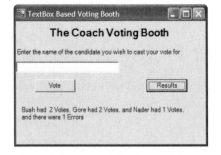

COACH'S TIP

You could choose to use a message box to display the results. This will be an assignment at the end of the chapter.

Problem Discussion

Your new application will take advantage of `ElseIf` and `Else` statements to total the votes more efficiently as well as keep a total of the improper votes. By using the `ElseIf` statement, you can process each vote more efficiently. By using the `Else` statement, you can capture all of the errors.

Problem Solution
Create Project and Form

Step 1: From the Start window, click on New Project. The New Project window will appear.

Step 2: Specify the name of the application as `ErrorTrackingVotingBooth`.

Step 3: Specify the location as `"C:\VB Net Coach\Chapter 4\Code\"`.

Step 4: Click on the OK button.

Step 5: Set the `Name` property of the form to `frmVoting`.

Step 6: Rename the file by right-clicking on the file name in the Solution Explorer and setting the name to `frmVoting.vb`.

Step 7: Set the `Text` property to `TextBox Based Voting Booth`.

Modify the Application's Code

You must modify the four code snippets associated with this application. The new code must first declare an additional variable, in the `Declarations` section of the form, to hold the number of errors encountered. This is seen in Figure 4.32.

Figure 4.32
Variable declaration for new voting application

```
Dim intBushCount As Integer
Dim intGoreCount As Integer
Dim intNaderCount As Integer
Dim intErrorCount As Integer
```

Then you must make sure that you initialize that variable to 0 in the constructor of the form. This is the same place you initialized the other variables in the application. This is seen in Figure 4.33.

```
Public Sub New()
    MyBase.New()

    'This call is required by the Windows Form Designer.
    InitializeComponent()

    'Add any initialization after the InitializeComponent() call
    intBushCount = 0
    intGoreCount = 0
    intNaderCount = 0
    intErrorCount = 0
End Sub
```

Figure 4.33   Initialize the variables to 0

Next, you need to modify the `btnVote` button so that it will use `ElseIf` and `Else` statements to process the vote efficiently and so that it now records the number of errors by using the `Else` statement. (See Figure 4.34.)

```
Private Sub btnVote_Click(...
    If (txtVote.Text = "Bush") Then
        intBushCount += 1
    ElseIf (txtVote.Text = "Gore") Then
        intGoreCount += 1
    ElseIf (txtVote.Text = "Nader") Then
        intNaderCount += 1
    Else
        intErrorCount += 1
    End If
    'Erase the vote
    txtVote.Text = ""
End Sub
```

Finally, you need to modify the btnResults button so that it will display the additional information. It is shown in Figure 4.35.

```
Private Sub btnResults_Click(...
    lblResults.Text = "Bush had " & Str(intBushCount) & _
                      " Votes, Gore had " & intGoreCount & _
                      " Votes, and Nader had " & intNaderCount & " Votes" & _
                      ", and there were " & intErrorCount & " Errors"
End Sub
```

Figure 4.35   Code for btnResults button

4.3 Compound Conditional Statements

Sometimes comparisons are not as simple as a single comparison. For instance, what happens if, while driving your car, you go through a red light? The answer depends. If you go through the light and it is red and another car is in the intersection, an accident occurs. If you go through the light and it is red and a police officer is there, you will get a ticket. If you go through the light and no car or police officer is there, you will get through the light safely. These more complex conditions are known as **compound conditional expressions**.

Visual Basic .NET gives you additional expression operators to help you map a problem or algorithm to a program. It is not uncommon to require **Boolean** logic operators like And, Or, and Not to assist in your representing a condition properly.

And is used to represent the logical "anding" of two conditions. If you are unfamiliar with Boolean logic, here is a simple truth table of all the possible conditions:

```
True  And True  = True
True  And False = False
False And True  = False
False And False = False
```

Or is used to represent the logical or. Here is a truth table of all of the possibilities:

True Or True = True
True Or False = True
False Or True = True
False Or False = False

In addition, Visual Basic .NET provides the **Not** operator to negate the value of an expression. Here is a truth table of all the possibilities:

Not True = False
Not False = True

Here are some sample expressions that evaluate to `True`:

(1 = 1) And (2 = 2)
(2 >= 1) Or (1 <> 1)
(2 >= 2) And (1 < 3)
(1 <= 2) Or (2 > 1)
(1 < 2) And (1 <> 2)
("CAT" = "CAT") And (1 < 2)
("a" <> "c") Or ("b" <> "c")
Not ("A" = "a")

Here are some samples of expressions that evaluate to `False`:

(1 = 2) Or (2 = 1)
(2 <= 1) Or (1 > 2)
(2 < 2) And (1 = 1)
(3 > 4) And (3 < 5)
(1 >= 2) Or (2 < 1)
Not (1 = 1)
("a" = "A") Or ("b" = "B")

DRILL 4.10

Indicate whether each expression evaluates to `True` or `False`.

```
1 Not (5 >= 4)
2 (-3 < -4) Or (1 = 1)
3 ("BOB" = "bob") And (2 >= 2)
4 (2 < 1) Or (5 <> 4)
5 (1 < 2) Or (4 >= 4)
6 Not (4 <= 4) And (1 <= 1)
```

If Statement Using an And Operator

You can use compound conditional expressions in a program the same way as with the previous conditional statements. Observe the following code snippet that shows the use of a compound conditional expression. The code assumes that a button, `btnCompoundIf`, has been created to contain the code. Additionally, three text boxes—`txtRetailPrice`, `txtSalePrice`, and `txtOutput` (all with their `Text` property empty)—have been created to hold the input and output of the user.

```
Private Sub btnCompoundIf_Click(...
    Dim sngRetailPrice As Single
    Dim sngSalesPrice As Single

    sngRetailPrice = Val(txtRetailPrice.Text)
    sngSalesPrice = Val(txtSalesPrice.Text)

    If ((sngRetailPrice = sngSalesPrice) And (sngRetailPrice > 100)) Then
        txtOutput.Text = "This product is not on sale and is expensive"
    Else
        txtOutput.Text = "This product may not be too expensive and " _
                         "may be on sale"
    End If
End Sub
```

What do you think would be contained in `txtOutput`:

1 If the user enters `50.25` for the retail price and `50.25` for the sales price?
2 If the user enters `125.13` for the retail price and `125.13` for the sales price?
3 If the user enters `150.00` for the retail price and `125.13` for the sales price?
4 If the user enters `99.90` for the retail price and `75.00` for the sales price?

With a Retail Price of 50.25 and a Sales Price of 50.25   When the application is executed and the button is clicked, the `If` statement is evaluated. When the user enters `50.25` for both the retail price and the sales price, then the `If` statement evaluates the expression by comparing the retail price to the sales price. Since both are equal to `50.25`, then that part of the expression evaluates to `True`. The second condition is then checked. The retail price is compared to `100`. Since the retail price is not greater than `100`, the comparison evaluates to `False`. Because the two subconditions are combined with an `And` operator, both must evaluate to `True` for the entire conditional expression to evaluate to `True`. Therefore, the conditional expression evaluates to `False` and the code associated with the `Else` statement is executed. The text `"This product may not be too expensive and may be on sale"` is assigned to the output text box.

With a Retail Price of 125.13 and a Sales Price of 125.13   When the application is executed and the button is clicked, the `If` statement is evaluated. When the user enters `125.13` for both the retail price and the sales price, then the `If` statement evaluates the expression by comparing the retail price to the sales price. Since both are equal to `125.13`, then that part of the expression evaluates to `True`. The second condition is then checked. The retail price is compared to `100`. This time the retail price is greater than `100`, so the comparison evaluates to `True`. Because the two subconditions are combined with an `And` operator, both must evaluate to `True` for the entire conditional expression to evaluate to `True`. Therefore, the conditional expression evaluates to `True` and the code associated with the `If` statement is executed. The text `"This product is not on sale and is expensive"` is assigned to the output text box.

With a Retail Price of 150.00 and a Sales Price of 125.13   When the application is executed and the button is clicked, the `If` statement is evaluated. When the user enters `150.00` and `125.13` for the retail price and the sales price, respectively, then the `If` statement evaluates the expression by comparing the retail price to the sales price. This time both are not equal, so the first subexpression evaluates to `False`. The second condition is then checked. The retail price is compared to `100`. The retail price is greater than `100`, so the comparison evaluates to `True`. Whether one or both subexpressions evaluate to `False` is irrelevant. As long as one of them evaluates to `False`, the entire expression will evaluate to `False`. Therefore, the conditional expression evaluates to `False` and the code associated with the `If` statement is executed. The text `"This product may not be too expensive and may be on sale"` is assigned to the output text box.

With a Retail Price of 99.90 and a Sales Price of 75.00   When the application is executed and the button is clicked, the `If` statement is evaluated. When the user enters `99.90` and `75.00` for the retail price and the sales price, respectively, then the `If` statement evaluates the expression by comparing the retail price to the sales price. This time both are not equal, so the first subexpression evaluates to `False`. The second condition is then checked. The retail price is compared to `100`. The retail price is not greater than `100`, so the comparison evaluates to `False`. Therefore, the conditional expression evaluates to `False` and the code associated with the `If` statement is executed. The text `"This product may not be too expensive and may be on sale"` is assigned to the output text box.

If Statement Using an Or Operator

Assume the following code for the `btnCompoundIf` exists in the same application as the previous example. Now however, you are demonstrating the use of an `Or` operator.

```
Private Sub btnCompoundIf_Click(...
    Dim sngRetailPrice As Single
    Dim sngSalesPrice As Single

    sngRetailPrice = Val(txtRetailPrice.Text)
    sngSalesPrice = Val(txtSalesPrice.Text)

    If ((sngRetailPrice = sngSalesPrice) Or (sngRetailPrice > 100)) Then
        txtOutput.Text = "This product is either not on sale or very expensive"
    Else
        txtOutput.Text = "This product is on sale and not expensive"
    End If
End Sub
```

What do you think would be contained in `txtOutput`:

1 If the user enters `50.25` for the retail price and `50.25` for the sales price?
2 If the user enters `125.13` for the retail price and `125.13` for the sales price?
3 If the user enters `150.00` for the retail price and `125.13` for the sales price?
4 If the user enters `99.90` for the retail price and `75.00` for the sales price?

With a Retail Price of 50.25 and a Sales Price of 50.25   When the application is executed and the button is clicked, the `If` statement is evaluated. When the user enters `50.25` for both the retail price and the sales price, then the `If` statement evaluates the expression by comparing the retail price to the sales price. Since both are equal to `50.25`, then that part of the expression evaluates to `True`. The second condition is then checked. The retail price is compared to `100`. Since the retail price is not greater than `100`, the comparison evaluates to `False`. Because the two subconditions are combined with an Or operator, only one of the subconditions must evaluate to True for the entire conditional expression to evaluate to True. Therefore, the conditional expression evaluates to True and the code associated with the If statement is executed. The text "This product is either not on sale or very expensive" is assigned to the output text box.

With a Retail Price of 125.13 and a Sales Price of 125.13   When the application is executed and the button is clicked, the If statement is evaluated. When the user enters 125.13 for both the retail price and the sales price, then the If statement evaluates the expression by comparing the retail price to the sales price. Since both are equal to 125.13, then that part of the expression evaluates to True. The second condition is then checked. The retail price is compared to 100. This time the retail price is greater than 100, so the comparison evaluates to True. Therefore, the conditional expression evaluates to True and the code associated with the If statement is executed. The text "This product is either not on sale or very expensive" is assigned to the output text box.

With a Retail Price of 150.00 and a Sales Price of 125.13   When the application is executed and the button is clicked, the If statement is evaluated. When the user enters 150.00 and 125.13 for the retail price and the sales price, respectively, then the If statement evaluates the expression by comparing the retail price to the sales price. This time both are not equal, so the first subexpression evaluates to False. The second condition is then checked. The retail price is compared to 100. The retail price is greater than 100, so the comparison evaluates to True. Therefore, the conditional expression evaluates to True and the code associated with the If statement is executed. The text "This product is either not on sale or very expensive" is assigned to the output text box.

With a Retail Price of 99.90 and a Sales Price of 75.00   When the application is executed and the button is clicked, the If statement is evaluated. When the user enters 99.90 and 75.00 for the retail price and the sales price, respectively, then the If statement evaluates the expression by comparing the retail price to the sales price. This time both are not equal, so the first subexpression evaluates to False. The second condition is then checked. The retail price is compared to 100. The retail price is not greater than 100, so the comparison evaluates to False. Therefore, the conditional expression evaluates to False and the code associated with the If statement is executed. The text "This product is on sale and not expensive" is assigned to the output text box.

If Statement Using a Not Operator

Assume the following code for the btnCompoundIf exists in the same application as the previous example. Now, however, you are using the Not operator.

```
Private Sub btnCompoundIf_Click(...
    Dim sngRetailPrice As Single
    Dim sngSalesPrice As Single

    sngRetailPrice = Val(txtRetailPrice.Text)
    sngSalesPrice = Val(txtSalesPrice.Text)

    If (Not (sngRetailPrice >= sngSalesPrice)) Then
        txtOutput.Text = "The Sales Price is greater than the Retail Price"
    Else
        txtOutput.Text = "The Sales Price is less than or equal to " _
                        "the Retail Price"
    End If
End Sub
```

What do you think would be contained in txtOutput:

1 If the user enters 50.25 for the retail price and 50.25 for the sales price?
2 If the user enters 49.95 for the retail price and 125.13 for the sales price?

With a Retail Price of 50.25 and a Sales Price of 50.25   When the application is executed and the button is clicked, the If statement is evaluated. When the user enters 50.25 for both the retail price and the sales price, then the If statement evaluates the expression by comparing the retail price to the sales price. This time the retail price is greater than or equal to the sales price, so the inner subexpression evaluates to True. Then the Not operator is applied to this result. When a Not operator is applied to True, the result is False. Therefore, the conditional expression evaluates to False and the code associated with the Else statement is executed. So the text "The Sales Price is less than or equal to the Retail Price" is assigned to the output text box.

With a Retail Price of 49.95 and a Sales Price of 125.15   When the application is executed and the button is clicked, the If statement is evaluated. When the user enters 49.95 and 125.15 for the retail price and the sales price, respectively, then the If statement evaluates the expression by comparing the retail price to the sales price. This time the retail price is not greater than or equal to the sales price, so the inner subexpression evaluates to False. Then the Not operator is applied to this result. When a Not operator is applied to False, the result is True. Therefore, the conditional expression evaluates to True and the code associated with the If statement is executed. So the text "The Sales Price is greater than the Retail Price" is assigned to the output text box.

DRILL 4.11

Use the same application as the previous drills, but change the code in the button as follows:

```
Private Sub btnCompoundIf_Click(...
    Dim sngRetailPrice As Single
    Dim sngSalesPrice As Single

    sngRetailPrice = Val(txtRetailPrice.Text)
    sngSalesPrice = Val(txtSalesPrice.Text)

    If ((sngRetailPrice >= sngSalesPrice) And _
        (Not (sngSalesPrice > 75))) Then
        txtOutput.Text = "This crazy drill outputs True"
    Else
        txtOutput.Text = "This crazy drill outputs False"
    End If
End Sub
```

What do you think would be contained in txtOutput:

1 If the user enters 99.95 for the retail price and 50.25 for the sales price?
2 If the user enters 199.95 for the retail price and 99.95 for the sales price?

Example: Improved Voting Booth Application
Problem Description

Our previous Voting Booth application allowed for the counting of votes for three candidates and a count of the number of incorrect votes. If this system were used in the real world, you would have a great number of incorrect votes that were really meant to be a vote for one of the three candidates.

Since you checked only the spelling for each name, what do you think would happen if you type `Al Gore` instead of `Gore`? The answer is that the vote would be counted as an incorrect vote.

Problem Discussion

There are many ways to solve this problem; one is to use compound conditional statements to check for the additional spellings of each name. The only modification required to the application would be to change the code in the `btnVote` button's `Click` event.

Problem Solution

Observe the modifications, shown in Figure 4.36, to the `btnVote` button that adds additional spellings for each candidate.

```
Private Sub btnVote_Click(...
    If (txtVote.Text = "Bush") Or (txtVote.Text = "George Bush") Then
        intBushCount += 1
    ElseIf (txtVote.Text = "Gore") Or (txtVote.Text = "Al Gore") Then
        intGoreCount += 1
    ElseIf (txtVote.Text = "Nader") Or (txtVote.Text = "Ralph Nader") Then
        intNaderCount += 1
    Else
        intErrorCount += 1
    End If

    'Erase the vote
    txtVote.Text = ""
End Sub
```

Figure 4.36   Code for `btnVote` button

4.4 Nested Conditional Statements

Compound conditional statements are useful for mapping real-world situations to the computer. However, if a part of the condition needs to be repeated more than once, it would be inefficient to repeat the check of that condition each time. Imagine you wanted to reward employees for their hard work. You were going to give them tickets to an event. Let's say you had tickets to a basketball game, a football game, the philharmonic, or the opera. You could start by asking if they would like to go to the basketball game, then ask about the football game, then the philharmonic, then finally the opera. If you added more choices, like baseball or hockey, wouldn't it be easier if you first asked if the person was a sports fan? If not, then you could ask them about the philharmonic or opera right away.

Nested conditional statements can do this. Figure 4.37 offers a graphical representation.

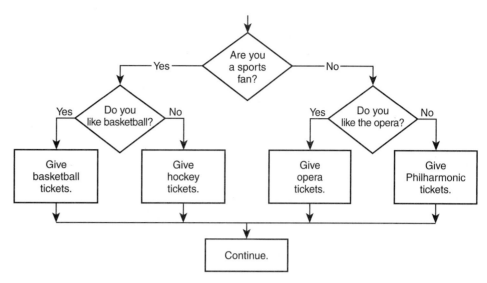

Figure 4.37
Nested conditional
statements

Visual Basic .NET provides the ability to nest conditional statements. It is simply a matter of placing one conditional statement inside another. This shouldn't add too much confusion; it simply requires treating the inner `If` statement as an individual `If` statement to be evaluated as you would any other statement.

Nested If Statements

The following code will loosely implement the flowchart seen in Figure 4.37. While it will not ask the questions depicted, it will process the answers to the three questions as if they were asked as portrayed in the flowchart.

The code assumes that a `btnCompoundConditional` button has been created to place the code and that three text boxes—`txtQuestion1`, `txtQuestion2`, and `txtOutput` (all with their `Text` property empty)—were created to hold the input and output.

See the following code as an example:

```
Private Sub btnCompoundConditional_Click(...
    If (txtQuestion1.Text = "Yes") Then
        If (txtQuestion2.Text = "Yes") Then
            txtOutput.Text = "Basketball"
        Else
            txtOutput.Text = "Hockey"
        End If
    Else
        If (txtQuestion2.Text = "Yes") Then
            txtOutput.Text = "Opera"
        Else
            txtOutput.Text = "Philharmonic"
        End If
    End If
End Sub
```

**COACH'S
WARNING**

For every `If` statement, you must have an `End If` statement. By indenting properly, you will find it easier to keep track of your nesting level.

What do you think would be contained in `txtOutput`:

1 If the user enters `"Yes"` in `txtQuestion1` and `"Yes"` in `txtQuestion2`?
2 If the user enters `"Yes"` in `txtQuestion1` and `"No"` in `txtQuestion2`?
3 If the user enters `"No"` in `txtQuestion1` and `"Yes"` in `txtQuestion2`?
4 If the user enters `"No"` in `txtQuestion1` and `"No"` in `txtQuestion2`?

User Enters "Yes" and "Yes"   When the program is executed and the button is clicked, the outer `If` statement is evaluated. Since `"Yes"` is equal to `"Yes"`, the conditional expression evaluates to `True`, and therefore all the statements until the `Else` are executed.

In this case, that means the first inner `If` statement is evaluated. Since the user entered `"Yes"` for the second question as well, the condition evaluates to `True`, and therefore the text `"Basketball"` is placed in the text box. Since the conditional expression in the inner `If` statement evaluated to `True`, none of the statements after the inner `Else` statement are executed. Since you previously determined that the outer `If` statement evaluated to `True`, then the outer `Else` statement is skipped as well.

User Enters "Yes" and "No"   When the program is executed and the button is clicked, the outer `If` statement is evaluated. Since `"Yes"` is equal to `"Yes"`, the conditional expression evaluates to `True`, and therefore all the statements until the `Else` are executed.

In this case, that means the first inner `If` statement is evaluated. Since the user entered `"No"` for the second question, the condition evaluates to `False`, and therefore the text `"Hockey"` is placed in the text box.

User Enters "No" and "Yes"   When the program is executed and the button is clicked, the outer `If` statement is evaluated. Since `"No"` is not equal to `"Yes"`, the conditional expression evaluates to `False`, and therefore all the statements after the `Else` are executed.

In this case, that means the second inner `If` statement is evaluated. Since the user entered `"Yes"` for the second question, the condition evaluates to `True`, and therefore the text `"Opera"` is placed in the text box. Since the conditional expression in the inner `If` statement evaluated to `True`, none of the statements after the inner `Else` statement are executed.

User Enters "No" and "No"   When the program is executed and the button is clicked, the outer `If` statement is evaluated. Since `"No"` is not equal to `"Yes"`, the conditional expression evaluates to `False`, and therefore all the statements after the `Else` are executed.

In this case, that means the second inner `If` statement is evaluated. Since the user entered `"No"` for the second question, the condition evaluates to `False`, and therefore the text `"Philharmonic"` is placed in the text box.

DRILL 4.12

Assume that a `btnCompoundConditional` button has been created to place the code and that two text boxes, `txtInput` and `txtOutput` (both with their `Text` property empty), were created to hold the input and output, respectively.

Also, assume the following code:

```
Private Sub btnCompoundConditional_Click(...
    Dim intDrillValue As Integer
    intDrillValue = Val(txtInput.Text)
    If (intDrillValue = 1) Then
        If (intDrillValue <= 1) Then
```

(continues)

```
                txtOutput.Text = "This will output, from the 1st Inner If"
            Else
                txtOutput.Text = "This will output, from the 1st Inner Else"
            End If
        Else
            If (intDrillValue < 1) Then
                txtOutput.Text = "This will output, from the 2nd Inner If"
            Else
                txtOutput.Text = "This will output, from the 2nd Inner Else"
            End If
        End If
End Sub
```

What do you think would be contained in `txtOutput`:

1 If the user enters 0 in `txtInput`?
2 If the user enters 1 in `txtInput`?
3 If the user enters 2 in `txtInput`?

Example: Improved Voting Booth Application
Problem Description

Imagine if instead of writing a Voting Booth application for a single presidential race, you needed to develop a Voting Booth application that could be used for additional races as well. For instance, let's change your current application to count votes for the presidential and vice presidential elections. For simplicity's sake, you will limit the candidates to George Bush and Al Gore for the presidency and Dick Cheney and Joe Lieberman for the vice presidency. (See Figure 4.38.) You can ignore the fact that you really don't vote for a vice president, because you don't really vote for a president either.

Figure 4.38
Improved Voting Booth
application

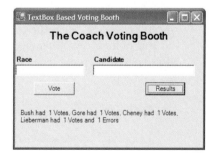

Problem Discussion

The changes required are not overly complex. You will still need a variable for each candidate to track the number of valid votes that they receive. You will also keep a single variable to track all of the improperly cast votes. Additionally, you will need to modify the results to display the additional candidates and modify the processing of the votes to handle the new race text box as well as the additional candidates.

Problem Solution

The code required for the additional variables needs to be declared in the `Declarations` section of the form. (See Figure 4.39.)

Figure 4.39
Declarations code

```
Dim intBushCount As Integer
Dim intGoreCount As Integer
Dim intCheneyCount As Integer
Dim intLiebermanCount As Integer
Dim intErrorCount As Integer
```

You would need to change the code for the `btnResults` button so that it outputs all of the results of the election. This can be seen in the code shown in Figure 4.40.

```
Private Sub btnResults_Click(...
    lblResults.Text = "Bush had " & intBushCount.ToString() & _
    " Votes, Gore had " & intGoreCount.ToString() & _
    " Votes, Cheney had " & intCheneyCount.ToString() & _
    " Votes, Lieberman had " & intLiebermanCount.ToString() & " Votes" & _
    " and " & intErrorCount.ToString() & " Errors"
End Sub
```

Figure 4.40　`btnResults'` `Click` event code

The main reason for selecting this example is to demonstrate the power of a nested conditional statement. If you didn't nest the conditional statements, your code would execute more slowly. Each time you check a candidate with the nonnested example, you have to recheck the condition to indicate whether this vote is for a president or a vice president. While this example will not produce a noticeable difference in the speed at which it executes, when the comparisons get either more complex or more numerous, this sort of inefficiency can become a real issue. Therefore, when a condition is repeatedly checked, consider using the nested form. See Figures 4.41–4.43.

```
Private Sub btnVote_Click(...
    If (txtRace.Text = "Pres") Then
        If (txtVote.Text = "Bush") Or (txtVote.Text = "George Bush") Then
            intBushCount += 1
        ElseIf (txtVote.Text = "Gore") Or (txtVote.Text = "Al Gore") Then
            intGoreCount += 1
        Else
            intErrorCount += 1
        End If
    ElseIf (txtRace.Text = "Vice") Then
        If (txtVote.Text = "Cheney") Or (txtVote.Text = "Dick Cheney") Then
            intCheneyCount += 1
        ElseIf (txtVote.Text = "Lieberman") Or _
            (txtVote.Text = "Joe Lieberman") Then
            intLiebermanCount += 1
        Else
            intErrorCount += 1
        End If
    Else
        intErrorCount += 1
    End If

    'Erase the vote
    txtVote.Text = ""
    txtRace.Text = ""
End Sub
```

Figure 4.41   btnVote's Click event code—correct code

```
Private Sub btnVote_Click(...
    If (txtRace.Text = "Pres") And _
        ((txtVote.Text = "Bush") Or (txtVote.Text = "George Bush")) Then
        intBushCount += 1
    ElseIf (txtRace.Text = "Pres") And _
        ((txtVote.Text = "Gore") Or (txtVote.Text = "Al Gore")) Then
        intGoreCount += 1
    ElseIf (txtRace.Text = "Vice") And _
        ((txtVote.Text = "Cheney") Or (txtVote.Text = "Dick Cheney")) Then
        intCheneyCount += 1
    ElseIf (txtRace.Text = "Vice") And _
        ((txtVote.Text = "Lieberman") Or _
         (txtVote.Text = "Joe Lieberman")) Then
        intLiebermanCount += 1
    Else
        intErrorCount += 1
    End If

    'Erase the vote
    txtVote.Text = ""
    txtRace.Text = ""
End Sub
```

Figure 4.42   btnVote's Click event code—incorrect code

```
intBushCount = 0
intGoreCount = 0
intCheneyCount = 0
intLiebermanCount = 0
intErrorCount = 0
```

4.5   Select Case Statements

As your applications become more complex, you may have many conditions to check. Using multiple If, ElseIf, and Else statements can become burdensome as well as look quite busy on the page. Visual Basic .NET gives you a better way to handle multiple options, the **Select Case** statement.

A Select Case statement gives the programmer the ability to shortcut the process of describing under what conditions certain code should be executed. The programmer must indicate an expression that the decision will be based on. Then the programmer indicates a series of cases with code associated with each. If the case matches the expression, then the code is executed. If no cases match the expression, then the statements associated with the **Case Else** would be executed.

```
Select Case Expression
    Case Possible Value or Range of Values
        Statement(s)
    Case Another Possible Value or Range of Values
        Statement(s)
    .
    .
    .

    Case Else
        Statement(s)
End Select
```

The expression in a Select Case statement may be

◆ a numeric variable
◆ a string variable
◆ a simple expression composed of operators and variables

The possible values in a **Case** statement may be

◆ a numeric constant
◆ a string constant
◆ a numeric variable
◆ a string variable
◆ a range of values
◆ a combination of the above

Select Case Statement with Numeric Values

You can use a Select Case statement in a program in the same way as conditional statements. Observe the following code snippet, which shows the use of a Select Case statement to determine how many dozens of roses are being ordered. The code assumes that a button, `btnSelectCase`, has been created to contain the code. Additionally, the text boxes `txtInput` and `txtOutput` (with its `Text` property empty) have been created to hold the input and output, respectively, of the user.

```
Private Sub btnSelectCase_Click(...
    Dim intExampleValue As Integer

    intExampleValue = Val(txtInput.Text)

    Select Case intExampleValue
        Case 12
            txtOutput.Text = "Your order of a dozen roses has been placed"
        Case 24
            txtOutput.Text = "Your order of two dozen roses has been placed"
        Case Else
            txtOutput.Text = "You must order either one or two dozen roses"
    End Select

End Sub
```

What do you think would be contained in `txtOutput`:

1 If the user enters `12` in the `txtInput` text box?
2 If the user enters `24` in the `txtInput` text box?
3 If the user enters `0` in the `txtInput` text box?

With the Number of Roses Equal to 12   When the program is executed and the button is clicked, the `Case` statement is evaluated. Since `intExampleValue` is equal to 12, the first case statement evaluates to `True`. Therefore, the value `"Your order of a dozen roses has been placed"` is assigned to the `txtOutput` text box. Once a `Case` statement is found to evaluate to `True`, the rest are ignored.

With the Number of Roses Equal to 24   If you changed the value of `intExampleValue` to 24, then the first case would evaluate to `False`. This would cause the next `Case` statement to be evaluated. Since `intExampleValue` equals 24, this would cause the second `Case` statement to evaluate to `True`. Therefore, the value `"Your order of two dozen roses has been placed"` is assigned to the `txtOutput` text box. Again, since a `Case` statement evaluated to `True`, the rest are ignored.

With the Number of Roses Equal to 0   Finally, if you changed the value of `intExampleValue` to 0, then not only would the first case evaluate to `False`, but so would the second. This would cause the `Case Else` statement to be evaluated. Therefore, the value `"You must order either one or two dozen roses"` is assigned to the `txtOutput` text box.

Select Case Statement with String Values

`Select Case` statements can also be used with `Strings`. Observe the following code snippet, which shows the use of `Strings`. The code assumes that a button, `btnSelectCase`, has been created to contain the code. Additionally, the text boxes `txtPlayer` and `txtOutput` (with its `Text` property empty) have been created to hold the input and output, respectively, of the user.

```
Private Sub btnSelectCase_Click(...
    Select Case txtPlayer.Text
        Case "Allen Iverson"
            txtOutput.Text = "Iverson Rules the NBA"
        Case "Theo Ratliff"
            txtOutput.Text = "Ratliff is the ultimate shot blocker"
        Case Else
            txtOutput.Text = "Try again"
    End Select
End Sub
```

What do you think would be contained in txtOutput:

1 If the user enters "Allen Iverson" in the txtPlayer text box?
2 If the user enters "Theo Ratliff" in the txtPlayer text box?
3 If the user enters "Michael Jordan" in the txtPlayer text box?

With "Allen Iverson" Entered in txtPlayer   When the application is executed and the button is clicked, the Case statement is evaluated. Since txtPlayer.Text is equal to "Allen Iverson", the first Case statement evaluates to True. Therefore, the value "Iverson Rules the NBA" is assigned to the txtOutput text box. Once a Case statement is found to evaluate to True, the rest are ignored.

With "Theo Ratliff" Entered in txtPlayer   If you changed the value of txtPlayer.Text to "Theo Ratliff", then the first Case statement would evaluate to False. This would cause the next Case statement to be evaluated. Since txtPlayer.Text equals "Theo Ratliff", this would cause the second Case statement to evaluate to True. Therefore, the value "Ratliff is the ultimate shot blocker" is assigned to the txtOutput text box. Again, since a Case statement evaluated to True, the rest are ignored.

With "Michael Jordan" Entered in txtPlayer   Finally, if you changed the value of txtPlayer.Text to "Michael Jordan", then not only would the first Case statement evaluate to False, but so would the second. This would cause the Case Else statement to be evaluated. Therefore, the value "Try again" is assigned to the txtOutput text box.

Select Case Statement with Multiple String Values

One great feature of a Select Case statement is the ability to indicate a Case as a series of Strings to compare against. If you wish the same code to execute for more than one String, simply list them one after another separated by commas. This can be seen in the following code, which illustrates the syntax of testing the value in VariableToTestAgainst against the strings listed in the Cases that follow.

```
Select Case VariableToTestAgainst
    Case "FirstString", "SecondString", "ThirdString"
        txtOutput.Text = "1st Output"
    Case "FourthString", "FifthString", "SixthString"
        txtOutput.Text = "2nd Output"
        .
        .
        .
    Case Else
        txtOutput.Text = "String Not Found"
End Select
```

Following is a simple example demonstrating how you can check for which sport an athlete plays. It takes advantage of the use of multiple `Strings` in a `Select Case` statement to simplify the code and assumes a text box `txtAthlete` has been created.

```
Select Case txtAthlete.Text
    Case "Serena Williams", "Martina Hingis", "Anna Kournikova"
        txtOutput.Text = "Tennis"
    Case "Sheryl Swoopes", "Katie Smith", "Brandy Reed"
        txtOutput.Text = "Basketball"
    Case "Marion Jones", "Michelle Kwan"
        txtOutput.Text = "Olympics"
    Case Else
        txtOutput.Text = "Some Other Event"
End Select
```

What do you think would be contained in `txtOutput`:

1 If the user enters `"Serena Williams"` in the `txtAthlete` text box?
2 If the user enters `"Katie Smith"` in the `txtAthlete` text box?
3 If the user enters `"Michael Jordan"` in the `txtAthlete` text box?

With "Serena Williams" Entered in txtAthlete When the program is executed and the button is clicked, the `Case` statement is evaluated. Since `txtAthlete.Text` contains `"Serena Williams"`, the first `Case` statement evaluates to `True`, since `"Serena Williams"` is one of the `Strings` listed. Therefore, the word `"Tennis"` is copied to `txtOutput.Text`. Since a `Case` statement evaluated to `True`, the rest are ignored.

With "Katie Smith" Entered in txtAthlete If you changed the value of `txtAthlete.Text` to `"Katie Smith"`, then the first `Case` statement would evaluate to `False` and the second `Case` statement would evaluate to `True`. Therefore, `"Basketball"` is copied to `txtOutput.Text`.

With "Michael Jordan" Entered in txtAthlete If you changed the value of `txtAthlete` to `"Michael Jordan"`, then the first three `Case` statements would evaluate to `False`. Therefore, the `Case Else` is executed and `"Some Other Event"` is copied to `txtOutput.Text`.

Select Case Statements with a Range of Values

`Select Case` statements can also be used with multiple values in each `Case` statement. Observe the following code snippet to evaluate a basketball score, which shows the use of a compound conditional expression and assumes a `txtPoints` text box has been created.

```
Private Sub btnSelectCase_Click()
    Dim intTotalPoints As Integer

    intTotalPoints = Val(txtPoints.Text)
    Select Case intTotalPoints
        Case 0 To 10
            txtOutput.Text = "Quite a bad night for Iverson"
        Case 11 To 20
            txtOutput.Text = "Allen should be able to do better"
        Case 21 To 30
            txtOutput.Text = "Not too shabby"
        Case Is > 30
```

(continues)

```
(continued)
                  txtOutput.Text = "He shoots, he scores!"
            Case Else
                  txtOutput.Text = "Error in Input"
      End Select
End Sub
```

What do you think would be contained in txtOutput:

1 If the user enters 0 in the txtPoints text box?
2 If the user enters 15 in the txtPoints text box?
3 If the user enters 30 in the txtPoints text box?
4 If the user enters 50 in the txtPoints text box?
5 If the user enters –5 in the txtPoints text box?

With 0 Entered in txtPoints   When the application is executed and the button is clicked, the Case statement is evaluated. Since intTotalPoints is equal to 0, the first Case statement evaluates to True. Therefore, the value "Quite a bad night for Iverson" is assigned to the txtOutput text box. Since a Case statement evaluated to True, the rest are ignored.

With 15 Entered in txtPoints   When the application is executed and the button is clicked, the Case statement is evaluated. Since intTotalPoints equals 15 and 15 is not in the range of 0 To 10, the first Case statement evaluates to False. Therefore, the second Case statement is evaluated. Since 15 is within the range of 11 To 20, the Case statement evaluates to True. Therefore, the value "Allen should be able to do better" is assigned to the txtOutput text box. Since a Case statement evaluated to True, the rest are ignored.

With 30 Entered in txtPoints   When the application is executed and the button is clicked, the Case statement is evaluated. Since intTotalPoints equals 30 and 30 is not in the range of 0 To 10 or 11 To 20, the first two Case statements evaluate to False. However, when the third Case statement is evaluated, it evaluates to True since 30 is greater than 20 and less than or equal to 30. Therefore, the value "Not too shabby" is assigned to the txtOutput text box. Since a Case statement evaluated to True, the rest are ignored.

With 50 Entered in txtPoints   When the application is executed and the button is clicked, the Case statement is evaluated. Since intTotalPoints equals 50 and 50 is not in the range of 0 To 10, or 11 To 20, or 21 To 30, the first three Case statements evaluate to False. Therefore, the fourth Case statement is evaluated. Since 50 is greater than 30, the fourth Case statement evaluates to True. Therefore, "He shoots, he scores!" is assigned to the txtOutput text box. Since a Case statement evaluated to True, the rest are ignored.

With –5 Entered in txtPoints   When the application is executed and the button is clicked, the Case statement is evaluated. Since intTotalPoints equals –5 and –5 is not in the range of 0 To 10, or 11 To 20, or 21 To 30, or > 30, the first four Case statements evaluate to False. Therefore, the fifth Case Else statement is evaluated, and the value "Error in Input" is assigned to the txtOutput text box. Since a Case statement evaluated to True, the rest are ignored.

You could have written this example without using a Case Else statement. Instead, you could have added one more Case statement that would check to see if TotalPoints was less than 0.

DRILL 4.13

The following code assumes that a button, `btnSelectCase`, has been created to contain the code. Additionally, the text boxes `txtInput` and `txtOutput` (with its `Text` property empty) have been created to hold the input and output, respectively, of the user.

```
Private Sub btnSelectCase_Click(...

    Dim intDrillValue As Integer

    intDrillValue = Val(txtInput.Text)

    Select Case intDrillValue
        Case Is < 0
            txtOutput.Text = "Error in Input"
        Case 0 To 20
            txtOutput.Text = "2nd Case Statement"
        Case 21 To 30
            txtOutput.Text = "3rd Case Statement"
        Case 31 To 50
            txtOutput.Text = "4th Case Statement"
        Case Is > 50
            txtOutput.Text = "5th Case Statement"
        Case Else
            txtOutput.Text = "Can I get here?"
    End Select
End Sub
```

What do you think would be contained in `txtOutput`:

1 If the user enters 0 in `txtInput`?
2 If the user enters 100 in `txtInput`?
3 If the user enters –50 in `txtInput`?
4 Is there any value the user can enter that will allow the `Case Else` statement to execute?

Example: Improved Compute Grade Application
Problem Description

The Compute Grade application from Section 4.2 determined a letter grade for a class given a numerical grade as input. Let's rewrite that example but implement it using a `Select Case` statement instead of `If`, `ElseIf`, and `Else` statement. To the user of the application it will appear that nothing has changed.

Problem Discussion

The only code that must change is in `btnCompute_Click()`. You can take advantage of the fact that you can list multiple `String` values to check against for a single case on a single line to greatly simplify the code.

Problem Solution

Examine the code in Figure 4.44.

```
Private Sub btnCompute_Click(...
    Dim intGrade As Integer 'Declare temporary variable

    intGrade = Val(txtNumericGrade.Text) 'Convert user input to an Integer

    'Compute Grade
    Select Case intGrade
        Case Is >= 90
            lblLetterGrade.Text = "A"
        Case Is >= 80
            lblLetterGrade.Text = "B"
        Case Is >= 70
            lblLetterGrade.Text = "C"
        Case Is >= 60
            lblLetterGrade.Text = "D"
        Case Else
            lblLetterGrade.Text = "F"
    End Select
End Sub
```

Figure 4.44 Improved btnCompute's Click event code

COACH'S TIP

You may be wondering why you have an If/ElseIf/Else construct if the Select Case is better. While a Select Case can replace the If/ElseIf/Else structure in many cases, it cannot do so in all cases. Observe that the Select Case structure evaluates an expression once at the top of the structure. If your If/ElseIf/Else structure evaluates the same expression each time, it can be replaced by a Select Case. However, if a different expression is evaluated in each ElseIf statement, it cannot be replaced. Both are useful and have their own place.

◆ 4.6 Case Study

Problem Description

This chapter's case study will be a continuation of last chapter's case study to compute the payroll of four workers for a company. In this application, you want to add the functionality to compute the pay of each worker at two different pay rates. In this case, you will have a rate of $25/hour for workers who are in the sales department and a rate of $15/hour for workers who are in the processing department.

You will need a set of text box controls that allow the user to indicate a department for each employee. Figure 4.45 demonstrates what the input to your application may look like.

Figure 4.46 shows the sample output for the input from Figure 4.45 after the btnCalculate button is clicked.

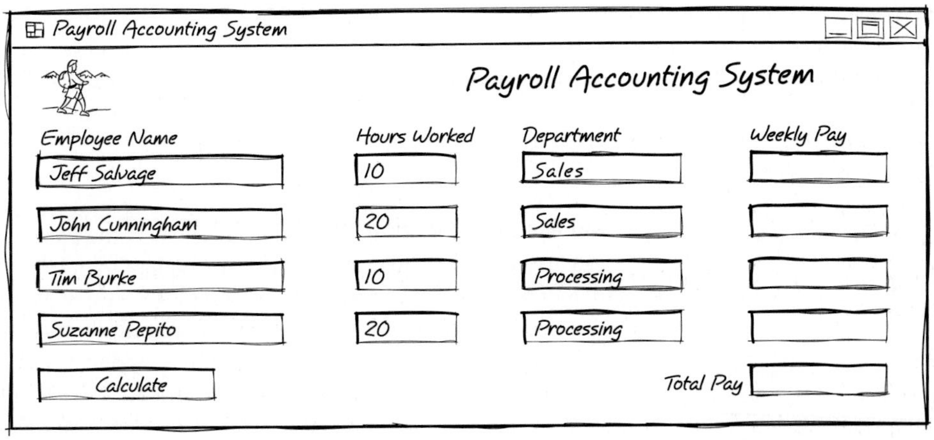

Figure 4.45
Sketch of Payroll
application

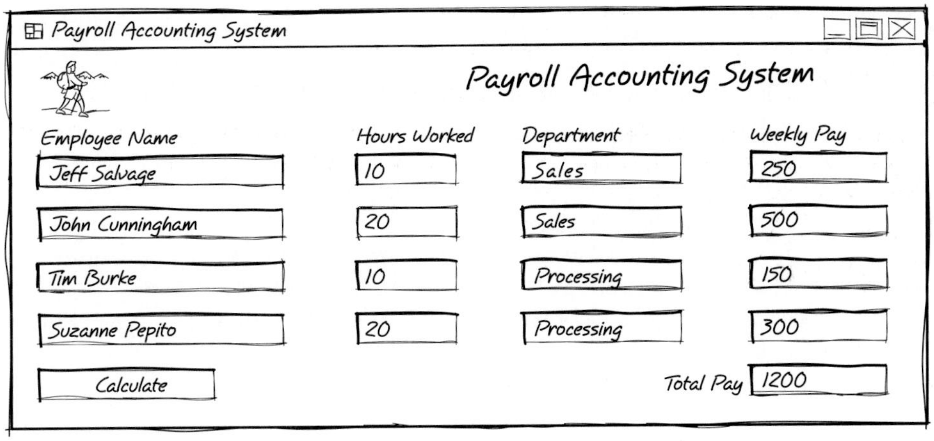

Figure 4.46
Sketch of execution
of Payroll application

Problem Discussion

The solution to the problem does not change much from the previous chapter's case study. The main difference is that you need to check which pay rate to use in the calculation of the weekly pay.

Again, most of the controls for your application were placed on the form in the previous chapter. You need only add the controls for the department label and text boxes. What you call the label control is unimportant. However, you should call the department text boxes `txtDept1`, `txtDept2`, `txtDept3`, and `txtDept4`.

Problem Solution

Although it is not required, the use of constants in this solution is desirable. You should code a constant to indicate the pay rates for the sales and processing departments. The constant for the sales department and processing department pay rates will be called `decSalesPayRate` and `decProcessingPayRate`, respectively. This way you can change either pay rate once and have it affect the entire application.

To set the constant, perform the following steps:

Step 1: Right-click the mouse button and click on `View Code`.
Step 2: Select the `Declarations` area of code.
Step 3: Type "`Const decSalesPayRate As Decimal = 25`".
Step 4: Type "`Const decProcessingPayRate As Decimal = 15`".

Your code should look like that shown in Figure 4.47.

Figure 4.47
General declarations section

```
Const decSalesPayRate As Decimal = 25
Const decProcessingPayRate As Decimal = 15
```

The btnCalculate button's Click event code must set each weekly pay's value to the number of hours worked multiplied by the pay rate associated with each employee's department. This value is first stored in a temporary variable and then in the weekly pay text box associated with the employee. Each weekly pay value is also added to a total weekly pay variable so that it can be output at the end of all the calculations. The code is shown in Figure 4.48, and the final application appears in Figure 4.49.

```
Private Sub btnCalculate_Click(...
        'Temporary Variables to Store Calculations
        Dim decTotalPay As Decimal
        Dim decWeeklyPay As Decimal

        'First Person's Calculations
        If (txtDept1.Text = "Sales") Then
            decWeeklyPay = decSalesPayRate * Val(txtHours1.Text)
        ElseIf (txtDept1.Text = "Processing") Then
            decWeeklyPay = decProcessingPayRate * Val(txtHours1.Text)
        Else
            decWeeklyPay = 0
        End If
        txtWeeklyPay1.Text = decWeeklyPay.ToString
        decTotalPay = decWeeklyPay

        'Second Person's Calculations
        If (txtDept2.Text = "Sales") Then
            decWeeklyPay = decSalesPayRate * Val(txtHours2.Text)
        ElseIf (txtDept2.Text = "Processing") Then
            decWeeklyPay = decProcessingPayRate * Val(txtHours2.Text)
        Else
            decWeeklyPay = 0
        End If
        txtWeeklyPay2.Text = decWeeklyPay.ToString()
        decTotalPay += decWeeklyPay

        'Third Person's Calculations
        If (txtDept3.Text = "Sales") Then
            decWeeklyPay = decSalesPayRate * Val(txtHours3.Text)
        ElseIf (txtDept3.Text = "Processing") Then
            decWeeklyPay = decProcessingPayRate * Val(txtHours3.Text)
        Else
            decWeeklyPay = 0
        End If
        txtWeeklyPay3.Text = decWeeklyPay.ToString()
```

(continues)

Figure 4.48 btnCalculate's Click event

(continued)

```
        decTotalPay += decWeeklyPay

        'Fourth Person's Calculations
        If (txtDept4.Text = "Sales") Then
            decWeeklyPay = decSalesPayRate * Val(txtHours4.Text)
        ElseIf (txtDept4.Text = "Processing") Then
            decWeeklyPay = decProcessingPayRate * Val(txtHours4.Text)
        Else
            decWeeklyPay = 0
        End If
        txtWeeklyPay4.Text = decWeeklyPay.ToString()
        decTotalPay += decWeeklyPay

        'Convert Total Pay to a string and copy to TextBox
        txtTotalPay.Text = decTotalPay.ToString()

    End Sub
```

Figure 4.48 (continued)

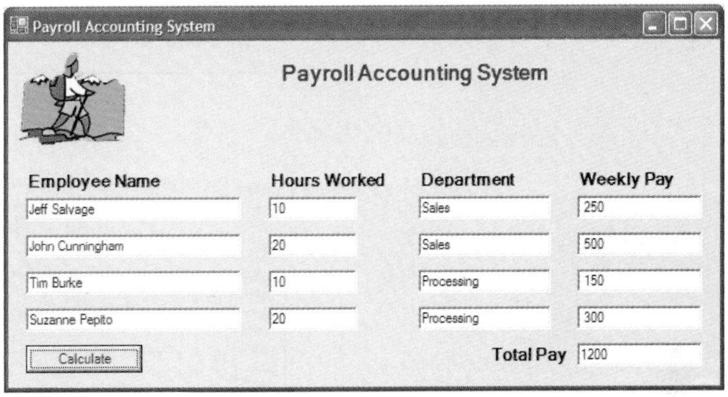

Figure 4.49
Final application

CORNER

Adding Functionality to the Message Box

In this chapter, you have learned how to code decisions into the applications you create. With a slight modification to the `MsgBox` command, you can ask the user a question and get an answer without having to create new forms.

If you want to ask a simple Yes/No question, you can ask it using the `MsgBox` command. The following code will ask the question "Should everyone in the class get an A?" and store the result in the variable `intAnswer`.

```
intAnswer = MsgBox("Should everyone in the class get an A?", _
            MsgBoxStyle.YesNo, "Question")
```

The message box would look like that shown in Figure 4.50.

Figure 4.50
Message box

You added another value to the `MsgBox` line. You added a parameter, `MsgBoxStyle.YesNo`, that tells the `MsgBox` command to display a Yes/No style message box. This is just one of many types of message boxes that can be used. When you change the parameter, other message boxes can be selected.

By using the following constants, you can create dialog boxes with the following buttons:

YesNo	Yes/No
YesNoCancel	Yes/No/Cancel
OKCancel	OK/Cancel
RetryCancel	Retry/Cancel

By using the following constants, you can check to see what the user's response was:

vbYes	Yes
vbNo	No
vbCancel	Cancel
vbOK	OK
vbRetry	Retry

Short Circuit Analysis of Conditional Statements

When an `If` or `ElseIf` statement was evaluated in previous versions of Visual Basic, every condition was evaluated whether or not it was necessary to do so. In Visual Basic .NET, the evaluation of conditional statements is performed using **short circuit analysis**. A very loose definition is that the conditional statement is evaluated as long as the outcome of the conditional statement is unknown. Once the outcome is determined, the evaluation of the conditional statement ceases.

When you use short circuit analysis, the performance of your applications increases. Imagine if you wanted to write a conditional statement that displayed whether the average of a series of homework grades was passing or failing.

You could use code as follows:

```
If (intNumberGrades > 0) And (intGradeTotal / intNumberGrades >= 65) Then
    MsgBox("Pass")
Else
    MsgBox("Fail")
End If
```

Without short circuit evaluation, if `intNumberGrades` equals 0, the execution of the code would cause a run-time error. However, with short circuit evaluation, the second condition never evaluates and the message box displays `"Fail"`.

DRILL 4.14

Determine if the following conditions and values cause all of the conditional expressions to be evaluated.

1

```
Dim intDrillValue As Integer
intDrillValue = 70

If ((intDrillValue >= 65) And (intDrillValue <= 75)) Then
```

2

```
Dim intDrillValue As Integer
intDrillValue = 70

If ((intDrillValue >= 65) Or (intDrillValue <= 75)) Then
```

3

```
Dim intDrillValue As Integer
intDrillValue = 70

If ((intDrillValue <= 65) Or (intDrillValue >= 75)) Then
```

COACH'S TIP

Remember, in order for a compound condition containing `And`s to evaluate to `True`, all of the conditions must evaluate to `True`. Therefore, if one condition evaluates to `False`, then the remaining conditions do not have to be checked.

Key Words and Key Terms

<
    An operator performing the less-than comparison.

>
    An operator performing the greater-than comparison.

<=
    An operator performing the less-than or equal-to comparison.

>=

An operator performing the greater-than or equal-to comparison.

=

An operator performing the equal-to comparison.

<>

An operator performing the not-equal-to comparison.

And

An operator used to perform the logical "anding" of two conditions.

Boolean

A variable data type that allows the storage of a Boolean value.

Case

A keyword that indicates the individual cases of a `Select Case` statement.

Case Else

The default case for a `Select` statement. Executes if all the other `Case` statements fail.

Compound Conditional Expression

An expression that involves more than one subexpression.

Else

A keyword that indicates what statement(s) should be executed when an `If` statement evaluates to `False`.

ElseIf

A keyword that indicates another condition to check and statement(s) that should be executed when the `If` statement evaluates to `False` but the `ElseIf` statement evaluates to `True`.

End If

A keyword that indicates the end of an `If` statement.

End Select

A keyword that indicates the end of a `Select Case` statement.

False

A keyword that indicates that an expression did not evaluate to `True`.

If

A keyword that indicates what statement(s) should be executed when the expression following it evaluates to `True`.

Nested Conditional Statement

A conditional statement that is written inside of another conditional statement.

Not

An operator used to negate a value or expression.

Or

An operator used to perform the logical "oring" of two conditions.

Select Case

A keyword that indicates the beginning of a `Select Case` statement.

Short Circuit Analysis

When a conditional statement is evaluated as long as the outcome of the conditional statement is unknown. Once the outcome is determined, the evaluation of the conditional statement ceases.

True

A keyword that indicates that an expression evaluated to `True`.

Answers to Chapter's Drills

Drill 4.1

1. (5 >= 4) evaluates to True. When the operator >= is used, the expression evaluates to True if the value to the left is greater than the value to the right (in this case, it is) or if the value to the left is equal to the value to the right (in this case, it is not). Since only one of these cases must be true for the expression to be evaluated to True, the expression is evaluated to True.

2. (-3 < -4) evaluates to False. When the operator < is used, the expression evaluates to True if the value to the left is less than the value to the right. Although the number 3 is less than the number 4, the value –3 is not less than the number –4.

3. (5 = 4) evaluates to False. When the operator = is used, the expression evaluates to True if the value to the left is exactly the same as the value to the right. Since 5 is the value on the left and 4 is the value on the right, the values are not the same.

4. (5 <> 4) evaluates to True. When the operator <> is used, the expression evaluates to True if the value to the left of the operator is not the same as the value to the right of the operator. Since 5 is not the same as 4, the expression evaluates to True.

5. (4 >= 4) evaluates to True. When the operator >= is used, the expression evaluates to True if the value to the left is greater than the value to the right (in this case, it is not) or the value to the left is the same as the value to the right (in this case, it is). Since only one of these cases must be true for the expression to be evaluated to True, the expression is evaluated to True.

6. (4 <= 4) evaluates to True. When the operator <= is used, the expression evaluates to True if the value to the left is less than the value to the right (in this case, it is not) or the value to the left is the same as the value to the right (in this case, it is). Since only one of these cases must be true for the expression to be evaluated to True, the expression is evaluated to True.

Drill 4.2

With 1 or 2 Entered in txtInput

If the user enters either 1 or 2 in the txtInput text box, then the value in the label lblOutput would be as follows:

```
 and the second statement prints
```

When the value stored in txtInput is equal to 1 or 2, then the If statement evaluates to False since neither value is greater than 2. Therefore, the first assignment to the lblOutput label is not performed. However, since the second statement has nothing to do with the If statement, it is executed.

With 3 Entered in txtInput

If the user enters 3 in the txtInput text box, the value in the label lblOutput would be as follows:

```
The first statement prints and the second statement prints
```

When the value stored in txtInput equals 3, then the If statement evaluates to True since 3 is greater than 2. Therefore, the first assignment to the lblOutput label is performed. Since the second statement has nothing to do with the If statement, it is executed as well.

Drill 4.3

With 1 Entered in txtInput

If the user enters 1 in the `txtInput` text box, then the value in the label `lblOutput` would be as follows:

```
The first statement prints and the second statement prints
```

When the value stored in `txtInput` equals 1, then the `If` statement evaluates to `True` since 1 is less than 2. Therefore, the first assignment to the `lblOutput` label is performed. Since the second statement has nothing to do with the `If` statement, it is executed as well.

With 2 or 3 Entered in txtInput

If the user enters either 2 or 3 in the `txtInput` text box, then the value in the label `lblOutput` would be as follows:

```
and the second statement prints
```

When the value stored in `txtInput` is equal to 2 or 3, then the `If` statement evaluates to `False` since neither value is less than 2. Therefore, the first assignment to the `lblOutput` label is not performed. However, since the second statement has nothing to do with the `If` statement, it is executed.

Drill 4.4

With 1 Entered in txtInput

If the user enters 1 in the `txtInput` text box, then the value in the label `lblOutput` would be as follows:

```
and the second statement prints
```

When the value stored in `txtInput` is equal to 1, then the `If` statement evaluates to `False` since 1 is not greater than or equal to 2. Therefore, the first assignment to the `lblOutput` label is not performed. However, since the second statement has nothing to do with the `If` statement, it is executed.

With 2 or 3 Entered in txtInput

If the user enters either 2 or 3 in the `txtInput` text box, then the value in the label `lblOutput` would be as follows:

```
The first statement prints and the second statement prints
```

When the value stored in `txtInput` equals 2 or 3, then the `If` statement evaluates to `True` since 2 and 3 are both greater than or equal to 2. Therefore, the first assignment to the `lblOutput` label is performed. Since the second statement has nothing to do with the `If` statement, it is executed as well.

Drill 4.5

With 1 or 2 Entered in txtInput

If the user enters either 1 or 2 in the `txtInput` text box, then the value in the label `lblOutput` would be as follows:

```
The first statement prints and the second statement prints
```

When the value stored in `txtInput` equals 1 or 2, then the `If` statement evaluates to `True` since 1 and 2 are both less than or equal to 2. Therefore, the first assignment to the `lblOutput` label is performed. Since the second statement has nothing to do with the `If` statement, it is executed as well.

With 3 Entered in txtInput

If the user enters 3 in the `txtInput` text box, then the value in the label `lblOutput` would be as follows:

```
and the second statement prints
```

When the value stored in `txtInput` is equal to 3, then the `If` statement evaluates to `False` since 3 is not less than or equal to 2. Therefore, the first assignment to the `lblOutput` label is not performed. However, since the second statement has nothing to do with the `If` statement, it is executed.

Drill 4.6

The value contained in `lblOutput` when the value entered by the user is 0 is:

```
This will output, because intDrillValue <= 1 and this is here as well
```

If the user enters 0, then `intDrillValue` is set to 0, and the expression (`intDrillValue <= 1`) evaluates to `True`. The code associated with the `If` statement is executed, and `"This will output, because intDrillValue <= 1"` is assigned to `lblOutput`. The code associated with the `Else` statement is therefore not executed. However, the last statement is executed because it is not in the `If` statement and therefore executes every time. So `" and this is here as well"` is concatenated to `lblOutput`.

The value contained in `lblOutput` when the value entered by the user is 1 is:

```
This will output, because intDrillValue <= 1 and this is here as well
```

If the user enters 1, then `intDrillValue` is set to 1, and the expression (`intDrillValue <= 1`) evaluates to `True`. The code associated with the `If` statement is executed, and `"This will output, because intDrillValue <= 1"` is assigned to `lblOutput`. The code associated with the `Else` statement is therefore not executed. However, the last statement is executed because it is not in the `If` statement and therefore executes every time. So `" and this is here as well"` is concatenated to `lblOutput`.

The value contained in `lblOutput` when the value entered by the user is 2 is:

```
Instead this outputs, because intDrillValue > 1 and this is here as well
```

If the user enters 2, then `intDrillValue` is set to 2, and the expression (`intDrillValue <= 1`) evaluates to `False`. Therefore, the code associated with the `If` statement is not executed. Instead, the code associated with the `Else` statement is. So `"Instead this outputs, because intDrillValue > 1"` is assigned to `lblOutput`. Finally, the last statement is executed because it is not in the `If` statement and therefore executes every time. So `" and this is here as well"` is concatenated to `lblOutput`.

Drill 4.7

The value contained in `lblOutput` when the value entered by the user is 0 is:

```
This will output, because intDrillValue < 1 and this is here as well
```

If the user enters 0, then `intDrillValue` is set to 0, and the expression (`intDrillValue < 1`) evaluates to `True`. The code associated with the `If` statement is executed, and "`This will output, because intDrillValue < 1`" is assigned to `lblOutput`. The code associated with the `Else` statement is therefore not executed. However, the last statement is executed because it is not in the `If` statement and therefore executes every time. So "` and this is here as well`" is concatenated to `lblOutput`.

The value contained in `lblOutput` when the value entered by the user is 1 is:

```
Instead this outputs, because intDrillValue >= 1 and this is here as well
```

If the user enters 1, then `intDrillValue` is set to 1, and the expression (`intDrillValue < 1`) evaluates to `False`. Therefore, the code associated with the `If` statement is not executed. Instead, the code associated with the `Else` statement is. So "`Instead this outputs, because intDrillValue >= 1`" is assigned to `lblOutput`. Finally, the last statement is executed because it is not in the `If` statement and therefore executes every time. So "` and this is here as well`" is concatenated to `lblOutput`.

The value contained in `lblOutput` when the value entered by the user is 2 is:

```
Instead this outputs, because intDrillValue >= 1 and this is here as well
```

If the user enters 2, then `intDrillValue` is set to 2, and the expression (`intDrillValue < 1`) evaluates to `False`. Therefore, the code associated with the `If` statement is not executed. Instead, the code associated with the `Else` statement is. So "`Instead this outputs, because intDrillValue >= 1`" is assigned to `lblOutput`. Finally, the last statement is executed because it is not in the `If` statement and therefore executes every time. So "` and this is here as well`" is concatenated to `lblOutput`.

Drill 4.8
With 600.00 Entered by the User

When the program is executed and the button is clicked, the `If` statement is evaluated. If the user enters `600.00`, then the `If` statement evaluates the expression by comparing the value entered to 100. Therefore, the conditional expression will evaluate to `True`. This causes all the statements until the `ElseIf` to be executed. Therefore, the purchase price is multiplied by `.05` and the result is converted to a `String`. So the value "`30`" is placed in the label `lblOutput`. Since the conditional expression in the `If` statement evaluated to `True`, none of the statements after the `ElseIf` or `Else` statements and before the `End If` statement are executed. Note this is not what you wanted to have happen! Because you evaluated the condition comparing the value to 100 first, it will evaluate to `True` when you really want the expression `> 500` to evaluate to `True`. The order you evaluate your conditions can make a difference.

With 250.00 Entered by the User

When the program is executed and the button is clicked, the `If` statement is evaluated. If the user enters `250.00`, then the `If` statement evaluates the expression by comparing the value entered to 100. Therefore, the conditional expression will evaluate to `True`. This causes all the statements until the `ElseIf` to be executed. Therefore, the purchase price is multiplied by `.05` and the result is converted to a `String`. So the value "`12.5`" is placed in the label `lblOutput`. Since the conditional expression in the `If` statement evaluated to `True`, none of the statements after the `ElseIf` or `Else` statements and before the `End If` statement are executed.

With 50.00 Entered by the User

Finally, if the user enters a value less than or equal to `100`, neither the `If` or `ElseIf` conditional expressions evaluate to `True`. Therefore, the statements after the `Else` statement and before the `End If` statement are executed.

So the text `"NO DISCOUNT"` is placed in the label `lblOutput`.

Drill 4.9

With –1 Entered by the User

When the application is executed and the button is clicked, the `If` statement is evaluated. If the user enters `–1`, then the `If` statement evaluates the expression by comparing the value entered to see if it is greater than `0`. Since `–1` is not greater than `0`, the conditional expression will evaluate to `False`. Therefore, the second condition will be evaluated in the `ElseIf` statement. The `ElseIf` condition compares `–1` to see if it is less than `0`. This time the conditional expression evaluates to `True`. This causes all the statements until the `Else` to be executed. So `"The number is negative"` is copied to the label `lblOutput`.

With 0 Entered by the User

When the application is executed and the button is clicked, the `If` statement is evaluated. If the user enters `0`, then the `If` statement evaluates the expression by comparing the value entered to see if it is greater than `0`. Since `0` is not greater than `0`, the conditional expression will evaluate to `False`. Therefore, the second condition will be evaluated in the `ElseIf` statement. The `ElseIf` condition compares `0` to see if it is less than `0`. Again, the conditional expression evaluates to `False`. Therefore, the `Else` statement is executed, copying `"I got a big zero"` to the label `lblOutput`.

With 1 Entered by the User

When the application is executed and the button is clicked, the `If` statement is evaluated. If the user enters `1`, then the `If` statement evaluates the expression by comparing the value entered to see if it is greater than `0`. Since `1` is greater than `0`, the conditional expression will evaluate to `True`, copying `"The number is positive"` to the label `lblOutput`.

Drill 4.10

Indicate whether each expression evaluates to `True` or `False`.

1. `Not (5 >= 4)` evaluates to `False`. The subexpression `(5 >= 4)` evaluates to `True`; however, the `Not` operator inverts the `True` to `False`. Therefore, the entire expression evaluates to `False`.

2. `(-3 < -4) Or (1 = 1)` evaluates to `True`. The subexpression `(-3 < -4)` evaluates to `False`; however, the other subexpression, `(1 = 1)`, evaluates to `True`. Since the two subexpressions are joined with an `Or` operator, only one of the subexpressions must evaluate to `True` for the entire expression to evaluate to `True`. Therefore, the expression evaluates to `True`.

3. `("BOB" = "bob") And (2 >= 2)` evaluates to `False`. The subexpression `("BOB" = "bob")` evaluates to `False` because even though the two strings have the same letters, they are not the same capitalization. Even though the second subexpression evaluates to `True`, it doesn't matter. When two subexpressions are joined with an `And` operator, both subexpressions must be `True` for the entire expression to evaluate to `True`.

4. `(2 < 1) Or (5 <> 4)` evaluates to `True`. The subexpression `(2 < 1)` evaluates to `False`. However, since an `Or` operator only requires one of the subexpressions to evaluate to `True`, then if the second subexpression evaluates to `True`, the entire expression would evaluate to `True`. Since `(5 <> 4)` evaluates to `True`, the entire expression evaluates to `True`.

5. (1 < 2) Or (4 >= 4) evaluates to True. The subexpression (1 < 2) evaluates to True. Since the two subexpressions are joined with an Or operator, the entire expression evaluates to True regardless of the evaluation of the second expression.

6. Not (4 <= 4) And (1 <= 1) evaluates to False. Since the two subexpressions are joined with an And operator, then they must both evaluate to True. The first subexpression, Not (4 <= 4), actually can be thought of as an expression with two subexpressions in itself. First, you have the subexpression (4 <= 4), which evaluates to True. However, when you apply the Not operator, that entire first subexpression evaluates to False. Therefore, the entire expression evaluates to False.

Drill 4.11
With a Retail Price of 99.95 and a Sales Price of 50.25

When the application is executed and the button is clicked, the If statement is evaluated. When the user enters 99.95 and 50.25 for the retail price and the sales price, respectively, then the If statement evaluates the expression by comparing the retail price to the sales price. Since 99.95 is greater than 50.25, then that part of the expression evaluates to True. The second condition is then checked. The sales price is compared to 75. Since the sales price is not greater than 75, the comparison evaluates to False. However, the Not operator has to be applied. This negates the False and the second subcondition evaluates to True. Because the two subconditions are combined with an And operator, both of the subconditions must evaluate to True for the entire conditional expression to evaluate to True. Therefore, the code associated with the If statement is executed, and the text "This crazy drill outputs True" is assigned to the output text box.

With a Retail Price of 199.95 and a Sales Price of 99.95

When the application is executed and the button is clicked, the If statement is evaluated. When the user enters 199.95 and 99.95 for the retail price and the sales price, respectively, then the If statement evaluates the expression by comparing the retail price to the sales price. Since 199.95 is greater than 99.95, then that part of the expression evaluates to True. The second condition is then checked. The sales price is compared to 75. Since the sales price is greater than 75, the comparison evaluates to True. However, the Not operator has to be applied. This negates the True and the second subcondition evaluates to False. Because the two subconditions are combined with an And operator, both of the subconditions must evaluate to True for the entire conditional expression to evaluate to True. Therefore, the code associated with the Else statement is executed. Therefore, the text "This crazy drill outputs False" is assigned to the output text box.

Drill 4.12
With 0 Entered

When the user enters 0, the expression (intDrillValue = 1) evaluates to False, since intDrillValue will contain 0. Therefore, you will process the code contained in the outer Else statement.

   The expression (intDrillValue < 1) evaluates to True, so "This will output, from the 2nd Inner If" is assigned to txtOutput.

With 1 Entered

When the user enters 1, the expression (intDrillValue = 1) evaluates to True, since intDrillValue will contain 1. Therefore, you will process the code contained in the inner If statement.

   The expression (intDrillValue <= 1) evaluates to True, so "This will output, from the 1st Inner If" is assigned to txtOutput.

With 2 Entered

When `intDrillValue` is set to 2, the expression (`intDrillValue = 1`) evaluates to `False`, since `intDrillValue` will contain 2. Therefore, you will process the code contained in the outer `Else` statement.

In executing the code contained within the outer `Else` statement, you must evaluate the second inner `If` statement. The expression (`intDrillValue < 1`) evaluates to `False`, so `"This will output, from the 2nd Inner Else"` is assigned to `txtOutput`.

Drill 4.13
With 0 Entered

When the user enters 0, the first `Case` statement evaluates to `False` and the next one is tried. Since `intDrillValue` equals 0 and 0 is in the range `0  To  20`, the second `Case` statement evaluates to `True`. Therefore, the value `"2nd Case Statement"` is assigned to the `txtOutput` text box. Since a `Case` statement evaluated to `True`, the rest are ignored.

With 100 Entered

When the user enters `100`, the first, second, third, and fourth `Case` statements all evaluate to `False` since 100 is not in the range of any of the values listed. However, when the fifth `Case` statement is tried, it evaluates to `True` since `intDrillValue` equals `100` and `100` is greater than 50. Therefore, the value `"5th Case  Statement"` is assigned to the `txtOutput` text box. Since a `Case` statement evaluated to `True`, the rest are ignored.

With –50 Entered

When the user enters `–50`, the first `Case` statement evaluates to the value `"Error in Input"` is assigned to the `txtOutput` text box. Since a `Case` statement evaluated to `True`, the rest are ignored.

Any Value Entered?

As to whether or not the `Case  Else` statement could ever execute, the answer is no. If you look at the ranges of all the other `Case` statements, you will find that every possible value for an `Integer` is covered in one of the cases. Therefore, no value could be entered by the user that would cause the `Case  Else` statement to execute.

Drill 4.14
1. When the variable `intDrillValue` equals 70, the first condition in the `If` statement evaluates to `True`. Since the compound condition uses an `And` operator, the second condition must be evaluated. In this case, the second condition also evaluates to `True`, so the entire expression evaluates to `True`.

2. When the variable `intDrillValue` equals 70, the first condition in the `If` statement evaluates to `True`. Since the compound condition uses an `Or` operator, the second condition does not have to be evaluated. Regardless of the evaluation of the second condition, the entire condition will evaluate to `True`.

3. When the variable `intDrillValue` equals 70, the first condition in the `If` statement evaluates to `False`. Since the compound condition uses an `Or` operator, the second condition must be evaluated. In this case, the second condition also evaluates to `False`, so the entire expression evaluates to `False`.

Additional Exercises
1. Indicate whether each of the following is true or false.

   a. An `If` statement can only have one `ElseIf` and `Else` statement associated with it.

b. It is possible to have an `ElseIf` statement without associating it with an `If` statement.

c. It is possible to have an `If` and `ElseIf` statement without an `Else` statement being associated with it.

2. Which of the following is not an operator to link conditions in a compound conditional expression?

   a. And   b. Maybe   c. Not   d. Or

3. Describe in your own words what would happen to an expression that had the `Not` operator applied to it twice, as in `Not ( Not ( ` *Expression* ` ) )`.

4. What is the advantage of using a nested conditional statement instead of a compound conditional statement?

5. When using a `Select Case` statement, which of the following statements would be used to signify the case to execute when none of the other cases are chosen?

   a. `Case Else`   b. `Else`

   c. `Else Case`   d. `Just In Case`

6. Which of the following expressions evaluate to `True`?

   a. `(2 >= 3)`
   b. `(-5 > -4) Or (1 <= 3)`
   c. `("BOB" <> "bob") And (3 >= 2)`
   d. `(1 < 1) Or (1 <> 1)`
   e. `(1 < 1) Or (2 <> 2)`
   f. `(4.3 <= 4.33) And (0 <= -1)`

7. What is the value in `txtOutput` after the following code is executed if `strExampleValue` is set to:

   a. `"XOX"`
   b. `"XXX"`
   c. `"OOX"`

```
Private Sub btnOutput_Click(...
    Dim strExampleValue As String
    strExampleValue = "XOX" 'or the other values


    If (strExampleValue = "XXX") Then
        txtOutput.Text = "Choice 1"
    ElseIf (strExampleValue = "OOO") Then
        txtOutput.Text = "Choice 2"
    ElseIf (strExampleValue = "OXO") Then
        txtOutput.Text = "Choice 3"
    Else
        txtOutput.Text = "Choice 4"
    End If
End Sub
```

8. What is the value in `txtOutput` after the following code is executed if `strExampleValue` is set to:

   a. `"XxX"`
   b. `"OOO"`
   c. `"OXO"`
   d. `"xox"`

```
Private Sub btnOutput_Click(...
    Dim strExampleValue As String
    strExampleValue = "XOX" 'or the other values

    If (strExampleValue = "XXX") And (strExampleValue = "xxx") Then
        txtOutput.Text = "Choice 1"
    ElseIf (strExampleValue = "OOO") And (strExampleValue = "ooo") Then
        txtOutput.Text = "Choice 2"
    ElseIf (strExampleValue = "XOX") And (strExampleValue = "xox") Then
        txtOutput.Text = "Choice 3"
    Else
        txtOutput.Text = "Choice 4"
    End If
End Sub
```

9. What is the value in txtOutput after the following code is executed if strExampleValue is set to:
    a. "XxX"
    b. "OOO"
    c. "OXO"
    d. "xox"

```
Private Sub btnOutput_Click(...
    Dim strExampleValue As String
    strExampleValue = "XOX" 'or the other values

    If (strExampleValue = "XXX") Or (strExampleValue = "xxx") Then
        txtOutput.Text = "Choice 1"
    ElseIf (strExampleValue = "OOO") Or (strExampleValue = "ooo") Then
        txtOutput.Text = "Choice 2"
    ElseIf (strExampleValue = "XOX") Or (strExampleValue = "xox") Then
        txtOutput.Text = "Choice 3"
    Else
        txtOutput.Text = "Choice 4"
    End If
End Sub
```

10. What is the value in txtOutput after the following code is executed if strExampleValue is set to:
    a. "XxX"
    b. "OOO"
    c. "OXO"
    d. "xox"

```
Private Sub btnOutput_Click(...
    Dim strExampleValue As String
    strExampleValue = "XOX" 'or the other values

    If Not (strExampleValue = "XXX") And (strExampleValue = "xxx") Then
        txtOutput.Text = "Choice 1"
    ElseIf (strExampleValue = "OOO") And Not (strExampleValue = "ooo") Then
        txtOutput.Text = "Choice 2"
    ElseIf (strExampleValue = "XOX") And Not (strExampleValue = "xox") Then
```

(continues)

(continued)

```
        txtOutput.Text = "Choice 3"
    Else
        txtOutput.Text = "Choice 4"
    End If

End Sub
```

11. What is the value in `txtOutput` after the following code is executed if `intExampleValue =`?

    a. 10
    b. 5
    c. 20
    d. 100
    e. 200

```
Private Sub btnOutput_Click(...
    Dim intExampleValue As Integer
    intExampleValue = 10 'or the other values

    Select Case intExampleValue
        Case Is < 100
            txtOutput.Text = "Less Than 100"
        Case 10
            txtOutput.Text = "Equals 10"
        Case Else
            txtOutput.Text = "Other"
    End Select
End Sub
```

12. What is the value in `txtOutput` after the following code is executed if `strExample = `?

    a. President
    b. PRESIDENT
    c. Vice Pres
    d. Vice President

```
Private Sub btnOutput_Click(...
    Dim strExampleValue As String
    strExampleValue = "President" 'or the other values

    Select Case strExampleValue
        Case "PRESIDENT"
            txtOutput.Text = "George Bush"
        Case "VICE PRESIDENT"
            txtOutput.Text = "Dick Cheney"
        Case Else
            txtOutput.Text = "Other"
    End Select
End Sub
```

13. Write an application that accepts two grades and outputs the larger of the two grades. If both grades are the same, output the word "EQUAL". The grades should be entered in two text boxes and output in a label.

14. Write an application that converts English units to metric units. The application should accept a value from the user to convert and units to convert from. Each value should be stored in its own text box. When the user clicks on a button, it should output the converted value in a label.

    1 inch = 2.54 centimeters

    1 gallon = 3.785 liters

    1 mile = 1.609 kilometers

    1 pound = .4536 kilograms

    Make sure that your application only accepts valid choices to convert.

    For example, when the user enters 20 in the first text box and miles in the second text box, the output in the label should be 32.18.

15. Write an application that accepts a single-digit integer and outputs the word that represents that number. The input should be in a text box and the output should be in a label. If a number other than a single digit is entered, the program should output "Error in Input".

    For example, if the digit 5 is entered, the word "Five" should be placed in the label.

16. Write an application that simulates a bank account for a single person. The application should initialize the bank account to a 0 balance. The balance of the bank account should be displayed in a label control. Develop the application so that it can accept deposits and withdrawals. Deposits and withdrawals should use two text boxes, one for the amount and the other to indicate whether or not it's a deposit or a withdrawal. It should not allow withdrawals that will lower the balance below 0. If such a withdrawal is attempted, a warning message should be displayed.

17. Add data validation to the case study in this chapter so that the application does not process a person's pay who has a negative value entered for hours worked.

18. Write a Hangman application. It should play Hangman, a game where one player picks a word and another player guesses the word by picking a letter at a time. If the letter exists in the word, then the letter is displayed in its proper place. If the letter is not found in the word, then the player is one step closer to losing. Each time a letter is not found, the next image in the sequence shown in Figure 4.51 is displayed. If the last figure is displayed, then the player has lost the game.

    In order to implement this with what you know so far, you need to set some limitations. The word to guess will need to be coded directly into the application for simplicity's sake. It should be set using constants. You also will need to limit the size of the word, let's say 10 characters. To draw the Hangman, you will need to create a series of graphic files. As each incorrect guess is made, the next graphic file is displayed. As each correct guess is made, display it in the proper place.

    The graphics should look like those shown in Figure 4.51.

Figure 4.51
Hangman images

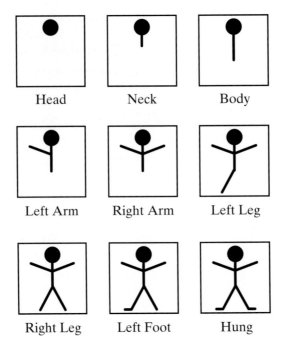

19. Write an application to simulate a vending machine. The vending machine should be preloaded with different types of candy and a quantity for each. Each candy needs a price and a code. The code would be a combination of a letter and number. For simplicity, just allow the letters to be an A, B, C, D, or E.

    The vending machine must have a mechanism to accept money. You can use a text box and a button to accept it, but you then would need to validate that each value is a valid denomination of currency. A better way is to create a button each for a nickel, dime, quarter, and dollar. As each button is clicked, add the appropriate amount to the total. Also, create a Change Return button to return the money entered to the user.

    Create a series of buttons to allow the entry of a digit from 1 to 3 and a letter from A to E so that the user can select a candy to purchase. Since each purchase is signified by a combination of a letter and a number, as the buttons are clicked, display the choice being made.

    Finally, add a button to make the purchase. It should validate that you have entered enough money to make the purchase, that you have selected a valid choice for a candy, and that candy still has a quantity greater than 0. The last step is to indicate how much money is returned as change.

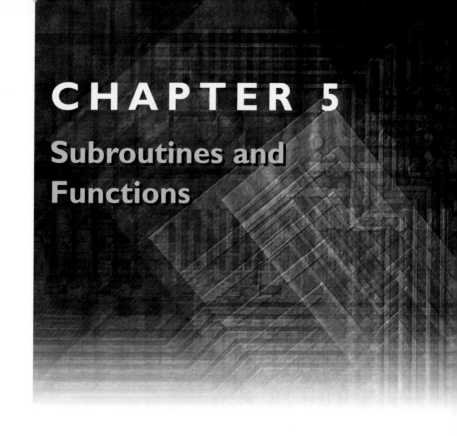

CHAPTER 5
Subroutines and Functions

CHAPTER
OBJECTIVES

- Explain various built-in functions
- Explain how to create your own subroutines and functions
- Introduce local variables
- Introduce return values
- Discuss pass by reference versus pass by value

5.1 What Are Subroutines and Functions?

As your applications grow, you need to break them into separate logical units. Indeed, you have already seen one way of accomplishing this.

Your applications are broken up into different controls that accomplish different tasks. Likewise, the code associated with accomplishing each task is separated from the code that accomplishes other tasks. These actions are referred to as events and are one way of breaking up code into smaller, more logical units. The event you are most familiar with so far is the `Click` event.

Another way to break up an application is by using either **functions** or **subroutines**. Functions and subroutines are used to make our programs more readable by breaking large amounts of code into smaller, more concise parts. By breaking code into functions and subroutines, code can be written once and reused often. This not only reduces the size of our application, but it will also reduce debugging time.

Imagine if you, as the developer, had to write an application that performed a complex mortgage calculation to determine the amount of principal you would have after a number of years of mortgage payments. Now imagine this calculation was required many times throughout your application. It would be far easier to have a routine to call, say `CalculatePrincipal`, than to have to repeat the calculation each time you required it.

Each time you had to repeat the calculation, you would not only waste space but also increase the likelihood of a typographical error and therefore cause your application to execute improperly. Functions and subroutines are the answer to this problem.

Functions and subroutines operate similarly but have one key difference. A function is used when a value is returned to the calling routine, while a subroutine is used when a desired task is needed, but no value is returned.

Invoking a Subroutine

A subroutine is used when a series of steps are required but no value is returned to the routine that called the subroutine. Subroutines are invoked using a subroutine name, as shown in the following syntax:

SubroutineName(ParameterList)

Invoking a subroutine can occur with parameters, as in the following example of a call to the `OutputMin` subroutine that accepts two `Integers` for parameters:

```
OutputMin(intValue1, intValue2)
```

Invoking a subroutine can also occur without parameters, as in the following example of a call to the `Message` subroutine that has no parameters:

```
Message()
```

Invoking a Function Call

A function by definition has a **return value**. Therefore, a function call must be assigned to a variable of the type that the function returns, as in the following syntax:

VariableName = FunctionName(ParameterList)

For example, the following code calls the `UCase` function to return an uppercase representation of a `String` that is passed as a parameter:

```
strVariableName = UCase("please uppercase this")
```

5.2 Built-In Functions

Before we demonstrate how to develop your own functions and subroutines, we will show a few useful built-in functions Visual Basic .NET provides.

Visual Basic .NET provides many built-in functions to assist your coding of applications. By using built-in functions you save time in coding and debugging work that has already been provided for you.

The following is a description of some of the most useful built-in functions in Visual Basic.

String Functions

Function Name: `UCase`

Function Description: Returns the `String` that is passed in all uppercase letters.

Common Uses: While `UCase` can be used when the desired output is required to be in all uppercase letters, it is commonly used when you wish to validate data entered by a user against a given string. In your voting booth applications, you needed to check multiple capitalizations for each vote recorded. By converting the vote to uppercase, you could have only checked it once.

Syntax: `String = UCase(String)`

Examples:

Function Call	Return Value
`UCase("Input String")`	`"INPUT STRING"`
`UCase("all lowercase")`	`"ALL LOWERCASE"`
`UCase("ALL UPPERCASE")`	`"ALL UPPERCASE"`
`UCase("UpPeR AnD lOwErCaSE")`	`"UPPER AND LOWERCASE"`

Previous Way of Coding Validation:

```
If (txtVote.Text = "Bush" Or txtVote.Text = "BUSH" Or _
    txtVote.Text = "bush") Then ...
```

Better Way of Coding Validation:

```
If (UCase(txtVote.Text) = "BUSH") Then ...
```

Function Name: `LCase`

Function Description: Returns the `String` that is passed converted to all lowercase letters.

Common Uses: `LCase` is very similar in use to `UCase`. While it is more common to use `UCase` for data validation, `LCase` can be used equally as well.

Syntax: `String = LCase(String)`

Examples:

Function Call	Return Value
`LCase("Input String")`	`"input string"`
`LCase("all lowercase")`	`"all lowercase"`
`LCase("ALL UPPERCASE")`	`"all uppercase"`
`LCase("UpPeR AnD lOwErCaSE")`	`"upper and lowercase"`

Function Name: `Trim`

Function Description: Returns a `String` with the same content, except the leading and trailing spaces are removed.

Common Uses: Often when data is gathered, additional spaces may exist before the first noncharacter or after the last nonblank character. It is good practice to remove these so that data may be presented cleanly.

Syntax: `String = Trim(String)`

Examples:

Function Call	Return Value
`Trim("   InputString")`	`"InputString"`
`Trim("InputString   ")`	`"InputString"`
`Trim("   InputString   ")`	`"InputString"`
`Trim("   Input String   ")`	`"Input String"`

Notice that although spaces are removed from the beginning and ending of the `String`, they are not removed from the middle, as seen in the fourth example.

The following code will initialize two `Strings`. One will contain a `String` that has the leading and trailing spaces removed by the `Trim` function. It is displayed between two vertical bars so that it will be obvious that the spaces have been removed. (See Figure 5.1.) The second `String` will be created in a similar manner; however, the spaces will not be removed. (See Figure 5.2.)

```
Dim strTest As String
Dim strWithBlanks As String
Dim strBorder As String
Dim strTrimmedOutput As String
Dim strUnTrimmedOutput As String

strTest = "  Hello  " 'Two spaces before and after
strBorder = "|"

strTrimmedOutput = strBorder & Trim(strTest) & strBorder
strUnTrimmedOutput = strBorder & strTest & strBorder

MsgBox(strTrimmedOutput)
MsgBox(strUnTrimmedOutput)
```

COACH'S TIP

Similar to the `Trim` function are the `RTrim` and `LTrim` functions, which trim a `String` only from the right or left side of the string, respectively.

Figure 5.1
First output

|Hello|

Figure 5.2
Second output

| Hello |

Function Name: `Space`

Function Description: Returns a `String` containing the number of spaces indicated by the parameter.

Common Uses: Often you wish to add spaces to set the total length of a `String` to an exact size. This is often used when working with fixed-width data files. We will demonstrate this in Chapter 9.

Syntax: `String = Space(Integer)`

Examples:

Function Call	Return Value
Space(5)	" "
Space(10)	" "
Space(0)	""
"Hello" & Space(10) & "Goodbye"	"Hello Goodbye"

Function Name: `Len`

Function Description: Returns the number of characters contained within a `String`.

Common Uses: `Len` is used to determine the size of a `String`.

Syntax: `Integer = Len(String)`

Examples:

Function Call	Return Value
Len("Inconceivable")	13
Len("Iocaine Powder")	14
Len("Hello, my name is Inigo Montoya. " & _ "You killed my father. Prepare to die.")	70
Len("")	0

Function Name: Left

Function Description: Returns the first N characters of a String where N is an Integer parameter indicating the number of characters to return. If N is greater than the number of characters in the String, then the String is returned. No extra spaces are added.

Common Uses: Often you are only concerned with the first few characters of a String. Left is a great way to look at only the beginning of a String.

Syntax: String = Microsoft.VisualBasic.Left(String, Integer)

 COACH'S TIP

The Left function, as well as the Right function that follows, is part of the Microsoft.VisualBasic object. You can call them by preceding the Left or Right function call with Microsoft.VisualBasic.

Examples:

Function Call	Return Value
Microsoft.VisualBasic.Left("Beginning of String", 5)	"Begin"
Microsoft.VisualBasic.Left("Beginning of String", 2)	"Be"
Microsoft.VisualBasic.Left("Beginning of String", 0)	""
Microsoft.VisualBasic.Left("Beginning of String", 20)	"Beginning of String"

The following code shows how you might use Left to determine if a person's full name belongs to either a man or a woman.

```
Dim strPerson1 As String
Dim strPerson2 As String
Dim strPerson3 As String
Dim strPerson4 As String

strPerson1 = "Mr. Jeff Salvage"
strPerson2 = "Ms. Charlene Nolan"
strPerson3 = "Mrs. Karen Charles"
strPerson4 = "Miss Lynn Bosko"

'Process Person1
```

(continues)

```
(continued)
If ("Mr." = Microsoft.VisualBasic.Left(strPerson1, 3)) Then
    MsgBox "Person 1 is a Man"
ElseIf ("Miss" = Microsoft.VisualBasic.Left(strPerson1, 4) Or _
        "Ms." = Microsoft.VisualBasic.Left(strPerson1, 3) Or _
        "Mrs." = Microsoft.VisualBasic.Left(strPerson1, 4)) Then
    MsgBox "Person 1 is a Woman"
Else
    MsgBox "Is Person 1 an Alien?"
EndIf

'Process Person2
If ("Mr." = Microsoft.VisualBasic.Left(strPerson2, 3)) Then
    MsgBox "Person 2 is a Man"
ElseIf ("Miss" = Microsoft.VisualBasic.Left(strPerson2, 4) Or _
        "Ms." = Microsoft.VisualBasic.Left(strPerson2, 3) Or _
        "Mrs." = Microsoft.VisualBasic.Left(strPerson2, 4)) Then
    MsgBox "Person 2 is a Woman"
Else
    MsgBox "Is Person 2 an Alien?"
EndIf

'Person3 and Person4 code could follow
```

Function Name: `Right`

Function Description: Returns the last N characters of a `String` where N is an `Integer` passed indicating the number of characters to return. If N is greater than the number of characters in the `String`, then the `String` is returned. No extra spaces are added.

Common Uses: Often you are only concerned with the last few characters of a `String`. `Right` is a great way to look at only the end of a `String`.

Syntax: `String = Right(String, Integer)`

Examples:

Function Call	Return Value
Microsoft.VisualBasic.Right("Ending of String", 5)	"tring"
Microsoft.VisualBasic.Right("Ending of String", 2)	"ng"
Microsoft.VisualBasic.Right("Ending of String", 0)	""
Microsoft.VisualBasic.Right("Ending of String", 20)	"Ending of String"

The following code shows how you might use `Right` to determine a person's suffix, as in, Jr., Sr., or Ph.D.

```
Dim strPerson1 As String
Dim strPerson2 As String
Dim strPerson3 As String

strPerson1 = "Nira Herrmann, Ph.D."
strPerson2 = "John Cunningham, Sr."
strPerson3 = "Bob Bruno, Jr."
```

(continues)

(continued)

```
'Process Person1
If ("Ph.D." = Microsoft.VisualBasic.Right(strPerson1, 5)) Then
    MsgBox "Person 1 has a doctorate degree."
ElseIf ("Sr." = Microsoft.VisualBasic.Right(strPerson1, 3)) Then
    MsgBox "Person 1 has a kid with the same name."
ElseIf ("Jr." = Microsoft.VisualBasic.Right(strPerson1, 3)) Then
    MsgBox "Person 1 has a father with the same name."
EndIf

'Person2 and Person3 code could follow
```

Function Name: `Mid`

Function Description: Returns a specific number of characters from a `String` allowing the developer to indicate where to start and how many characters to return. The first parameter is the source `String`. The second is an `Integer` indicating the starting position to copy from. The third parameter is optional and indicates the number of characters to copy. If the third parameter is left out, all characters from the starting position are returned.

Common Uses: Often you wish to extract a portion of a `String` to use separately from the rest of the `String`. This is often the case when working with fixed-width data files. We will demonstrate this in Chapter 9.

Syntax: `String = Mid(String, Starting Position, Optional Length)`

Examples:

Function Call	Return Value
Mid("This is the String", 6, 2)	"is"
Mid("This is the String", 9, 3)	"the"
Mid("This is the String", 13, 4)	"Stri"
Mid("This is the String", 8)	" the String"

Function Name: `InStr`

Function Description: Returns the position of the first occurrence of a substring that is searched for in the `String` passed.

Common Uses: `InStr` can be used to tell us if a `String` has a certain substring contained within it. It operates much like searching a document for a word.

Syntax: `Long = InStr(String to be Searched, Search String)`

Examples:

Function Call	Return Value
InStr("This is a very", "is")	3
InStr("ab ab ab", "ab")	1
InStr("ab ab ab", "a")	1
InStr("ab ab ab", "c")	0

DRILL 5.1

What is the output of the following code?

```
MsgBox UCase("What is the output?")
```

DRILL 5.2

What is the output of the following code?

```
MsgBox Microsoft.VisualBasic.Left("What is the output?", 4)
```

DRILL 5.3

What is the output of the following code?

```
MsgBox Microsoft.VisualBasic.Right("What is the output?", 4)
```

DRILL 5.4

What is the output of the following code?

```
MsgBox UCase(Microsoft.VisualBasic.Left("What is the output?", 4))
```

DRILL 5.5

What is the output of the following code?

```
MsgBox Microsoft.VisualBasic.Left("What is the output?", 4) & _
                      Space(5) & Trim("  ?  ")
```

Conversion Functions

Function Name: `Str`

Function Description: Returns a `String` representation of the numeric value passed to it. By default it will place a single space in front of the first numeric character.

Common Uses: Visual Basic .NET will not allow you to assign a value of one data type to a variable of another data type. Avoid future problems by manually converting numeric values to `Strings` before assigning them to either a variable of type `String` or a `Text` attribute in a control.

Syntax: `String = Str(Numeric Value)`

Examples:

```
'Proper conversion
Dim strDestination As String
Dim intSource As Integer

intSource = 1

strDestination = Str(intSource)
```

The following is a demonstration of an improper conversion. Depending on your settings, you may or may not be allowed to perform it.

```
'Improper conversion
Dim strDestination As String
Dim intSource As Integer

intSource = 1

strDestination = intSource
```

Here is another example of an improper conversion (depending upon the settings of your system) that will not become apparent until you run the application. The code attempts to convert a `String` variable to a `String` value. Since the conversion is trying to go from a `String` to a `String`, it causes an error.

```
'Run-time Error
Dim strDestination As String
Dim strSource As String

strSource = "Source"

strDestination = Str(strSource)
```

Function Name: `Val`

Function Description: Returns a numeric representation of the `String` value passed to it. `Val` will convert a `String` to a numeric until it reaches a character that is not a numeric value, a decimal point, or a white-space character. Once an unrecognizable character is read, conversion stops at that point.

Common Uses: `Val` is used much in the same manner as `Str`, except in the opposite direction.

Syntax: `Numeric Value = Val(String)`

Examples:

Function Call	Return Value
Val("199.11")	199.11
Val(" 199.11 ")	199.11
Val(" 1 99.1 1")	199.11
Val(" 199 ")	199
Val("$199.11")	0
Val("1,199.11")	1
Val(" ")	0
Val("123abc")	123
Val("abc123")	0

```
'Proper conversion
Dim intDestination As Integer
Dim strSource As String

strSource = "1"

intDestination = Val(strSource)
```

Function Name: CDate

Function Description: Returns a Date representation of the String value passed to it. While this sounds simple, there are multiple date formats. CDate will consider your computer's system setting as the valid Date format.

Common Uses: CDate is used when a Date representation is needed. Often a date can be stored in a String when it is gathered from a fixed-width or comma-delimited file. If proper operations are going to be performed on the date, then it is necessary to store it in its native format.

Syntax: Date = CDate(String)

Examples:

```
Dim dteToday As Date
Dim strToday As String
Dim strTomorrow As String
Dim dteTomorrow As Date

strToday = "September 30, 2001"
dteToday = CDate(strToday)

'See Coach's Tip for explanation of the DateAdd function
dteTomorrow = DateAdd(DateInterval.Day, 1, dteToday)
strTomorrow = CStr(dteTomorrow)

MsgBox(strTomorrow)
```

COACH'S TIP

The `DateAdd` function will perform a mathematical calculation for you with the date type. It would be convenient if Visual Basic .NET allowed you to add to a date using the + operator. However, what should Visual Basic .NET add? Do you mean to add a day, month, or year? Therefore, the `DateAdd` function is provided. The first parameter indicates the units of that you wish to add for a `Date`. Some of the choices for an interval are `DateInterval.Day`, `DateInterval.Month`, or `DateInterval.Year`. The second parameter is the number of units you wish to add. Finally, the third parameter is the variable or constant you wish to add a date to.

COACH'S TIP

There are many conversion functions to assist your handling of the many data types in Visual Basic .NET. They all basically operate the same way; the value passed to them is converted to the type in the name of the function. Here is a list to assist you. For more information, check out the MSDN.

```
CBool(expression) 'Convert to a Boolean value
CDate(expression) 'Convert to a Date value
CDbl(expression) 'Convert to a Double value
CDec(expression) 'Convert to a Decimal value
CInt(expression) 'Convert to an Integer value
CLng(expression) 'Convert to a Long value
CSng(expression) 'Convert to a Single value
CStr(expression) 'Convert to a String value
```

DRILL 5.6

What is the output of the following code?

```
Dim sngValue1 As Single
Dim strValue2 As String

sngValue1 = 1.1
strValue2 = Str(sngValue1)

MsgBox(strValue2)
```

DRILL 5.7

What is the output of the following code?

```
Dim strValue As String

strValue = Str("A")
MsgBox(strValue)
```

Mathematical Functions

Function Name: `Int, Fix`

Function Description: Returns the `Integer` portion of the numerical value passed to it.

Common Uses: `Int` or `Fix` are used when you wish to convert a numerical value to an integer without regard for the decimal value. It performs a truncation of the number. Imagine if you needed to know how many complete dozens of an item you have. You could perform the calculation as follows: `Int(intQuantity/12)`.

Syntax: `Integer = Int(Numerical Value)`
`Integer = Fix(Numerical Value)`

Examples:

Function Call	Return Value
`Int(199.11)`	199
`Int(0.1)`	0
`Int(1.5)`	1
`Int(0.99999)`	0
`Fix(199.11)`	199
`Fix(0.1)`	0

COACH'S TIP

When programming, there are many ways to accomplish the same result. In the previous example, you could also calculate the number of dozens by using the `Integer` divide operator, \. The `Integer` divide operator will divide a number and return the whole number portion of the quotient. Therefore, `intQuantity\12` will result in the number of dozens.

COACH'S WARNING

While `Int` and `Fix` return the same values for positive numbers, they do not necessarily return the same values for negative numbers. While `Int` will return the first negative number less than or equal to the number passed, `Fix` will return the first negative number greater than or equal to the number passed.

Function Call	Return Value
`Int(-199.11)`	−200
`Int(-0.1)`	−1
`Fix(-199.11)`	−199
`Fix(-0.1)`	0

DRILL 5.8

What is the output of the following code?

```
MsgBox (Str(Int(-9.9)))
```

DRILL 5.9

What is the output of the following code?

```
MsgBox (Str(Fix(-9.9)))
```

Miscellaneous Functions

Function Name: IsNumeric

Function Description: Returns True if the value passed to it evaluates to a numeric data type, otherwise it returns False.

Common Uses: IsNumeric can be used to verify that a value can be evaluated as a number. Instead of possibly getting either inaccurate results or a run-time error, by using IsNumeric, a proactive approach to error handling can be achieved.

Syntax: Boolean = IsNumeric(Expression)

Examples:

Function Call	Return Value
IsNumeric("199.11")	True
IsNumeric(199.11)	True
IsNumeric("ABC")	False
IsNumeric("123ABC")	False
IsNumeric("1,999")	True
IsNumeric("$1,1999")	True
IsNumeric("50%")	False
IsNumeric("One")	False

Further Example:

```
If IsNumeric(txtInput.Text) Then
    intTotal = intTotal + Val(txtInput.Text)
Else
    MsgBox("Not a number", , "IsNumeric Error")
End If
```

Function Name: IsDate

Function Description: Returns True if the value passed to it evaluates to a valid Date, otherwise it returns False.

Common Uses: IsDate can be used when you are about to convert a value to a Date representation. Instead of possibly getting either inaccurate results or a run-time error, by using IsDate, a proactive approach to error handling can be achieved.

Syntax: `Boolean = IsDate(Expression)`

Examples:

Function Call	Return Value
`IsDate("January 1, 2001")`	True
`IsDate("1/1/2001")`	True
`IsDate("1/1/01")`	True
`IsDate(#1/1/01#)`	True
`IsDate(1/1/2001)`	False, the value needs either quotes or pound signs around it
`IsDate("Today")`	False, the string today is not a date, just the characters that make up the word Today

Function Name: `Today`

Function Description: Returns the current system date.

Common Uses: `Today` can be used anytime the developer wishes to access the system date. While it is returned as a variant, it can be used as a native date format or converted to a `String` representation.

Syntax: `Date = Today()`

Examples:

```
'Code to display Yesterday's Date in a MessageBox
Dim dteToday As Date
Dim dteYesterday As Date
Dim strYesterday As String

dteToday = Today()
dteYesterday = DateAdd(DateInterval.Day, -1, dteToday)
strYesterday = CStr(dteYesterday)
MsgBox(strYesterday)
```

Function Name: `TimeOfDay`

Function Description: Returns the current system time.

Common Uses: `TimeOfDay` can be used anytime the developer wishes to access the system time. While it is returned as a variant, it can be used as a native date format or converted to a `String` representation. You can store a `Time` in the `DateTime` data type.

Syntax: `DateTime = TimeOfDay()`

Examples:

```
'Code to display the time now in a MessageBox
Dim dteExactTime As DateTime
dteExactTime = TimeOfDay()
MsgBox(dteExactTime.ToString())
```

Function Name: Rnd

Function Description: Returns a pseudo random decimal number that is greater than or equal to 0 and less than 1. By passing Rnd an optional numeric parameter, you can further control the type of random number you generate. See the MSDN for more details.

Common Uses: Random numbers are required for a great many reasons. Imagine if you wished to create a video game where aliens were attacking. A random number generator can determine a random number of aliens and a random position on the screen for each alien. Often, random number generators are also used for simulations. In Visual Basic .NET you can use the Rnd function to simulate a random event. By combining the output of the Rnd function with some basic mathematics, random numbers can be generated within a given range.

Syntax: Variant = Rnd()

Examples:

Function Call	Return Value
Int(Rnd()*3)	Generates a random number from 0 to 2
Int(Rnd()*3)+1	Generates a random number from 1 to 3
Int(Rnd()*6)+1	Generates a random number from 1 to 6
(Int(Rnd()*6) + 1) + (Int(Rnd()*6) + 1)	Generates a random number from 2 to 12 similar to rolling a pair of dice

COACH'S TIP

When you use the Rnd function, each time you run the application the same sequence of random numbers will be generated. By adding the keyword Randomize, with a parameter, to the application before the calls to Rnd, new sequences of random numbers will be generated each time the application is run. In order for Randomize to generate a different list each time the application is run, a different value must be passed to the Randomize function call. See the MSDN for more details.

Function Name: Format

Function Description: Returns a String representation of the expression passed formatted according to instructions passed to it in the second parameter. Format may be used to improve the appearance of numbers, dates, times, or string values.

Common Uses: Format is used anytime the user needs to beautify the output of a value.

Syntax: String = Format(Expression, String)

Second Parameter:

Standard Format	Description
Currency	Displays the number as a monetary value. A dollar sign precedes the number that is formatted to two decimal places. If a number requires it, a comma is placed to the left of every three digits (except for the two for the decimal places). If the number is negative, it is enclosed in parentheses.
Date	There are many "Standard" date formats. `"General Date"` will format a date/time as mm/dd/yyyy and hh:mm:ss if there is a time. Other formats include: `"Long Date"`—Displays full names in the date `"Medium Date"`—Displays abbreviated names in date `"Short Date"`—Displays as mm/dd/yy
Fixed	Displays the number with two decimal places and at least one digit to the left of the decimal place.
Percent	Displays the number as a percentage. It multiplies the number passed by 100 (with two decimal places) and places a percent sign to the right.
Standard	Displays a number with two decimal places. If the number requires it, a comma is placed to the left of every three digits (except for the two for the decimal places). If the number is negative, a negative sign is displayed to the left of the number.
Time	There are many "Standard" time formats: `"Long Time"`—Displays as hh:mm:ss PM `"Medium Time"`—Displays as hh:mm PM `"Short Time"`—Displays as hh:mm

Examples:

Function Call	Return Value
Format(123.1, "Currency")	$123.10
Format(#03/03/2001#, "Short Date")	3/3/2001
Format(123.1, "Fixed")	123.10
Format(.1231, "Percent")	12.31%
Format(123.1, "Standard")	123.10
Format(#10:30:01#, "Long Time")	10:30:01 AM

Custom format strings can be made by combining different predetermined format characters.

Format Character	Description
0	A 0 in the format string is replaced by the digit from the expression that belongs in that space. If there is no digit for that space, the 0 is displayed.
#	When a format string specifies a #, if the expression has a digit in the position where the # is, the digit is displayed, otherwise nothing is displayed.
decimal point	Forces a decimal place to be displayed. Does not necessarily force a digit to be displayed to the right.
comma	Places a comma in the number. Usually used in the standard position, every three digits to the left of the decimal place.

COACH'S TIP

There are many more formatting options. Check out the MSDN for more specifics.

Examples:

Function Call	Return Value
Format(123.1, "00000.00")	00123.10
Format(0, "00000.00")	00000.00
Format(123.1, "00000")	00123
Format(123.1, "######.##")	123.1
Format(123.1, "0###.##")	0123.1
Format(123.1, "0,###.##")	0,123.1

COACH'S TIP

The many options of the Format function may be overwhelming. Instead, you might try using either FormatCurrency, FormatDateTime, FormatPercent, or FormatNumber. These functions, while having options of their own, are an easy way to format a value to a currency, date, percent, or number.

```
Function Call                  Return Value
FormatCurrency(199.33)         $199.33
FormatDateTime(Now())          12/29/2001 9:42:15 AM
FormatPercent(.55)             55.00%
FormatNumber("123.11")         123.11
```

DRILL 5.10

What is the range of values produced by the following code?

```
MsgBox Str(Int(Rnd()*100))
```

DRILL 5.11

What is the range of values produced by the following code?

```
MsgBox Str(Int(Rnd()*10+3))
```

DRILL 5.12

What is the `String` produced by the following call to `Format`?

```
Format(1111.1111, "Standard")
```

DRILL 5.13

What is the `String` produced by the following call to `Format`?

```
Format(452.23, "0000.000")
```

DRILL 5.14

What is the `String` produced by the following call to `Format`?

```
Format(#03/01/2001#, "Date")
```

5.3   Writing Functions and Subroutines

While the functions built into Visual Basic .NET are useful, they are not all-inclusive. There are countless functions and subroutines that developers wish were built into Visual Basic .NET, but unfortunately, they are not. Because it would be impossible to predict all the routines developers require, you have the ability to create your own.

More often than not, applications development requires coding of your own functions and subroutines. The syntax for a creating your own function is as follows:

```
Scope Function FunctionName(ParameterList) As ReturnType
    BodyOfFunction()
End Function
```

Coding a Function

A function is declared with a scope of either `Private` or `Public`. Usually, functions will be written as `Private`, indicating that they are usable only in the form that they are coded. However, if you specify a `Public` scope, then the function would be visible to other forms. (So far you have not learned how to create multiple forms in a project.)

Using the `Function` keyword makes the distinction between a function and subroutine.

The `FunctionName` is used to differentiate this function from any others. Naming a function follows the same rules as naming a variable. You have already seen function names when you used the built-in functions like `UCase`, `IsDate`, or `Str`.

The `ParameterList` is a list of variables that will be passed to the function. **Parameters** are passed to functions so that the function can perform its operation on many different values. A parameter list is specified by specifying the parameter name, the keyword `As`, and then the data type of the parameter. If more than one parameter is listed, the list of variables passed are separated by commas. Although less probable, it is possible that a function does not require any parameters.

The `ReturnType` is the type of value that is returned from the function. When a function is written, it must return a value of the same data type as specified by the `ReturnType`. A value is returned using the following syntax:

Return *ReturnValue*

The `BodyOfFunction` is the code that accomplishes the function's task.

Example: Max Function

Here is an example of a function that returns the maximum of two `Integers`. It compares the first parameter, `intValue1`, to the second parameter, `intValue2`. If the first parameter is greater than the second parameter, then the first parameter is the value returned from the function. If the first parameter is not greater than the second parameter, then the second parameter is returned. You may be wondering what happens if the first parameter equals the second parameter. While not explicitly tested for, when the first parameter equals the second parameter, `Max` returns the second parameter.

COACH'S TIP

Ignore the keyword `ByVal` for now; it will be explained shortly.

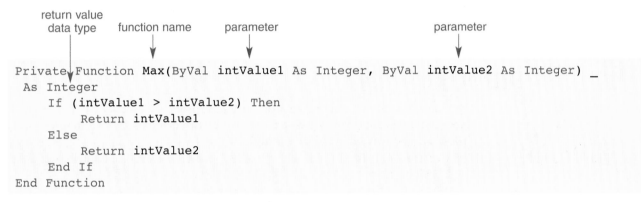

```
Private Function Max(ByVal intValue1 As Integer, ByVal intValue2 As Integer) _
As Integer
    If (intValue1 > intValue2) Then
        Return intValue1
    Else
        Return intValue2
    End If
End Function
```

COACH'S TIP

A function name is used in two places. The first can be seen in the previous code. It is used in the declaration of the function itself.

The second can be seen in the following code where the `Max` function is called and the result is set to the `intMaximum` variable.

```
Dim intMaximum As Integer
intMaximum = Max(1, 2)
MsgBox("The Maximum value is " & Str(intMaximum))
```

Example: PayRate Function

Here is an example of a function that returns the pay rate of a department. This is the same calculation you have performed in your case study. However, now you can use the function `PayRate` to simplify your payroll calculation. The function accepts the department as a `String` parameter and returns the pay rate associated with the department. Note that the function assumes a valid department, otherwise it will return `0`.

```
'Declare constants for entire application, place in declarations areas of code
Const sngSalesPayRate As Single = 25
Const sngProcessingPayRate As Single = 15
```

(continues)

(continued)

```
Const sngManagementPayRate As Single = 75
Const sngPhonePayRate As Single = 10

'Declare PayRate function
Private Function PayRate(ByVal strDepartment As String) As Single
    Select Case strDepartment
        Case "Sales"
            Return sngSalesPayRate
        Case "Processing"
            Return sngProcessingPayRate
        Case "Management"
            Return sngManagementPayRate
        Case "Phone"
            Return sngPhonePayRate
        Case Else
            Return 0
    End Select
End Function
```

 COACH'S TIP

You may have noticed that the keyword `ByVal` appears before a parameter. Visual Basic .NET will allow you to pass a parameter by two methods: `ByVal` and `ByRef`. These methods will be explained shortly.

 COACH'S TIP

This may be obvious, but notice that there is no `Return` statement in a subroutine. Since no value is returned, there is no need for a `Return` statement.

Coding a Subroutine

The coding of a subroutine does not vary much from the coding of a function. The only difference is that a subroutine cannot directly return a resulting value.

The syntax for a subroutine is as follows:

```
Scope Sub SubroutineName(ParameterList)
        Body of Subroutine
End Sub
```

Example: ThankYouMessage Subroutine

The `ThankYouMessage` subroutine simply outputs a message in a message box. This particular subroutine contains no parameters. A subroutine does not require parameters. They are strictly optional. The code follows:

```
Private Sub ThankYouMessage()
        MsgBox("Thank You Pat Croche for a Great Basketball Team!")
End Sub
```

Example: DisplayGrade Subroutine

Here is a subroutine that accepts an `Integer` parameter that indicates a person's average and displays a `MessageBox` containing the letter grade associated with the person's average.

```
Private Sub DisplayGrade(ByVal intStudentAverage As Integer)
    Select Case intStudentAverage
        Case 90 To 100
            MsgBox("A")
        Case 80 To 89
            MsgBox("B")
        Case 70 To 79
            MsgBox("C")
        Case 60 To 69
            MsgBox("D")
        Case Else
            MsgBox("F")
    End Select
End Sub
```

The `DisplayGrade` subroutine could be called from a button and pass a value contained in a text box to the subroutine. Note how the following code converts the text box value to an `Integer` before it's passed.

```
Private Sub btnDisplayGrade_Click(...
    DisplayGrade(Int(txtStudentGrade.Text))
End Sub
```

Example: InitializePicture Subroutine

Subroutines can be used to change the properties of a control. Observe the following subroutine, `InitializePicture`. It accepts a picture box as the first parameter and a `String` containing the new picture file location and name as the second parameter. The subroutine will set the `Picture` attribute to the new file name and set the `TabStop` and `BorderStyle` attributes to 0. The code follows.

```
Private Sub InitializePicture(ByVal picControl As PictureBox, _
                    ByVal strNewPicture As String)

    picControl.Image = Image.FromFile(strNewPicture)
    picControl.TabStop = False
    picControl.BorderStyle = 0

End Sub
```

The `InitializePicture` subroutine could be called from a button as shown in the following code:

```
Private Sub btnInitialize_Click(...

    InitializePicture(picPicture1, "c:\VB Coach\Chapter 5\DontTouchThis.jpg")

End Sub
```

COACH'S TIP

When passing parameters to a function or subroutine, you must match the data types of the parameters you are passing with the data types of the parameters in the function's or subroutine's declaration. For example, if a subroutine is declared with two parameters of data types `Integer` and `String`, then any call to that subroutine must have two parameters. The first must be an `Integer` and the second must be a `String`.

DRILL 5.15

Given the following definitions of three subroutines, show which of the following subroutine calls are valid (assuming that `Option Strict` is On):

```
Private Sub DrillSub1(ByVal  intDrillValue As Integer, _
                      ByVal  strDrillValue As String)

End Sub

Private Sub DrillSub2(ByVal  strDrillValue As String, _
                      ByVal  intDrillValue As Integer)

End Sub
Private Sub DrillSub3(ByVal  strStringValue As Integer, _
                      ByVal  intIntegerValue As String)

End Sub
```

```
Dim intVal1 As Integer
Dim strVal2 As String
Dim intVal3 As Integer
Dim sngVal4 As Single

DrillSub1(intVal1, strVal2)
DrillSub1(strVal2, intVal1)
DrillSub1(intVal3, strVal2)
DrillSub2(intVal1, intVal3)
DrillSub2(sngVal4, intVal1)
DrillSub2(strVal2, intVal1)
DrillSub3(intVal1, strVal2)
DrillSub3(strVal2, intVal1)
DrillSub3(intVal1, intVal3)
```

Local Variables

Many times when you are writing a function or subroutine, data must be stored temporarily within the routine. The value being stored will only be required during the execution of the routine and then not required after the routine is exited. These **local variables** are declared in the same manner as the other variables you declared.

When you declare a variable within a function or subroutine, it is only accessible from within the function or subroutine where it is declared. Attempts to access a local variable from outside the routine where it is defined will result in a compile error.

COACH'S WARNING

Often beginner programmers will declare every variable to be either global to the application or the form that they are developing. While this may appear to be an easy way to program, this method is fraught with errors.

Applications with too many global variables can cause the developer to inadvertently use a variable that was meant for another purpose. Imagine if you wrote an application that had many loops. If you used the variable `intLoopCounter` for each loop, it is possible that one loop's execution would affect another's execution by changing the common variable.

Applications with too many global variables can waste memory. If every variable needs to be declared at once, the maximum memory allocation required may be larger than with local variables.

COACH'S TIP

A local variable goes out of scope when the block of code that it has been defined in is exited.

Example: Final Purchase Price

Imagine if you wished to write a subroutine that output the tax and final price of a purchase when passed the purchase amount. You may assume that the tax rate is stored in a constant called `sngSalesTaxRate`.

```
Private Sub PurchasePrice(ByVal dblPurchasePrice As Double)
Dim dblTax As Double
'sngSalesTaxRate is declared as a constant earlier in the program

dblTax = dblPurchasePrice * sngSalesTaxRate
MsgBox("Purchase Price: " & dblPurchasePrice.ToString & _
       "Sales Tax: " & dblTax.ToString & _
       "Final Price: " & (dblPurchasePrice*dblTax).ToString)

End Sub
```

5.4 Pass By Reference and Pass By Value

Visual Basic .NET allows you to declare a function or subroutine with parameters that are either a copy (**pass by value**) or a reference (**pass by reference**) to the original value. This is something that may seem trivial; indeed, you wrote your first functions and subroutines without worrying much about it. However, as your applications become more complex, this issue will become important.

You may be wondering, which way is better? It depends largely on your concerns. If you wish your application to run quickly, then passing large parameters by reference will increase performance. However, the speed comes at the risk that the original value passed can be altered unexpectedly by the routine that is called.

COACH'S TIP

Pass by value is usually slower than pass by reference because when a large parameter is passed by value, the computer must copy the entire parameter and pass it to the routine. However, when the computer passes a parameter by reference, it simply passes its original location, and all references to that parameter are made from the original.

Visual Basic .NET's parameter passing defaults to pass by value for subroutine or function calls. Parameters like `Integers`, `Booleans`, and `Decimals` are relatively small and do not benefit from passing the parameter by reference. However, passing large `String` variables and complex controls by value could waste time.

Since these are often the values that will be passed as a parameter, it seems a natural choice to default parameter passing to by value. To give the developer maximum flexibility, Visual Basic allows us to specify either pass by reference or pass by value.

Specifying a parameter as pass by value is accomplished by placing the keyword `ByVal` in front of a parameter, as in the following declaration of a subroutine:

```
Private Sub SubroutineName(ByVal Parameter1 As Type)
```

Similarly, by placing the keyword `ByRef` in front of a parameter, the parameter will be passed by reference. If you do not specify either, it is as if you have placed a `ByVal` keyword, since the default value is by value.

```
Private Sub SubroutineName(ByRef Parameter1 As Type)
```

COACH'S TIP

You can mix the specification of by reference or by value within a single subroutine call. Observe the following subroutine declaration, where the first parameter is declared as pass by value and the second parameter is declared as pass by reference.

```
Private Sub SubroutineName(ByVal Param1 As Type, ByRef Param2 As Type)
```

Before we show you a practical use for pass by reference, practice the following drills:

DRILL 5.16

Assuming the `Mystery` function has been defined as follows, what is the output of the following code?

```
'Declare variables
Dim intTestValue As Integer
Dim intReturnValue As Integer

'Initialize intTestValue
intTestValue = 5

'Display value of intTestValue before call to Mystery
MsgBox("The value of intTestValue before the call = " & _
    intTestValue.ToString)
```

(continues)

DRILL 5.16 (continued)

```
'Call the Mystery Function
intReturnValue = Mystery(intTestValue)

'Output the return value and intTestValue
MsgBox("The return value from the call to Mystery is " & _
      intReturnValue.ToString)
MsgBox("The value of intTestValue after the call = " & _
      intTestValue.ToString())


Private Function Mystery(ByRef intMaxNum As Integer) As Integer
    Dim intValue As Integer
    intValue = 0

    intValue += intMaxNum
    intMaxNum = intMaxNum - 1
    intValue += intMaxNum
    intMaxNum = intMaxNum - 1
    intValue += intMaxNum
    intMaxNum = intMaxNum - 1

    Return intValue
End Function
```

DRILL 5.17

What is the output of the code in Drill 5.16 when the `intMaxNum` parameter is changed to pass by value by changing the function declaration as follows?

```
Private Function Mystery(ByVal intMaxNum As Integer) As Integer
```

DRILL 5.18

Assuming the `DrillRoutine` subroutine has been defined as follows, what is the output of the following code?

```
Dim intTestValue1 As Integer
Dim intTestValue2 As Integer

intTestValue1 = 5
intTestValue2 = 7

DrillRoutine(intTestValue1, intTestValue2)
MsgBox(Str(intTestValue1) & " " & Str(intTestValue2))

Private Sub DrillRoutine(ByVal intParam1 As Integer, _
                         ByRef intParam2 As Integer)
    intParam1 = 10
    intParam2 = 20
End Sub
```

DRILL 5.19

Assuming the `DrillRoutine` subroutine has been defined as follows, what is the output of the following code?

```
Dim intTestValue1 As Integer
Dim intTestValue2 As Integer

intTestValue1 = 5
intTestValue2 = 7
DrillRoutine(intTestValue1, intTestValue2)
MsgBox(Str(intTestValue1) & " " & Str(intTestValue2))

Private Sub DrillRoutine(ByRef intParam1 As Integer, _
                         ByRef intParam2 As Integer)
    intParam1 = 10
    intParam2 = 20
End Sub
```

DRILL 5.20

Assuming the `DrillRoutine` subroutine has been defined as follows, what is the output of the following code?

```
Dim intTestValue1 As Integer
Dim intTestValue2 As Integer

intTestValue1 = 5
intTestValue2 = 7

DrillRoutine(intTestValue1, intTestValue2)
MsgBox(Str(intTestValue1) & " " & Str(intTestValue2))

Private Sub DrillRoutine(ByVal intTestValue1 As Integer, _
                         ByVal intTestValue2 As Integer)
    intTestValue1 = 10
    intTestValue2 = 20
End Sub
```

DRILL 5.21

Assuming the `DrillRoutine` subroutine has been defined as follows, what is the output of the following code?

```
Dim intTestValue1 As Integer
Dim intTestValue2 As Integer

intTestValue1 = 5
intTestValue2 = 7
```

(continues)

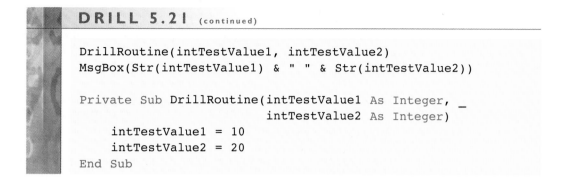

```
DrillRoutine(intTestValue1, intTestValue2)
MsgBox(Str(intTestValue1) & " " & Str(intTestValue2))

Private Sub DrillRoutine(intTestValue1 As Integer, _
                         intTestValue2 As Integer)
    intTestValue1 = 10
    intTestValue2 = 20
End Sub
```

DRILL 5.21 (continued)

Example: Compute Change Application Utilizing Pass By Reference
Problem Description

You will develop an application that will accept as input a purchase price and an amount paid. The application will output the change due to the person in the highest denominations of the bills and change. Assume that you can give change in denominations of $100, $50, $20, $10, $5, $1, 25 cents, 10 cents, 5 cents, and 1 cent.

Observe the behavior of the application if the purchase price is $511.13 and the amount paid is $600.00. The output, in a label, shows the denominations required to give a total of $88.87 in change. The application looks as shown in Figure 5.3.

Figure 5.3
Make Change application

Problem Discussion

So far all the examples of functions and routines could have been written either as pass by value or pass by reference. Here's a perfect example of where you actually need pass by reference so that you can develop an elegant solution to the problem. The application may seem simple in its definition, but it requires some thought to develop an efficient solution.

The solution requires figuring out the total number of each denomination (starting with the largest) you can return. As each number of bills or coins is determined, you must account for the corresponding amount so that you do not count the same money multiple times.

The easiest way to accomplish this is to write a single function that computes the maximum amount of the denomination passed that can be returned. Once the number is computed, the corresponding amount can be reduced from the remaining money. That way, you can pass the function 100 and determine the number of hundred dollar bills that can be returned to the purchaser. Then you can pass the function 50 and determine the number of fifty dollar bills that can be returned to the purchaser. This continues until all the denominations of money are computed.

Problem Solution

You are going to break your problem into sections. The first is simple—it passes the text box controls' values to the MakeChange subroutine that will start the actual *work* of the application.

```
Private Sub btnMakeChange_Click(...
    MakeChange(Val(txtPurchasePrice.Text), Val(txtAmountPaid.Text))
End Sub
```

The MakeChange subroutine will be the *driver* of the application. It accepts a purchase price and the amount paid. It outputs the correct change. Instead of complicating MakeChange, you call a support function called PrintBills. PrintBills does the real work. Once you calculate the amount of change required, MakeChange calls PrintBills with each denomination that you can give as change. PrintBills then outputs the amount given for that denomination and reduces the amount of change remaining to be given by said amount.

```
Private Sub MakeChange(ByVal dblPurchasePrice As Double, _
                ByVal dblAmountPaid As Double)
    'Variable to store the amount of change remaining
    Dim dblTotalChange As Double

    'Compute initial amount of change
    dblTotalChange = dblAmountPaid - dblPurchasePrice
    'Determine how many hundred dollar bills should be returned
    PrintBills(dblTotalChange, 100)
    'Determine how many fifty dollar bills should be returned
    PrintBills(dblTotalChange, 50)
    'Determine how many twenty dollar bills should be returned
    PrintBills(dblTotalChange, 20)
    'Determine how many ten dollar bills should be returned
    PrintBills(dblTotalChange, 10)
    'Determine how many five dollar bills should be returned
    PrintBills(dblTotalChange, 5)
    'Determine how many dollar bills should be returned
    PrintBills(dblTotalChange, 1)
    'Determine how many quarters should be returned
    PrintBills(dblTotalChange, 0.25)
    'Determine how many dimes should be returned
    PrintBills(dblTotalChange, 0.1)
    'Determine how many nickels should be returned
    PrintBills(dblTotalChange, 0.05)
    'Determine how many pennies should be returned
    PrintBills(dblTotalChange, 0.01)
End Sub
```

PrintBills calculates the largest number of the current denomination by converting the result of the division to an Integer. Since the calculation returns an Integer value, it can be used directly as the amount of that denomination. Then the rest of the function simply selects the proper wording for that denomination.

```
Private Sub PrintBills(ByRef dblTChange As Double, ByVal dblDenomination As Double)
    'Variable to store the number of bills of the current denomination returned
    Dim intNumBills As Integer

    'Compute the number of bills
    intNumBills = Int(dblTChange / dblDenomination)

    'Compute the amount of change remaining
    dblTChange = dblTChange - dblDenomination * intNumBills

    'If there is at least one bill/coin then output the amount
    If (intNumBills > 0) Then
        'If the denomination is a bill (1, 5, 10, 20, 50, or 100)
        If (dblDenomination >= 1) Then
            'Output the bill information
            lblChange.Text &= "$" & dblDenomination & " bills:" & intNumBills

        'Otherwise the denomination is a coin (penny, nickel, dime, quarter)
        Else
            'Check if it is quarter
            If (dblDenomination = 0.25) Then
                lblChange.Text &= "Quarters: "
            'Check if it is dime
            ElseIf (dblDenomination = 0.1) Then
                lblChange.Text &= "Dimes: "
            'Check if it is nickel
            ElseIf (dblDenomination = 0.05) Then
                lblChange.Text &= "Nickels: "
            'Otherwise there are pennies
            Else
                lblChange.Text &= "Pennies: "
            'Otherwise it is more than one penny
            End If

            'Add the number of coins
            lblChange.Text &= intNumBills.ToString
        End If

        'Add a new line to the output
        lblChange.Text &= vbNewLine
    End If
End Sub
```

The use of pass by reference may not be readily apparent in the elegance of the solution. Since `TotalChange` is passed from `MakeChange` to `PrintBills` by reference, the changes made to `dblTChange` in `PrintBills` are remembered in `TotalChange` when the application returns to the `MakeChange` subroutine. If `TotalChange` was passed by value, this application will not work.

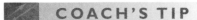

COACH'S TIP

An important point that beginner programmers often miss is that variables are passed by position, not by name. Notice the parameters for `MakeChange` are `dblTChange` and `dblDenomination`. This means that the first parameter will always be the current change and the second parameter will always be the current denomination, regardless of the variable name used to pass it.

In the example you use `dblTotalChange` as the variable to pass for `dblTChange` and you use a series of constants to pass for `dblDenomination`.

◆ 5.5 Case Study

Problem Description

You wish to modify the case study from Chapter 4 so that instead of displaying a weekly pay, you display a gross pay, tax, and net pay for each employee. Additionally, you wish to display a total gross pay, tax, and net pay for all the employees. With the added knowledge of built-in functions, you can also format the monetary values to appear as currency values. For simplicity's sake, you will compute the tax at a single rate of 28%.

The completed application should look as shown in Figure 5.4.

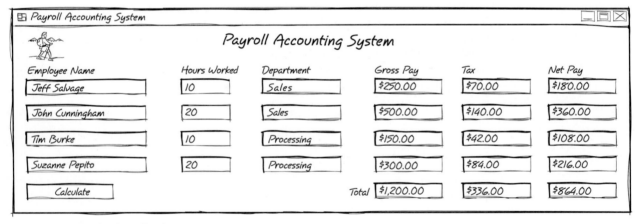

Figure 5.4   Sketch of application

Problem Discussion

With the additional knowledge of subroutines, you can add this functionality and actually shrink the size of your code. Since the calculations required are the same for each employee, you can write one routine that accepts the text boxes for each employee as parameters. You do not need to pass the employee name text box to the subroutine, since it is not used in the calculations.

Problem Solution

You need to remove the text boxes from Chapter 4's solution for weekly pay and add text boxes for gross pay, tax, and net pay. You need one for each of the four employees. You also need variables to store the total gross pay, total tax, and total net pay. You can place these in the common declarations section of code along with the constants. This code follows:

```
'Constants to Hold Pay Rates and Tax Rate

Const intSalesPayRate = 25
Const intProcessingPayRate = 15
Const intManagementPayRate = 50
Const intPhonePayRate = 10
Const sngTaxRate = 0.28


'Temporary Variables to Store Calculations
Dim dblTmpTotalGross As Double
Dim dblTmpTotalTax As Double
Dim dblTmpTotalNet As Double
```

Next you must add a subroutine to compute the gross pay, tax, and net pay for a single employee. You need to pass it the number of hours worked and the department so that you can compute the necessary values. Additionally, you need to pass it the three text boxes that will store the results. Once you have the necessary parameters, the code is similar to the previous chapter's solution. You are going to add three local variables: `dblGrossPay`, `dblTax`, and `dblNetPay`. Although the local variables are not required, they will make your programming easier. A `Select Case` statement will determine which pay rate to use based upon the department stored in a text box. The gross pay is then calculated and stored in the local variable `dblGrossPay`. With the gross pay calculated, you can calculate the tax and net pay for the employee and store the results in the local variables `dblTax` and `dblNetPay`, respectively.

With all the necessary values calculated, the next step is to store the results, properly formatted, into their respective text boxes. You can format the monetary values using the `FormatCurrency` function.

The final step is just to add the calculated values to the variables storing the total gross pay, tax, and net pay.

The code follows:

```
Private Sub ComputePay(ByVal txtHours As TextBox, ByVal txtDept As TextBox, _
                ByVal txtGross As TextBox, ByVal txtTax As TextBox, _
                ByVal txtNet As TextBox)

    Dim dblGrossPay As Double 'Stores the calculated gross value
    Dim dblTax As Double 'Stores the calculated tax
    Dim dblNetPay As Double 'Stores the calculated net pay

    Select Case txtDept.Text
        Case "Sales"
            dblGrossPay = Val(txtHours.Text) * intSalesPayRate
        Case "Processing"
            dblGrossPay = Val(txtHours.Text) * intProcessingPayRate
        Case "Management"
            dblGrossPay = Val(txtHours.Text) * intManagementPayRate
        Case "Phone"
            dblGrossPay = Val(txtHours.Text) * intPhonePayRate
        Case Else
            MsgBox("Error in input")
            dblGrossPay = 0
    End Select


    dblTax = dblGrossPay * sngTaxRate 'Compute Tax
    dblNetPay = dblGrossPay - dblTax 'Compute Net Pay
```

(continues)

(continued)

```
'Format Output
txtGross.Text = FormatCurrency(dblGrossPay)
txtTax.Text = FormatCurrency(dblTax)
txtNet.Text = FormatCurrency(dblNetPay)

'Add to totals
dblTmpTotalGross += dblGrossPay
dblTmpTotalTax += dblTax
dblTmpTotalNet += dblNetPay

End Sub
```

COACH'S TIP

Although you have not seen objects like text boxes passed to subroutines before, the concept and procedure is the same as passing any other variable.

With the addition of the ComputePay subroutine, your btnCalculate_Click event becomes almost trivial. You pass the proper parameters for each of the four employees, and then you copy the totals to their respective text boxes. (See Figure 5.5.)

```
Private Sub btnCalculate_Click(...

    'First Person's Calculations
    ComputePay(txtHours1, txtDept1, txtGross1, txtTax1, txtNet1)

    'Second Person's Calculations
    ComputePay(txtHours2, txtDept2, txtGross2, txtTax2, txtNet2)

    'Third Person's Calculations
    ComputePay(txtHours3, txtDept3, txtGross3, txtTax3, txtNet3)

    'Fourth Person's Calculations
    ComputePay(txtHours4, txtDept4, txtGross4, txtTax4, txtNet4)


    'Copy the Totals to their TextBoxes
    txtTotalGross.Text = FormatCurrency(dblTmpTotalGross)
    txtTotalTax.Text = FormatCurrency(dblTmpTotalTax)
    txtTotalNet.Text = FormatCurrency(dblTmpTotalNet)

End Sub
```

Figure 5.5
Final application

Payroll Accounting System

Employee Name	Hours Worked	Department	Gross Pay	Tax	Net Pay
Jeff Salvage	10	Sales	$250.00	$70.00	$180.00
John Cunningham	20	Sales	$500.00	$140.00	$360.00
Tim Burke	10	Processing	$150.00	$42.00	$108.00
Suzanne Pepito	20	Processing	$300.00	$84.00	$216.00
Calculate		Totals	$1,200.00	$336.00	$864.00

CORNER

With the ability to write your own subroutines and functions comes a new option when using a Debugger.

When you step through your application, you have a choice of whether you wish to step through every line of code or skip over code like function calls.

Observe the following simple application, as illustrated in Figure 5.6. It contains a button to roll a die five times. The result will be displayed in a message box.

Figure 5.6   RollDice application

Observe the following code that calls the `RollDice` function and returns the total value of the die rolled five times.

```
Private Sub btnRoll_Click(...
    'Variable to store 5 rolls of the dice
    Dim intTotal As Integer

    'Call the RollDice function and store the results
    intTotal = RollDice()

    'Output the result
    MsgBox(Str(intTotal))

End Sub


Private Function RollDice() As Integer
    Dim intTotal As Integer

    intTotal = 0
```

(continues)

(continued)

```
        intTotal += Rnd() * 6 + 1 'First Roll
        intTotal += Rnd() * 6 + 1 'Second Roll
        intTotal += Rnd() * 6 + 1 'Third Roll
        intTotal += Rnd() * 6 + 1 'Fourth Roll
        intTotal += Rnd() * 6 + 1 'Fifth Roll


        Return intTotal
    End Function
```

Notice that the code defines the same local variable in both routines. This is completely acceptable. A local variable is only visible within the function that is defined. Therefore, another local variable with the same name can exist in another function. Also note that this function does not have any parameters. Nothing is either sent or received by the function. This is also completely acceptable.

While you could step through this example by pressing the <F11> key or selecting Step Into from the Debug menu, you can skip the tracing of the function call by either hitting the <F10> key or selecting Step Over from the Debug menu. (See Figures 5.7 and 5.8.)

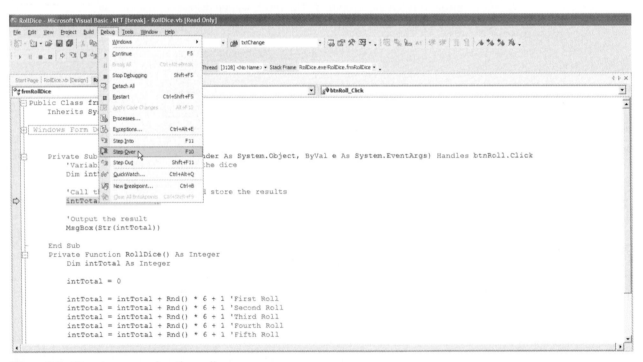

Figure 5.7   Stepping over a function call

Conditional Statements with Function Calls

Visual Basic .NET has one more twist when evaluating conditional statements. If a function call is made within a conditional expression, all of the conditional expressions are evaluated regardless of whether or not a condition can be short-circuited.

Visual Basic .NET does this because usually if a function call is embedded in a conditional statement, the desire was for the function to be called consistently.

Observe the following application, as illustrated in Figure 5.9. It computes a homework average and then determines whether a student passes. Due to the generosity of

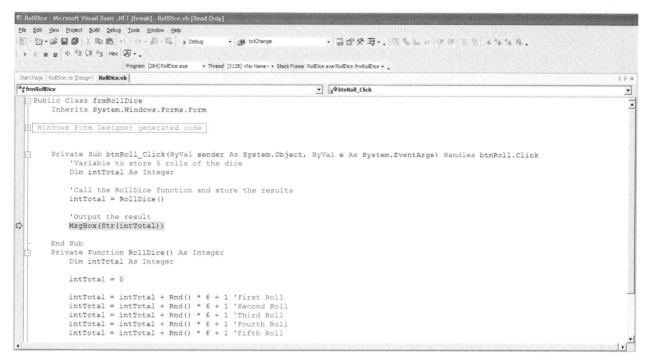

Figure 5.8 After stepping over a function call

Figure 5.9
Final Grade Calculator

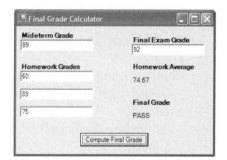

the teacher in this class, as long as the student passes the midterm exam or the final exam, or the homework averages to a passing grade, the student will pass the class.

To implement this grading scheme, the following code is used:

```
Private Sub butCompute_Click(...
    'If the midterm grade or the Final exam grade is >= 65
    'ComputeHomeworkAverage will still be called
    If (Val(txtMidtermGrade.Text) >= 65) Or (Val(txtFinalExamGrade.Text) >= 65) _
        Or (ComputeHomeworkAverage()) Then
        lblFinalGrade.Text = "PASS"
    Else
        lblFinalGrade.Text = "FAIL"
    End If
End Sub


Private Function ComputeHomeworkAverage() As Boolean
    'Declare variable to store the homework average
    Dim sngHomeworkAverage As Single
```

(continues)

(continued)
```
'Compute the homework average
sngHomeworkAverage = (Val(txtHomeworkGrade1.Text) + _
                      Val(txtHomeworkGrade2.Text) + _
                      Val(txtHomeworkGrade3.Text)) / 3


'Output the homework average formatted to 2 decimal places
lblHomeworkAverage.Text = Format(sngHomeworkAverage, "0.00")

'return true if the homework average is passing
If (sngHomeworkAverage >= 65) Then
    Return True
Else
    Return False
End If

End Function
```

With short circuit analysis you would expect that once the midterm grade was evaluated as greater than or equal to 65 it would not evaluate the remaining conditions. However, the final condition is the evaluation of the return value of a function. Since a function is called within the condition, all the conditions are evaluated.

If the final condition was not evaluated, then the `ComputeHomeworkAverage` function would not be called and the label `lblHomeworkAverage` would not contain the average of the homework.

Key Words and Key Terms

Function
A modular piece of code used to organize a program into more readable, maintainable parts that returns a single value.

Parameter
A variable that accepts a value from the function that calls it.

Subroutine
A modular piece of code used to organize a program into more readable, maintainable parts that does not return any values.

Local variables
A variable that is defined within a routine that is visible only within the area of code that it was defined.

Pass by value
A method of passing a variable where a copy of the original value is used by the function. Any changes made to this copy do not affect the original value.

Pass by reference
A method of passing a variable where a reference to the original value is used by the function. Any changes made to this reference are reflected in the original value.

Return value
The value passed back from a function to the function that called it.

Answers to Chapter's Drills

Drill 5.1
The output of the code is as follows:

```
WHAT IS THE OUTPUT?
```

The code calls the `UCase` function with the parameter `"What is the output?"`, which converts all the characters to uppercase. The question mark remains unaffected.

Drill 5.2
The output of the code is as follows:

```
What
```

The code calls the `Left` function with two parameters. The first, `"What is the output?"`, is a `String`. The second, 4, indicates how many characters from the left of the `String` should be returned.

Drill 5.3
The output of the code is as follows:

```
put?
```

The code calls the `Right` function with two parameters. The first, `"What is the output?"`, is a `String`. The second, 4, indicates how many characters from the right of the `String` should be returned. Note that the question mark is one of those four characters.

Drill 5.4
The output of the code is as follows:

```
WHAT
```

The code calls both the `Left` and the `UCase` functions. The `Left` function is called with two parameters. The first, `"What is the output?"`, is a `String`. The second, 4, indicates how many characters from the left of the `String` should be returned. Therefore, the `Left` function returns `"What"`, which is passed to the `UCase` function as its parameter. `UCase` then converts its parameter to uppercase, giving us the output `"WHAT"`.

Drill 5.5
The output of the code is as follows:

```
What      ?
```

The output of the code is actually the combination of three function calls: `Left`, `Space`, and `Trim`. First, `Left` is called with the parameters `"What is the output?"` and 4 and returns `"What"`. The return value `"What"` is appended with the return values of the other two functions. `Space` is called with 5, so it returns a `String` of five spaces, `"     "`. `Trim` is passed the `String` `"  ?  "` and returns a `String` with the spaces to the left and right removed. Therefore, `Trim` returns a `String` with the single character `"?"` returned. When all three return values are appended, the value `"What      ?"` is passed to `MsgBox` and output.

Drill 5.6
The output of the code is as follows:

```
1.1
```

The code starts by assigning the value `1.1` to the variable `sngValue1`. `Value1` is of the type `Single`; therefore, when you wish to assign it to the variable `strValue2`, you use the `Str` function to convert the value stored in the variable `sngValue1` to the variable `strValue2`. Finally, the value is output in a `MessageBox`.

Drill 5.7
The output of the code is as follows:

The code does not produce output. The code may not compile, depending on your system's settings. The `Str` function is expecting a numeric value for its parameter and will not execute.

Drill 5.8
The output of the code is as follows:

```
-10
```

The output of the code is produced by first calculating the result of the call to the function `Int`, which returns the `Integer` portion of the number passed to it. In this case it is -10, because the `Int` function will return the first negative number less than or equal to the number passed. Then the `Str` function is called to convert the result to a `String` so that it may be displayed in a message box.

Drill 5.9
The output of the code is as follows:

```
-9
```

The output of the code is produced by first calculating the result of the call to the function `Fix`, which returns the `Integer` portion of the number passed to it. In this case it is -9, because the `Fix` function will return the first negative number greater than or equal to the number passed. Then the `Str` function is called to convert the result to a `String` so that it may be displayed in a message box.

Drill 5.10
The `Rnd` function generates a value greater than or equal to 0 and less than 1. When multiplied by 100, it will generate a value greater than or equal to 0 and less than 100. This value is then converted to an integer and then output. Therefore, the range of values are `Integers` from 0 to 99.

Drill 5.11
The `Rnd` function generates a value greater than or equal to 0 and less than 1. When multiplied by 10, it will generate a value greater than or equal to 0 and less than 10. By adding 3 to this generated value, the number generated is greater than or equal to 3 and less than 13. This value is then converted to an integer and then output. Therefore, the range of values are `Integers` from 3 to 12.

Drill 5.12
The `Format` function converts the input value of `1111.1111` to a representation that includes standard comma placement and two decimal places of accuracy. Therefore the value would be `1,111.11`.

Drill 5.13
The `Format` function converts the input value of `452.23` to a representation that does not include commas, four digits before the decimal place, and has three decimal places of accuracy. Therefore, the value would be `0452.230`.

Drill 5.14

You will not get expected results because `Date` is not a standard format.

Drill 5.15

In order for each subroutine call to be valid, the data type of each parameter passed must match the data type of the parameter in the exact order as specified in the subroutine definition.

In the first subroutine call, `DrillSub1(intVal1, strVal2)`, the subroutine is expecting a parameter of the data type `Integer` followed by a parameter of the data type `String`. Since `intVal1` is declared as an `Integer` and `strVal2` is declared as a `String`, this is a **valid** subroutine call.

In the second subroutine call, `DrillSub1(strVal2, intVal1)`, the subroutine is expecting a parameter of the data type `Integer` followed by a parameter of the data type `String`. Since `intVal1` is declared as an `Integer` and `strVal2` is declared as a `String`, this is an **invalid** subroutine call. The data types of the parameters were correct but in the wrong order.

In the third subroutine call, `DrillSub1(intVal3, strVal2)`, the subroutine is expecting a parameter of the data type `Integer` followed by a parameter of the data type `String`. Since `intVal3` is declared as an `Integer` and `strVal2` is declared as a `String`, this is a **valid** subroutine call.

In the fourth subroutine call, `DrillSub2(intVal1, intVal3)`, the subroutine is expecting a parameter of the data type `String` followed by a parameter of the data type `Integer`. Since `intVal1` is declared as an `Integer` and `intVal3` is declared as an `Integer`, this is an **invalid** subroutine call. The data type of the second parameter was correct but the first parameter was incorrect.

In the fifth subroutine call, `DrillSub2(sngVal4, intVal1)`, the subroutine is expecting a parameter of the data type `String` followed by a parameter of the data type `Integer`. Since `sngVal4` is declared as a `Single` and `intVal1` is declared as an `Integer`, this is an **invalid** subroutine call. The data type of the second parameter was correct but the first parameter was incorrect.

In the sixth subroutine call, `DrillSub2(strVal2, intVal1)`, the subroutine is expecting a parameter of the data type `String` followed by a parameter of the data type `Integer`. Since `strVal2` is declared as a `String` and `intVal1` is declared as an `Integer`, this is a **valid** subroutine call.

In the seventh subroutine call, `DrillSub3(intVal1, strVal2)`, the subroutine is expecting a parameter of the data type `Integer` followed by a parameter of the data type `String`. Even though the parameter names are named as if they were the opposite, the name of the parameter does not matter. The only issue is the data types of the parameters. Since `strVal2` is declared as a `String` and `intVal1` is declared as an `Integer`, this is a **valid** subroutine call.

In the eighth subroutine call, `DrillSub3(strVal2, intVal1)`, the subroutine is expecting a parameter of the data type `Integer` followed by a parameter of the data type `String`. Even though the parameter names are named as if they were the opposite, the name of the parameter does not matter. The only issue is the data types of the parameters. Since `intVal1` is declared as an `Integer` and `strVal2` is declared as a `String`, this is an **invalid** subroutine call.

In the ninth subroutine call, `DrillSub3(intVal1, intVal3)`, the subroutine is expecting a parameter of the data type `Integer` followed by a parameter of the data type `String`. Even though the parameter names are named as if they were the opposite, the name of the parameter does not matter. The only issue is the data types of the parameters. Since `intVal1` is declared as an `Integer`, it is a valid parameter; however, since `intVal3` is also declared as an `Integer`, this is an **invalid** subroutine call.

Drill 5.16
The output of the code is as follows:

```
The value of intTestValue before the call = 5
The return value of the call to Mystery is 12
The value of intTestValue after the call = 2
```

The code passes the value `intTestValue`, by reference, to the function `intSumValues`. Then `intSumValues` returns an `Integer` that is the result of a series of calculations. The result is 12, so 12 is returned. However, since the value passed is done so by reference, when `intMaxValue` is changed in the `Mystery` function, the original value for `intTestValue` is also changed. Therefore, when the 1 is subtracted three times from `intTestValue`, the result, 2, is stored in the original variable and eventually output by the application.

Drill 5.17
The output of the code is as follows:

```
15 5
```

The code passes the value `intTestValue`, by value, to the function `intSumValues`. Then `intSumValues` returns an `Integer` that is the sum of all the values between the value passed and 1. Since this time the value passed is done so by value, when `intMaxValue` is changed in the `Do While` loop, the original value for `intTestValue` remains the same as it was before the call to `intSumValues`.

Drill 5.18
The output of the code is as follows:

```
5 20
```

The code passes the value `intTestValue1`, by value, as well as `intTestValue2`, by reference, to the function `DrillRoutine`. Within `DrillRoutine`, the value of the first parameter, `intParam1`, is set to 10. Since the first parameter was passed by value, it does not affect the value of the variable `intTestValue1` outside the subroutine. Additionally, `DrillRoutine` sets the value of the second parameter, `intParam2`, to 20. Since the second parameter is passed by reference, it changes the value of `intTestValue2` outside the subroutine. Therefore, the values 5 and 20 are output in the message box.

Drill 5.19
The output of the code is as follows:

```
10 20
```

The code passes the values `intTestValue1` and `intTestValue2`, by reference, to the function `DrillRoutine`. Within `DrillRoutine`, the value of the first parameter, `intParam1`, is set to 10. Since the first parameter was passed by reference, it also changes the value of the variable `intTestValue1` outside the subroutine. Additionally, `DrillRoutine` sets the value of the second parameter, `intParam2`, to 20. Since the second parameter is passed by reference, it changes the value of `intTestValue2` outside the subroutine. Therefore, the values 10 and 20 are output in the message box.

Drill 5.20
The output of the code is as follows:

```
5  7
```

The code passes the values `intTestValue1` and `intTestValue2`, by value, to the function `DrillRoutine`. Within `DrillRoutine`, the value of the first parameter, `intParam1`, is set to 10. Since the first parameter was passed by value, it does not affect the value of the variable `intTestValue1` outside the subroutine. This is true even though they are named the same. Additionally, `DrillRoutine` sets the value of the second parameter, `intParam2`, to 20. Since the second parameter is passed by value, it also does not change the value of `intTestValue2` outside the subroutine. Therefore, the values 5 and 7 are output in the message box.

Drill 5.21
The output of the code is as follows:

```
5  7
```

Even though you did not specify whether the parameters are pass by value or pass by reference, the parameters are considered passed by value since that is the default.

Additional Exercises

1. What is the value of the `String` produced by the following expression?

```
UCase("all lower") & LCase("####0.00")
```

2. What is the value of the `String` produced by the following expression?

```
Left("Hey what's that?", 3) & Right("We have to go now!", 4)
```

3. What is the value of the `String` produced by the following expression?

```
LCase(UCase(Left("Hey what's that?", 3) & Right("We have to go now!", 4)))
```

4. What is the value of the `String` produced by the following expression?

```
Trim(Space(10) & "A" & Space(10))
```

5. What is the value of the `String` produced by the following expression?

```
InStr("I really want to be on The Real World", "real")
```

6. What is the value of the `String` produced by the following expression?

```
InStr("I really want to be on The Real World", "REAL")
```

7. What is the value produced by the following expression?

```
Fix(-9.3 - 2.1 - 1.2)
```

8. What is the value produced by the following expression?

```
Int(9.3 - 2.1 - 1.2)
```

9. Will the following two sets of code produce the same results? If not, explain why.

```
Function Version1(ByVal sngValue As Single) As Single
    Return(Rnd(Int(sngValue)))
End Function

Function Version2(ByVal sngValue As Single) As Single
    Return(Int(Rnd(sngValue)))
End Function
```

10. Write the code required to generate a random number in the range of 1 to 10,000.
11. Write the code required to generate a random number in the range of 5 to 15.
12. What is the value produced by the following expression?

```
Format(99.123, "00.0")
```

13. Write a function called `JustTheEnds` that accepts two parameters. The first is the `String` that will be processed. The second is an `Integer` indicating the number of characters to combine from the beginning and ending of the `String` as the return value. Therefore, if `JustTheEnds` is passed `"WHAT COULD THIS BE?"`, 3, then the function should return `"WHABE?"`

14. Write a function called `Greater` that accepts two `Integer` parameters and returns `True` if the first parameter is greater than the second parameter. Otherwise it should return `False`.

15. Write a function called `Max3` that accepts three `Integer` parameters and returns the maximum value of the three parameters.

16. Write a function called `Middle` that accepts three `Integer` parameters and returns the middle value of the three parameters.

17. Write a function called `SalesTax` that accepts two parameters. The first parameter, `dblPurchasePrice`, should be of type `Double`. The second parameter, `sngPercentageTax`, should be of type `Single`. The function should compute and return the sales tax of the item purchased.

18. Write a function called `RestofString` that accepts two parameters. The first is the `String` to be processed. The second is a `String` to search for within the first `String`. If the `String` is found, return a `String` containing the remainder of the `String` after the first occurrence of the search `String`. If the `String` is not found, return an empty `String`. Therefore, if `RestofString` is called with `"Hello, I must be going"` and `"I"`, the function will return `" must be going"`.

INTERVIEW

An Interview with Aric Levin

Aric Levin is the Vice President of Technology at Westside Technologies, a consulting firm that designs and implements advanced information management systems based on Microsoft Technologies. Among other projects, Aric manages the software development efforts and infrastructure needs of one of Westside Technologies' major clients, Sound Dogs, the premier sound design team for Hollywood's feature film industry. Aric started as one of the software developers who created Sounddogs.com, the host site of their vast sound effects library, with over 70,000 sound effects.

How do the new features of VB.NET affect your job of developing?

A lot of the new features will be helping us to port the new application to VB.NET. There are major advantages which will be from the user experience on the Web site to advanced remote management. The use of .NET Web Controls will help us provide a more compatible and easy-to-use interface for our customers. Web caching will allow us to provide more data to our users faster, as well as new sorting and paging methods. Development will be made simpler due to the code-behind feature of ASP.NET, allowing us to completely separate the presentation tier from the business tier. .NET Assemblies will replace the current COM+ components.

The administration will be a big boost for Sound Dogs. Having the ability to easily create mobile forms can cut down response time for Customer Service problems.

One of the biggest advantages for us will be the use of Web Services.

Why was VB.NET chosen to create the Sound Dogs Effects Library?

Sound Dogs sells sound effect files over the Internet using an automated system. VB was primarily chosen for the low cost of maintenance, and high connectivity value (i.e., it could easily connect with components from inside the company as well as outside). As the effect library website grew, we were able to scale it up, using more and more advanced technologies that VB let us produce. At each point, there were no other design tools that would let us produce this quality of

software, with this rate of scalability at the cost we were paying our developers.

Currently we have started to use VB.NET in some of the sections of the Web site, mostly for administration. It has become a very easy way to add new features to the site, debug existing pages, and provide added security. We will be able to extend our existing services to not only customers but also other applications and systems. We are now at the beginning of the analysis phase for the next version of the site, and will probably start major development within a couple of months. We are certain that ASP.NET (VB.NET and CS.NET) will enhance the user experience on the site, and provide easy management for out support personnel.

Has it been difficult or relatively easy to update the Library to new versions of VB? How will Visual Basic .NET enhance the site?

The site was continually upgraded to incorporate new VB features. When we started, we were using Visual Basic 4 with a custom CGI interface. We have since moved to a fully transactional system, using stored procedures, ASP, different VB components running on different systems and several systems distributing the overall processing load.

VB.NET will allow us to extend our services to end users and sound-effect consumers with very little overhead. We will be able to offer extended services to programs that want to integrate our sound effects search and retrieval directly into their end-user applications. VB.NET's Web development platform will be a welcomed enhancement to our development systems.

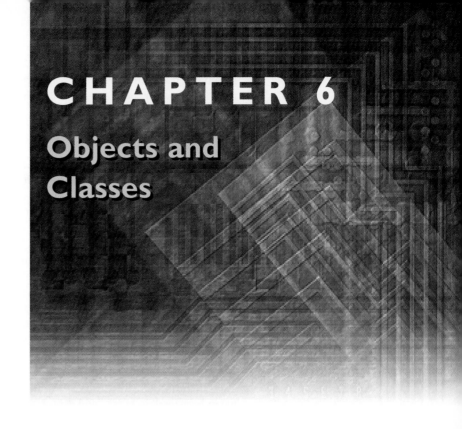

CHAPTER 6
Objects and Classes

CHAPTER
OBJECTIVES

◆ Describe the introductory concepts of object-oriented development

◆ Relate the concepts of object-oriented development to real-world examples

◆ Demonstrate many of the built-in objects and their methods

◆ Explain how to create your own objects

Objects like labels, text boxes, and command buttons are included in Visual Basic .NET. Objects are the basic building blocks of a program. They make the development of complex applications easier because you do not have to concern yourself with the creation of objects and their properties. However, the basic objects included in Visual Basic .NET are not enough. Sometimes a programmer needs more tools. This chapter explains how to create and use these tools and provides some examples and ideas for their use.

Visual Basic .NET allows you to create your own objects both by code and visually from existing objects contained within Visual Basic .NET. Since the concepts involved in creating objects start simplistically but grow more and more complex as you exploit the many features of object-oriented development, only the basic ways for creating objects will be introduced in this chapter. The more complex features will be explained in Chapter 10.

6.1 Object-Oriented Development Concepts

Many computer languages throw the term object-oriented programming around, but what is it? A *real* object-oriented programming language supports three basic concepts: **encapsulation**, **polymorphism**, and **inheritance**.

Confused? Most people are. So instead of delving straight into a confusing array of terms and concepts, let's take a step back for a discussion about real-world objects. Then once you understand the concepts, it will be easy for you to relate the terms of object-oriented programming to the analogy. This will provide a good parallel to introduce many sometimes-confusing terms.

A Real-World Example

Think about an object that everyone is familiar with, a TV. If I asked you to explain exactly how a TV works, could you do it? Could you explain every detail of how a show is broadcast and displayed? I doubt it. I certainly cannot; however, that does not stop me from watching the latest episode of *Buffy the Vampire Slayer*.

How about another question: How is a TV built? Well, I can't tell you all the details of that either, but somewhere someone has designed a set of blueprints that specifically outline the necessary parts and their configuration. These blueprints would specify the internal and external characteristics that define how the TV would operate.

There are a great many variations in television design. TVs now come in different shapes, sizes, method of display—the list goes on and on. If I had a set of blueprints for the latest 65-inch HDTV, I would have the information required to build a great TV, but I couldn't watch Buffy staking vampires on the blueprint.

However, if someone created a TV from those specifications and placed it in front of me, then I would be ready to watch whatever show I wanted.

Of course, the TV probably would not come set to the exact station that I wanted when I received it. Nor would it probably be set to the volume level and brightness that I desired. Does this mean that I will have to go through the blueprints and determine the exact inner workings of the TV to change some of its settings? Of course not, because the TV comes with an interface in the form of a remote control. This interface allows the user to set certain of the TV's characteristics to specific values.

Object-Oriented Concepts

Just as real-world objects need specifications to detail the design of an object, so do **objects** that you will develop in Visual Basic .NET. In Visual Basic .NET, you use a **class** to describe the properties and actions associated with an object in the same manner as a blueprint describes the properties and functionality of a TV.

Just as you do not have access to the inner workings of a TV, a developer should not allow access to the properties of a class except by specific routines that the developer creates. These routines are referred to as **methods** of the class.

Just as the blueprint for a TV does not serve as a functioning TV, a class does not serve as a functioning version of the item you are creating. The class must be *built* just as your TV is assembled. When you wish to create a functioning version of the class, you must create an object. While the computer does not have an assembly line to create an object, it does have to allocate the memory required for the object and initialize any variables. This process of creating an object from a class is known as **instantiating** an object.

So now that you are familiar with a few object-oriented terms, the question remains: How object-oriented is Visual Basic .NET? Let's look at the three terms introduced earlier and see if Visual Basic .NET implements some or all of them.

Encapsulation

During the course of the day, you are used to using many real-world objects without concerning yourself with the details of how they work internally. You use these objects with an interface that restricts your use to predefined tasks.

A television has a series of controls on the outside for the viewer to turn it on or off, change the channel, and adjust the picture. You are restricted from making other changes to the television by the box that surrounds it.

Encapsulation enables the programmer designing the class to dictate what types of operations are permissible upon a class without permitting other programmers access to the inner workings of the class. In essence, the class designer allows other programmers to have the complexity of a class hidden and ensures that other programmers can only use the class in ways intended by the programmer designing the class.

You have used objects like text boxes, labels, and buttons without knowledge of their internal workings. The properties and events accessed only allowed you to manipulate the objects in ways predetermined by the developers of the objects.

Imagine if you had an `Integer` variable that was supposed to represent the minute portion of a time. You would not want to the value to be beyond the range of 0 to 59. An `Integer` could be between the range of –2,147,483,648 to 2,147,483,647. By creating a minute object that restricts the value to a range of 0 to 59, the class provides a user interface over the data.

Polymorphism

There are many types of televisions. Currently, you can choose from a black and white, a color, an HDTV, a picture tube, an LCD, or a projection television. While all of these televisions have different features, they are all commonly referred to as TVs. These TVs have many of the same functions, even though these functions might operate differently from set to set.

Try switching the channels on a bunch of different sets. Do they all do the same thing? The channel up button or switch will generally move to the next channel. However, depending upon the set, any of the following actions can occur.

◆ The television is set to the next numerical channel above the current one.
◆ The television is set to the next valid channel above the current one.
◆ The television is set to the next numerical channel above the current one and it briefly displays the new channel number.

While there are many other possibilities, you get the idea. The concept of having one name but a different behavior depending upon the object it belongs to is known as polymorphism. You are already familiar with polymorphism in Visual Basic .NET. Many of the controls that you have built your applications from have properties, methods, or events with the same name but take on a slightly different meaning from control to control. When polymorphism is implemented well, you may not even be aware that something out of the ordinary has occurred.

Indeed, in its simplest form, you have been using polymorphism when you perform the basic mathematical operations. Regardless of the data type you wish to perform addition or subtraction on, you use operators like + or –. You do not require a different operator to perform an addition for each data type. Imagine how cumbersome it would be if you had to use a different operator to add `Integer`, `Single`, and `Double` variables. Similarly, when you design objects that have similar functions, it is helpful to design them with polymorphism in mind.

Inheritance

One of the keys to efficient development of applications is the ability to reuse the code that you previously developed. One way programmers accomplish this is to cut and paste code from one project to another. A better method, inheritance, is to build new classes from previous ones without modifying the original code.

Often when you develop a class, you realize after developing it that you may need another class that is very similar. Beginning programmers will copy the original class, make any changes necessary, and rename the old class. While this works in the short term, it is problematic in the long term. Imagine if you have created many classes using this method. Then after using the new classes in various programs, you discover that there was a bug in the original code. Now you must go back and modify the code in all the classes you copied the bug into. With inheritance, if you modify the original class, all the classes based on that change would be updated automatically.

The other problem, although not quite as severe, is the waste of a lot of unnecessary disk space by having multiple copies of the source code each time you copy it.

A simple example of using inheritance is to create a class called `Person`. A `Person` would have properties like `FirstName`, `LastName`, `Address`, `City`, `State`, `Zip`, and `PhoneNumber`.

If you then wanted to develop a `Student` class, by inheriting the properties of the `Person` class, you can simply add the properties specific to being a student: `Major`, `GPA`, `TotalCredits`, and so on. The actual explanation of how to code with inheritance will appear in Chapter 10.

DRILL 6.1

Match the following terms to the closest example.

a	inheritance	1	When a function takes on different meanings based upon what object is being used.
b	polymorphism	2	The hiding of the details of the implementation from a developer.
c	encapsulation	3	The ability to create a new class based on the definition of an existing one.
d	instantiation	4	The "blueprint" of an object.
e	class	5	The creation of an object from a class.

DRILL 6.2

Specify all the properties and functions of your television set. It will be impossible for you to get the same solution as found in the back of the chapter because your television most likely varies from the one used to write the solution. However, your answer should have the same major properties and methods.

6.2 Using Built-In Objects

Visual Basic .NET comes with many built-in objects ready for you to use. Indeed, you have been using them without even being aware of it. Our very first application involved using built-in objects on the toolbox that you placed on a form. These objects included labels, text boxes, picture boxes, and buttons.

Can you name any other objects that you have been using? How about `Strings`? Not all objects are visual in nature. Indeed, there are many ways of adding objects to your application. The most intuitive way to add an object to your application is to drag a predefined object onto your form. However, this only works with objects built into the toolbox.

Let's look at the `String` class to demonstrate the other ways you can declare and instantiate objects.

String Class

You are already familiar with declaring variables of the type `String`.

```
Dim strName As String
```

When you declare an object in this way, which is the same way you declare `Integer`, `Single`, and `Double` variables, the object is considered a structure or value type variable. Structures will be defined in Chapter 8; however, there is only a subtle difference between using them and using reference type objects. For purposes of discussion, you can still refer to them as objects.

As far as the difference is concerned, you only need concern yourself with the difference in declaring, allocating, and deallocating value type objects from reference type objects. This will be explained in greater detail as you proceed; for now do not worry about the intricacies but just know that value type variables are automatically deallocated when the routine they are declared within is exited.

Reference type variables will be discussed shortly, but first you will investigate many of the features of the `String` class that you have yet to explore. By learning how to exploit the built-in objects included with Visual Basic .NET, you will aid your understanding of objects, making creating your own objects easier.

There are a great many routines that can be executed upon the data stored in the `String` built into the `String` class. These routines are commonly referred to as methods of the class. In general, methods come in two varieties.

Some methods and functions perform a series of tasks and pass a value back to the calling routine. An example of this is if you had an object that stored a list of items purchased on a Web site. It might be necessary to have a checkout procedure call a method that calculates the sales tax. The result of the calculation could be returned to the checkout procedure.

Other methods and subroutines will perform a series of tasks but not pass a value back. When you display values in a message box, you call a routine that outputs the result of the method but does not return a value.

To access a list of them, just type a period after the object's name. Observe how if you declare an object called `strTest` you can see the list of methods. (See Figure 6.1.)

Figure 6.1
Showing the `String` classes methods

The simplest methods are ones that do not require any further specification. Let's look at how you might output the `strName` String from `"Jeff Salvage"` to `"JEFF SALVAGE"`. The difference between the two `Strings` is that the second contains the uppercase of each letter in the first `String`.

To accomplish this, you must call the `ToUpper` method. To call a method, you must type the name of the object, followed by a period, followed by the name of the method, followed by a set of parentheses. Therefore, to output the `strName` String to uppercase, you use the following code:

```
MsgBox(strName.ToUpper())
```

Similarly, if you wish to display the entire `String` in lowercase letters, you use the `ToLower` method as demonstrated in the following code:

```
MsgBox(strName.ToLower())
```

In both of these cases, the methods returned a value to the `MsgBox` function. The value returned was the converted `String`. The original `String` was not altered in any way.

The syntax for calling methods like this is as follows:

```
ObjectName.MethodName()
```

Other methods require additional information, known as parameters, which further specify the action performed by the method. A parameter is passed to a method by placing it between the parentheses. The syntax for passing a single parameter to a method is as follows:

```
ObjectName.MethodName(Parameter)
```

An example of a method that accepts a parameter is the `Substring` method. The `Substring` method allows you to access a portion of the `String`. In its simplest form it accepts an `Integer` parameter indicating the starting location of the `String` you wish to return. `Substring` will then return the `String` starting at that location until the end of the `String`.

Observe the following example, which declares a `String` called `strName` and initializes it to `"Jeff Salvage"`. It outputs the portion of the `String` starting at the location 5, which in this example is `"Salvage"`.

```
Dim strName As String
strName = "Jeff Salvage"
MsgBox(strName.Substring(5))
```

COACH'S TIP

When counting locations in a `String`, you start with the first letter being the location 0. The second letter is at location 1. The remaining letters in the `String` follow this pattern so the nth character is located at position n–1. While this is confusing, using a pattern like this leads to a more efficient program. Also remember that spaces count as a location.

If more than one parameter is required, the parameters are separated by commas. Therefore, the syntax for calling a method with two parameters is:

```
ObjectName.MethodName(Parameter1, Parameter2)
```

An example of this can also be shown using the `Substring` method that requires two parameters. When you place two parameters, the `Substring` method returns a portion of the `String` starting at the location specified by the first parameter and the number of characters returned as the second parameter.

Observe the following example, which declares a `String` called `strName` and initializes it to `"Jeff Salvage"`. It outputs the portion of the `String` starting at the location 5 and 3 characters. In this example, the output would be `"Sal"`.

```
Dim strName As String
strName = "Jeff Salvage"
MsgBox(strName.Substring(5, 3))
```

If a method requires more than two parameters, as many parameters as are required can be passed as long as commas separate the parameters.

COACH'S TIP

Be very careful when passing parameters. You must pass parameters of the data type specified by the method's definition. Fortunately, Visual Basic .NET makes it easy to determine what the definition is. Observe how when you type the object name, a dot, and the method name, followed by the open parenthesis, the parameter list and its definition pop up. (See Figure 6.2.)

Figure 6.2
Help with parameters is provided for you

```
Dim strName As String
strName = "Jeff Salvage"
strName.Substring(
```
1 of 2 ▾ Substring (**startIndex As Integer**) As String
startIndex:
    The starting character position of a substring in this instance.

COACH'S TIP

Here's another trick. Notice how Figure 6.2 shows that you are at definition 1 of 2. That means there is another definition for how parameters may be passed to this method. By pressing the <Down arrow> key you can see additional definitions. See the second definition in Figure 6.3.

Figure 6.3
Additional parameter lists are available

```
Dim strName As String
strName = "Jeff Salvage"
strName.Substring(
```
2 of 2 ▾ Substring (**startIndex As Integer**, length As Integer) As String
startIndex:
    The index of the start of the substring.

If you wish to return to the first definition, just press the <Up arrow> key.

Methods for the String Class

Here is a list of some of the methods available for the `String` class. Learning them is good practice for learning methods, but it is also good to learn because they will increase your power when you are working with `Strings`.

Previously we mentioned that there are two types of methods. All of the `String` class methods are functions. They return a value that is the result of the method. In all of these methods, the original value of the `String` is not changed in any way.

Method Name: `ToUpper`

Method Description: Returns the `String` that is passed in all uppercase letters.

Common Uses: While `ToUpper` can be used when the desired output is required to be in all uppercase letters, it is commonly used when you wish to validate data entered by a user against a given string. In your Voting Booth applications, you needed to check multiple capitalizations for each vote recorded. By converting the vote to uppercase, you could have only checked it once.

Syntax: `String = strStringVariable.ToUpper()`

Examples:

Invoke Method	Return Value
strStringVariable = "Input String" strStringVariable.ToUpper()	"INPUT STRING"
strStringVariable = "all lowercase" strStringVariable.ToUpper()	"ALL LOWERCASE"
strStringVariable = "ALL UPPERCASE" strStringVariable.ToUpper()	"ALL UPPERCASE"
strStringVariable = "UpPeR AnD lOwErCaSE" strStringVariable.ToUpper()	"UPPER AND LOWERCASE"

Previous Way of Coding Validation:

```
If (txtVote.Text = "Bush" Or txtVote.Text = "BUSH" Or _
    txtVote.Text = "bush") Then ...
```

Better Way of Coding Validation:

```
If (txtVote.Text.ToUpper() = "BUSH") Then ...
```

 COACH'S TIP

The previous code may have seemed a little odd. Placing the `.ToUpper()` after the `txtVote.Text` is allowed because a method of the `String` class may be invoked from any valid `String`. Since the `txtVote.Text` property accesses a `String`, you may invoke a method by coding a dot and the method name following it.

Here is a simple piece of code to further demonstrate the concept of a function returning a value. The original `String`, called `strOriginalValue`, will not be changed even though it will be used with the method `ToUpper` to assign a value to `strNewValue`. Then `strOriginalValue` remains "lowercase" and the code assigns "LOWERCASE" to `strNewValue`.

The code assigns a `String` variable, `strOriginalValue`, the `String` "lowercase". Then the `String` variable `strNewValue` is assigned the return value from the call to the method `ToUpper` from `strOriginalValue`.

As stated previously, the original value of the `String` is not changed in any way. The `String` `strNewValue` is assigned the original `String` converted to uppercase. When both `Strings` are output in message boxes, you will see that `strOriginalValue` is still "lowercase" and `strNewValue` is "LOWERCASE".

```
Dim strOriginalValue As String
Dim strNewValue As String

strOriginalValue = "lowercase"
strNewValue = strOriginalValue.ToUpper()
MsgBox(strOriginalValue)
MsgBox(strNewValue)
```

Function Name: ToLower

Function Description: Returns the String that is passed converted to all lowercase letters.

Common Uses: ToLower is very similar in use to ToUpper. While it is more common to use ToUpper for data validation, ToLower can be used equally as well.

Syntax: String = strStringVariable.ToLower()

Examples:

Invoke Method	Return Value
strStringVariable = "Input String" strStringVariable.ToLower()	"input string"
strStringVariable = "all lowercase" strStringVariable.ToLower()	"all lowercase"
strStringVariable = "ALL UPPERCASE" strStringVariable.ToLower()	"all uppercase"
strStringVariable = "UpPeR AnD lOwErCaSE" strStringVariable.ToLower()	"upper and lowercase"

Function Name: Trim

Function Description: Returns a String with the same content, except the leading and trailing spaces are removed.

Common Uses: Often when data is gathered, additional spaces may exist before the first noncharacter or after the last nonblank character. It is good practice to remove these so that data may be presented cleanly.

Syntax: String = strStringVariable.Trim()

Examples:

Invoke Method	Return Value
strStringVariable = " InputString" strStringVariable.Trim()	"InputString"
strStringVariable = "InputString " strStringVariable.Trim()	"InputString"
strStringVariable = " InputString " strStringVariable.Trim()	"InputString"
strStringVariable = " Input String " strStringVariable.Trim()	"Input String"

Notice that although spaces are removed from the beginning and ending of the String, they are not removed from the middle as in the fourth example.

The following code will initialize two Strings. One will contain a String that has had the leading and trailing spaces removed by the Trim method. It is displayed between two vertical bars so that it will be obvious that the spaces have been removed. (See Figure 6.4.) The second String will be created in a similar manner, however the spaces will not be removed. (See Figure 6.5.)

```
Dim strTest As String
Dim strWithBlanks As String
Dim strBorder As String
Dim strTrimmedOutput As String
Dim strUnTrimmedOutput As String

strTest = "  Hello  " 'Two spaces before and after
strBorder = "|"

strTrimmedOutput = strBorder & strTest.Trim() & strBorder
strUnTrimmedOutput = strBorder & strTest & strBorder

MsgBox(strTrimmedOutput)
MsgBox(strUnTrimmedOutput)
```

Figure 6.4
First output

| |Hello| |

Figure 6.5
Second output

| | Hello | |

Function Name: Substring

Function Description: Returns a specific number of characters from a String allowing you to indicate where to start and how many characters to return. The first parameter is an Integer indicating the starting position of the characters to return. The second parameter is optional and indicates the number of characters to return. If the second parameter is left out, all characters from the starting position are returned.

Common Uses: Often you wish to extract a portion of a String for use separately from the rest of the String. This is often used when working with fixed-width data files. This will be demonstrated in Chapter 9.

Syntax: String = strStringVariable.Substring(Integer (Starting Position), Optional Integer(Length))

Examples:

Invoke Method	Return Value
strStringVariable = "This is the String" strStringVariable.Substring(5, 2)	"is"
strStringVariable = "This is the String" strStringVariable.Substring (8, 3)	"the"
strStringVariable = "This is the String" strStringVariable.Substring(12, 4)	"Stri"
strStringVariable = "This is the String" strStringVariable.Substring(7)	" the String"

COACH'S TIP

Remember that a String's first index is 0. Also remember that spaces count!

Function Name: Length

Function Description: Returns the number of characters contained within a String.

Common Uses: Length is used to determine the size of a String.

Syntax: Integer = strStringVariable.Length()

Examples:

Invoke Method	Return Value
strStringVariable = "Inconceivable" strStringVariable.Length()	13
strStringVariable = "Iocaine Powder" strStringVariable.Length()	14
strStringVariable = "Hello, my name is Inigo Montoya." & _ " You killed my father. Prepare to die." strStringVariable.Length()	70
strStringVariable = "" strStringVariable.Length()	0

DRILL 6.3

Which of the following calls to the methods of the `String` class are correct?

```
a strStringVariable.ToUpper()
b strStringVariable.ToUpper("This will work")
c strStringVariable.Length(10)
d strStringVariable.Trim()
e strStringVariable.SubString("This will work", 10)
f strStringVariable.SubString("This will work", 10, 2)
g strStringVariable.SubString(10)
h strStringVariable.SubString(10, 2)
i strStringVariable.GiveMeAnA()
```

DRILL 6.4

What is the output of the following code?

```
strStringVariable = "Do or do not, there is no try."
MsgBox(strStringVariable.ToUpper())
```

DRILL 6.5

What is the output of the following code?

```
strStringVariable = "Do or do not, there is no try."
MsgBox(strStringVariable.ToLower())
```

DRILL 6.6

What is the output of the following code?

```
strStringVariable = "Do or do not, there is no try."
MsgBox(strStringVariable.SubString(14))
```

DRILL 6.7

What is the output of the following code?

```
strStringVariable = "Do or do not, there is no try."
MsgBox(strStringVariable.SubString(14,5))
```

DRILL 6.8

What is the output of the following code?

```
strStringVariable = "Do or do not, there is no try."
MsgBox(strStringVariable.Length().ToString)
```

DRILL 6.9

What is the output of the following code?

```
strStringVariable = "Do or do not, there is no try."
MsgBox(strStringVariable.ToUpper().ToLower())
```

Text Box Viewed as an Object

Another object you have already become familiar with is the text box. So far, you have added a text box to your project by dragging it from the toolbox and placing it on a form. You have seen that a text box contains properties. You have already modified properties such as `Name`, `Text`, `Color`, and `Font`. Although you have not used them, a text box also contains methods to perform actions upon the text box.

When using Microsoft Word or Excel, you are familiar with using the Paste function. You can cut or copy text onto a clipboard. Then when you issue the Paste command, whatever was contained in the clipboard is copied to the current position in your document. A similar feature is available via a method in the text box class. Observe how you may call the `Paste` method of a text box in the following code:

```
Private Sub btnPaste_Click(...
    txtEmployee1.Paste()
End Sub
```

The code simply calls the `Paste` method of the `txtEmployee1` text box when the button is clicked and copies the contents of the clipboard to the `Text` property of the text box.

While the methods can be called in the same manner as any other methods, declaring a text box in code must be accomplished differently.

Reference Versus Value Types

Earlier we mentioned that Visual Basic .NET uses the approach that everything is an object. You have already experienced that there are many different types of objects in Visual Basic .NET. Some objects like text boxes and picture boxes are visible on forms. It is easy to comprehend that objects such as these are complex in their design. Indeed, each object requires different specifications and uses a different amount of computer memory when added to your form. By providing many different types of objects, Visual Basic .NET allows you to use an object that meets the requirements of your application without wasting computer resources.

Compare a text box and a label object. You could use a text box in place of a label and not allow the user to enter a value; however, this would be a waste of resources. Similarly, Visual Basic .NET provides different objects, in the form of simple data types, to store numerical values. While Visual Basic .NET could have provided only one data type for numerical values, `Short`, `Integer`, and `Long` data types were provided to allow you to select the data type with the size and range requirements you will use in your application when working with whole numbers. In addition, data types like `Single`, `Double`, and `Decimal` exist for handling floating point numbers.

Visual Basic .NET delineates further between objects, because there are two ways to allocate the resources required for instantiating an object. When an object requires a small amount of the computer's memory, it will access it from a high-speed structure called the stack.

There are a lot of reasons why a complex object should not be allocated on a stack. When objects become more complex or the exact number of objects required is unknown at the time the application is written, allocating them on a stack is problematic. Either too much space is required or determining the exact amount of space becomes difficult.

If Visual Basic .NET tried to allocate all objects in this manner, the system would run out of stack space and cause an error. Therefore, larger objects like text and picture boxes are allocated from a slower but larger structure called the run-time heap. By balancing the allocation of resources, your application will run more efficiently.

Visual Basic .NET differentiates the two types of allocation by classifying objects as either a value or reference type. Value types are objects that are allocated on the stack and are used to improve performance when dealing with simple data types. All numeric data types as well as `Booleans`, `Dates`, and `Char` data types are all examples of value types. Value types are stored on the stack so that they can be allocated, accessed, and deallocated quickly and efficiently. Technically objects of this type are called structures; however, the only significant difference between a structure and an object in Visual Basic .NET is the way their memory is allocated. This should not concern you other than you will have to learn a slightly different way to allocate and deallocate objects in code other than the ones just mentioned.

Reference type variables like text boxes, labels, picture boxes, and buttons as well as user-defined objects are stored on the run-time heap.

Declaring and Instantiating Reference Data Types

An object can be declared from a reference data type using the following syntax:

```
Dim ObjectName As DataType
```

When you declare an object called `ObjectName` of a reference data type, you have not actually allocated memory for the data type, but you have a reference for that data type. You may think of a reference to a data type as similar to an index in the back of a book. The index indicates what and where the information is that you wish to read, and by following it you get the information you want. The information still must be created, in our case allocated, and initialized to the value you wish to store there.

By using the following code, you may allocate the memory required for that data type:

```
ObjectName = New Datatype()
```

Once the variable has been declared, it can be accessed in the same manner as with value type variables.

Declaring a Text Box in Code

Observe the following code that declares an object of the data type text box, allocates it, and initializes some of its properties:

```
Dim txtName As TextBox 'Declares an object of type text box
txtName = New TextBox() 'Allocates an object of type text box

txtName.Name = "txtName" 'Assigns the Name property the value txtName
txtName.Text = "" 'Clears the Text property
```

However, because a text box is an object that is placed on a form in a specific location and with a specific size, the previous code is not enough to properly specify a text box. You must specify a text box's `Location` and `Size`. Observe the Properties window in Figure 6.6. It shows the `Location` and `Size` for a text box.

Figure 6.6
`Location` and `Size` properties shown

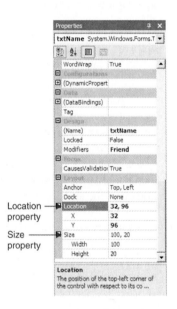

Notice they are not a single value. The size and location are actually objects themselves. These objects must be allocated dynamically using the keyword **New**. Additionally, they must be initialized to some value(s). An explanation of the initialization of objects will appear in greater detail later in the chapter, but for now just accept that you can place the values you need to initialize the object to in between parentheses with a comma separating them.

The following code initializes the text box's `Location` and `Size` objects:

```
txtName.Location = New Point(100, 100) 'Set the Location of the text box
txtName.Size = New Size(100, 20) 'Set the size of the text box
```

The final step is to add the text box to the forms `Controls` object. By adding it to the form, the form knows that the text box exists and it can interact with it.

```
Controls.Add(txtName) 'Add the text box to the form's controls object
```

6.3   Creating Your Own Classes

Despite the wide variety of data types available in Visual Basic .NET, sometimes the right type just doesn't exist. With Visual Basic .NET, developers have the power to create and define their own types. You might need to combine several variable types to create a record. This is easy to do, and it gives you the power to control all of the variables at once.

Classes in Visual Basic .NET can be created in a few ways. The simplest way is to create a class in code. Let's create a `Counter` class that is similar to the application you created in Chapter 3. Your new `Counter` class will allow you to create an object that will store an `Integer` value. The value will start at `1` and can be incremented by `1`. It can also be reset to `0`, but not to any other value.

A class can be thought of as being composed of three sets of definitions. To define a class and all of its attributes and methods, you enclose all of the contents using the following syntax.

```
Public Class ClassName
    'Properties definitions go here

    'Property Get/Set statements go here

    'Methods go here
End Class
```

`Public Class` are keywords that indicate to Visual Basic .NET that you are creating a class.

ClassName indicates the name of the class. A class name follows the same rules as when you create a variable name.

`End Class` are keywords that indicate to Visual Basic .NET that you have finished specifying the creation of a class.

The property definitions of a class that you define are conceptually the same as properties in the objects you are already familiar with. In a label object, the property `Text` was used to display text of a form. The `Text` is a property that could be declared as a `String`.

The property `Get/Set` statements allow you to detail how you will allow users of the class to access the individual properties defined for the class. For instance, in the `Counter` class, a rule was dictated that a counter can only be set to `0`. With a property `Set` statement, you can specify that the only value that can be set is a `0`, otherwise you would indicate that an error has occurred.

Methods of a class allow you to write subroutines and functions that have access to all of the properties defined within the class. Methods are how other objects and routines interact with the class you are defining.

Here are the steps entailed in creating the `Counter` class.

Step 1: Select `Add Class` from the `Project` menu. The window as seen in Figure 6.7 will appear.

Step 2: Specify the name of the class by changing `Class1.vb` to `Counter.vb`. Then click on the Open button.

Observe the changes to the development environment. The keywords `Public Class` and `End Class` enclose the `Counter` class and the new file is included in the Solution Explorer. (See Figure 6.8.)

Figure 6.7
New class window

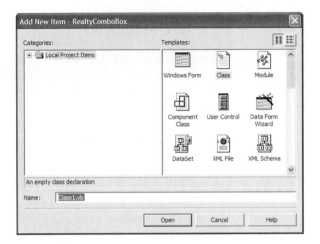

Figure 6.8   Development environment with new class added

Step 3: You must specify the properties of the class. Properties are in essence the variables of the class. For the `Counter` class, only one value must be stored, the current state of the counter. Therefore, only one property is required. An `Integer` property must be created to store the current value of the counter. The property is declared within the class definition. A property is defined with the following syntax:

```
Scope PropertyName As Datatype
```

The `Scope` of a property determines how visible this property is to other parts of the application. The scope can be `Public`, `Private`, or `Protected`. A `Public` scope gives the entire application access to the property, while a `Private` scope only allows methods from the class the property is defined within to have access to it. The `Protected` scope deals with more advanced concepts in object-oriented development and will be skipped for now.

The rules for specifying a data type for a property are the same as for declaring a variable. Therefore, a data type can be an `Integer`, `Single`, `String`, text box, and so on.

You now know enough to declare all of the properties for your `Counter` class. The code follows:

COACH'S TIP

When declaring properties in a class, you should start each property name with the letter m, for module, and then use the same naming convention as when declaring variables.

```
Public Class Counter
    Private mintCurrentCount As Integer
End Class
```

In order to allow properties to be accessed, Visual Basic .NET provides special functions to allow the developer to access each of the properties. If you do not want a property to be accessed directly, you could leave out the property function and it would not be accessible outside the class.

The functions are called `Get` and `Set`. `Get` allows you to specify what property variable is returned when the property is accessed. `Set` allows you to specify what property variable is set when you assign a value to the property.

The syntax for the `Get` and `Set` routines for a property are as follows:

```
Public Property PropertyName() As Datatype
     Get
          Return PropertyVariableName
     End Get
     Set
          PropertyVariableName = Value
     End Set
End Property
```

The *PropertyName* is the name of the property as it appears to the developer. The *PropertyVariableName* is the name of the property variable accessible only within the class and its methods.

In most cases, the coding of your `Get` routine will be minimal. Usually, you are just returning the `Private` property to another routine.

If there are no rules restricting the values that can be set to a property, then your `Set` statement can simply assign the quantity being passed in the `Value` parameter to the `Private` property. However, in the case of the `Counter` class, you only want to allow the counter to be set to `0`. Therefore, you must add code to the `Set` statement to check that the value being set is acceptable. If not, you can display an error message in a message box.

The `Get` and `Set` routines for your `Counter` class are as follows:

```
Public Property CurrentValue() As String
     Get
          Return mintCurrentCount
     End Get
     Set(ByVal Value As String)
          If (Value = 0) Then
               mintCurrentCount = Value
          Else
               MsgBox("You have attempted to set the counter to a value other" & _
                    " than 0")
          End If
     End Set
End Property
```

While you haven't learned enough to completely use your class yet, try Drills 6.10 and 6.11 to make sure you understand the syntax of creating a class definition, its properties, and property statements.

DRILL 6.10

Given the following declaration for a class, indicate which of the following references to a property are accessible.

```
Public Class DVD
    Private mTitle As String
    Private mYearOfRelease As Integer

    Public Property Title() As String
        Get
            Return mTitle
        End Get
        Set
            mTitle = Value
        End Set
    End Property
    Public Property YearOfRelease() As Single
        Get
            Return mYearOfRelease
        End Get
        Set
            mYearofRelease = Value
        End Set
    End Property
End Class
```

a.	b.	c.
Dim Shrek As DVD	Dim Shrek As DVD	Dim Shrek As DVD
Shrek = New DVD	Shrek = New DVD	Shrek = New DVD
Shrek.Title = "Shrek"	Shrek.mTitle = "Shrek"	Shrek.YearOfRelease = 2001

d.	e.	f.
Dim Shrek As DVD	Dim test As DVD	Dim test As DVD
Shrek = New DVD	test = New DVD	test = New DVD
Shrek.mYearOfRelease = 2001	MsgBox(test.Title)	MsgBox(test.mTitle)

g.	h.
Dim test As DVD	Dim test As DVD
test = New DVD	test = New DVD
MsgBox(test.YearOfRelease.ToString())	MsgBox(test.mYearOfRelease.ToString())

DRILL 6.11

Given the following declaration for a class, indicate which of the following references to a property are accessible.

```
Public Class DVD
    Private Title As String
    Private YearOfRelease As Integer

    Public Property mTitle() As Single
        Get
            Return Title
        End Get
        Set
            Title = Value
        End Set
    End Property
    Public Property mYearOfRelease() As Single
        Get
            Return YearOfRelease
        End Get
        Set
            YearofRelease = Value
        End Set
    End Property
End Class
```

a.	b.
Dim Shrek As DVD	Dim Shrek As DVD
Shrek = New DVD	Shrek = New DVD
Shrek.Title = "Shrek"	Shrek.mTitle = "Shrek"
c.	d.
Dim Shrek As DVD	Dim Shrek As DVD
Shrek = New DVD	Shrek = New DVD
Shrek.YearOfRelease = 2001	Shrek.mYearOfRelease = 2001

Writing Methods

While the ability to store different values in one construct is a huge advantage, you also need the ability to perform operations upon the properties stored within the class.

A method is an easy way to accomplish this.

By providing public methods to a class, you can control the way developers access the properties you specify. You have two choices as to the type of method that you can create. The simplest is a subroutine and will be explained here. Later the function method, which is slightly more complicated, will be explained.

The syntax for writing a simple subroutine method is as follows:

```
Public Sub MethodName()
    'Body of Method
End Sub
```

The keywords `Public Sub` specify the beginning of a subroutine that will be called `MethodName`. `MethodName` is the name of the routine and can be named using the same rules as were used for declaring a variable. The parentheses following `MethodName` are required, but for now nothing will be placed in between them.

The body of the method will be instructions that you wish to execute when the method is called. The keywords `End Sub` specify the end of the subroutine.

In our example, you might want to create a method that allows the user to call a `Reset` routine that sets the counter back to 0. Observe the following code that implements this functionality.

```
'Method to reset the counter to 0
Public Sub Reset()
    mintCurrentCount = 0
End Sub
```

A counter wouldn't be very useful without the ability to add or subtract 1 from it. So here is the code to increment or decrement the counter.

```
'Method to add 1 to the counter
Public Sub Increment()
    mintCurrentCount += 1
End Sub

'Method to subtract 1 from the counter
Public Sub Decrement()
    mintCurrentCount -= 1
End Sub
```

Writing Methods with Parameters

Often you will wish a method to provide different functionality depending upon **parameters** that are provided. Imagine you wanted to create a subroutine that allowed the user to enter a day of the week and the subroutine would output the employee's pay for that day.

If only one parameter were to be passed to a subroutine, the syntax would be as follows:

```
Public Sub MethodName(ParameterName As Datatype)
    'Body of Method
End Sub
```

The only difference between the declaration of a method with parameters and one without is the addition of code in between the parentheses. This code indicates the name and type of the parameter that will be passed to the method. The parameter name is used to reference the parameter within the method. It can be named using the same rules as were used for declaring a variable. The data type can be any valid data type such as an `Integer`, `String`, or text box.

Once a parameter is declared, it can be accessed within the method just as any of the properties of the class can.

The code to create a method called `LargeIncrement` that accepts a parameter called `intAmount` of the `Integer` type is as follows:

```
'Method to allow increments by more than 1 to the counter
Public Sub LargeIncrement(ByVal intAmount As Integer)
    mintCurrentCount += intAmount
End Sub
```

If more than one parameter is to be passed, you can create a method with as many parameters as you wish by separating the individual parameters with commas. The following code shows you the syntax for creating a method with three parameters, although this can be extended to as many parameters as you like.

```
Public Sub MethodName(ParameterName As Datatype, ParameterName As Datatype, _
                      ParameterName As Datatype)
      'Body of Method
End Sub
```

Sometimes it's difficult to see how all the pieces fit together, so here's the entire class as it would appear in Visual Basic. NET.

```
Public Class Counter
'Properties
Private mintCurrentCount As Integer

'Property statements
Public Property CurrentValue() As String
    Get
        Return mintCurrentCount
    End Get
    Set(ByVal Value As String)
        If (Value = 0) Then
            mintCurrentCount = Value
        Else
            MsgBox("You have attempted to set the counter to a value" & _
                " other than 0")
        End If
    End Set
End Property

'Method to reset the counter to 0
Public Sub Reset()
    mintCurrentCount = 0
End Sub

'Method to add 1 to the counter
Public Sub Increment()
    mintCurrentCount += 1
End Sub

'Method to subtract 1 from the counter
Public Sub Decrement()
    mintCurrentCount -= 1
End Sub

'Method to allow increments by more than 1 to the counter
Public Sub LargeIncrement(ByVal intAmount As Integer)
    mintCurrentCount += intAmount
End Sub

End Class
```

Example: Employee Class

Let's create an Employee class that stores an employee's name, hourly wages, and number of hours worked on each weekday during the week. The class should be written so that all of its properties can be set and modified. Additionally, the user should be able to output the daily or weekly pay for the employee.

Here are the steps entailed in creating the Employee class.

Step 1:   Select Add Class from the Project menu.

Step 2:   Specify the name of the class by changing Class1.vb to Employee.vb.

Step 3:   You must specify the properties of the class. You will require a property for each value you wish to be stored in an object created from this class. You will require a FirstName and LastName property of type String as well as MondayHours, TuesdayHours, WednesdayHours, ThursdayHours, and FridayHours of type Single. Additionally, you need a property, HourlyRate, of type Single that will store the rate of pay for the employee. Whether or not you need a property to store the employee's weekly pay is a matter of choice. You can either store it or simply calculate it whenever you need it. To save memory in your object, you will not store it as a property.

The code follows:

```
Public Class Employee
    Private mstrFirstName As String
    Private mstrLastName As String
    Private msngMondayHours As Single
    Private msngTuesdayHours As Single
    Private msngWednesdayHours As Single
    Private msngThursdayHours As Single
    Private msngFridayHours As Single
    Private msngHourlyRate As Single
End Class
```

Step 4:   You must add a Property statement for each property. The Get and Set routines for your Employee class are as follows:

```
Public Property FirstName() As String
    Get
        Return mstrFirstName
    End Get
    Set
        mstrFirstName = Value
    End Set
End Property

Public Property LastName() As String
    Get
        Return mstrLastName
    End Get
    Set
        mstrLastName = Value
    End Set
End Property

Public Property MondayHours() As Single
    Get
```

(continues)

(continued)

```
                    Return msngMondayHours
        End Get
        Set
                    msngMondayHours = Value
        End Set
    End Property
    Public Property TuesdayHours() As Single
        Get
                    Return msngTuesdayHours
        End Get
        Set
                    msngTuesdayHours = Value
        End Set
    End Property
    Public Property WednesdayHours() As Single
        Get
                    Return msngWednesdayHours
        End Get
        Set
                    msngWednesdayHours = Value
        End Set
    End Property
    Public Property ThursdayHours() As Single
        Get
                    Return msngThursdayHours
        End Get
        Set
                    msngThursdayHours = Value
        End Set
    End Property
    Public Property FridayHours() As Single
        Get
                    Return msngFridayHours
        End Get
        Set
                    msngFridayHours = Value
        End Set
    End Property
    Public Property HourlyRate() As Single
        Get
                    Return msngHourlyRate
        End Get
        Set
                    msngHourlyRate = Value
        End Set
    End Property
```

Step 5:   In your example, imagine if you wanted to output the weekly pay of the employee. A method could be written that adds up the individual total hours worked during the week and multiplies the result by the hourly rate. This value could then be output in a message box. Observe the following code that implements this functionality:

```
Public Sub OutputWeeklyPay()
    MsgBox ((msngHourlyRate*(msngMondayHours + msngTuesdayHours + _
            msngWednesdayHours + msngThursdayHours + _
            msngFridayHours)).ToString, _
        MsgBoxStyle.OKOnly,"Weekly Pay")
End Sub
```

Step 6: Finally, you should code a method called OutputDailyPay that accepts a parameter called strDayOfWeek of the String type, as follows:

```
Public Sub DailyPay(ByVal strDayOfWeek As String)
    Select Case strDayOfWeek.ToUpper
        Case "MONDAY"
            MsgBox(msngMondayHours.ToString)
        Case "TUESDAY"
            MsgBox(msngTuesdayHours.ToString)
        Case "WEDNESDAY"
            MsgBox(msngWednesdayHours.ToString)
        Case "THURSDAY"
            MsgBox(msngThursdayHours.ToString)
        Case "FRIDAY"
            MsgBox(msngFridayHours.ToString)
        Case Else
            MsgBox("Invalid day of the week entered")
    End Select
End Sub
```

COACH'S TIP

The ToUpper method of the String class was used so you wouldn't have to check the different capitalizations of each day of the week. By uppercasing the parameter, you can check the all capitals case and it will match any capitalization of the day of the week.

Creating an Object from a Class

When you define a class, all that you have accomplished is creating a model for declaring objects. In order to create an object of a class you must instantiate it. You can use the following syntax:

```
Dim objName As New ClassName()
```

The statement will declare and instantiate an object called objName of the class ClassName. If you do not wish to declare and instantiate an object in the same statement, you can separate them. Sometimes this is desirable, because you may not require the object in all cases and it would be a waste of resources to allocate it early. Why then should you declare the object early? Remember that variables in Visual Basic .NET are visible only in the scope of the code they are declared. Therefore, if you declared it exactly where you needed it, it might not be visible to the rest of the code. The syntax for declaring and instantiating an object separately is as follows:

```
Dim objName As ClassName
'Other code goes here
objName = New ClassName()
```

Therefore, if you wanted to declare an Employee object called JeffSalvage, you could use the following code:

```
Dim JeffSalvage As New Employee()
```

COACH'S TIP

You can also declare a class in one line and then allocate its memory in another, as demonstrated in Section 6.2.

```
Dim objName As ClassName()
objName = New ClassName()
```

Setting and Accessing Properties

Once an object has been instantiated, you will want to set its individual properties. Imagine that you want to set the object you just instantiated to the following values:

Property	Value
FirstName	Jeff
LastName	Salvage
MondayHours	7
TuesdayHours	9
WednesdayHours	8.5
ThursdayHours	7.5
FridayHours	8.0
HourlyWage	125.00

You are familiar with setting object properties through the Properties window; however, with an object declared from code you do not have this option available. Therefore, you need another syntax.

```
ObjectName.PropertyName = PropertyValue
```

So to declare an object `JeffSalvage` and set all the properties to the values in the previous chart, you would require the following code:

```
Dim JeffSalvage As New Employee()
JeffSalvage.FirstName = "Jeff"
JeffSalvage.LastName = "Salvage"
JeffSalvage.MondayHours = 7
JeffSalvage.TuesdayHours = 9
JeffSalvage.WednesdayHours = 8.5
JeffSalvage.ThursdayHours = 7.5
JeffSalvage.FridayHours = 8
JeffSalvage.HourlyRate = 125
```

Calling a Method

Once an object has been instantiated, its methods can be called. Calling a method is often referred to as invoking a method and can be accomplished using the following syntax:

ObjectName.*MethodName*()

Therefore, to invoke the method `OutputWeeklyPay` of the object `JeffSalvage`, you use the following code:

```
JeffSalvage.OutputWeeklyPay()
```

To invoke the method `OutputDailyPay` of the object `JeffSalvage` with the parameter `"Monday"`, you use the following code:

```
JeffSalvage.OutputDailyPay("Monday")
```

Constructors

Often as you are developing, you will find it helpful to code special methods called **constructors** to assist you in specifying how an object is initialized.

Constructors usually take one of two forms. Either you wish to provide default values to an object so that you can be sure what the values of an object are at the start, or you wish to provide a shortcut to the developer so that all or many of the properties can be initialized in a shorter amount of code.

You are already familiar with objects that have default values. If you declare a numeric variable, the variable is initialized to 0. If you add a text box to the form, its `Text` and `Name` properties default to `Text1`. These values are set by constructors that the developers of Visual Basic .NET created for these objects.

The easiest constructor to implement is the default constructor. It is called when an object is instantiated without any parameters being passed to it. The syntax for a constructor with no parameters is as follows:

```
Public Sub New()
' Initializations go here
End Sub
```

Therefore, if you wanted to default the hours worked each day to 8 and the hourly rate to $25.00 an hour, you could use the following code:

```
Public Sub New()
    msngMondayHours = 8
    msngTuesdayHours = 8
    msngWednesdayHours = 8
    msngThursdayHours = 8
    msngFridayHours = 8
    msngHourlyRate = 25
End Sub
```

When you place a text box on the form, more than just the `Text` and `Name` properties are set. The `Location` property is set to the specific X and Y coordinates of where you place the text box. Similarly, the `Size` property is set to the specific X and Y size of the text box. These values must be passed to the constructor of the text box. Often you will wish to create constructors that allow the setting of all the class's properties. This requires more code than the default constructor.

In order to set each property, you must pass a parameter to the method for each property you are setting. The parameter name must be different from the name of the property you will set it with. There is no difference in the way you declare the parameter for a constructor and any other method you might write.

Once you have declared all of the parameters, all that is left is for you to assign each property its corresponding parameter. The code for a constructor of this style can be seen in the following code:

```
Public Sub New(ByVal strFirstName As String, ByVal strLastName As String, _
               ByVal sngMondayHours As Single, _
               ByVal sngTuesdayHours As Single, _
               ByVal sngWednesdayHours As Single, _
               ByVal sngThursdayHours As Single, _
               ByVal sngFridayHours As Single, _
               ByVal sngHourlyRate As Single)
    mstrFirstName = strFirstName
    mstrLastName = strLastName
    msngMondayHours = sngMondayHours
    msngTuesdayHours = sngTuesdayHours
    msngWednesdayHours = sngWednesdayHours
    msngThursdayHours = sngThursdayHours
    msngFridayHours = sngFridayHours
    msngHourlyRate = sngHourlyRate
End Sub
```

In order for you to create more than one constructor, each constructor that you create must contain a different combination of types for the parameter list. This means that you can have one constructor with a parameter list of an `Integer` and a `String`, and another constructor of a parameter list of a `String` and an `Integer`, but you cannot have two constructors with an `Integer` and a `String` in the same order. The name that you give the parameters does not affect this situation.

Invoking a Constructor

You cannot specifically invoke a constructor whenever you wish. A constructor is called once, when the object is instantiated. If no parameters are passed to the object when it is instantiated, the default constructor is called (if it has been coded). If parameters are passed, then the compiler matches the type and order the parameters are given to one that you coded. If they match, that constructor is called. You can code as many constructors as you wish, as long as they differ in the sequence of data types for the parameters.

DRILL 6.12

Given the following definitions of three methods, show which of the following method calls are valid (assuming that `Option Strict` is On):

```
Private Sub DrillMethod1(ByVal intDrillValue As Integer, _
                         ByVal strDrillValue As String)

End Sub

Private Sub DrillMethod2(ByVal strDrillValue As String, _
                         ByVal intDrillValue As Integer)

End Sub

Private Sub DrillMethod3(ByVal strStringValue As Integer, _
                         ByVal intIntegerValue As String)

End Sub
```

(continues)

```
Dim intVal1 As Integer
Dim strVal2 As String
Dim intVal3 As Integer
Dim sngVal4 As Single


DrillMethod1(intVal1, strVal2)
DrillMethod1(strVal2, intVal1)
DrillMethod1(intVal3, strVal2)
DrillMethod2(intVal1, intVal3)
DrillMethod2(sngVal4, intVal1)
DrillMethod2(strVal2, intVal1)
DrillMethod3(intVal1, strVal2)
DrillMethod3(strVal2, intVal1)
DrillMethod3(intVal1, intVal3)
```

Example: Clock
Problem Description

Let's create a class that would store the information for a clock, display the current time, and allow the time to be incremented by one second at a time. While your `Clock` class will not keep actual time or increment time automatically, it will serve as an excellent example to demonstrate many of the new constructs you were just introduced to.

Problem Discussion

For simplicity, your clock will keep military time and should track hours, minutes, and seconds. Therefore, you will need three attributes, all of which will be stored as `Shorts`.

To define a class and all of its attributes and methods, enclose all of the contents using the following syntax:

```
Public Class Clock
    'Properties Definitions Go Here

    'Property Get/Set Statements Go Here

    'Methods Go Here
End Class
```

While it is not required to list the properties first, then the property `Get/Set` statements, and finally the methods, it is a good convention to follow.

Problem Solution

Observe how your `Clock` class is defined using the same syntax you are already familiar with.

```
Public Class Clock
```

Next you must declare any properties required for your class.

```
Private mshtHour As Short
Private mshtMinute As Short
Private mshtSecond As Short
```

Next you must create any Get/Set statements required for the new properties.

```
Public Property Hour() As Short
    Get
        Return mshtHour
    End Get
    Set(ByVal Value As Short)
        mshtHour = Value
    End Set
End Property

Public Property Minute() As Short
    Get
        Return mshtMinute
    End Get
    Set(ByVal Value As Short)
        mshtMinute = Value
    End Set
End Property

Public Property Second() As Short
    Get
        Return mshtSecond
    End Get
    Set(ByVal Value As Short)
        mshtSecond = Value
    End Set
End Property
```

By convention, it is a good practice to list all of the constructors before listing any additional methods.

In your implementation you are going to code two constructors. The first will be the default constructor that will accept no parameters. It will initialize the clock to 12:00.

```
Public Sub New()
    mshtHour = 12
    mshtMinute = 0 'Not really necessary, 0 is the default
    mshtSecond = 0 'Not really necessary, 0 is the default
End Sub
```

The second constructor will accept parameters for the hour, minute, and second to initialize your clock. All parameters must be present in order for this constructor to be called.

```
Public Sub New(ByVal shtHour As Short, ByVal shtMinute As Short, _
            ByVal shtSecond As Short)
    mshtHour = shtHour
    mshtMinute = shtMinute
    mshtSecond = shtSecond
End Sub
```

The next method to implement is to display the time. This implementation is fairly straightforward. If you wish to display the time in an H:M:S format, you can use the `Integer` class's method, `.ToString`, to perform the type conversion to convert the `Integer` to a `String` for purposes of display.

```
Public Sub OutputTime()
    MsgBox(mshtHour.ToString & ":" & mshtMinute.ToString & _
        ":" & mshtSecond.ToString)
End Function
```

The final method, `Increment`, will increment the time by 1 second. When you increment the seconds by 1 second, you must check if the total number of seconds equals 60. If it does, then you must set the seconds back to 0 and increment the total number of minutes. If the number of minutes now equals 60, then you must set the total number of minutes to 0 and increment the total number of hours by 1. Finally, if the total number of hours equals 24, then you reset the total number of hours to 0. The code follows:

```
Public Sub Increment()
    mshtsecond += 1
    If (mshtSecond = 60) Then
        mshtSecond = 0
        mshtMinute += 1
        If (mshtMinute = 60) Then
            mshtMinute = 0
            mshtHour = mshtHour + 1
            If mshtHour = 24 Then
                mshtHour = 0
            End If
        End If
    End If
End Sub
```

Finally, you end the declaration of the class with the following code:

```
End Class
```

Methods Using Functions

You may have noticed that all of the methods written so far either perform an assignment or output a result. While these operations are valuable, you will also have the need for a method to perform a calculation and return the result.

I mentioned earlier that there were two types of methods. The second type of method is a function. The only difference between a function method and a subroutine method is that a function method must return a value.

You have used methods like this before. All of the `String` methods introduced did not change the value of the `String` they were invoked from but returned a new `String` with the operation performed upon it.

To create a method that returns a value, use the following syntax:

```
Public Function MethodName(ParameterName As Datatype) As Datatype
    'Body of Method
End Function
```

The declaration of a function method is very similar. Instead of using the keyword `Sub` in the first and last line of the routine, you use the keyword `Function`. The method name and parameter list is identical to a subroutine method. Notice that this syntax shows one parameter, but a function method can have any number of parameters.

The main difference in the declaration is the addition of the keyword `As` followed by a data type. The data type must be declared indicating the type of variable that will be returned from the function.

Observe the following example of a method that returns the current time in your `Clock` class as a `String` as opposed to outputting the time as a `String`.

```
Public Function Time() As String
     Return(mintHour.ToString & ":" & mintMinute.ToString & _
          ":" & mintSecond.ToString)
End Function
```

Observe the following example, which demonstrates the declaration of an object called `MyTime` from the `Clock` class and an object called `strOutputTime` from the `String` class. It will be initialized to 8:00 AM and then `strOutputTime` will be assigned a `String` representation of the time by calling the `Time` method of the `Clock` class. Finally, you will output the `String` representation of the time using the `MsgBox` subroutine.

```
Dim MyTime As New Clock(8, 0, 0) 'Declare and Instantiate a Clock object
Dim strTime As String 'Declare a String object

strTime = MyTime.Time() 'Set the strTime to a String representation of the time

MsgBox(strTime) 'Output the Time
```

COACH'S CORNER

There are a great many objects built into Visual Basic .NET. While it would be too lengthy to explain all of them, here are a few of the most widely used objects that are located on the toolbox. Most of these objects are ones that you are already familiar with from using the Internet. **Check boxes**, **radio buttons**, **combo boxes**, and **list boxes** should all be familiar.

Check Box Control

A check box control is extremely useful when you want to toggle a value between checked or unchecked. A selected check box control will be indicated as one with a check mark visible. An unselected check box control is indicated as an empty box. A check box control can easily represent values that are either true/false or yes/no.

The ability to turn on or off the control makes the use of the check box control ideal for situations where a value is included or excluded from a list. Figure 6.9 shows how using a series of check boxes allows users to enter the characteristics of a house they may wish to purchase.

Figure 6.9
The Coach Realty with
check boxes

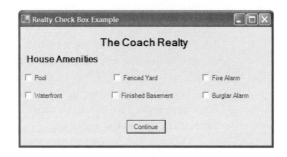

While a check box can be placed on a form in the same manner as any other control from the toolbox, care must be taken so that the check box is drawn large enough to fit the value you intend to place in the `Text` property. Of course, if you find you need to make the check box larger, you can do so by clicking on it and dragging the corner of the outline for the check box.

Once a check box is placed on the form, you should set the `Name` and `Text` properties. The `Name` property should reflect the intent of the check box and begin with the prefix `chk`. The `Text` property of a check box is similar to the `Text` property of a label control. Whatever you enter as the `Text` property will be displayed to the right of the check box.

When you run an application with a form containing a check box, you may click on the check box to select it or unselect it. However, typically the user of the application cannot change the text associated with it.

Within the application you need the ability to determine whether a check box is checked or unchecked by accessing the `Checked` property. If the check box is checked, it will return `True`, otherwise it will return `False`.

Example: Oscar Voting Application with Check Boxes
Problem Description

The addition of check box controls allows you to improve the interface of your Voting Booth application. While it may have been possible for you to spell the names of presidential candidates properly, what are the odds that you could spell all the names of the best actors and actresses nominated for an Oscar award? Probably pretty slim. The check box interface is an improvement. Instead of simply rewriting the Voting Booth application you created in Chapter 4, let's create an entirely new one for the Oscar awards.

With a check box, you do not have to worry about the spelling of the candidates' names—you can redesign the interface so that it uses check box controls instead of text box controls to gather the votes. Figure 6.10 shows the newly designed Oscar Nomination application.

Problem Discussion

In your previous Voting Booth application, you could only enter a vote for one person and one race at a time. Now you can easily select the candidates you want from both awards presented on this screen and not have to worry about data entry problems. You can also change the way you indicate the winner of the award. All too often programmers will continue to do things the same way they have done them in the past. When new interface options are available, you should rethink the way you develop your application. In this case, instead of showing the results in a label, you will indicate the number of votes for each candidate next to their respective check box. This can be seen in Figure 6.11.

Figure 6.10
Sketch of the Oscar
Nomination application

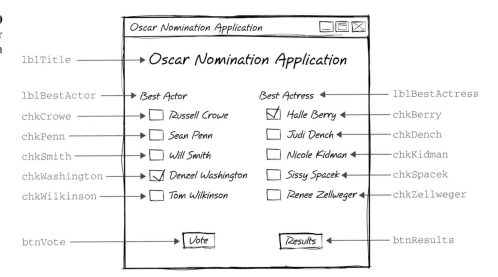

Figure 6.11
Oscar Nomination application with results and check boxes

Problem Solution

By now you can place controls on the form without the need for step-by-step instructions. Place the three labels, 10 check boxes, and two buttons in their appropriate places.

You need to declare a `Short` variable for each candidate to store the number of votes they receive. Place the following code in the form's `Declarations` section.

```
'Variables to store votes for Best Actor
Dim shtCroweCount As Short
Dim shtPennCount As Short
Dim shtSmithCount As Short
Dim shtWashingtonCount As Short
Dim shtWilkinsonCount As Short

'Variables to store votes for Best Actress
Dim shtBerryCount As Short
Dim shtDenchCount As Short
Dim shtKidmanCount As Short
Dim shtSpacekCount As Short
Dim shtZellwegerCount As Short
```

When the `btnResults` button is clicked, you will append the number of votes each candidate received to the `Text` property of their check box. You will also add a set of parentheses around the number of votes to improve readability.

```
Private Sub btnResults_Click(...
    chkCrowe.Text &= " (" & shtCroweCount.ToString & ")"
    chkPenn.Text &= " (" & shtPennCount.ToString & ")"
    chkSmith.Text &= " (" & shtSmithCount.ToString & ")"
    chkWashington.Text &= " (" & shtWashingtonCount.ToString & ")"
    chkWilkinson.Text &= " (" & shtWilkinsonCount.ToString & ")"
    chkBerry.Text &= " (" & shtBerryCount.ToString & ")"
    chkDench.Text &= " (" & shtDenchCount.ToString & ")"
    chkKidman.Text &= " (" & shtKidmanCount.ToString & ")"
    chkSpacek.Text &= " (" & shtSpacekCount.ToString & ")"
    chkZellweger.Text &= " (" & shtZellwegerCount.ToString & ")"
End Sub
```

When the voter clicks on the btnVote button, you must account for their vote and clear the check box control. As mentioned earlier, a selected check box will have a value of True. Therefore, inspect each check box for True, increment the appropriate variable, and reset the check box value to False. This can be seen in the following code:

```
Private Sub btnVote_Click(...
    If (chkCrowe.Checked = True) Then 'Process vote for Russell Crowe
        shtCroweCount += 1
        chkCrowe.Checked = False 'Erase Vote
    End If
    If (chkPenn.Checked = True) Then 'Process vote for Sean Penn
        shtPennCount += 1
        chkPenn.Checked = False 'Erase Vote
    End If
    If (chkSmith.Checked = True) Then 'Process vote for Will Smith
        shtSmithCount += 1
        chkSmith.Checked = False 'Erase Vote
    End If
    If (chkWashington.Checked = True) Then 'Process vote for Denzel Washington
        shtWashingtonCount += 1
        chkWashington.Checked = False 'Erase Vote
    End If
    If (chkWilkinson.Checked = True) Then 'Process vote for Tom Wilkinson
        shtWilkinsonCount += 1
        chkWilkinson.Checked = False 'Erase Vote
    End If
    If (chkBerry.Checked = True) Then 'Process vote for Halle Berry
        shtBerryCount += 1
        chkBerry.Checked = False 'Erase Vote
    End If
    If (chkDench.Checked = True) Then 'Process vote for Judi Dench
        shtDenchCount += 1
        chkDench.Checked = False 'Erase Vote
    End If
    If (chkKidman.Checked = True) Then 'Process vote for Nicole Kidman
        shtKidmanCount += 1
        chkKidman.Checked = False 'Erase Vote
    End If
    If (chkSpacek.Checked = True) Then 'Process vote for Sissy Spacek
        shtSpacekCount += 1
        chkSpacek.Checked = False 'Erase Vote
```

(continues)

(continued)
```
    End If
    If (chkZellweger.Checked = True) Then 'Process vote for Renee Zellweger
        shtZellwegerCount += 1
        chkZellweger.Checked = False 'Erase Vote
    End If
End Sub
```

If you think about your implementation, you might realize that you developed the application with the same basic problem that the Florida voting machines had. It allows voters to vote more than once!

It is possible to add code to prevent duplicate votes from being counted, but then you are in no better shape than the Floridian machines. You could add code that warns a voter that they have double-voted and make sure they change the vote before it counts. However, it is better to prevent the mistake from happening in the first place. The solution is discussed in the next section. You will use a radio button control instead of a check box control.

Radio Button Control

A radio button control is extremely useful when you want to allow a user to enter a value from a list of values but only allow one item from the list to be selected. Figure 6.12 shows an example of an information form for a realty company. This form contains several radio buttons that allow the user to enter the range of income for a person. Notice that an income of under $30,000 is indicated. When you use a radio button, only one of the options may be selected at a time.

Figure 6.12
Realty application using radio buttons

Radio buttons can also be placed on the form from the toolbox; however, an issue exists when you wish to have more than one set of information stored as radio buttons within a single form. This can be seen in Figure 6.13.

Figure 6.13
Multiple sets of radio buttons on a form

The problem is that you wish to record a value for a Personal Income and a House Price simultaneously. If you place radio buttons directly on the form, you will not be able to achieve this.

Instead, you must first place a container control such as a **group box** or panel control on the form. You need one group box control for each group of radio buttons you desire. See the form in Figure 6.14, which was created correctly with a group box control for Personal Income and another group box control for House Price.

Figure 6.14
Correct multiple sets of radio buttons on a form

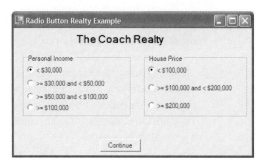

COACH'S TIP

When using a group box or panel control to contain other controls like radio buttons, place the group box on the control first. Then create each of the controls to be contained on the group box directly on the group box control itself. By doing this, you will be able to move all the controls contained within the group box by moving the group box itself.

Example: Improved Oscar Nomination Application with Radio Buttons
Problem Description

Now you can correct your problem of the Oscar Nomination application allowing double votes. Florida would be so jealous! Al Gore might even have become president. By using a series of radio buttons, you can allow only one candidate to be selected for each race. See the Figure 6.15 showing the newly designed Oscar Nomination application.

Figure 6.15
Improved Oscar Nomination application

COACH'S TIP

The prefix for a group box is `grp`.

Problem Discussion

Notice that the two sets of radio buttons are grouped in separate group box controls. If they weren't, then all the radio buttons on the form would be treated as one group, so you couldn't vote in both the Best Actor and the Best Actress categories at the same time.

Notice in Figure 6.16 that you display the results of the voting in the same manner that you did in the check box implementation.

Figure 6.16
Results shown using new application

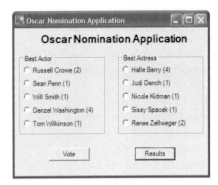

Problem Solution

The code for the `btnResults` button is very similar to the code you used for check boxes instead of radio buttons. When the `btnResults` button is clicked, you append the results of each candidate to the `Text` property associated with the radio button.

```
Private Sub btnResults_Click(...
    rbCrowe.Text &= " (" & shtCroweCount.ToString & ")"
    rbPenn.Text &= " (" & shtPennCount.ToString & ")"
    rbSmith.Text &= " (" & shtSmithCount.ToString & ")"
    rbWashington.Text &= " (" & shtWashingtonCount.ToString & ")"
    rbWilkinson.Text &= " (" & shtWilkinsonCount.ToString & ")"
    rbBerry.Text &= " (" & shtBerryCount.ToString & ")"
    rbDench.Text &= " (" & shtDenchCount.ToString & ")"
    rbKidman.Text &= " (" & shtKidmanCount.ToString & ")"
    rbSpacek.Text &= " (" & shtSpacekCount.ToString & ")"
    rbZellweger.Text &= " (" & shtZellwegerCount.ToString & ")"
End Sub
```

The code for the `btnVote` button is also very similar to the code for the check box version of the Voting Booth application. If the value of the radio button is `True`, then you add 1 to the appropriate candidate's counter. To reset the radio button, you reset it back to `False`.

```
Private Sub Vote_Click(...
    If (rbCrowe.Checked = True) Then 'Process vote for Russell Crowe
        shtCroweCount += 1
        rbCrowe.Checked = False 'Erase Vote
    ElseIf (rbPenn.Checked = True) Then 'Process vote for Sean Penn
        shtPennCount += 1
        rbPenn.Checked = False 'Erase Vote
    ElseIf (rbSmith.Checked = True) Then 'Process vote for Will Smith
```

(continues)

(continued)

```
        shtSmithCount += 1
        rbSmith.Checked = False 'Erase Vote
    ElseIf (rbWashington.Checked = True) Then 'Process vote for Denzel Washington
        shtWashingtonCount += 1
        rbWashington.Checked = False 'Erase Vote
    ElseIf (rbWilkinson.Checked = True) Then 'Process vote for Tom Wilkinson
        shtWilkinsonCount += 1
        rbWilkinson.Checked = False 'Erase Vote
    ElseIf (rbBerry.Checked = True) Then 'Process vote for Halle Berry
        shtBerryCount += 1
        rbBerry.Checked = False 'Erase Vote
    ElseIf (rbDench.Checked = True) Then 'Process vote for Judi Dench
        shtDenchCount += 1
        rbDench.Checked = False 'Erase Vote
    ElseIf (rbKidman.Checked = True) Then 'Process vote for Nicole Kidman
        shtKidmanCount += 1
        rbKidman.Checked = False 'Erase Vote
    ElseIf (rbSpacek.Checked = True) Then 'Process vote for Sissy Spacek
        shtSpacekCount += 1
        rbSpacek.Checked = False 'Erase Vote
    ElseIf (rbZellweger.Checked = True) Then 'Process vote for Renee Zellweger
        shtZellwegerCount += 1
        rbZellweger.Checked = False 'Erase Vote
    End If
End Sub
```

The remainder of the code for this application is the same as in the check box version.

 COACH'S TIP

One difference between the solution with radio buttons and the solution with check boxes is that since only one value can be picked from a radio button, the individual radio buttons are compared using an If/ElseIf structure instead of a series of If statements like the check box example.

Combo Box and List Box Controls

Radio buttons and check boxes are excellent ways of allowing a user to enter values from a list of predetermined choices. However, what happens if the number of choices to choose from is rather large? With our current methods, you would have a problem. Imagine if you had to create a form with many more awards on it. You would have to list each and every nominee on the form in a separate check box or radio button. This would not only take a long time, but it would also produce applications that are unwieldy in size.

Combo and list boxes are excellent ways to solve this problem. The next two figures show how your Realty application would look using a set of combo boxes (Figure 6.17) and list boxes (Figure 6.18).

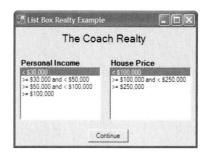

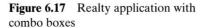

Figure 6.17   Realty application with combo boxes

Figure 6.18   Realty application with list boxes

As you can see, a combo box takes up much less space than the radio buttons you previously used. Fortunately, this reduction in space does not come at the cost of usability. With a combo box, the currently selected value is displayed. You can see this in the House Price combo box. However, when a combo box is clicked on, all of its possible values are displayed and can be selected from. This is shown in the Personal Income combo box.

The list box is a compromise between the methods used with combo boxes and radio buttons. The developer can choose how many elements of the list are displayed at once. In Figure 6.18, all of the list items are displayed. However, you will learn how to limit the number of items displayed when you develop a new version of the Oscar Nomination application. When the number of list items is greater than the space allowed to display them, a scroll bar will appear on the right side of the list box allowing the user to display the remainder of the list.

The steps in using a combo or list box are not very different from the other controls in this chapter, with the exception of the `Items` property. The `Items` property is actually an object called a collection (explained in Chapter 10). For now all that you need to know is that you can enter the list of values to appear with the `String Collection Editor` that appears when you click on the `Items` property of either the combo or list box. (See Figure 6.19.)

Figure 6.19
Enter list items into a combo box

To determine what value has been selected, use the `SelectedItem` property. It will return a `String` containing the selected item.

Example: Improved Oscar Nomination Application with Combo Boxes

Problem Description

With the addition of the combo and list box controls, you can greatly increase the amount of information that you can display on a single form. Instead of just showing two awards, you could show many more. Observe Figure 6.20, which demonstrates the newly created Oscar Nomination application that shows three awards in the same space that you had two awards before. In this case, you default each combo box to be blank. When you click on the combo box, a list of every nominee for the award drops down. When you click on the individual nominee, that nominee is selected from the list. Figure 6.21 demonstrates the application developed with list boxes. You can see in the Best Actor category that only two of the candidates are displayed. The scroll bar to the right of the control will allow the user to select the nondisplayed candidates.

Problem Discussion

Both forms are created almost identically. See the following properties and the values you need to set them to for creating both applications.

Problem Solution

In both applications, you must modify the code of the application. The variables required for both applications are the same. You must create new counters for the additional candidates in the new races.

```
'Variables to store votes for Best Actor
Dim shtCroweCount As Short
Dim shtPennCount As Short
Dim shtSmithCount As Short
Dim shtWashingtonCount As Short
Dim shtWilkinsonCount As Short

'Variables to store votes for Best Actress
Dim shtBerryCount As Short
Dim shtDenchCount As Short
Dim shtKidmanCount As Short
Dim shtSpacekCount As Short
Dim shtZellwegerCount As Short

'Variables to store votes for Best Picture
Dim shtLordRingsCount As Short
Dim shtBeautifulMindCount As Short
Dim shtGosfordParkCount As Short
Dim shtInTheBedroomCount As Short
Dim shtMoulinRougeCount As Short
```

You must modify the `btnVote_Click` routine to handle the new categories and controls. The easiest way to track the votes is to use a `Select Case` statement for each race. You can access the value selected in the combo box by accessing the `Text` property. Then you compare that value to one spelling of the candidate's name (the one in the `Items` property), since you know the only possible spelling.

The code is nearly identical between the combo and list box implementations. The only real difference is in the names of the controls. The two sets of code follow.

Figure 6.20 Oscar Nomination application with combo boxes

Figure 6.21 Oscar Nomination application with list boxes

To create the new Oscar Nomination application with combo boxes, you must add three combo boxes and labels as follows:

Label lblBestActor

Text: Best Actor

ComboBox cboBestActor

Items: Russell Crowe

Sean Penn

Will Smith

Denzel Washington

Tom Wilkinson

DropDownStyle: DropDownList

Label lblBestActress

Text: Best Actress

ComboBox cboBestActress

Items: Halle Berry

Judy Dench

Nicole Kidman

Sissy Spacek

Renee Zellweger

DropDownStyle: DropDownList

Label lblBestPicture

Text: Best Picture

ComboBox cboBestPicture

Items: Lord of the Rings

A Beautiful Mind

Gosford Park

In the Bedroom

Moulin Rouge

DropDownStyle: DropDownList

To create the new Oscar Nomination application with list boxes, you must add three list boxes and labels as follows:

Label lblBestActor

Text: Best Actor

ListBox lstBestActor

Items: Russell Crowe

Sean Penn

Will Smith

Denzel Washington

Tom Wilkinson

Label lblBestActress

Text: Best Actress

ListBox lstBestActress

Items: Halle Berry

Judy Dench

Nicole Kidman

Sissy Spacek

Renee Zellweger

Label lblBestPicture

Text: Best Picture

ListBox lstBestPicture

Items: Lord of the Rings

A Beautiful Mind

Gosford Park

In the Bedroom

Moulin Rouge

```
'Combo box implementation
Private Sub btnVote_Click(...
    'Process Best Actor vote
    Select Case cboBestActor.SelectedItem
        Case "Russell Crowe"
            shtCroweCount += 1
        Case "Sean Penn"
            shtPennCount += 1
        Case "Will Smith"
            shtSmithCount += 1
        Case "Denzel Washington"
            shtWashingtonCount += 1
        Case "Tom Wilkinson"
            shtWilkinsonCount += 1
    End Select
    cboBestActor.SelectedIndex = -1 'Reset the Combo Box to unselected

    'Process Best Actress vote
    Select Case cboBestActress.SelectedItem
        Case "Halle Berry"
            shtBerryCount += 1
        Case "Judi Dench"
            shtDenchCount += 1
        Case "Nicole Kidman"
            shtKidmanCount += 1
        Case "Sissy Spacek"
            shtSpacekCount += 1
        Case "Renee Zellweger"
            shtZellwegerCount += 1
    End Select
    cboBestActress.SelectedIndex = -1 'Reset the Combo Box to unselected

    'Process Best Picture vote
    Select Case cboBestPicture.SelectedItem
        Case "The Lord of the Rings"
            shtLordRingsCount += 1
        Case "A Beautiful Mind"
            shtBeautifulMindCount += 1
        Case "Gosford Park"
            shtGosfordParkCount += 1
        Case "In the Bedroom"
            shtInTheBedroomCount += 1
        Case "Moulin Rouge"
            shtMoulinRougeCount += 1
    End Select
    cboBestPicture.SelectedIndex = -1 'Reset the Combo Box to unselected
End Sub


'List box implementation
Private Sub btnVote_Click(...
    'Process Best Actor vote
    Select Case lstBestActor.SelectedItem
```

(continues)

(continued)

```
        Case "Russell Crowe"
            shtCroweCount += 1
        Case "Sean Penn"
            shtPennCount += 1
        Case "Will Smith"
            shtSmithCount += 1
        Case "Denzel Washington"
            shtWashingtonCount += 1
        Case "Tom Wilkinson"
            shtWilkinsonCount += 1
    End Select
    lstBestActor.SelectedIndex = -1 'Reset the List Box to unselected

    'Process Best Actress vote
    Select Case lstBestActress.SelectedItem
        Case "Halle Berry"
            shtBerryCount += 1
        Case "Judi Dench"
            shtDenchCount += 1
        Case "Nicole Kidman"
            shtKidmanCount += 1
        Case "Sissy Spacek"
            shtSpacekCount += 1
        Case "Renee Zellweger"
            shtZellwegerCount += 1
    End Select
    lstBestActress.SelectedIndex = -1 'Reset the List Box to unselected

    'Process Best Picture vote
    Select Case lstBestPicture.SelectedItem
        Case "The Lord of the Rings"
            shtLordRingsCount += 1
        Case "A Beautiful Mind"
            shtBeautifulMindCount += 1
        Case "Gosford Park"
            shtGosfordParkCount += 1
        Case "In the Bedroom"
            shtInTheBedroomCount += 1
        Case "Moulin Rouge"
            shtMoulinRougeCount += 1
    End Select
    lstBestPicture.SelectedIndex = -1 'Reset the List Box to unselected
End Sub
```

COACH'S TIP

You may have wondered why the `SelectedIndex` of each list box was set to `-1`. A list box may have an index of `0` to 1 less than the number of items contained in its `Items` collection. By setting it to `-1`, you are ensuring that no item is selected in the list box.

Finally, you need to change the code to display the results for all three races. For lack of a better way to display the results, you will append each nominee's vote count to the end of the appropriate list item.

This will require you to learn a concept that will be further explained in Chapter 8. If you do not completely grasp it now, do not worry. To access each list item individually requires you to access them in the order that they appear in the `Items` collection. The first item in a collection is referred to by its position in the collection. This position is referred to as an index. The first value in the collection is assigned an index number of 0, the second value an index of 1, the third value an index of 2, and so on. This is very similar to accessing individual characters in a `String`. The first character is at position 0, the second character at position 2, and so on. Therefore, in the `cboBestActor` combo box, Russell Crowe would have an index of 0, Sean Penn would have an index of 1, Will Smith would have an index of 2, Denzel Washington would have an index of 3, and Tom Wilkinson would have an index of 4.

To access each item in the list, you place the index within parentheses.

```
'Combo box implementation
Private Sub btnResults_Click(By...
    'Best Actor Results
    cboBestActor.Items(0) &= " (" & shtCroweCount & ")"
    cboBestActor.Items(1) &= " (" & shtPennCount & ")"
    cboBestActor.Items(2) &= " (" & shtSmithCount & ")"
    cboBestActor.Items(3) &= " (" & shtWashingtonCount & ")"
    cboBestActor.Items(4) &= " (" & shtWilkinsonCount & ")"

    'Best Actress Results
    cboBestActress.Items(0) &= " (" & shtBerryCount & ")"
    cboBestActress.Items(1) &= " (" & shtDenchCount & ")"
    cboBestActress.Items(2) &= " (" & shtKidmanCount & ")"
    cboBestActress.Items(3) &= " (" & shtSpacekCount & ")"
    cboBestActress.Items(4) &= " (" & shtZellwegerCount & ")"

    'Best Picture Results
    cboBestPicture.Items(0) &= " (" & shtLordRingsCount & ")"
    cboBestPicture.Items(1) &= " (" & shtBeautifulMindCount & ")"
    cboBestPicture.Items(2) &= " (" & shtGosfordParkCount & ")"
    cboBestPicture.Items(3) &= " (" & shtInTheBedroomCount & ")"
    cboBestPicture.Items(4) &= " (" & shtMoulinRougeCount & ")"
End Sub


'List box implementation
Private Sub btnResults_Click(...
    'Best Actor Results
    lstBestActor.Items(0) &= " (" & shtCroweCount & ")"
    lstBestActor.Items(1) &= " (" & shtPennCount & ")"
    lstBestActor.Items(2) &= " (" & shtSmithCount & ")"
    lstBestActor.Items(3) &= " (" & shtWashingtonCount & ")"
    lstBestActor.Items(4) &= " (" & shtWilkinsonCount & ")"

    'Best Actress Results
    lstBestActress.Items(0) &= " (" & shtBerryCount & ")"
    lstBestActress.Items(1) &= " (" & shtDenchCount & ")"
    lstBestActress.Items(2) &= " (" & shtKidmanCount & ")"
    lstBestActress.Items(3) &= " (" & shtSpacekCount & ")"
    lstBestActress.Items(4) &= " (" & shtZellwegerCount & ")"
```

(continues)

(continued)

```
     'Best Picture Results
     lstBestPicture.Items(0) &= " (" & shtLordRingsCount & ")"
     lstBestPicture.Items(1) &= " (" & shtBeautifulMindCount & ")"
     lstBestPicture.Items(2) &= " (" & shtGosfordParkCount & ")"
     lstBestPicture.Items(3) &= " (" & shtInTheBedroomCount & ")"
     lstBestPicture.Items(4) &= " (" & shtMoulinRougeCount & ")"
End Sub
```

Manually Adding List Items

While Visual Basic .NET provides an easy interface to add items to the collection for a combo or list box, it is not always convenient to do so interactively. Often you will want to add or remove values of the `Items` collection for a combo or list box programmatically. Imagine if instead of the applications you write being predefined, you create an application that allows a user to customize the form without having access to the source code of the application. While you do not know enough to create a truly useful application yet, it is worth showing how to do this now.

This can be seen in the following code, which illustrates the syntax of adding an item to the combo box.

ComboBoxName.`Items.Add(`*"Item to Add"*`)`

By repeatedly calling `Add`, you can add as many values to the `Items` collection as you desire.

If instead of creating the list of nominees at design time you choose to set them programmatically, the code would be as follows:

```
cboBestActor.Items.Add("Russell Crowe")
cboBestActor.Items.Add("Sean Penn")
cboBestActor.Items.Add("Will Smith")
cboBestActor.Items.Add("Denzel Washington")
cboBestActor.Items.Add("Tom Wilkinson")
```

The method is the same for list boxes:

`ListBox.Items.Add(`*"Item to Add"*`)`

```
lstBestActor.Items.Add("Russell Crowe")
lstBestActor.Items.Add("Sean Penn")
lstBestActor.Items.Add("Will Smith")
lstBestActor.Items.Add("Denzel Washington")
lstBestActor.Items.Add("Tom Wilkinson")
```

◆ 6.4 Case Study

Problem Description

Rewrite your `Employee` class from earlier in the chapter to track and process additional information. Instead of just tracking the hours worked during each day of the week, create an object that can track the hours worked, the hours billed, and the project number the hours are billed to. Often when employees are contracted to other companies, they must track their time so that the client can be billed appropriately. It is fairly common for an employee to work more hours than they bill. Nonbillable hours must also be tracked because employees would not be very happy if they did not get paid for the work that they did. While the original `Employee` class tracked the workweek as Monday through Friday, you should not restrict your workweek in this manner. Therefore, create a billing cycle of five days so that a person does not have to work on a specific day of the week.

Additionally, you should provide a mechanism to output the net profit, amount billed, and amount paid in wages during a billable cycle.

Problem Discussion

There are many ways to tackle this problem. You might think about writing a single class called `Employee` that solves all the problems. This can be very cumbersome.

When working with classes it is best to break up your problem into smaller, easier-to-solve problems. Therefore, you will code this solution by creating three classes instead of one. There is no one clear way to break up a problem; however, if you try to divide the work into logical objects that contain only the data and method required of that object, you will find that building your complex object will be quite simple.

Problem Solution

Therefore, you are going to start by creating an object to track the information pertaining to the workday. This object, `WorkDay`, will track the date, the hours worked, the hours billed, and the project the hours were billed to. You should create a `Property` statement for each property. Additionally, you should create a default constructor as well as one that accepts parameters. While not required, it is not a bad idea to create a method called `NonBillableHours` that computes the number of hours worked that were not billable. The construction of this class is fairly straightforward and is shown in the following code:

```
Public Class WorkDay
    Private mdteDayWorked As Date
    Private msngHoursWorked As Single
    Private msngHoursBilled As Single
    Private mintProjectNumber As Integer

    'Default constructor
    Public Sub New()
        mdteDayWorked = Today()
        msngHoursWorked = 0
        msngHoursBilled = 0
        mintProjectNumber = 0
    End Sub

    'Constructor with parameters
    Public Sub New(ByVal dteDayWorked As Date, _
                ByVal sngHoursWorked As Single, _
                ByVal sngHoursBilled As Single, _
                ByVal intProjectNumber As Integer)
        mdteDayWorked = dteDayWorked
        msngHoursWorked = sngHoursWorked
        msngHoursBilled = sngHoursBilled
        mintProjectNumber = intProjectNumber
    End Sub
```

(continues)

(continued)

```
    'Property Statements
    Public Property DayWorked() As Date
        Get
            Return mdteDayWorked
        End Get
        Set(ByVal Value As Date)
            mdteDayWorked = Value
        End Set
    End Property

    Public Property HoursWorked() As Single
        Get
            Return msngHoursWorked
        End Get
        Set(ByVal Value As Single)
            msngHoursWorked = Value
        End Set
    End Property

    Public Property HoursBilled() As Single
        Get
            Return msngHoursBilled
        End Get
        Set(ByVal Value As Single)
            msngHoursBilled = Value
        End Set
    End Property

    Public Property ProjectNumber() As Integer
        Get
            Return mintProjectNumber
        End Get
        Set(ByVal Value As Integer)
            mintProjectNumber = Value
        End Set
    End Property

    'Method to return the total number of non-billable work hours
    Public Function NonBillableHours() As Single
        Return msngHoursWorked - msngHoursBilled
    End Function
End Class
```

The next class, `BillingCycle`, will allow the combining of five `WorkDay` objects into one billing cycle. The `BillingCycle` class will require five properties. Each property will be a `WorkDay` object and represent one day that an employee worked. The constructor for this class is not required but is desired. Either the user of the class would have to allocate a `WorkDay` as needed, or you can create a constructor to allocate the `WorkDay` objects when the `BillingCycle` object is instantiated. Additionally, methods should be created to return the total hours billable, the total hours worked, and the total hours worked that were nonbillable during a billing cycle.

```
Public Class BillingCycle
    Private mDay1 As WorkDay
    Private mDay2 As WorkDay
    Private mDay3 As WorkDay
    Private mDay4 As WorkDay
    Private mDay5 As WorkDay

    'Default constructor
    Public Sub New()
        mDay1 = New WorkDay()
        mDay2 = New WorkDay()
        mDay3 = New WorkDay()
        mDay4 = New WorkDay()
        mDay5 = New WorkDay()
    End Sub

    'Property Statements
    Public Property Day1() As WorkDay
        Get
            Return mDay1
        End Get
        Set(ByVal Value As WorkDay)
            mDay1 = Value
        End Set
    End Property
    Public Property Day2() As WorkDay
        Get
            Return mDay2
        End Get
        Set(ByVal Value As WorkDay)
            mDay2 = Value
        End Set
    End Property
    Public Property Day3() As WorkDay
        Get
            Return mDay3
        End Get
        Set(ByVal Value As WorkDay)
            mDay3 = Value
        End Set
    End Property
    Public Property Day4() As WorkDay
        Get
            Return mDay4
        End Get
        Set(ByVal Value As WorkDay)
            mDay4 = Value
        End Set
    End Property
    Public Property Day5() As WorkDay
        Get
            Return mDay5
        End Get
```

(continues)

(continued)

```
        Set(ByVal Value As WorkDay)
            mDay5 = Value
        End Set
    End Property


    'Method returning the total hours working in this billing cycle
    Public Function TotalHoursWorked() As Single
        Return (mDay1.HoursWorked + mDay2.HoursWorked + mDay3.HoursWorked + _
            mDay4.HoursWorked + mDay5.HoursWorked)
    End Function


    'Method returning the total hours billed in this billing cycle
    Public Function TotalHoursBilled() As Single
        Return (mDay1.HoursBilled + mDay2.HoursBilled + mDay3.HoursBilled + _
            mDay4.HoursBilled + mDay5.HoursBilled)
    End Function


    'Method returning the total hours worked that were
    'not billable in this billing cycle
    Public Function TotalNonBillableHours() As Single
        Return (mDay1.NonBillableHours + mDay2.NonBillableHours + _
            mDay3.NonBillableHours + mDay4.NonBillableHours + _
            mDay5.NonBillableHours)
    End Function


End Class
```

Finally, you will create an `Employee` class. By creating a `WorkDay` and `BillableCycle` object, you will find most of the work is already done for you. The `Employee` class should have properties for the employee's first name, last name, wage, and billable rate and the last billing cycle. A default constructor as well as one that accepts parameters should be created. `Property` statements for all of the class's properties should also be created. Methods should be created to return the total wages, total billables, and net profit for the billing cycle. Each can be calculated by combining the information obtained from the methods of the object containing the last billing cycle with the financial information stored in the `Employee` object. Finally, you will create a method that outputs the financial information. This can be implemented by calling the previous methods implemented for the `Employee` class.

```
Public Class Employee
    Private mstrFirstName As String
    Private mstrLastName As String
    Private msngHourlyWage As String
    Private msngBillableRate As String
    Private mLastBillingCycle As BillingCycle

    'Default Constructor
    Public Sub New()
        mstrFirstName = ""
        mstrLastName = ""
        msngHourlyWage = 0
        msngBillableRate = 0
```

(continues)

(continued)

```
        mLastBillingCycle = New BillingCycle() 'Allocate a Billing Cycle
    End Sub


    'Constructor with Parameters
    Public Sub New(ByVal strFirstName As String, ByVal strLastName As String, _
                ByVal sngHourlyWage As Single, _
                ByVal sngBillableRate As Single)
        mstrFirstName = strFirstName
        mstrLastName = strLastName
        msngHourlyWage = sngHourlyWage
        msngBillableRate = sngBillableRate
        mLastBillingCycle = New BillingCycle()
    End Sub


    'Property Statements
    Public Property FirstName() As String
        Get
            Return mstrFirstName
        End Get
        Set(ByVal Value As String)
            mstrFirstName = Value
        End Set
    End Property


    Public Property LastName() As String
        Get
            Return mstrLastName
        End Get
        Set(ByVal Value As String)
            mstrLastName = Value
        End Set
    End Property


    Public Property HourlyWage() As Single
        Get
            Return msngHourlyWage
        End Get
        Set(ByVal Value As Single)
            msngHourlyWage = Value
        End Set
    End Property
    Public Property BillableRate() As Single
        Get
            Return msngBillableRate
        End Get
        Set(ByVal Value As Single)
            msngBillableRate = Value
        End Set
    End Property
    Public Property LastBillingCycle() As BillingCycle
        Get
            Return mLastBillingCycle
        End Get
```

(continues)

(continued)

```
        Set(ByVal Value As BillingCycle)
            mLastBillingCycle = Value
        End Set
    End Property


    'Method to return the total wage paid this billing cycle
    Public Function BillingCycleWage() As Single
        Return msngHourlyWage * mLastBillingCycle.TotalHoursWorked
    End Function


    'Method to return the total amount billed during this billing cycle
    Public Function BillingCycleBillables() As Single
        Return msngBillableRate * mLastBillingCycle.TotalHoursBilled
    End Function


    'Method to return the net profit earned during this billing cycle
    Public Function BillingCycleNetProfit() As Single
        Return BillingCycleBillables() - BillingCycleWage()
    End Function


    'Method to output the net profit, amount billed, and wage paid
    'during this billing cycle
    Public Sub OutputStatus()
        MsgBox(mstrFirstName & " " & mstrLastName & _
              "'s Net Profit for the billing cycle is " _
              & Format(BillingCycleNetProfit(), "Currency"))
        MsgBox(mstrFirstName & " " & mstrLastName & _
              "'s Billables for the billing cycle is " _
              & Format(BillingCycleBillables(), "Currency"))
        MsgBox(mstrFirstName & " " & mstrLastName & _
              "'s Wage for the billing cycle is " _
              & Format(BillingCycleWage(), "Currency"))
    End Sub
End Class
```

With your `Employee` class created, you can see how easy it is to store the information of a billing cycle in an object and display a summary of the results.

```
'Declare and instantiate an Employee called JeffSalvage
Dim JeffSalvage As New Employee("Jeff", "Salvage", 125, 200)

'Enter the hours billed, hours worked and date of the first day
'of the last billing cycle for Jeff Salvage
JeffSalvage.LastBillingCycle.Day1.HoursBilled = 8
JeffSalvage.LastBillingCycle.Day1.HoursWorked = 8
JeffSalvage.LastBillingCycle.Day1.DayWorked = #4/8/2002#
JeffSalvage.LastBillingCycle.Day1.ProjectNumber = 101

'Enter the hours billed, hours worked and date of the second day
'of the last billing cycle for Jeff Salvage
JeffSalvage.LastBillingCycle.Day2.HoursBilled = 9
JeffSalvage.LastBillingCycle.Day2.HoursWorked = 8
```

(continues)

(continued)

```
JeffSalvage.LastBillingCycle.Day2.DayWorked = #4/9/2002#
JeffSalvage.LastBillingCycle.Day2.ProjectNumber = 101

'Enter the hours billed, hours worked and date of the third day
'of the last billing cycle for Jeff Salvage
JeffSalvage.LastBillingCycle.Day3.HoursBilled = 7
JeffSalvage.LastBillingCycle.Day3.HoursWorked = 8
JeffSalvage.LastBillingCycle.Day3.DayWorked = #4/10/2002#
JeffSalvage.LastBillingCycle.Day3.ProjectNumber = 101

'Enter the hours billed, hours worked and date of the fourth day
'of the last billing cycle for Jeff Salvage
JeffSalvage.LastBillingCycle.Day4.HoursBilled = 6
JeffSalvage.LastBillingCycle.Day4.HoursWorked = 8
JeffSalvage.LastBillingCycle.Day4.DayWorked = #4/11/2002#
JeffSalvage.LastBillingCycle.Day4.ProjectNumber = 101

'Enter the hours billed, hours worked and date of the fifth day
'of the last billing cycle for Jeff Salvage
JeffSalvage.LastBillingCycle.Day5.HoursBilled = 8
JeffSalvage.LastBillingCycle.Day5.HoursWorked = 8
JeffSalvage.LastBillingCycle.Day5.DayWorked = #4/12/2002#
JeffSalvage.LastBillingCycle.Day5.ProjectNumber = 101

'Output the net profit, wage, and billables for Jeff Salvage
JeffSalvage.OutputStatus()
```

 COACH'S TIP

Review the previous solution. Observe how because each object provided methods to calculate totals about the information stored within it that you did not have a complex job of calculating to implement the `Employee` class. By developing your classes carefully, you will save yourself from a great deal of frustration later.

Key Words and Key Terms

Check Box
> A control that allows the user to select or deselect individual items.

Class
> A template for creating objects defining properties and methods.

Combo Box
> A control that allows the user to select an item from a predetermined list of choices. Only the selected item is displayed, unless the combo box is clicked on.

Constructor
> A special method that is called automatically when an object is instantiated.

Encapsulation
> Restricting the access of data from programmers.

Group Box
> A control that allows the user to group other controls together.

Inheritance

The ability to create a class from another defintion of a class.

Instantiate

The act of creating an object from a class.

List Box

A control that allows the user to select an item from a predetermined list of choices. Some or all of the items in the list are displayed at once.

Method

A function or subroutine defined within a class.

New

A keyword used to create an object from a class.

Object

The instantiation of a class.

Parameter

A variable passed to a method from another routine.

Polymorphism

The concept of using a single name for different behaviors depending upon the object it belongs to.

Radio Button

A control that allows the user to select a single item from a set controls.

Answers to Chapter's Drills

Drill 6.1

The following is the matching of terms and examples.

a. inheritance	3. The ability to create a new class based on the definition of an existing one.
b. polymorphism	1. When a function takes on different meanings based upon what object is being used.
c. encapsulation	2. The hiding of the details of the implementation from a developer.
d. instantiation	5. The creation of an object from a class.
e. class	4. The "blueprint" of an object.

Drill 6.2

While all television sets are different, the following is a list of the properties and methods for my television set.

Properties

Volume Level: Specifies the current volume between 0 and 30.

Brightness: Specifies how bright the screen is with a value between 0 and 20.

Contrast: Specifies the contrast level of the screen between 0 and 20.

Power On/Off: Indicates whether the power of the TV is on or off.

Methods

Volume Up: Changes the volume level by increasing it by 1.

Volume Down: Changes the volume level by decreasing it by 1.

Channel Up: Changes the current channel by increasing it by 1.

Channel Down: Changes the current channel by increasing it by 1.

Power Toggle: Changes the power to the opposite of the current state.

Direct Entering of Channel: Allows a channel number to be entered directly.

Return: Sets the channel to the previous channel.

TV/Video: Changes the display to the opposite of the current state. Either it can be set for television watching or the VCR.

Mute: Sets the volume level to 0.

Drill 6.3

a. This is a **valid** call to the method `ToUpper`. `ToUpper` is a method of the `String` class that converts the characters stored within the `String` to uppercase and returns the result. No parameters are required.

b. This is an **invalid** call to the method `ToUpper`. `ToUpper` is a method of the `String` class that converts the characters stored within the `String` to uppercase and returns the result. No parameters are required, but one is supplied.

c. This is an **invalid** call to the method `Length`. `Length` is a method of the `String` class that returns an `Integer` indicating the number of characters in the `String`. No parameters are required, but one is supplied.

d. This is a **valid** call to the method `Trim`. `Trim` is a method of the `String` class that strips leading and trailing blank characters from the characters stored within the `String` and returns the result. No parameters are required.

e. This is an **invalid** call to the method `SubString`. `SubString` is a method of the `String` class that returns a portion of the characters stored within the `String`. The first parameter must be an `Integer` indicating the first character to be contained within the resulting `String`. As the first parameter here is a `String`, a compile error will occur.

f. This is an **invalid** call to the method `SubString`. `SubString` is a method of the `String` class that returns a portion of the characters stored within the `String`. The first parameter must be an `Integer` indicating the first character to be contained within the resulting `String`. As the first parameter here is a `String`, a compile error will occur.

g. This is a **valid** call to the method `SubString`. `SubString` is a method of the `String` class that returns a portion of the characters stored within the `String`. The first parameter must be an `Integer` indicating the first character to be contained within the resulting `String`. If no other parameters are specified, the method will return a `String` containing characters starting with the location of the first parameter and include all the remaining characters in the `String`.

h. This is a **valid** call to the method `SubString`. `SubString` is a method of the `String` class that returns a portion of the characters stored within the `String`. The first parameter must be an `Integer` indicating the first character to be contained within the resulting `String`. The second parameter, while optional, if present will determine the number of characters to return.

i. This is an **invalid** call because the method `GiveMeAnA` does not exist in the `String` class.

Drill 6.4

The `String` `"DO OR DO NOT, THERE IS NO TRY."` is displayed in the message box. When the `ToUpper` method is called, a `String` is returned that contains the same characters as in the original `String`, but they are all converted to uppercase. Punctuation like commas and periods are not affected.

Drill 6.5

The String "do or do not, there is no try." is displayed in the message box. When the ToUpper method is called, a String is returned that contains the same characters as in the original String, but they are all converted to uppercase. Punctuation like commas and periods are not affected.

Drill 6.6

The String "there is no try." is displayed in the message box. The first character displayed is the 15th in the String. Remember, the 1st character is at position 0. Since no 2nd parameter is specified, all the remaining characters in the String are returned.

Drill 6.7

The String "there" is displayed in the message box. The first character displayed is the 15th in the String. Remember, the 1st character is at position 0. Then, including the first character displayed, five characters are displayed.

Drill 6.8

The total number of characters in the String is 30, so "30" is output in the message box. Remember, spaces, commas, and periods are all counted as characters.

Drill 6.9

The String "do or do not, there is no try." is displayed in the message box. When the ToUpper method is called, a String is returned that contains the same characters as in the original String, but they are all converted to uppercase. However, then the method ToLower is invoked upon the String that was returned. ToLower returns the String in all lowercase.

Drill 6.10

a. This assignment is **valid**. The Title property is made accessible by the Public Property statement in the class definition.

b. This assignment is **invalid**. The mTitle property is declared as Private to the class and can only be accessed through another routine.

c. This assignment is **valid**. The YearOfRelease property is made accessible by the Public Property statement in the class definition.

d. This assignment is **invalid**. The mYearOfRelease property is declared as Private to the class and can only be accessed through another routine.

e. The accessing of the property is **valid**. The Title property is made accessible by the Public Property statement in the class definition.

f. The accessing of the property is **invalid**. The mTitle property is declared as Private to the class and can only be accessed through another routine.

g. The accessing of the property is **valid**. The YearOfRelease property is made accessible by the Public Property statement in the class definition.

h. The accessing of the property is **invalid**. The mYearOfRelease property is declared as Private to the class and can only be accessed through another routine.

Drill 6.11

This drill is obviously very similar to Drill 6.10. The major difference is that the m in the private class variables has been placed on the Public Property methods instead of the variables themselves. The use of the m is a convention that should, but does not have to, be followed. It is important to realize the accessibility of Private variables and

`Public Property` methods is determined by the scope indicated, not by the way you name them.

   a. This assignment is **invalid**. The `Title` variable is declared as `Private` to the class and can only be accessed through another routine.

   b. This assignment is **valid**. The `mTitle` property is made accessible by the `Public Property` statement in the class definition.

   c. This assignment is **invalid**. The `YearOfRelease` variable is declared as `Private` to the class and can only be accessed through another routine.

   d. This assignment is **valid**. The `mYearOfRelease` property is made accessible by the `Public Property` statement in the class definition.

Drill 6.12

In order for each subroutine call to be valid, the data type of each parameter passed must match the data type of the parameter in the exact order as specified in the subroutine definition.

In the first subroutine call, `DrillMethod1(intVal1, strVal2)`, the subroutine is expecting a parameter of the data type `Integer` followed by a parameter of the data type `String`. Since `intVal1` is declared as an `Integer` and `strVal2` is declared as a `String`, this is a **valid** subroutine call.

In the second subroutine call, `DrillMethod1(strVal2, intVal1)`, the subroutine is expecting a parameter of the data type `Integer` followed by a parameter of the data type `String`. Since `intVal1` is declared as an `Integer` and `strVal2` is declared as a `String`, this is an **invalid** subroutine call. The data types of the parameters were correct but in the wrong order.

In the third subroutine call, `DrillMethod1(intVal3, strVal2)`, the subroutine is expecting a parameter of the data type `Integer` followed by a parameter of the data type `String`. Since `intVal3` is declared as an `Integer` and `strVal2` is declared as a `String`, this is a **valid** subroutine call.

In the fourth subroutine call, `DrillMethod2(intVal1, intVal3)`, the subroutine is expecting a parameter of the data type `String` followed by a parameter of the data type `Integer`. Since `intVal1` is declared as an `Integer` and `intVal3` is declared as an `Integer`, this is an **invalid** subroutine call. The data types of the second parameter were correct but the first parameter was incorrect.

In the fifth subroutine call, `DrillMethod2(sngVal4, intVal1)`, the subroutine is expecting a parameter of the data type `String` followed by a parameter of the data type `Integer`. Since `sngVal4` is declared as a `Single` and `intVal1` is declared as an `Integer`, this is an **invalid** subroutine call. The data types of the second parameter were correct but the first parameter was incorrect.

In the sixth subroutine call, `DrillMethod2(strVal2, intVal1)`, the subroutine is expecting a parameter of the data type `String` followed by a parameter of the data type `Integer`. Since `strVal2` is declared as a `String` and `intVal1` is declared as an `Integer`, this is a **valid** subroutine call.

In the seventh subroutine call, `DrillMethod3(intVal1, strVal2)`, the subroutine is expecting a parameter of the data type `Integer` followed by a parameter of the data type `String`. Even though the parameter names are named as if they were the opposite, the name of the parameter does not matter. The only issue is the data types of the parameters. Since `strVal2` is declared as a `String` and `intVal1` is declared as an `Integer`, this is a **valid** subroutine call.

In the eighth subroutine call, `DrillMethod3(strVal2, intVal1)`, the subroutine is expecting a parameter of the data type `Integer` followed by a parameter of the data type `String`. Even though the parameter names are named as if they were the opposite, the name of the parameter does not matter. The only issue is the data types of the parameters. Since `intVal1` is declared as an `Integer` and `strVal2` is declared as a `String`, this is an **invalid** subroutine call.

In the ninth subroutine call, `DrillMethod3(intVal1, intVal3)`, the subroutine is expecting a parameter of the data type `Integer` followed by a parameter of the data type `String`. Even though the parameter names are named as if they were the opposite, the name of the parameter does not matter. The only issue is the data types of the parameters. Since `intVal1` is declared as an `Integer`, it is a valid parameter; however, since `intVal3` is also declared as an `Integer`, this is an **invalid** subroutine call.

Additional Exercises

1. _____ is the concept of hiding data within an object.

   a. Encapsulation   b. Polymorphism   c. Inheritance
   d. Instantiation   e. None of these

2. _____ is the concept that new objects can be created by extending the definitions of previously constructed objects.

   a. Encapsulation   b. Polymorphism   c. Inheritance
   d. Instantiation   e. None of these

3. _____ allows different objects to perform different functionality with the same method name.

   a. Encapsulation   b. Polymorphism   c. Inheritance
   d. Instantiation   e. None of these

4. Allocating memory for an object is known as _____.

   a. Deallocating   b. Instantiating   c. Referencing
   d. Inheriting   e. None of these

Questions 5–8 are true or false.

5. A class may be thought of as the blueprint for creating an object.

6. When an object created from the `String` class's `ToUpper` method is called, the object's characters are converted to uppercase and the result is stored within the object itself.

7. Value type variables require the use of the `New` keyword when declaring and allocating the variable.

8. What is the output of the following code?

```
Dim strName As String
strName = "Jeff Salvage"
MsgBox(strName.ToUpper().SubString(4))
```

9. What is the output of the following code?

```
Dim strName As String
strName = "Jeff Salvage"
MsgBox(strName.Length().ToString)
```

10. What is the output of the following code?

```
Dim strName As String
strName = "Jeff Salvage"
MsgBox(strName.Substring(5))
```

11. Objects created from classes that you have written are _____.

    a. Value Types   b. Reference Types

Questions 12–19 are true or false.

12. Properties within a class declared with a `Private` scope cannot be accessed from methods within that class.

13. All properties must be accessible outside the object.

14. Only one constructor may exist for a class.

15. Methods can be both functions and subroutines.

16. A check box control is useful when you only want one value to be selected from a list of values.

17. A combo box control is useful because it does not require a lot of space on the form.

18. A check box control usually does not require the `Text` field to be initialized.

19. You can set up different sets of radio buttons by setting a property within the control to select which set it would belong to.

20. Which of the following are reference type objects?

    a. Single   b. Integer   c. Double   d. text box   e. combo box

21. Rank the following controls in the order, from smallest to largest, of the amount of space required on the form to display a list of information. If two require the same amount of space, indicate so.

    a. check box   b. combo box   c. list box   d. radio buttons

22. Which control can contain other controls in it?

    a. check box   b. combo box   c. group box   d. list box
    e. radio buttons   f. text box

23. If you were designing a form to gather the possible majors (notice plural) a student is interested in, which control would you use to gather the information?

    a. check box   b. combo box   c. group box   d. list box
    e. radio buttons   f. text box

24. If you were designing a form to gather the name of students' favorite teacher, which control would you use to gather the information and why did you pick it? Assume there were 100 teachers at the school.

    a. check box   b. combo box   c. group box   d. list box
    e. radio buttons   f. text box

25. If you were designing a form to gather the names of the car companies (notice plural) that the user liked, which control would you use to gather the information? Also, indicate why you picked it.

    a. check box   b. combo box   c. group box   d. list box
    e. radio buttons   f. text box

26. Write a class called `Employee`. It should have properties of `FirstName`, `LastName`, `Salary`, `Position`, `Password`, and `YearsOfEmployment`. It should have Property methods to set and access the `FirstName`, `LastName`, `Position`, and `YearsOfEmployment` properties. There should also be a constructor to initialize all of the properties. A method should exist to set the `Salary` that requires a password. A method, `GiveRaise`, should exist to give an employee a raise. It should require a password.

27. Write a class called `Student`. It should have properties of `FirstName`, `LastName`, `CreditsCompleted`, `GPA`, and `Major`. It should have `Property` methods to set and access the `FirstName`, `LastName`, and `Major` properties. There should be a constructor that accepts `FirstName`, `LastName`, and `Major` and initializes `GPA` to 0 and `CreditsCompleted` to 0. A `RecordGrade` grade method should exist that will accept a grade and the number of credits for the course. `RecordGrade` should calculate the new `GPA` and store that as well. Finally, there should be an `OutputStudent` method that outputs all of their information in a message box.

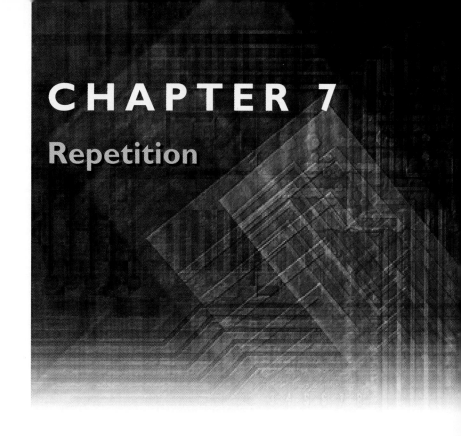

CHAPTER 7
Repetition

CHAPTER
OBJECTIVES

- ◆ Introduce the concept of executing code more than once
- ◆ Introduce the concept of **For loops**
- ◆ Introduce the concept of **Do While loops**
- ◆ Introduce the concept of **Do Until loops**
- ◆ Introduce nested loops

Chapter 1 introduced various algorithms. Throughout the first six chapters, many constructs were introduced to help you implement algorithms similar to the ones discussed. However, until now, an important construct, repetition, had been skipped. In Chapter 1, the algorithm to brush one's teeth stated that you would "Move the toothbrush back and forth across your teeth" and "Repeat until all teeth are well cleaned." The ability to repeat a step until a condition is met will now be explained.

In Visual Basic .NET, the ability to perform a statement or series of statements over and over again is accomplished in three ways: For loops, Do loops, and While loops.

7.1 For Loops

The choice of loop construct is mainly one of style. In fact, any loop construct can be represented using any of the other loop constructs. However, usually there is a natural choice of looping construct for your problem. A For loop is selected when the loop starts at a specific value, increments by a set amount, and terminates at a specific value.

Do and While loops are similar but are typically used when the initial condition(s) and/or terminating condition(s) are comparisons between more dynamic conditions.

The For loop is very versatile with lots of options. This does not have to be confusing. If you break the loop into separate components, understand the order in which they are executed, and evaluate them carefully, the evaluation of For loops can be simple.

COACH'S WARNING

It is important to master conditional expression evaluation in the decision-making chapter before attempting to learn Visual Basic .NET's looping constructs. The evaluation of conditional expressions and looping expressions are exactly the same. The conditional expression evaluation section in Chapter 4 is stated in more detail than in this chapter.

The following is a syntax for the `For` loop:

```
For  LoopCounter = InitialValue  To  TerminatingValue
        ' Program Statement(s)
Next  LoopCounter
```

Follow this sequence for the correct evaluation of a `For` loop:

1 The `LoopCounter` is set to the value `InitialValue`.
2 The `LoopCounter` is compared to the `TerminatingValue`. If the `LoopCounter` is greater than the `TerminatingValue`, go to step 6. Otherwise, continue with the execution of the loop.
3 The program statements contained in the body of the loop are executed.
4 The value `LoopCounter` is incremented.
5 Go to step 2.
6 Exit the loop.

Observe the flowchart in Figure 7.1 demonstrating the behavior of the `For` loop.

COACH'S TIP

The repeated nature of a loop is often referred to as iterating.

Figure 7.1
Flowchart of a `For` loop

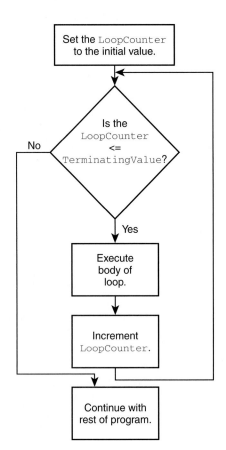

The following is an example of a `For` loop that adds up all the values between 1 and 3 and then displays the result in a message box:

```
Private Sub btnOutput_Click(...
    Dim intSum As Integer
    Dim intCounter As Integer
    intSum = 0

    For intCounter = 1 To 3
        intSum += intCounter
    Next intCounter

    MsgBox(intSum.ToString())

End Sub
```

> **COACH'S TIP**
>
> Remember += is a shortcut operator. The code could have been written intSum = intSum + intCounter.

To help you completely understand the execution of the `For` loop, trace through the following example using the Debugger. Since you do not wish to step through all of the form's initialization routines, follow these steps to start debugging when the `btnOutput` button is clicked.

Entering the Debugger

Step 1: Click the left mouse button on the first line of the `Click` event for the `btnForLoop` button.

Step 2: Right-click and a pop-up menu will appear.

Step 3: Click on the `Run to Cursor` menu option.

Step 4: When the application executes, click on the `btnForLoop` button. A window like the one shown in Figure 7.2 will appear.

Figure 7.2 Trace of `For` loop

In order to trace the execution with continuous feedback, you might want the value of `intSum` and `intCounter` to be displayed during the entire execution of the For loop. You can accomplish this with the `Watch Window`.

The `Watch Window` is a special window that can be opened when the Debugger is running. It allows programmers to list values that they wish to be continuously displayed while the program is being traced. Previously, if you wanted to display the contents of a variable or control, you would mouse over the reference in the code.

With this application, there are two values that are worth displaying: `intSum` and `intCounter`. To display them in a `Watch Window`, follow these steps:

Step 1:   Right-click on the `intSum` variable name.

Step 2:   Select the `Add Watch` option.

Step 3:   The `Watch Window` with the `intSum` variable and its current value appear.

Step 4:   Right-click on the `intCounter` variable name.

Step 5:   Select the `Add Watch` option.

Step 6:   The `Watch Window` with the `intSum` variable and its current value appear.

Initially, both `intSum` and `intCounter` are equal to 0. This is shown in Figure 7.3.

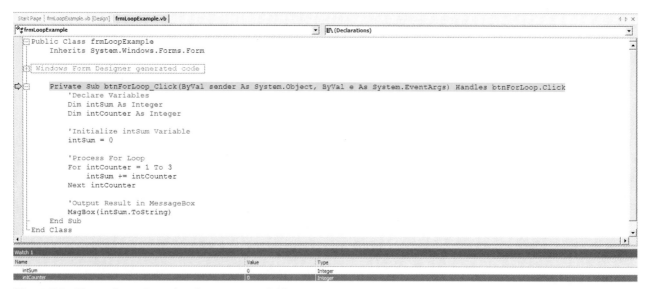

Figure 7.3   Trace of For loop showing Watch variables

Step 1:   When you press the `<F11>` key, the application steps into the `btnForLoop_Click()` event. Since variable declarations are not really programming lines that execute (they only allocate space), you proceed to the first programming line. This is shown in Figure 7.4, where you are about to execute the statement highlighted in yellow.

Step 2:   Although you do not observe a difference when initializing `intSum` to 0, you do so to ensure that it contains 0. `Integers` will be defaulted to 0, so no change is observed in the `Watch Window` when you press the `<F10>` key. This is seen in Figure 7.5.

Step 3:   When you press the `<F10>` key the next time, you execute the first line of the For loop. This initializes the value of the `intCounter` variable to 1. This is seen in Figure 7.6, where the `Watch Window` displays the value of `intCounter` now equaling 1.

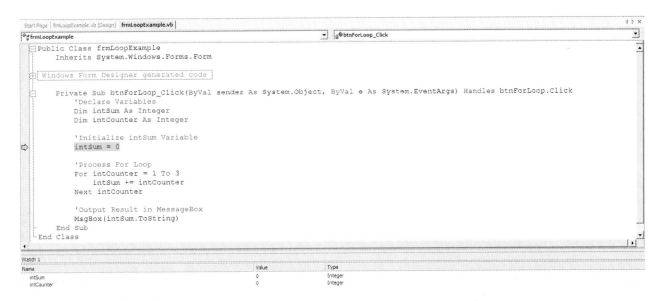

Figure 7.4 Trace of For loop

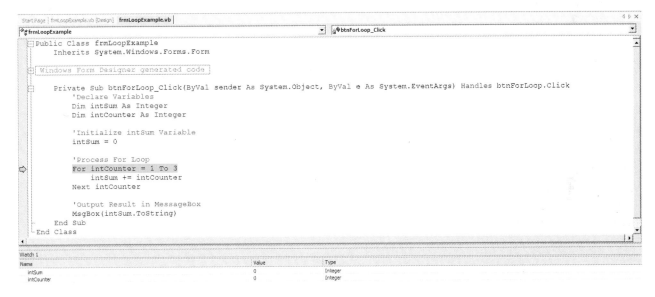

Figure 7.5 Trace of For loop

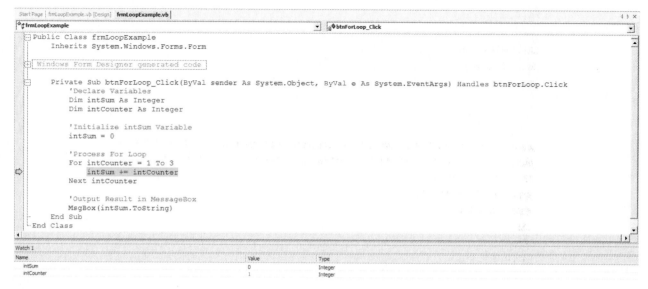

Figure 7.6   Trace of `For` loop

COACH'S TIP

Notice that the variable whose value changed has turned red in the Watch Window.

Step 4: You are now ready to execute the body of the `For` loop for the first time. If you press the `<F10>` key again, you execute the body of the loop and add `intCounter` to `intSum`. Since the `intCounter` is equal to 1 and the `intSum` is equal to 0, the result of the addition is 1. This is stored in `intSum`. Figure 7.7 shows the changed value of `intSum` and that you are ready to execute the increment statement of the loop.

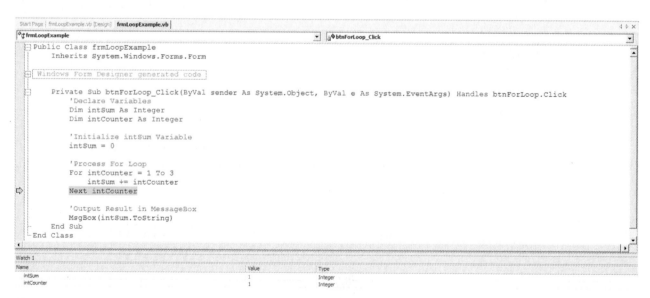

Figure 7.7   Trace of `For` loop

Step 5: By pressing the `<F10>` key again, you execute the increment statement of the `For` loop. This increases the value of the `intCounter` variable by 1. Therefore, `intCounter` now equals 2. This is seen in Figure 7.8.

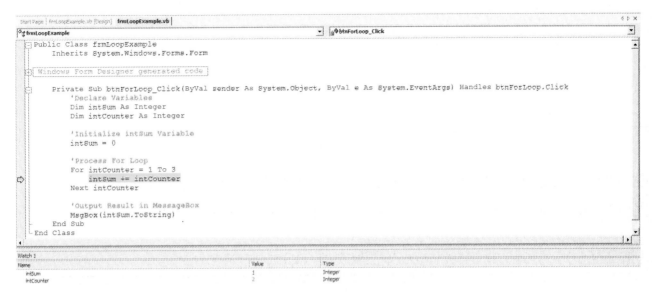

Figure 7.8 Trace of For loop

Step 6: When you press the <F10> key again, intCounter is compared to 3. Since 2 is less than 3, you continue by executing the body of the loop. This time, the intCounter variable equals 2, so 2 is added to the value of the intSum variable, 1, and intSum is set to 3. (See Figure 7.9.)

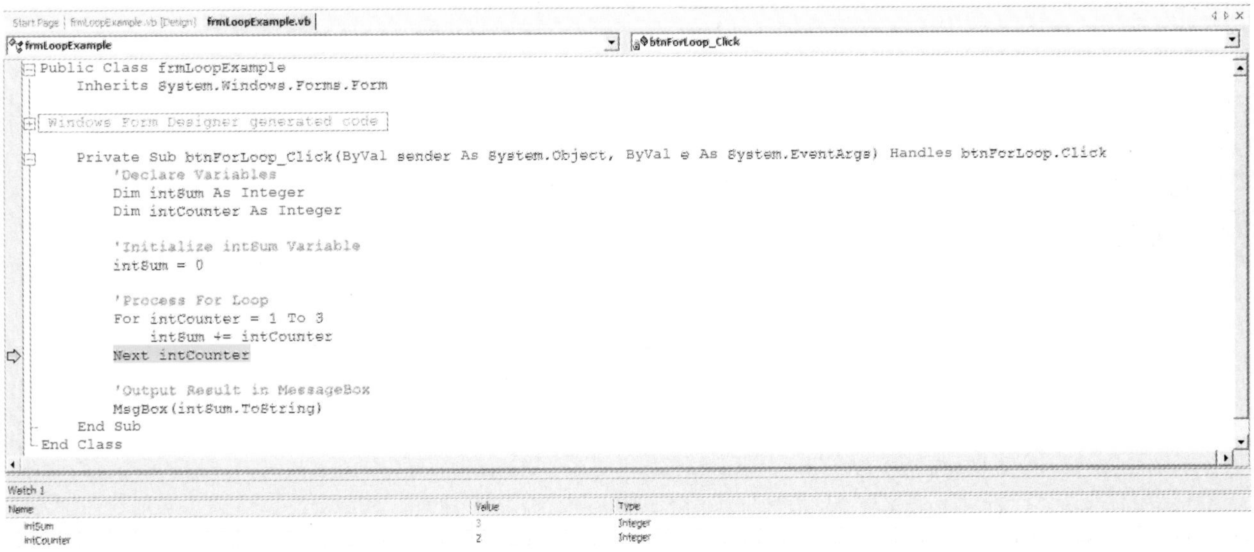

Figure 7.9 Trace of For loop

Step 7: When you press the <F10> key again, intCounter increments again. This increases the value of the intCounter variable by 1. Therefore, intCounter now equals 3. (See Figure 7.10.)

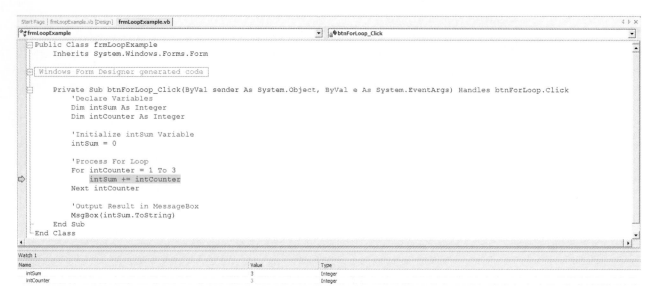

Figure 7.10   Trace of `For` loop

Step 8: When you press the `<F10>` key again, the body of the `For` loop executes once again. This time, the `intCounter` variable equals 3, so 3 is added to the value of the `intSum` variable, 3, and the `intSum` variable is set to 6. This is shown in Figure 7.11.

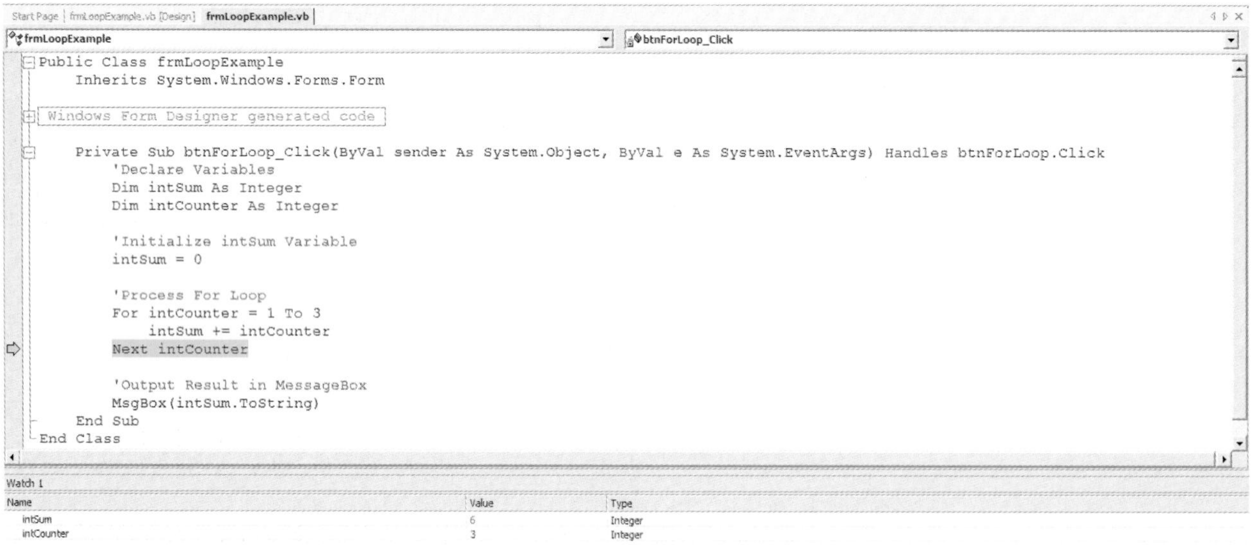

Figure 7.11   Trace of `For` loop

Step 9: When you press the `<F10>` key again, the increment statement of the `For` loop executes for the third time. This increases the value of the `intCounter` variable by 1. Therefore, `intCounter` now equals 4. Since the value of `intCounter`, 4, is not less than or equal to 3, the execution of the loop halts. This is seen in Figure 7.12.

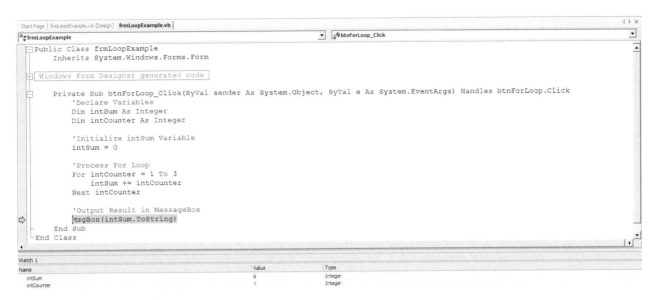

Figure 7.12   Trace of `For` loop

Step 10:   When you press the `<F10>` key again, the `MsgBox` function is executed. The result is displayed in Figure 7.13.

Figure 7.13
Output of `For` loop

6

Click on the OK button to complete the execution of this routine.

Incrementing by Values Other than 1

Often real-world situations require that your loops increment the value by something other than the default value of 1.

Visual Basic .NET allows you to use the **Step** option of the `For` statement to specify an increment size other than 1. The following is the syntax of a `For` loop with the `Step` option:

```
For LoopCounter = InitialValue To TerminatingValue Step Amount
    Program Statement(s)
Next LoopCounter
```

The only difference between this and the first `For` loop introduced is that by adding the `Step` keyword, you can indicate a value, `Amount`, that will be added to the `LoopCounter` on each iteration of the loop.

The following is an example of a `For` loop that adds up all the odd values between 1 and 5 and displays the result in a message box. By starting at 1, and adding 2 to `intCounter` on each iteration of the loop, only odd numbers are added to the `intSum` variable. This is shown in the following code:

```
Private Sub btnOutput_Click(...
    Dim intSum As Integer
    Dim intCounter As Integer
    intSum = 0
```

(continues)

COACH'S TIP

To convert from a numeric value to a `String`, use the built-in conversion method `ToString`.

(continued)

```
For intCounter = 1 To 5 Step 2
    intSum += intCounter
Next intCounter


MsgBox(intSum.ToString())
End Sub
```

Decrementing the Loop Counter

In addition to incrementing the loop counter, a loop counter can be decremented by simply indicating a negative value for the step size. The execution of a `For` loop with a loop counter that decrements is the same as before, but instead of adding the value indicated as the step size, it subtracts it.

See the following code, which displays the numbers from 5 through 1 in the label `lblOutput`:

COACH'S TIP

Remember, `&=` is a shortcut operator. The code could have been written
`lblOutput.Text = lblOutput.Text & intCounter. ToString & " "`.

```
Private Sub btnOutput_Click(...
    Dim intCounter As Integer

    For intCounter = 5 To 1 Step -1
        lblOutput.Text &= intCounter.ToString & " "
    Next intCounter

End Sub
```

The code initializes the `intCounter` variable to 5 and loops until the `intCounter` variable is less than 1. Each iteration of the loop decrements the `intCounter` variable by 1. Within the body of the loop, the `intCounter` variable's string value is appended to the `lblOutput` label along with a space character for clarity.

The output of the execution of the previous code is shown in Figure 7.14.

Figure 7.14
Decrement loop example output

5 4 3 2 1

For Drills 7.1 through 7.9, assume that a label, `lblOutput`, and a button, `btnOutput`, have been created.

DRILL 7.1

What is the value in `lblOutput`'s `Text` property after the following code has been executed?

```
Private Sub btnOutput_Click(...
    Dim intCounter As Integer

    For intCounter = 6 To 10
        lblOutput.Text &= intCounter.ToString & " "
    Next intCounter

End Sub
```

DRILL 7.2

What is the value in lblOutput's Text property after the following code has been executed?

```
Private Sub btnOutput_Click(...
    Dim intCounter As Integer

    For intCounter = 1 To 10 Step 4
        lblOutput.Text &= intCounter.ToString + " "
    Next intCounter
End Sub
```

DRILL 7.3

What is the value in lblOutput's Text property after the following code has been executed?

```
Private Sub btnOutput_Click(...
    Dim intCounter As Integer

    For intCounter = 10 To 0 Step -2
        lblOutput.Text &= intCounter.ToString + " "
    Next intCounter

End Sub
```

DRILL 7.4

What is the value in lblOutput's Text property after the following code has been executed?

```
Private Sub btnOutput_Click(...
    Dim intCounter As Integer
    Dim intValue As Integer

    intValue = 1
    For intCounter = 1 To 10 Step 2
        intValue *= intCounter
    Next intCounter

    lblOutput.Text = intValue.ToString

End Sub
```

DRILL 7.5

What is the value in `lblOutput`'s `Text` property after the following code has been executed?

```
Private Sub btnOutput_Click(...
    Dim intCounter As Integer

    For intCounter = 1 To 10 Step -2
        lblOutput.Text &= intCounter.ToString & " "
    Next intCounter
End Sub
```

DRILL 7.6

What is the value in `lblOutput`'s `Text` property after the following code has been executed?

```
Private Sub btnOutput_Click(...
    Dim intCounter As Integer

    For intCounter = -10 To -5 Step 1
        lblOutput.Text &= intCounter.ToString & " "
    Next intCounter
End Sub
```

DRILL 7.7

What is the value in `lblOutput`'s `Text` property after the following code has been executed?

```
Private Sub btnOutput_Click(...
    Dim intCounter As Integer

    For intCounter = -10 To -5 Step 2
        lblOutput.Text &= intCounter.ToString & " "
    Next intCounter
End Sub
```

DRILL 7.8

What is the value in lblOutput's Text property after the following code has been executed?

```
Private Sub btnOutput_Click(...
    Dim intCounter As Integer

    For intCounter = 2 To 10 Step 5
        lblOutput.Text &= intCounter.ToString & " "
    Next intCounter

    lblOutput.Text &= intCounter.ToString
End Sub
```

DRILL 7.9

What is the value in lblOutput's Text property after the following code has been executed?

```
Private Sub btnOutput_Click(...
    Dim sngCounter As Single

    For sngCounter = 1 To 5 Step .5
        lblOutput.Text &= sngCounter.ToString & " "
    Next sngCounter
End Sub
```

Now that you have a strong mastery of the syntax of the For loop, let's write some applications that take advantage of them and the Visual Basic .NET interface.

Example: Investment Application
Problem Description

Create an application that allows the user to enter an initial investment amount, the percentage return on investment per year, and the number of years of the investment. The application should output in a message box the final value of the investment.

See Figures 7.15 and 7.16, showing the initial input form and the message box displaying the result, respectively.

Figure 7.15 Investment input form   **Figure 7.16** Results message box

Problem Discussion

The problem can be solved by accepting the initial investment, the percentage returned on investment, and the duration in three text boxes. The application will require a `For` loop to calculate the return on investment for each year and then add it to the subtotal. Each additional year's return on investment calculation should be calculated from the subtotal, not the original investment amount.

Problem Solution

Three text boxes and three labels must be added to the form. The text boxes should be called `txtInitialInvestment`, `txtPercentageReturn`, and `txtDuration`. In addition, a button must be created with the following code included in its `Click` event:

```
Private Sub btnCalculate_Click(...
    'Declare local variables
    Dim sngValue As Single
    Dim intLoopCounter As Integer
    Dim sngPercentageReturn As Single
    Dim intDuration As Integer

    'Initialize variables to values stored in TextBoxes
    sngValue = Val(txtInitialInvestment.Text)
    intDuration = Val(txtDuration.Text)
    sngPercentageReturn = Val(txtPercentageReturn.Text)

    'Process Loop
    For intLoopCounter = 1 To intDuration
        sngValue = sngValue + (sngValue * sngPercentageReturn / 100)
    Next intLoopCounter

    MsgBox(FormatCurrency(sngValue))
End Sub
```

COACH'S TIP

Notice that the previous `For` loop used a variable as the upper bound of the `For` loop. This is a fairly common occurrence and does not present any problem.

The code computes the final investment by adding the previous year's investment to the product of the previous year's investment times the percentage return of the investment. When the loop terminates, the final value of the investment is displayed in a message box.

List Box Example

When list boxes were introduced earlier, an additional feature of a list box was skipped. Often the entry of information can be simplified by allowing a user to select more than one item from the list at the same time.

Imagine if you had an application that allowed a user to select three flavors of ice cream plus one topping for a sundae. You could use a radio button to select the topping and a list box with the ability to select more than one item for the ice cream flavors. Then you could output the type of sundae selected.

Observe the following application, which displays the message box when three flavors of ice cream are selected (Figure 7.17) and then the button `btnOrderSundae` is clicked (Figure 7.18).

The three toppings—Hot Fudge, Chocolate, and Butterscotch—are represented by the radio buttons `rbHotFudge`, `rbChocolate`, and `rbButterscotch`, respectively. The flavors—Vanilla, Chocolate, Strawberry, Cookies and Cream, Coffee, Peach, and Rocky Road—are represented in a list box.

When you set the `SelectionMode` property of the list box to `MultiSimple`, the application will allow more than one item from a list box to be selected. If a user clicks

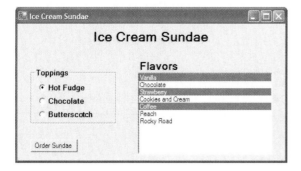

Figure 7.17   Ice cream sundae interface

Figure 7.18   Ice cream sundae output

on an item, the item becomes selected. If a user clicks on the same item again, it becomes deselected. Since the list box has the `MultiSelect` property set, the list box will not deselect the previously selected items when another one is selected.

Determining which items of the list box are selected can be achieved by stepping through the `SelectedItems` collection of the list box. By looping through the collection, starting at an index of 0 and looping until the `Count` equals `SelectedItems` `-1`, you can determine which items were selected from the list box. The name of a selected item is returned by using the following syntax:

ListBoxName`.SelectedItems(ItemIndex)`

The number of items in the `SelectedItems` collection can be determined by using the following syntax:

`ListBox.SelectedItems.Count`

Your application does not require checking a single item. Instead, you must check all the items to see if they have been selected. The easiest way to accomplish this is to use a `For` loop. Observe the following code for the `btnOrderSundae` button, which calls a message box with your specific order. First, it appends the type of sundae information; then it determines the types of ice cream selected. The process is a bit complicated because you should use the proper grammar for commas and the word "and" in your answer.

```
Private Sub btnOrderSundae_Click(...
    'Declare Variables
    Dim intSelectedCounter As Integer
    Dim strOutputString As String

    'Initialize Variables
    strOutputString = "A "

    'Select Type of Sundae
    If (rbHotFudge.Checked = True) Then
        strOutputString &= "Hot Fudge "
    Else If (rbChocolate.Checked = True) Then
        strOutputString &= "Chocolate "
    Else If (rbButterscotch.Checked = True) Then
        strOutputString &= "Butterscotch "
    End If
```

(continues)

(continued)

```
    strOutputString &= "Sundae with "

    'Select Ice Cream Flavors
    For intSelectedCounter = 0 To lstFlavors.SelectedItems.Count - 1
        If (intSelectedCounter = lstFlavors.SelectedItems.Count - 1) Then
            strOutputString &= "and "
        End If

        strOutputString &= lstFlavors.SelectedItems(intSelectedCounter)

        If (intSelectedCounter < 2) Then
            strOutputString &= ", "
        End If
    Next intSelectedCounter

    strOutputString &= " Ice Cream"

    MsgBox(strOutputString)
End Sub
```

You could write the code to a specific number of total flavors; however, with accessing the number of selected items, you can loop through just the flavors selected. This way, if you choose to add more flavors, you do not have to modify the last index value.

You might think you are done, but you would be wrong. Your application does not meet all the requirements specified. The problem was to write an application that allowed the selection of three ice cream flavors. Well, what happens if you select more or fewer than three flavors? Right now, nothing. A good programmer will validate the data entered to ensure the proper selection has been made. The following code should be added to the end of our code instead of just displaying the `strOutputString` variable automatically.

```
If (lstFlavors.SelectedItems.Count = 3) Then
    MsgBox (strOutputString)
Else
    MsgBox ("You did not select 3 flavors")
End If
```

COACH'S WARNING

Visual Basic .NET allows the developer to write a `For` loop so that the code can exit within the middle of the loop if a condition occurs. While this is valid Visual Basic .NET coding, it should be avoided in almost every case. Usually, the need to exit within the middle of a loop indicates a poorly designed loop.

If you need to exit a `For` loop, all that is required is that you type `Exit For`.

Observe the following example, which sets up a loop to add the numbers from 1 to 10 but drops out of the loop at 5.

(continues)

```
Private Sub LoopExample()
    Dim intLoopCounter As Integer
    Dim intTotal As Integer

    intTotal = 0

    For intLoopCounter = 1 To 10
        If (intLoopCounter = 5) Then
            Exit For
        End If
    intTotal += intLoopCounter
    Next intLoopCounter
    MsgBox(intTotal.ToString)
End Sub
```

7.2 Do Loops

Another loop construct in Visual Basic .NET is the `Do While` loop. Often it's used when the repeating process is not controlled by counting with a fixed-step amount, as in a `For` loop. Instead, use the `Do While` construct when the loop will continue while a certain condition evaluates to `True`. There are actually a number of formats that you may use `Do` loops with—the choice is yours. Pick the one that best maps to the problem you are trying to solve.

First Do Loop Construct

The following is the syntax of the code to use for the `Do` loop when testing if a condition evaluates to `True`, before executing any program statements, and to continue executing the statements while the condition evaluates to `True`:

```
Do While (Condition)
    Program Statement(s)
Loop
```

The next four applications all accomplish the same goal, but do so using different looping constructs.

Each application displays a message box asking whether you wish to continue. If you answer `Yes`, then it prompts you again until you select `No`. Once `No` has been selected, it displays the number of times `Yes` was selected.

The choice of construct is totally one of style; however, one usually is most appropriate for the problem you are trying to solve. Assume a form has been created for each application with a single button. The button's `Click` event code is shown.

```
'Version #1
Private Sub btnDoLoop_Click(...
    'Variable Declaration
    Dim intCounter As Integer
    Dim intAnswer As Integer
```

(continues)

(continued)

```
    'Variable Initialization
    intCounter = 0
    intAnswer = vbYes

    'Do While Loop
    Do While (intAnswer = vbYes)
        intAnswer = MsgBox("Continue?", vbYesNo)
        If (intAnswer = vbYes) Then
            intCounter += 1
        End If
    Loop

    'Output Results
    MsgBox("Number of Continues = " & intCounter.ToString)
End Sub
```

Version #1 of the application declares an `Integer` variable to store the number of times you indicated you wished to continue. The variable is initialized to 0. Another `Integer` variable is declared to store the answer the message box receives. Because of the looping construct picked for this version, you need to initialize the `intAnswer` variable to `vbYes` so it will enter the body of the loop the first time.

Then the `Do` loop displays the first message box and waits for an answer. Once received, if the answer is `Yes`, it adds 1 to the counter. Then the loop condition is checked. If it is `Yes`, the loop continues. Once the loop terminates, a message box displaying the total is called.

Second Do Loop Construct

Another form of the `Do` loop is used when you wish the loop to execute until a given condition evaluates to `True`. Its syntax follows:

```
Do Until (Condition)
    Program Statement(s)
Loop
```

Version #2 of the application changes the looping construct to use an `Until` statement. This program is virtually identical except for the condition to check for the case that the loop should terminate upon. The code follows:

```
'Version #2
Private Sub btnDoLoop_Click(...
    'Variable Declaration
    Dim intCounter As Integer
    Dim intAnswer As Integer

    'Variable Initialization
    intCounter = 0
    intAnswer = vbYes

    'Do Until Loop
    Do Until (intAnswer = vbNo)
        intAnswer = MsgBox("Continue?", vbYesNo)
        If (intAnswer = vbYes) Then
            intCounter += 1
```

(continues)

(continued)

```
        End If
    Loop

    'Output Results
    MsgBox("Number of Continues = " & intCounter.ToString)
End Sub
```

Third Do Loop Construct

Still another form of the Do loop is used when you wish to execute the program statements at least once and continue to execute the statement while the condition evaluates to True. The syntax follows:

```
Do
    Program Statement(s)
Loop While (Condition)
```

The benefit of this looping construct is that, by allowing the application to assume that the loop will execute at least once, you do not have to initialize the intAnswer variable. You'll see that it will be set to your answer before it is ever compared. The code follows:

```
'Version #3
Private Sub btnDoLoop_Click(...
    'Variable Declaration
    Dim intCounter As Integer
    Dim intAnswer As Integer

    'Variable Initialization
    intCounter = 0

    'Do...While Loop
    Do
        intAnswer = MsgBox("Continue?", vbYesNo)
        If (intAnswer = vbYes) Then
            intCounter += 1
        End If
    Loop While (intAnswer = vbYes)

    'Output Results
    MsgBox("Number of Continues = " & intCounter.ToString)
End Sub
```

This application is very similar to the other examples; it just contains one less step.

Fourth Do Loop Construct

The final looping construct is used when you wish to execute the program statements at least once and continue to execute them until the given condition evaluates to True. The syntax follows:

```
Do
    Program Statement(s)
Loop Until (Condition)
```

The previous application can be rewritten with an `Until` statement instead of a `While` statement. This requires you to change the condition. Either program is correct—it's simply a matter of style.

```
'Version #4
Private Sub btnDoLoop_Click(...
    'Variable Declarations
    Dim intCounter As Integer
    Dim intAnswer As Integer

    'Variable Initialization
    intCounter = 0

    'Do ... Until Loop
    Do
        intAnswer = MsgBox("Continue?", vbYesNo)
        If (intAnswer = vbYes) Then
            intCounter += 1
        End If
    Loop Until (intAnswer = vbNo)

    'Output Results
    MsgBox("Number of Continues = " & intCounter.ToString)
End Sub
```

The only change in the application is that we changed the condition to check for a No response. When the value of `intAnswer` equals `vbNo`, the loop terminates.

So which choice of looping construct did you think most fit the needs of the application developed? I would have selected either the third or fourth version, since they would not require the initialization of the `intAnswer` variable. But again, remember that this is a matter of style.

For Drills 7.10 through 7.15, assume that a label, `lblOutput`, and a button, `btnOutput`, have been created.

DRILL 7.10

What is the value in `lblOutput`'s `Text` property after the following code has been executed?

```
Private Sub btnOutput_Click(...
    Dim intCounter As Integer

    intCounter = 5
    Do While (intCounter > 0)
        intCounter -= 1
        lblOutput.Text &= intCounter.ToString & " "
    Loop
End Sub
```

DRILL 7.11

What is the value in lblOutput's Text property after the following code has been executed?

```
Private Sub btnOutput_Click(...
    Dim intCounter As Integer
    intCounter = 0

    Do Until (intCounter = 10)
        intCounter += 2
        lblOutput.Text &= intCounter.ToString & " "
    Loop

End Sub
```

DRILL 7.12

What is the value in lblOutput's Text property after the following code has been executed?

```
Private Sub btnOutput_Click(...
    Dim intCounter As Integer

    intCounter = 0
    Do Until (intCounter > 0)
        intCounter -= 3
        lblOutput.Text &= intCounter.ToString & " "
    Loop
End Sub
```

DRILL 7.13

What is the value in lblOutput's Text property after the following code has been executed?

```
Private Sub btnOutput_Click(...
    Dim intCounter As Integer

    intCounter = 0

    Do
        intCounter += 3
        lblOutput.Text &= intCounter.ToString & " "
    Loop Until (intCounter > 5)
End Sub
```

DRILL 7.14

What is the value in lblOutput's Text property after the following code has been executed?

```
Private Sub btnOutput_Click(...
    Dim intCounter As Integer

    intCounter = 0

    Do
        intCounter += 3
        lblOutput.Text &= intCounter.ToString & " "
    Loop While (intCounter < 10)
End Sub
```

DRILL 7.15

What is the value in lblOutput's Text property after the following code has been executed?

```
Private Sub btnOutput_Click(...
    Dim intCounter As Integer

    intCounter = 0
    Do
        intCounter = intCounter + 3
        lblOutput.Text &= intCounter.ToString & " "
    Loop While (intCounter > 10)
End Sub
```

COACH'S TIP

It is very easy to write an infinite loop. Infinite loops go on forever and can lead to major problems. Take care when writing loops to ensure that your loops have proper terminating conditions.

Example: Vampire Counting Application
Problem Description

An old story once claimed to prove the impossibility of the existence of vampires. The story alleged that a vampire needed to take a victim each night in order to survive. However, the victim became a vampire as well. That would mean each night, the number of vampires would double. With the world's population at approximately 6 billion, how long would it take for everyone to become a vampire?

Problem Discussion

Although any type of loop construct can be used to solve the problem, the use of a Do loop makes more sense than a For loop, since you do not know the number of times the loop will execute.

Problem Solution

Create an application that contains a button btnComputeDays with the following code and display the result in a message box:

```
Private Sub btnComputeDays_Click(...
    Dim dblNumVampires As Double
    Dim intNumDays As Integer

    dblNumVampires = 1

    Do While (dblNumVampires < 6000000000#)
        dblNumVampires *= 2
        intNumDays = intNumDays + 1
    Loop
    MsgBox(intNumDays.ToString)
End Sub
```

The code involves a few issues to point out. First, the choice of variable to hold the count of the number of vampires is not straightforward. A variable that can store a value in the billions is required. Neither an `Integer` nor a `Long` is large enough, so you must choose a `Double`. However, for the number of days, you can use an `Integer` variable type. This is because the number of days required is only 33, so you can see the world is safe from vampires or the world would already be filled with vampires if even one had ever existed.

COACH'S TIP

Notice the # after the number representing 6 billion. The # was added automatically when 6000000000 was typed to indicate the size of the variable.

Also, remember that `dblNumVampires *= 2` is equivalent to writing `dblNumVampires = dblNumVampires * 2`.

Example: Distance Conversion Application
Problem Description

When competing in a race, distances are often given in either miles or kilometers. Write an application that will accept a total distance, the interval to display the conversion for, and the units (miles or kilometers) the distance is measured in. Output a chart of distances showing both the number of kilometers and number of miles at the given interval. The application should look like Figure 7.19.

Figure 7.19
Distance Conversion
application

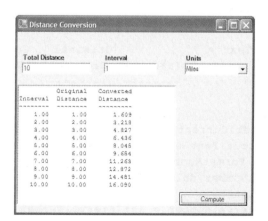

Problem Discussion

The problem requires some form of looping mechanism. While either a For or a Do loop can be used, the solution shown uses a Do loop. Since you do not know the number of times your loop will execute, unless you calculate it, it is simpler to use a Do loop that outputs the interval, distance in the original units, and the converted distance for each interval until the total distance is reached.

Problem Solution

Create three text boxes. The first two, txtTotalDistance and txtInterval, are created as usual. The third, txtOutput, should have the property MultiLine set to True. Then add a combo box, cboConversionFrom, that contains two list values, Miles and Kilometers. Add three labels so the purposes of the text boxes and combo box are easily understood. Finally, add a button, btnCompute, with the following code associated with its Click event:

```
Private Sub btnCompute_Click(...
    'Variable Declarations
    Dim dblCurrentDistance As Double
    Dim dblTotalDistance As Double
    Dim dblInterval As Double
    Dim intIntervalNumber As Integer
    Dim dblConvertValue As Double

    'Constant Declarations
    Const dblConvertFromKilometers As Double = 0.6215
    Const dblConvertFromMiles As Double = 1.609

    'Initialize Variables
    dblCurrentDistance = Val(txtInterval.Text)
    dblInterval = Val(txtInterval.Text)
    dblTotalDistance = Val(txtTotalDistance.Text)
    intIntervalNumber = 1


    'Select Conversion Factor
    If (cboConversionFrom.Text = "Miles") Then
        dblConvertValue = dblConvertFromMiles
    Else
        dblConvertValue = dblConvertFromKilometers
    End If

    'Display Header
    txtOutput.Text = "            Original    Converted" & vbNewLine & _
                "Interval  Distance     Distance" & vbNewLine & _
                "--------  --------     --------" & vbNewLine

    'Generate Chart
    Do Until (dblCurrentDistance > dblTotalDistance)
        txtOutput.Text &= FormatNumber(intIntervalNumber, 2).PadLeft(8) & _
        " " & FormatNumber(dblCurrentDistance, 2).PadLeft(9) & " " & _
        FormatNumber(dblCurrentDistance * dblConvertValue, 3).PadLeft(11) & _
        vbNewLine
        intIntervalNumber = intIntervalNumber + 1
```

(continues)

(continued)

```
            dblCurrentDistance = dblCurrentDistance + dblInterval
        Loop
End Sub
```

7.3 Nested Loops

Just as `If` statements could be nested to execute conditional statements within other conditional statements, loops can be nested within other loops. The execution of a **nested loop** is no different than the execution of loops you already have experience with.

When a loop is nested within another loop, the execution of the inner loop occurs completely for each iteration of the outer loop. Try Drills 7.16 through 7.19 to improve your understanding of nested loops.

DRILL 7.16

What is the value in `lblOutput`'s `Text` property after the following code has been executed?

```
Private Sub btnNested_Click(...
    Dim intOuterCounter As Integer
    Dim intInnerCounter As Integer

    For intOuterCounter = 1 To 3 Step 1
        For intInnerCounter = 1 To 3 Step 1
            lblOutput.Text &= intInnerCounter.ToString & " "
        Next intInnerCounter
    Next intOuterCounter
End Sub
```

COACH'S TIP

The `Next intInnerCounter` statement in the previous drill closes the innermost `For` loop. It is important when working with nested loops to indent properly so that the intent of the programmer is made clear. Otherwise, it is easy to get confused as to which `For` loop the `Next` statement belongs.

DRILL 7.17

What is the value in `lblOutput`'s `Text` property after the following code has been executed?

```
Private Sub btnNested_Click(...
    Dim intOuterCounter As Integer
    Dim intInnerCounter As Integer
    Dim intTotal As Integer

    intTotal = 0
    For intOuterCounter = 1 To 5 Step 2
```

(continues)

```
            For intInnerCounter = 1 To 3 Step 2
                intTotal = intTotal + intInnerCounter
            Next intInnerCounter
        Next intOuterCounter

        lblOutput.Text = intTotal.ToString

End Sub
```

DRILL 7.18

What is the value in lblOutput's Text property after the following code has been executed?

```
Private Sub btnNested_Click(...
    Dim intInnerCounter As Integer
    Dim intOuterCounter As Integer

    intOuterCounter = 0

    Do
        intInnerCounter = 0
        intOuterCounter = intOuterCounter + 3
        lblOutput.Text &= intOuterCounter.ToString & " "
        Do
            lblOutput.Text &= intInnerCounter.ToString & " "
            intInnerCounter += 2
        Loop While (intInnerCounter < 5)
    Loop While (intOuterCounter < 5)
End Sub
```

DRILL 7.19

What is the value in lblOutput's Text property after the following code has been executed?

```
Private Sub btnNested_Click(...
    Dim intInnerCounter As Integer
    Dim intOuterCounter As Integer

    intOuterCounter = 5
    intInnerCounter = 0

    Do
        intOuterCounter = intOuterCounter - 2
        lblOutput.Text &= intOuterCounter.ToString & " "
        Do
            lblOutput.Text &= intInnerCounter.ToString & " "
            intInnerCounter += 2
        Loop While (intInnerCounter < 5)
    Loop While (intOuterCounter > 0)
End Sub
```

7.4 Setting Breakpoints with the Debugger

In the previous section, loops were demonstrated that executed many times. If you wish to use a Debugger to trace through a program to track down an error, it may take a very long time to find the error. This is especially true if you know that the error occurs after the inner loop of a nested loop executes. Fortunately, the Visual Basic .NET Debugger provides a **breakpoint**.

A breakpoint allows the programmer to set the Debugger to execute until it reaches a specific line of code. Observe the following code, which contains two nested `For` loops. To demonstrate the use of a breakpoint, you will set the code to stop each time after the inner `For` loop executes. You will also set `Watch` variables on both loop counters.

```
Private Sub btnDebug_Click(...
    Dim intInnerCounter As Integer
    Dim intOuterCounter As Integer
    Dim intSum As Integer

    intSum = 0

    For intOuterCounter = 1 To 3
        For intInnerCounter = 1 To 100
                intSum += intInnerCounter
        Next intInnerCounter
    Next intOuterCounter

    lblOutput.Text = intSum.ToString

End Sub
```

In order to set the application to trace properly, follow these steps:

Step 1:   Create a form with a label called `lblOutput`.
Step 2:   Add a button called `btnDebug`.
Step 3:   Place the previous code in the button's `Click` event.
Step 4:   Click on the `Form1.vb*` tab.
Step 5:   Right-click on the `intInnerCounter` variable.
Step 6:   Click on the `Add Watch` menu item.
Step 7:   Right-click on the `intOuterCounter` variable.
Step 8:   Click on the `Add Watch` menu item.
Step 9:   Right-click on the `intSum` variable.
Step 10:   Click on the `Add Watch` pop-up menu item.
Step 11:   Click to the left of the `Next intOuterCounter` statement to place a breakpoint on that line.

Your application should look like that shown in Figure 7.20.

Notice that the last line of code the application will execute is a maroon color with a maroon circle in the left margin. Also notice that the `Watch` variables are all initially at 0.

You are now ready to execute the application until it reaches the breakpoint. This will cause the application to completely execute the inner `For` loop and stop.

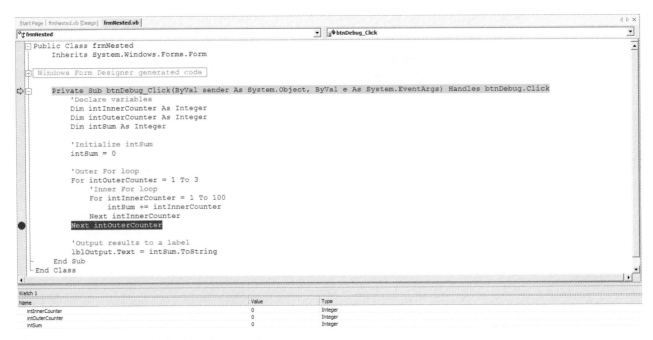

Figure 7.20 Initial setup for breakpoint example

Step 12: Click on the Play button in the toolbar. The application will run for a short time, and then your screen will look similar to Figure 7.21.

Figure 7.21 Visual Basic .NET environment after the breakpoint is reached for the first time

Since the inner `For` loop has executed 100 times, the value `intInnerCounter` is equal to `101`. This make sense. Since `intInnerCounter` is greater than `100`, the inner loop terminates. Also notice that `intSum` is equal to `5050`, which is the value you get when all the numbers from `1` to `100` are summed. Finally, notice that the `intOuterCounter` equals `1`, since it has not yet been incremented.

Step 13:   Click on the Play button in the toolbar again to execute the inner `For` loop a second time. The application will run for a short time, and then your screen will look similar to Figure 7.22.

Figure 7.22   Visual Basic .NET environment after the breakpoint is reached for the second time

Even though the inner `For` loop has executed an additional 100 times, the value `intInnerCounter` is still equal to `101`. This is because `intInnerCounter`'s value was reset to 1 at the beginning of the execution of the loop. The `intSum` variable is now double what it was before, `10100`. This is because an additional `5050` was added to the total during the second complete execution of the inner `For` loop. Finally, notice that the `intOuterCounter` equals `2`.

Step 14:   Click on the Play button in the toolbar again to execute the inner `For` loop a third time. The application will run for a short time, and then your screen will look similar to Figure 7.23.

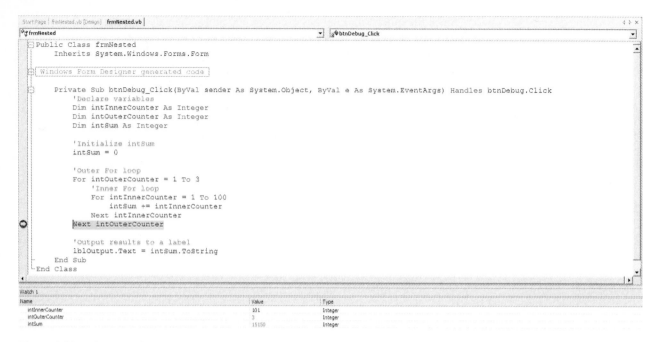

Figure 7.23   Visual Basic .NET Environment after the breakpoint is reached for the third time

Again the inner `For` loop has executed an additional 100 times. This time `intSum` is equal to `15150`, since an additional `5050` was added to it during the third complete execution of the inner `For` loop. Finally, notice that the `intOuterCounter` equals 3.

Step 15:   Click on the Play button in the toolbar again, and the program will finish its execution and display the final results. (See Figure 7.24.)

Figure 7.24
Final output of breakpoint example

> 15150

7.5   Use of the MS Flex Grid Control

With the introduction of loops, an additional control becomes very useful, the Microsoft flex grid. It is not one of the default controls in the toolbox, so you will have to manually add it to the toolbar when we want to use it in a solution.

Step 1:   Right-click on the toolbox.

Step 2:   Click on the `Customize Toolbox` menu option.

Step 3:   The window shown in Figure 7.25 appears.

Step 4:   Scroll down until the MS flex grid control appears. Note that your window may have slightly different options.

Step 5:   Click the check box associated with the MS flex grid.

Step 6:   Notice that the MS flex grid control now appears in the toolbar (see Figure 7.26).

Figure 7.25   Add Component window   **Figure 7.26**   Flex grid control

An MS flex grid looks similar to a spreadsheet application. It contains rows and columns. The box where a row and column intersect is known as a **cell**. A cell, which can be specified by its row and column, can be set to contain a string value.

Now you can create an application that will allow entry of sets of data and display all the sets in one control.

Example: Student Grades Application
Problem Description

Write an application that accepts a student's first name, last name, and GPA. The program should allow the addition of as many students as desired.

Problem Discussion

The application should look like that shown in Figure 7.27.

Figure 7.27
Student Grades application

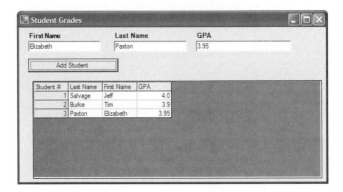

Step 1: This form requires adding three text boxes to store each student's information: `txtFirst`, `txtLast`, and `txtGPA`. Additionally, you need to add an MS flex grid (`grdStudents`) to contain all of the students' information. Finally, a button is required to process each student's information and place it in the MS flex grid.

In order to use an MS flex grid, you need to specify the number of rows and columns in the grid. In the example, the grid has four rows and four columns. The property for the number of rows is appropriately called `Rows`. Likewise, the number of columns is called `Cols`. Setting them is simply a matter of indicating the number of each that you wish. You may do so programmatically or from the Properties window.

In addition, you need to set the labels for the grid. The most appropriate place for this code is in the form's initialization routine. Your labels appear gray because you used the default of an MS flex grid so that the first row and column are fixed. You can create or remove more fixed rows and columns by setting the properties `FixedRows` and `FixedColumns`. If you set them to 0, there will be no fixed rows or columns.

However, to set each individual cell of the grid, you need to indicate the specific row and column that you want to set. This is accomplished with the `Row` and `Col` properties, respectively. Complicating the matter is the fact that the first `Row` and `Col` are specified with 0, not 1.

Figure 7.28 displays the row and column position of each cell with the format (row, column).

Figure 7.28
MS flex grid's indices

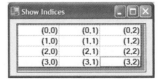

Step 2: You should now understand enough to write the code for the constructor of the form, which will initialize the grid column headers. The code follows:

```
Public Sub New()
        MyBase.New()

        'This call is required by the Windows Form Designer.
        InitializeComponent()

        'Add any initialization after the InitializeComponent() call
        grdStudents.Rows = 1
        grdStudents.Cols = 4

        grdStudents.Row = 0

        grdStudents.Col = 0
        grdStudents.Text = "Student #"

        grdStudents.Col = 1
        grdStudents.Text = "Last Name"

        grdStudents.Col = 2
        grdStudents.Text = "First Name"

        grdStudents.Col = 3
        grdStudents.Text = "GPA"

    End Sub
```

Step 3: Each time the button is clicked, you wish to increase the number of rows by one and copy the values in the text box to the newly created cells of the MS flex grid. The code for the `Click` event of the `btnAddStudent` button is as follows:

```
Private Sub btnAddStudent_Click(...
        'Increase the number of rows in the grid by 1
        grdStudents.Rows += 1

        'Set the current row index equal to the number of rows -1
        grdStudents.Row = grdStudents.Rows - 1

        'Set the Student Number
        grdStudents.Col = 0
        grdStudents.Text = grdStudents.Row

        'Set the Last Name
        grdStudents.Col = 1
        grdStudents.Text = txtLast.Text

        'Set the First Name
        grdStudents.Col = 2
        grdStudents.Text = txtFirst.Text

        'Set the GPA
        grdStudents.Col = 3
        grdStudents.Text = txtGPA.Text
End Sub
```

MS Flex Grid Example with Nested Loops

Suppose you wanted to add the functionality to the previous application so you could search the grid for a particular `String`. You could write a single `For` loop that compared the first name and last name columns with the `String` that you are looking for. However, suppose you increased the number of columns of data tracked for each student. You could add a student's major and year at school to your grid. Then you have two choices: You could hard code the additional columns to search within the existing `For` loop, or you could write a series of nested `For` loops that searched each column and row for the `String`. The latter approach is preferable because often additional columns are added to grids as your program grows more complex. If the routine is written in the latter manner, you can write it once and not have to modify it. Furthermore, if the routine is written as a function, you can write it once and use it anytime to search a grid for a specific value. Your new application looks like that shown in Figure 7.29.

Figure 7.29
Advanced Flex grid example
application

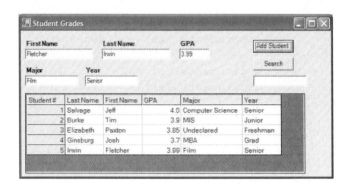

Step 1:   Add the controls shown in Figure 7.29 to the form.

Step 2:   The code for the `btnSearch` button's `Click` event is simple. The `Click` event will call the `SearchGrid` function, which you will write, and pass it two parameters: the grid and search string from the `txtSearch` text box. If the function returns `True`, you will output a message in a message box indicating the search value was found. Otherwise, you will output a message box indicating the search value was not found.

```
Private Sub btnSearch_Click(...
    If (SearchGrid(grdStudents, txtSearch.Text)) Then
        MsgBox("The searched value was found")
    Else
        MsgBox("The searched value was not found")
    End If
End Sub
```

COACH'S TIP

Code reuse is an extremely important programming practice to develop.

You could have written the search code directly into the `btnSearch` button, but if you write this code as a function, you can reuse it in other applications.

Step 3:   The `SearchGrid` function will step through each cell in the grid and compare its contents to see if the cell contains that exact `String`. If the `String` is found, the function's return value is set to `True`. However, if the entire grid is searched and the value is not found, the function will return `False`. The code follows:

```
Function SearchGrid(ByVal grdGrid As Object, _
                    ByVal strSearchString As String) As Boolean
    'Declare variables
    Dim intRow As Integer
    Dim intColumn As Integer

    'Loop through each row
    For intRow = 0 To grdGrid.Rows - 1
        grdGrid.Row = intRow

        'Loop through each column
        For intColumn = 0 To grdGrid.Cols - 1
            grdGrid.Col = intColumn
            If (grdGrid.Text = strSearchString) Then
                Return True
            End If
        Next intColumn
    Next intRow

    'If you reach here, the value is not in the grid
    Return False
End Function
```

◆ 7.6 Case Study

Problem Description

With the addition of the MS flex grid control and loops, there is no longer the need to limit the number of employees in your Payroll Accounting System. Now the Payroll Accounting System can be improved so that you can enter the information about each employee, one at a time.

Figure 7.30 demonstrates what your application will look like. Figure 7.31 shows the result of clicking the button.

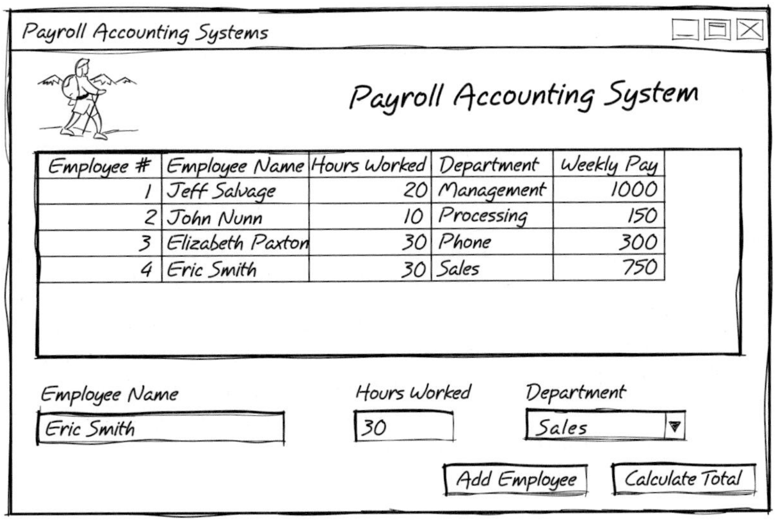

Figure 7.30
Sketch of application

Figure 7.31
Output when Calculate
Total is clicked

Problem Discussion

The problem can be solved by either calculating the total weekly pay as each employee's data is entered or all at once when the user has finished entering all the employees' data. To reinforce use of loops, you will solve the problem using the latter solution.

Problem Solution

Many parts of this application are similar to solutions in earlier chapters. You still need the constants (introduced in Chapter 3) to indicate the pay rates of each type of employee. They are declared in the following code, which should be listed in the `Declarations` section:

```
Const intSalesPayRate = 25
Const intProcessingPayRate = 15
Const intManagementPayRate = 50
Const intPhonePayRate = 10
```

You need to initialize the grid so that its labels are visible when the application is executed. The code should be located in the form's constructor.

```
Public Sub New()
    MyBase.New()

    'This call is required by the Windows Form Designer.
    InitializeComponent()

    'Add any initialization after the InitializeComponent() call

    grdEmployees.Rows = 1
    grdEmployees.Cols = 5

    grdEmployees.Row = 0
    grdEmployees.Col = 0
    grdEmployees.Text = "Employee #"


    grdEmployees.Col = 1
    grdEmployees.Text = "Employee Name"

    grdEmployees.Col = 2
    grdEmployees.Text = "Hours Worked"

    grdEmployees.Col = 3
    grdEmployees.Text = "Department"

    grdEmployees.Col = 4
    grdEmployees.Text = "Weekly Pay"

End Sub
```

Although you do not need a series of text boxes and combo boxes as before, you need text boxes to enter the employee's name and hours worked, as well as a combo box for the department. You also need a button that will add the new employee's information to the grid. This code follows:

```
Private Sub btnAddEmployee_Click(...
    grdEmployees.Rows = grdEmployees.Rows + 1 'Increase the number of rows by 1

    grdEmployees.Row = grdEmployees.Rows - 1 'Set the current row

    grdEmployees.Col = 0
    grdEmployees.Text = grdEmployees.Rows - 1 'Set the employee #

    grdEmployees.Col = 1
    grdEmployees.Text = txtEmployee.Text 'Set the employee name

    grdEmployees.Col = 2
    grdEmployees.Text = txtHours.Text 'Set the hours worked

    grdEmployees.Col = 3
    grdEmployees.Text = cboDepartment.Text 'Set the department

    grdEmployees.Col = 4
    'First Week's Calculations
      Select Case cboDepartment.Text
        Case "Sales"
            grdEmployees.Text = (Val(txtHours.Text) * intSalesPayRate).ToString
        Case "Processing"
            grdEmployees.Text = (Val(txtHours.Text) * _
                            intProcessingPayRate).ToString
        Case "Management"
            grdEmployees.Text = (Val(txtHours.Text) * _
                            intManagementPayRate).ToString
        Case "Phone"
            grdEmployees.Text = (Val(txtHours.Text) * intPhonePayRate).ToString
      End Select
End Sub
```

The final code required calculates the total weekly pay and displays it in a message box. The code follows:

```
Private Sub btnCalculateTotal_Click(...
    Dim intCurrentRow As Integer
    Dim sngTotal As Single

    sngTotal = 0
    intCurrentRow = 1
    grdEmployees.Col = 4


    Do While (grdEmployees.Rows > intCurrentRow)
        grdEmployees.Row = intCurrentRow
        sngTotal += Val(grdEmployees.Text)
```

(continues)

(continued)

```
            intCurrentRow += 1
    Loop

    MsgBox(FormatCurrency(sngTotal))
End Sub
```

The final application is shown in Figure 7.32.

Figure 7.32
Final application

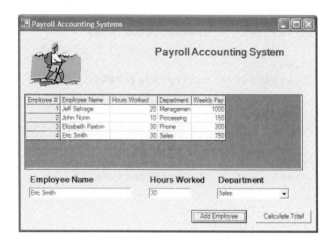

CORNER

Dynamic Flex Grid Resizing

Sometimes it is difficult to determine the exact size of a grid column before the application is run by the user. If you wish, you can change the setting of the `FlexGrid`'s `AllowUserResizing` property from the default, `flexResizeNone`, to the setting `flexResizeColumns`. This will allow the user to resize the width of the columns by clicking on the column line divider and pulling it in the desired direction. By setting the property to `flexResizeRows`, you will allow the user to resize the height of the rows by clicking on the row line divider and pulling it in the desired direction. Finally, if you wish to let the user modify both the column and row widths, you can set the property to `flexResizeBoth`.

Keyboard Shortcuts

As your applications grow in size, controlling the flow of their execution by the `TabIndex` (explained in Chapter 2's Coach's Corner) property or the mouse can become inconvenient. Many Windows applications contain keyboard shortcuts that allow the user to use a keyboard sequence to perform actions easily.

Visual Basic .NET allows us to attach keyboard shortcuts to buttons with a minimum of effort. See the modified Student Search application in Figure 7.33. It looks almost the same as before. The only difference is that the first letter of the caption on each of the buttons has an underscore.

To create a keyboard shortcut, place an ampersand in front of the letter of the `Text` that you wish to be the shortcut. Therefore, the `btnAddStudent` button's `Text` property would be `&Add  Student`, while the `btnSearch` button would have its `Text` property set to `&Search`.

Figure 7.33
Keyboard shortcut example

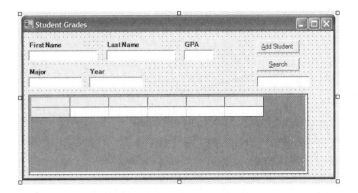

COACH'S WARNING

Do not create two shortcuts to the same letter. All shortcuts must be to a unique letter.

Pressing the <A> key while holding the <ALT> key has the same effect as clicking the btnAddStudent button. Similarly, pressing the <S> key while holding the <ALT> key has the same effect as clicking the btnSearch button.

Key Words and Key Terms

Breakpoint
An option in the Debugger to stop the execution of the code at a particular point.

Cell
The box where a row and column intersect in an grid.

Do Until Loop
A structure that is repeated as long as a given condition does not evaluate to True.

Do While Loop
A structure that is repeated as long as a given condition evaluates to True.

For Loop
A structure that is repeated a fixed number of times.

Nested Loop
A loop structure that has another loop structure defined within it.

Step
The amount by which the For loop index is incremented on each iteration of the loop.

Answers to Chapter's Drills

Drill 7.1
The output is as follows:

```
6 7 8 9 10
```

When the button is clicked, the code executes as follows: First the intCounter variable is initialized to 6. Since 6 is less than or equal to 10, the body of the For loop executes. This appends a "6" and a space to the lblOutput label. Then the loop counter, intCounter, is incremented by 1 to 7.

Since 7 is less than or equal to 10, the body of the For loop executes again. This time a "7" and a space are appended to lblOutput. Once again, intCounter is incremented by 1, to 8.

Since 8 is less than or equal to 10, the body of the For loop executes again. This time an "8" and a space are appended to lblOutput. Once again, intCounter is incremented by 1, to 9.

Since 9 is less than or equal to 10, the body of the For loop executes again. This time a "9" and a space are appended to lblOutput. Once again, intCounter is incremented by 1, to 10.

Since 10 is less than or equal to 10, the body of the For loop executes again. This time a "10" and a space are appended to lblOutput. Once again, intCounter is incremented by 1, to 11.

Since 11 is not less than or equal to 10, the loop terminates.

Drill 7.2
The output is as follows:

```
1  5  9
```

When the button is clicked, the code executes as follows: First the intCounter variable is initialized to 1. Since 1 is less than or equal to 10, the body of the For loop executes. This appends a "1" and a space to the lblOutput label. Then the loop intCounter, intCounter, is incremented by 4 to 5.

Since 5 is less than or equal to 10, the body of the For loop executes again. This time a "5" and a space are appended to lblOutput. Once again, intCounter is incremented by 4, to 9.

Since 9 is less than or equal to 10, the body of the For loop executes again. This time a "9" and a space are appended to lblOutput. Once again, intCounter is incremented by 4, to 13.

Since 13 is not less than or equal to 10, the loop terminates.

Drill 7.3
The output is as follows:

```
10  8  6  4  2  0
```

When the button is clicked, the code executes as follows: First the intCounter variable is initialized to 10. Since 10 is greater than or equal to 0, the body of the For loop executes. This appends a "10" and a space to the lblOutput label. Then the loop counter, intCounter, is decremented by 2 to 8.

Since 8 is greater than or equal to 0, the body of the For loop executes again. This time an "8" and a space are appended to lblOutput. Once again, intCounter is decremented by 2, to 6.

Since 6 is greater than or equal to 0, the body of the For loop executes again. This time a "6" and a space are appended to lblOutput. Once again, intCounter is decremented by 2, to 4.

Since 4 is greater than or equal to 0, the body of the For loop executes again. This time a "4" and a space are appended to lblOutput. Once again, intCounter is decremented by 2, to 2.

Since 2 is greater than or equal to 0, the body of the For loop executes again. This time a "2" and a space are appended to lblOutput. Once again, intCounter is decremented by 2 to 0.

Since 0 is greater than or equal to 0, the body of the For loop executes again. This time a "0" and a space is appended to lblOutput. Once again, intCounter is decremented by 2, to –2.

Since –2 is not greater than or equal to 0, the loop terminates.

Drill 7.4
The output is as follows:

```
945
```

When the button is clicked, the code executes as follows: First the variable `intValue` is initialized to 1. Then the `For` loop is entered and the `intCounter` variable is initialized to 1. Since 1 is less than or equal to 10, the body of the `For` loop executes. This appends `intValue` multiplied by 1 and stores it back in `intValue`. In this case, 1 is multiplied by 1, so `intValue` equal 1 after the body of the loop executes. Then the loop counter, `intCounter`, is incremented by 2 to 3.

Since 3 is less than or equal to 10, the body of the `For` loop executes again. This time `intValue` is multiplied by 3 and the result, 3, is stored in `intValue`. Once again, `intCounter` is incremented by 2, to 5.

Since 5 is less than or equal to 10, the body of the `For` loop executes again. This time `intValue` is multiplied by 5 and the result, 15, is stored in `intValue`. Once again, `intCounter` is incremented by 2, to 7.

Since 7 is less than or equal to 10, the body of the `For` loop executes again. This time `intValue` is multiplied by 7 and the result, 105, is stored in `intValue`. Once again, `intCounter` is incremented by 2, to 9.

Since 9 is less than or equal to 10, the body of the `For` loop executes again. This time `intValue` is multiplied by 9 and the result, 945, is stored in `intValue`. Once again, `intCounter` is incremented by 2, to 11.

Since 11 is not less than or equal to 10, the loop terminates.

Drill 7.5

The output is as follows:

This was a trick question! Although the `For` loop is coded to count from 1 to 10, you set the `Step` value to -2. This will cause `intCounter` to count down. Since you cannot count down from 1 to 10, the loop never executes. Therefore, the label is never appended, so it displays nothing.

Drill 7.6

The output is as follows:

```
-10  -9  -8  -7  -6  -5
```

When the button is clicked, the code executes as follows: First the `For` loop is entered and the `intCounter` variable is initialized to -10. Since -10 is less than or equal to -5, the body of the `For` loop executes. This appends a `"-10"` and a space to the `lblOutput` Label. Then the loop counter, `intCounter`, is incremented by 1 to -9.

Since -9 is less than or equal to -5, the body of the `For` loop executes again. This time a `"-9"` and a space are appended to `lblOutput`. Once again, `intCounter` is incremented by 1, to -8.

Since -8 is less than or equal to -5, the body of the `For` loop executes again. This time a `"-8"` and a space are appended to `lblOutput`. Once again, `intCounter` is incremented by 1, to -7.

Since -7 is less than or equal to -5, the body of the `For` loop executes again. This time a `"-7"` and a space are appended to `lblOutput`. Once again, `intCounter` is incremented by 1, to -6.

Since -6 is less than or equal to -5, the body of the `For` loop executes again. This time a `"-6"` and a space are appended to `lblOutput`. Once again, `intCounter` is incremented by 1, to -5.

Since -5 is less than or equal to -5, the body of the `For` loop executes again. This time a `"-5"` and a space are appended to `lblOutput`. Once again, `intCounter` is incremented by 1, to -4.

Since –4 is not less than or equal to –5, the loop terminates.

Drill 7.7
The output is as follows:

```
-10  -8  -6
```

When the button is clicked, the code executes as follows: First the For loop is entered and the intCounter variable is initialized to –10. Since –10 is less than or equal to –5, the body of the For loop executes. This appends a "-10" and a space to the lblOutput label. Then the loop counter, intCounter, is incremented by 2 to –8.

Since –8 is less than or equal to –5, the body of the For loop executes again. This time a "-8" and a space are appended to lblOutput. Once again, intCounter is incremented by 2, to –6.

Since –6 is less than or equal to –5, the body of the For loop executes again. This time a "-6" and a space are appended to lblOutput. Once again, intCounter is incremented by 2, to –4.

Since –4 is not less than or equal to –5, the loop terminates.

Drill 7.8
The output is as follows:

```
2  7  12
```

When the button is clicked, the code executes as follows: First the For loop is entered and the intCounter variable is initialized to 2. Since 2 is less than or equal to 2, the body of the For loop executes. This appends a "2" and a space to the lblOutput label. Then the loop counter, intCounter, is incremented by 5 to 7.

Since 7 is less than or equal to 10, the body of the For loop executes again. This time a "7" and a space are appended to lblOutput. Once again, intCounter is incremented by 5, to 12.

Since 12 is not less than or equal to 10, the loop terminates. However, in this case our processing is not complete. The value, 12, contained in the variable intCounter remains and is appended to lblOutput as the last statement of the button's code.

Drill 7.9
The output is as follows:

```
1  1.5  2  2.5  3  3.5  4  4.5  5
```

When the button is clicked, the code executes as follows: First the For loop is entered and the sngCounter variable is initialized to 1. Since 1 is less than or equal to 5, the body of the For loop executes and "1" and a space are added to the lblOutput. The step amount is .5, so the counter is incremented to 1.5.

Since 1.5 is less than or equal to 5, the body of the For loop executes again. This time a "1.5" and a space are appended to lblOutput. Once again, sngCounter is incremented by .5, to 2.

Since 2 is less than or equal to 5, the body of the For loop executes again. This time a "2" and a space are appended to lblOutput. Once again, sngCounter is incremented by .5, to 2.5.

This process continues until the loop counter is greater than 5 and the loop terminates.

Drill 7.10

The output is as follows:

```
4  3  2  1  0
```

When the button is clicked, the code executes as follows: First the `intCounter` variable is initialized to 5. Then the `Do` loop is entered and the `intCounter` is compared to see if it is greater than 0. Since 5 is greater than 0, the body of the `Do` loop executes. Then 1 is subtracted from `intCounter` so that `intCounter` now equals 4. Therefore, a `"4"` and a space are appended to the `lblOutput` label.

The looping condition is then evaluated. Since 4 is greater than 0, the body of the `Do` loop executes again. Again, 1 is subtracted from `intCounter`, setting `intCounter` equal to 3. This time a `"3"` and a space are appended to `lblOutput`.

Again, the looping condition is then evaluated. Since 3 is greater than 0, the body of the `Do` loop executes again. Again, 1 is subtracted from `intCounter`, setting `intCounter` equal to 2. Therefore, a `"2"` and a space are appended to `lblOutput`.

Again, the looping condition is then evaluated. Since 2 is greater than 0, the body of the `Do` loop executes again. Again, 1 is subtracted from `intCounter`, setting `intCounter` equal to 1. Therefore, a `"1"` and a space are appended to `lblOutput`.

Again, the looping condition is then evaluated. Since 1 is greater than 0, the body of the `Do` loop executes again. Again, 1 is subtracted from `intCounter`, setting `intCounter` equal to 0. Even though 0 is not greater than 0, you continue with the execution of the body of the `Do` loop, because the looping condition is not checked again until after the execution of the entire body of the loop. Therefore, a `"0"` and a space are appended to `lblOutput`.

Now, when 0 is compared to 0, it is no longer greater than 0, so the loop terminates.

Drill 7.11

The output is as follows:

```
2  4  6  8  10
```

When the button is clicked, the code executes as follows: First the `intCounter` variable is initialized to 0. Then the `Do` loop is entered and the `intCounter` is compared to see if it is equal to 10. If it is, the loop terminates. Since 0 is not equal to 10, the body of the `Do` loop executes. Then 2 is added to `intCounter` so that `intCounter` now equals 2. Therefore, a `"2"` and a space are appended to the `lblOutput` label.

The looping condition is then evaluated. Since 2 is not equal to 10, the body of the `Do` loop executes again. Again, 2 is added to the `intCounter`, setting `intCounter` equal to 4. This time a `"4"` and a space are appended to `lblOutput`.

The looping condition is then evaluated. Since 4 is not equal to 10, the body of the `Do` loop executes again. Again, 2 is added to the `intCounter`, setting `intCounter` equal to 6. This time a `"6"` and a space are appended to `lblOutput`.

The looping condition is then evaluated. Since 6 is not equal to 10, the body of the `Do` loop executes again. Again, 2 is added to the `intCounter`, setting `intCounter` equal to 8. This time an `"8"` and a space are appended to `lblOutput`.

Again, the looping condition is then evaluated. Since 8 is not equal to 10, the body of the `Do` loop executes again. Again, 2 is added to `intCounter`, setting `intCounter` equal to 10. Even though the `intCounter` variable is now equal to 10, you continue with the execution of the body of the `Do` loop, because the looping condition is not checked again until after the execution of the entire body of the loop. Therefore, a `"10"` and a space are appended to `lblOutput`.

Now, when 10 is compared to 10, they are equal and the loop terminates.

Drill 7.12
The output is as follows:

This was a trick question! There is no output. Actually, the application will enter into an infinite loop. Since intCounter starts at 0 and has 3 subtracted from it continuously, the condition checking to see if it is greater than 0 will never evaluate to True. Since you used an Until statement instead of a While statement, the loop will execute until the expression evaluates to True, which is never.

Drill 7.13
The output is as follows:

```
3  6
```

When the button is clicked, the code executes as follows: First the intCounter variable is initialized to 0. Then the Do loop is entered and 3 is added to intCounter, setting it equal to 3. Then a "3" and a space are appended to the lblOutput label. Now the loop condition is checked and 3 is compared to 5.

Since 3 is not greater than 5, the body of the Do loop executes again. Then 3 is added to the intCounter, setting intCounter equal to 6. This time a "6" and a space are appended to lblOutput.

Again, the looping condition is then evaluated. However, since 6 is greater than 5, the loop terminates.

Drill 7.14
The output is as follows:

```
3  6  9  12
```

When the button is clicked, the code executes as follows: First the intCounter variable is initialized to 0. Then the Do loop is entered and 3 is added to intCounter, setting it equal to 3. Then a "3" and a space are appended to the lblOutput label. Now the loop condition is checked and 3 is compared to 10.

Since 3 is less than 10, the body of the Do loop executes again. Then 3 is added to the intCounter, setting intCounter equal to 6. This time a "6" and a space are appended to lblOutput.

Since 6 is less than 10, the body of the Do loop executes again. Then 3 is added to the intCounter, setting intCounter equal to 9. This time a "6" and a space are appended to lblOutput.

Since 9 is less than 10, the body of the Do loop executes again. Then 3 is added to the intCounter, setting intCounter equal to 12. This time a "9" and a space are appended to lblOutput.

Again, the looping condition is then evaluated. However, since 12 is greater than 10, the loop terminates.

Drill 7.15
The output is as follows:

```
3
```

When the button is clicked, the code executes as follows: First the intCounter variable is initialized to 0. Then the Do loop is entered and 3 is added to intCounter, setting it equal to 3. Then a "3" and a space are appended to the lblOutput label. Now the loop condition is checked and 3 is compared to 10.

Since 3 is not greater than 10, the body of the loop terminates. Notice that although the condition never evaluated to True, the body of the loop executed once.

Drill 7.16
The output is as follows:

```
1 2 3 1 2 3 1 2 3
```

When the button is clicked, the code executes as follows: First the outer loop is entered with the intOuterCounter variable initialized to 1. Then the inner loop is entered with the intInnerCounter variable initialized to 1. You then process the inner loop in its entirety.

Since the inner loop starts at 1 and ends at 3, the value "1 2 3" is assigned to lblOutput. Then the intOuterCounter variable is incremented by 1 to 2. Since 2 is less than or equal to 3, you reexecute the inner loop.

Since no reference to intOuterCounter is made in the inner loop, it executes identically as before. Thus "1   2   3" is appended to lblOutput. Therefore, lblOutput now contains the String "1 2 3 1 2 3". Then the intOuterCounter variable is incremented by 1 again, to 3. Since 3 is still less than or equal to 3, you reexecute the inner loop again.

As before, the execution of the inner loop appends "1 2 3" to lblOutput, so it contains "1 2 3 1 2 3 1 2 3" after the inner loop completes executing for the third time. When the intOuterCounter variable is incremented again, it sets intOuterCounter to 4. Thus the outer loop terminates.

Drill 7.17
The output is as follows:

```
12
```

When the button is clicked, the code executes as follows: First the intTotal variable is initialized to 0. Then the outer loop is entered with the intOuterCounter variable initialized to 1. Next the inner loop is entered with the intInnerCounter variable initialized to 1. You then process the inner loop in its entirety.

Since the inner loop starts at 1, it is added to intTotal. Therefore, intTotal equals 1. Then intInnerCounter is incremented by 2, so that after the first iteration of the loop, it equals 3. Since 3 is less than or equal to 3, the inner loop executes again.

This time when intInnerCounter is added to Total, it adds 3, so intTotal equals 4. When intInnerCounter is incremented by 2, the value of intInnerCounter after the second iteration of the inner loop is 5. Since 5 is not less than or equal to 3, you terminate executing the inner loop. The intOuterCounter variable is then incremented by 2 to 3. Since 3 is less than or equal to 5, the inner loop is executed again.

Since no reference to intOuterCounter is made in the inner loop, it executes identically as before. Thus 4 is added to intTotal. The intOuterCounter variable is again incremented by 2, to 5. Since 5 is less than or equal to 5, the inner loop is executed again.

Once again, 4 is added to intTotal during the execution of the inner loop. Finally, when intOuterCounter is incremented by 2 again, this time to 7, the outer loop terminates with the value of intTotal being 12.

Drill 7.18
The output is as follows:

```
3 0 2 4 6 0 2 4
```

When the button is clicked, the code executes as follows: First the
`intOuterCounter` variable is initialized to 0. Then the outer loop is entered with
`intInnerCounter` initialized to 0 and 3 added to `intOuterCounter`. `lblOutput`
is then assigned the value in `OuterCounter`, `"3  "`.

The inner loop is then entered, with the value of `intInnerCounter` appended to
`lblOutput`. Then 2 is added to `intInnerCounter`. Since `intInnerCounter` is
equal to 2 and 2 is less than 5, the inner loop executes again.

This time, the value of `intInnerCounter`, 2, is appended to `lblOutput`, so that
it now equals `"3  0  2  "`. Once again 2 is added to `intInnerCounter`, and since the
value of `InnerCounter`, 4, is less than 5, the inner loop executes again. Once again, 2
is added to `InnerCounter`, but now that `intInnerCounter` equals 6, it is no longer
less than 5, so the inner loop terminates.

The outer loop condition is then checked. Since `intOuterCounter` still equals 3,
and 3 is less than 5, the entire outer loop executes again. First, `intInnerCounter` is
reset to 0. Then `intOuterCounter` has 3 added to it, equaling 6. The
`intOuterCounter` is then appended to `lblOutput`, so `lblOutput` now equals `"3
0 2 4 6"`.

The inner loop executes exactly as it did before, and therefore `"0  2  4"` is appended to `lblOutput`, so that `lblOutput` now equals `"3  0  2  4  6  0  2  4"`. Finally, the
value of `intOuterCounter`, 6, is compared to 5, and since it is not less than or equal
to it, the outer loop terminates.

Drill 7.19
The output is as follows:

```
3 0 2 4 1 6 -1 8
```

When the button is clicked, the code executes as follows: First the
`intOuterCounter` variable is initialized to 5 and the `intInnerCounter` variable is
initialized to 0. Then the outer loop is entered with `intOuterCounter` decremented
by 2, so that it now equals 3. This is appended to `lblOutput`, so that `lblOutput` now
equals `"3"`.

The inner `Do` loop is entered and the value of `intInnerCounter` is appended to
`lblOutput`, so that `txtOutput` now equals `"3   0"`. Then 2 is added to
`intInnerCounter`, so that `intInnerCounter` now equals 2. Since 2 is less than 5,
the inner loop continues to execute.

The value of `intInnerCounter` is appended to `lblOutput` so that `lblOutput`
now equals `"3  0  2"`. Then 2 is added to `InnerCounter`, so that `intInnerCounter`
now equals 4. Since 4 is less than 5, the inner loop continues to execute.

The value of `intInnerCounter` is appended to `lblOutput` so that `lblOutput`
now equals `"3   0   2   4"`. Then 2 is added to `intInnerCounter`, so that
`intInnerCounter` now equals 6. Since 6 is not less than 5, the inner loop terminates.

The outer `Do` loop's condition is then checked. Since `intOuterCounter` equals 3,
it is greater than 0 and the outer loop executes again. First, 2 is subtracted from
`intOuterCounter` and its new value, 1, is appended to `lblOutput`. Thus
`lblOutput` now equals `"3 0 2 4 1"`.

The inner `Do` loop is entered for a second time, and the value of
`intInnerCounter`, 6, is appended to `lblOuput`, so that `lblOutput` now equals `"3
0 2 4 1 6"`. Then 2 is added to `intInnerCounter`, so that `intInnerCounter`
now equals 8. Since 8 is not less than 5, the inner loop terminates.

The outer `Do` loop's condition is then checked. Since `intOuterCounter` equals 1, it is greater than 0 and the outer loop executes again. First, 2 is subtracted from `intOuterCounter` and its new value, -1, is appended to `lblOutput`. Therefore, `lblOutput` now equals "3 0 2 4 1 6 -1".

The inner `Do` loop is entered for a third time, and the value of `intInnerCounter`, 8, is appended to `lblOutput`, so that `lblOutput` now equals "3 0 2 4 1 6 8". Then 2 is added to `intInnerCounter`, so that `intInnerCounter` now equals 10. Since 10 is not less than 5, the inner loop terminates.

The outer `Do` loop's condition is then checked. Since `intOuterCounter` equals -1, it is not greater than 0 and so the outer loop terminates.

Additional Exercises

Questions 1–5 are true or false.

1. A `Step` amount in a `For` loop must be an `Integer` value.

2. Loops may only be nested one level deep. In other words, you can nest one loop inside another, but not a loop inside a loop inside another loop.

3. Breakpoints can only be used in conjunction with loops.

4. `For` loops can `Step` in positive or negative increments.

5. An MS flex grid's indices start at 1.

6. What is the value in the label `lblOutput` after the following code has been executed?

```
Dim intCounter As Integer


For intCounter = 10 To 1 Step -3
    lblOutput.Text &= intCounter.ToString & " "
Next intCounter
```

7. What is the value in the label `lblOutput` after the following code has been executed?

```
Dim intCounter As Integer


For intCounter = -1 To 1 Step 2
    lblOutput.Text &= intCounter.ToString & " "
Next intCounter
```

8. What is the value in the label `lblOutput` after the following code has been executed?

```
Dim intCounter As Integer


intCounter = 10
Do
    intCounter = intCounter - 2
    lblOutput.Text &= intCounter.ToString & " "
Loop Until (intCounter <= 5)
```

9. What is the value in the label `lblOutput` after the following code has been executed?

```
Dim intCounter As Integer

intCounter = 0
Do
    intCounter = intCounter + 2
    lblOutput.Text &= intCounter.ToString & " "
Loop While (intCounter > 5)
```

10. What is the value in the label `lblOutput` after the following code has been executed?

```
Dim intCounter As Integer

intCounter = -10
Do
    intCounter = intCounter + 2
    lblOutput.Text &= intCounter.ToString & " "
Loop While (intCounter > 10)
```

11. What is the value in the label `lblOutput` after the following code has been executed?

```
Dim sngCounter As Single
Dim sngTotal As Single

sngTotal = 0

For sngCounter = 0.5 To 3.5 Step 0.5
    sngTotal += sngCounter
Next sngCounter

lblOutput.Text = sngTotal.ToString
```

12. Write an application that computes the number of days in this year's month of February. Remember, in three out of every four years, the number of days equals 28. However, in one out of every four years, the number of days equals 29. Do not use a math trick to figure it out. Hint: Set a variable to the first day of the month and then increment it through all the days in the month. While you are incrementing the day of the month, keep track of the number of times you increment it and you will have your answer.

13. Write an application that computes the number of paydays in a single month. Assume that the company pays employees every Friday. Hint: The `Weekday` function will return `vbFriday` when the date passed to it is a Friday.

14. Chris just bought a Corvette. His payment is $790.50 a month. How many hours (round up to the nearest full hour) does it take for him to work to pay for his car each month? Because he didn't pay attention in class, his part-time job is flipping burgers, for which he is paid $5.50/hour. Unfortunately, he doesn't remember the `Divide` statement, so you must solve this problem using a loop instead of a simple calculation.

15. Create an application that contains two text boxes, called `txtHeight` and `txtWidth`. Additionally, create a label called `lblOutput` that will display a rectangle in Courier font when a positive height and length are entered in their respective text boxes. The rectangle should be "drawn" with asterisks and be completely filled in. Trigger the application drawing the rectangle on a button's `Click` event.

16. Create the same application as in Exercise 15, this time drawing the rectangle as hollow.

17. Write an application to compute the approximate odds of rolling an exact value when two dice are rolled. Each die has a value from 1 to 6. By rolling two dice, you can generate a value from 2 to 12. The application should roll the set dice 1,000 times and determine what percentage of time the desired combination is rolled. You should validate that the value you are checking for is a valid roll. (Hint: To simulate the roll of the dice, use the `Rnd` function.)

18. A person has a bank account containing $5,000. Each year the person withdraws $500 but gets 5% interest on the remaining amount. Write a function that returns the amount of money remaining in 10 years.

19. A person has the option to get $10,000 a day for a period of time, or $1 the first day and have the amount double each day. Write a function that computes the number of days required for the latter option to produce a greater total of money for the person receiving it.

20. Change the case study in Section 7.6 so that the user can enter the name of an employee and a message box displays that person's total pay. If the person is not found, display an appropriate message.

21. Change the case study in Section 7.6 so that the user can enter the name of an employee and the rows corresponding to that employee in the grid are removed. All remaining employees after the one deleted should be moved up in the grid. Make sure that you reduce the total number of rows in the grid by the number of rows deleted. Also, if the employee is not found, display a message box indicating the employee was not found.

INTERVIEW

An Interview with Joe Hummel

Joe Hummel is a Computer Scientist specializing in traditional CS education as well as Windows-based technologies such as VB, COM, MTS/COM+, and .NET. He works as a trainer for DevelopMentor, and is a professor of Computer Science at Lake Forest College. Joe received bachelor degrees in Math and Computer Science from Allegheny College and his Masters in Computer Science from the University of Michigan. At the University of California, Irvine, he focused on programming language design and optimizing compilers, and received his Ph.D. in Computer Science. He is co-author of Addison-Wesley's *Effective Visual Basic: How to Improve Your VB/COM+ Applications*.

Aside from teaching, what kinds of projects are you working on?

I'm developing courseware for a Windows training firm called *DevelopMentor*, and also I'm working on a reference manual for VB.NET. Visual Basic has always lacked what I felt is a proper language reference manual, so I'm trying to write that book for VB.NET. Finally, I'm developing a summer workshop for CS faculty on the topics of .NET, Windows applications, Web applications, and component-based, distributed system design. The goal is to empower faculty so they may introduce .NET and related concepts into their respective curriculums.

What are some of the challenges of using VB.NET? Do you have any suggestions for overcoming them?

The biggest challenge is for existing VB6 users. VB.NET offers some significant additions to the language, and it's not always clear how to use these new features. For example, VB.NET now offers multi-threading. Should all your Apps be multi-threaded? Definitely not. Multi-threading is hard to get right, and only appropriate in certain situations (like a web server that has to respond to potentially hundreds of client requests at the same time). As another example, VB.NET now supports both interfaces and inheritance—when should these be used, when should you use one over the other, both, or neither? Students with a good education in CS and object-oriented design will feel right at home in VB.NET, while the rest of us :-) have lots to learn before we can use VB.NET safely and effectively.

Do you have any advice for students entering the computer field using VB.NET?

Master the concepts, not where the semicolons go. The language isn't important, it's the concepts: programming logic, data structures, algorithms, software design, user-interface design, concurrency, etc. To be successful in the workplace you'll need to master different operating systems and programming languages, and be able to learn new concepts quickly. If all you know is VB, make sure you branch out and learn more about real OOP (VB6 is not truly OO), database access via SQL, and whatever else you can about computer science. VB is not the be-all-end-all, it's just another language for expressing your thoughts, better in some cases and worse in others. I like using VB, but mostly because it's fun, not because it's the best language. VB.NET is a much better language than VB6, but it still shouldn't be the only language in your repertoire.

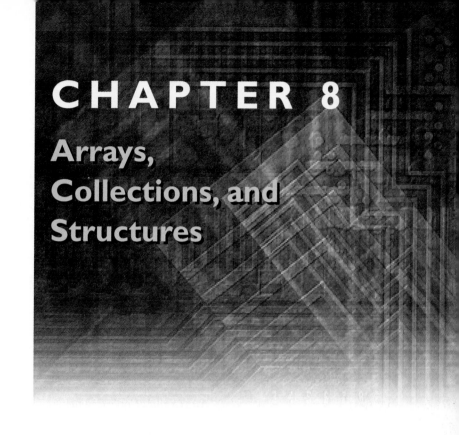

- Introduce arrays
- Introduce multidimensional arrays
- Explain how to use collections and why they are easy to store and access values
- Introduce structures

CHAPTER 8

Arrays, Collections, and Structures

What would you do if you lacked the ability to use controls like the MS flex grid to store multiple values simultaneously? Controls like the MS flex grid expand on the concept of a programming construct called an **array**. An array allows you to store multiple values of a data type in a single variable. An MS flex grid allows you to do this and provides an interface for the user to see the results graphically. Sometimes you will wish to store values without showing them to the user as with an MS flex grid.

While arrays give you an extremely efficient method of storing data, their rigid structure makes it challenging to delete values or store values of different data types. Visual Basic .NET provides the collection object to allow you to store objects in a single construct of different data types with the ability to easily add, access, and delete values.

8.1 Arrays

You can think of an array and its individual values as similar to calling a friend's house that has a fancy answering machine. The machine would have different mailboxes for each person in the house: 0 for Bill, 1 for Jerome, 2 for Kordell, and so on. You call the house with a single phone number, just as you will reference an array with a single variable name. Then to access the individual people in the house, you use an index representing the mailbox, as you will access the individual elements in an array by using an index.

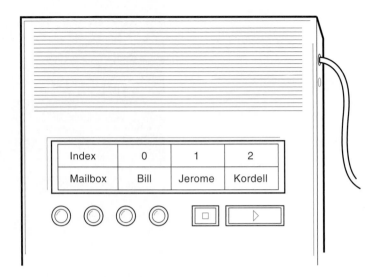

An array is declared using the following syntax:

`Dim` *ArrayName*`(`*UpperBound*`)` `As` *Datatype*

When defining an array, its name obeys the same rules as when declaring a variable. Therefore, an array name begins with a letter and may be followed by any number of letters, underscores, or digits. An array name can be as small as one letter or as large as 255 letters, underscores, and digits.

Individual values within an array are selected by using an index. The lowest index of an array is 0, while the **upper bound** of the array is the highest index in the array. An index must be a `Short`, an `Integer`, or a `Long` data type.

The data type is any valid variable like a `Short`, an `Integer`, or a `String`.

For example, the following code will define an array of six `Short` values called `shtGrades`. Remember, an array index starts at 0 and ends at the upper bound. With valid indexes from 0 to 5, you have six elements.

`Dim shtGrades(5) As Short`

Pictorially, the array would be represented as follows:

Array shtGrades						
Index	0	1	2	3	4	5
Values Relating to Index	0	0	0	0	0	0

COACH'S TIP

When an array is declared, the individual elements within the array are initialized in the same manner as variables of the data type the array is composed of. In this case, the array is declared as `Shorts`. Since `Shorts` initialize to 0, the individual components of the array are initialized to 0.

To access an individual value in an array, you place the subscript of the value you wish to access inside the parentheses. This can be seen using the following syntax:

ArrayName `(` *Index* `)`

Thus if you wanted to output the value stored in the array, `shtGrades`, at index 3, you could do so in a message box using the following code:

```
MsgBox(shtGrades(3).ToString())
```

Imagine if you had the following six grades: 90, 80, 77, 100, 95, and 67. If you wanted to store these grades, in order, into the array `shtGrades`, you would use the following code:

```
shtGrades(0) = 90
shtGrades(1) = 80
shtGrades(2) = 77
shtGrades(3) = 100
shtGrades(4) = 95
shtGrades(5) = 67
```

Graphically, the array would appear as follows:

Array shtGrades						
Index	0	1	2	3	4	5
Values Relating to Index	90	80	77	100	95	67

Arrays of Other Data Types

Arrays can be used to store values of other types of data besides numerical data. Arrays can be created from any data types. The following code shows how you can create an array of five `Strings` and initialize them to `"Allen Iverson"`, `"Aaron McKie"`, `"Eric Snow"`, `"Matt Harpring"`, and `"Derrick Coleman"`.

```
Dim strSixersNames(4) As String

strSixersNames(0) = "Allen Iverson"
strSixersNames(1) = "Aaron McKie"
strSixersNames(2) = "Eric Snow"
strSixersNames(3) = "Matt Harpring"
strSixersNames(4) = "Derrick Coleman"
```

If you wanted to store the salary of each player in terms of millions of dollars, you could store them in an array of `Single` variables. Therefore, if the salaries of each player were $7 million for Allen Iverson, $5.5 million for Aaron McKie, $4 million for Eric Snow, $2.7 million for Matt Harpring, and $8 million for Derrick Coleman, you could store them in the following code:

```
Dim sngSixersSalaries(4) As Single

sngSixersSalaries(0) = 7
sngSixersSalaries(1) = 5.5
sngSixersSalaries(2) = 4
sngSixersSalaries(3) = 2.7
sngSixersSalaries(4) = 8
```

COACH'S WARNING

Notice that the same indexes were used for each player's name and salary. This must be done if you want to associate the name with the salary.

DRILL 8.1

If an array has five elements, what is the highest index of a valid element in the array?

DRILL 8.2

How many elements are defined in the following array declaration?

```
Dim strDrillArray(5) As String
```

DRILL 8.3

Write the code required to declare an array of five `Strings` called `strDrillArray`. Then initialize the array to the following values: `"First Value"`, `"Second Value"`, `"Third Value"`, `"Fourth Value"`, and `"Fifth Value"`.

DRILL 8.4

Write the code required to declare an array of 1,000 `Integers` called `intDrillArray` with an index whose lower bound is 0 and upper bound is 999. Then initialize the array so that each element contains the value of its index. Hint: Use a loop.

COACH'S TIP

The data type of all of the elements of an array must be the same data type!

Stepping Through an Array

Many applications that utilize an array will require you to perform some action upon every element in the array. When this occurs you can use a `For` loop that steps from an index of 0 to the array's upper bound.

Imagine you wished to output all of the values in the array `strSixersNames`. You could use the following code:

```
Dim shtSixerName As Short

For shtSixerName = 0 To 4
    MsgBox(strSixersNames(shtSixerName))
Next
```

However, the code assumes that you know the upper bound of the array. While you will often know the upper bound, it is convenient to use the `UBound` function to determine the upper bound of an array. By passing an array to `UBound`, the upper bound of the array is returned. The following shows the previous code rewritten using `UBound` to determine the highest value of the loop.

```
Dim shtSixerName As Short

For shtSixerName = 0 To UBound(strSixersNames)
    MsgBox(strSixersNames(shtSixerName))
Next
```

The final way to loop is actually the simplest. You can loop through the array by stepping through each element of the array. You do not have to concern yourself with lower or upper bounds. All you have to do is declare a variable with the same data type as the array that you wish to step through. Then you can step through the array by using the following syntax:

```
Dim VariableName As Datatype

For Each VariableName In ArrayName
    Do something with VariableName
Next
```

Therefore, by using the For Each looping statement, you can simplify your loop further. See the following code:

```
Dim strSixerName As String

For Each strSixerName In strSixersNames
    MsgBox(strSixerName)
Next
```

Example: TV Ratings
Problem Description

Create an application that rates a TV show from 1 to 5, with 5 being the best and 1 being the worst. The user should enter the rating with a combo box so that only a value of 1 to 5 can be entered. As each rating is entered, the application should track how many of each rating is selected and display them on the form after 10 ratings are entered. (See Figure 8.1.)

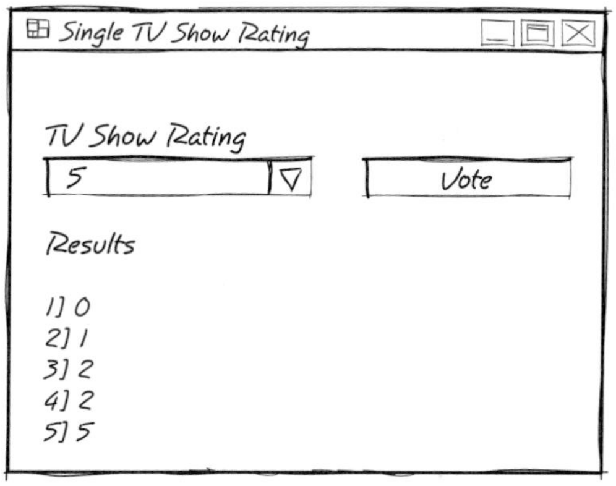

Figure 8.1
Sketch of TV ratings
program

Problem Discussion

You could write the application so that the total number of each rating is stored in a separate variable. You could create variables like `shtRating1`, `shtRating2`, `shtRating3`, `shtRating4`, and `shtRating5` and then increment each one every time a vote is cast corresponding to the appropriate variable. Observe the following code that implements a rating system employing this strategy.

First, you would declare the five variables to store the total of each rating, as well as a variable to store the total number of votes, in the `Declarations` section of the application.

```
'Code to be placed in the Declarations Section
Dim shtRating1 As Short
Dim shtRating2 As Short
Dim shtRating3 As Short
Dim shtRating4 As Short
Dim shtRating5 As Short
Dim shtTotalVotes As Short
```

Next, you would need to process each vote as the Voting button is clicked. You must track the total number of votes and output the result when all the votes have been cast. You can process each individual vote by using a `Select Case` statement and setting up a case for each possible vote.

```
Private Sub btnVote_Click(...
    'Check each possible vote.
    Select Case cboRating.Text
        Case "1"
            shtRating1 += 1
        Case "2"
            shtRating2 += 1
        Case "3"
            shtRating3 += 1
        Case "4"
            shtRating4 += 1
        Case "5"
            shtRating5 += 1
    End Select

    'Increment the number of votes processed
    shtTotalVotes += 1

    'If all ten votes have been processed then output the results
    If (shtTotalVotes = 10) Then
        Call OutputResults()
    End If

End Sub
```

To simplify the processing of the results, you can move code that displays the results into another subroutine.

```
Private Sub OutputResults()
    lblResults.Text = "1]   " & shtRating1.ToString & vbNewLine & _
    "2]   " & shtRating2.ToString & vbNewLine & _
    "3]   " & shtRating3.ToString & vbNewLine & _
    "4]   " & shtRating4.ToString & vbNewLine & _
    "5]   " & shtRating5.ToString
End Sub
```

COACH'S TIP

You can use the constant vbNewLine to make Strings appear on the next line of output.

You might not think that was a lot of wasted code; however, if you increased the choice of ratings from 1–5 to 1–100, your application's code would grow considerably. You obviously need a better approach.

An array is the perfect solution. Arrays allow a programmer to create a single variable that can store multiple values. These values can be referenced by an index similar to the index in an MS flex grid.

If you create a simple form with a single combo box that contains only the values 1, 2, 3, 4, and 5 and a button to process the votes, you can store each rating's votes in an array of Shorts. You will see that, aside from having fewer variables to deal with, you will also simplify the execution of the code.

While storing all of the votes in a single variable is convenient, having a lower bound of 0 is not always convenient. For example, if you wished to create an array of five Shorts to store your ratings from 1 to 5, it would seem logical for your array to be indexed from 1 to 5. However, due to performance issues, Visual Basic .NET forces you to start indexing from 0.

This can add a little confusion to some applications, but with care it is not too much of a burden. Observe the following code, which declares an array of five Shorts with an index from 0 to 4.

```
Dim shtRatings(4) As Short
```

This would allocate an array that looks as follows:

Array shtRatings					
Index	0	1	2	3	4
Values	0	0	0	0	0

If you have an array like this, you can store each of the results in one of the array elements; however, because the array index starts at 0 instead of 1, you have a problem.

The easiest solution would be to say that you are going to rate programs from 0 to 4 so that the ratings match the indexes. This is the worst possible solution. As a developer, you should not force a change to the way business is handled just to make your life simpler.

You have two viable solutions.

First, you could store the rating's votes in the array element indexed by 1 less than the rating's number. This would mean a rating of 1 would be stored at the index 0, a rating of 2 would be stored at the index of 1, a rating of 3 would be stored at the index of 2, a rating of 4 would be stored at the index of 3, and a rating of 5 would be stored at the index of 4.

Pictorially, it would look as follows:

Array shtRatings					
Index	0	1	2	3	4
Values Relating to Index	1	2	3	4	5

The other option would be to simply declare an array with one more value and ignore the values stored in the element at index 0. Pictorially, this would look as follows:

Array shtRatings						
Index	0	1	2	3	4	5
Values Relating to Index	Ignored	1	2	3	4	5

While the second solution requires an additional value to be declared in the array, the code is simpler, which will make the application smaller even with the wasted space in the array. Furthermore, the application will execute faster, so it is definitely the superior choice.

Problem Solution

With that, you now understand enough about arrays to rewrite your rating application. First, add the code required in the `Declarations` section: an array and a single variable to store the total number of votes.

```
'Code to be placed in the Declarations Section
Dim shtRatings(5) As Short
Dim shtTotalVotes As Short
```

The processing of the vote event is so simple that you can combine the code for storing the vote and outputting the results. Since each vote corresponds to the index in the array where the total of that vote is counted, you can directly add 1 to the rating voted for by using the current vote as an index for the array. Thus you can avoid using a `Select Case` statement. In addition, instead of having to list each variable separately when you output the results, you can use a `For` loop to step through the array and display each individual value. The code follows:

```
Private Sub btnRatings_Click(...
    'Declare variables
    Dim strOutputString As String
    Dim shtVote As Short

    'Add 1 to the current rating
    shtRatings(Val(cboRating.Text)) += 1

    'Add 1 to the total number of votes
    shtTotalVotes += 1

    'Check if all the votes have been entered
    If (shtTotalVotes = 10) Then
        'Build the output string by looping through the array
        For shtVote = 1 To 5
            strOutputString &= "   " & shtVote.ToString() & "] " & _
                        shtRatings(shtVote).ToString() & vbNewLine
```

(continues)

(continued)

```
        Next shtVote
        'Copy the output string to the label
        lblResults.Text = strOutputString
    End If

End Sub
```

COACH'S WARNING

Values that you wish to store in an array do not always map themselves directly to the indexes in an array as in the previous ratings example; however, arrays can still be used.

Initializing Arrays at Time of Declaration

While individual array values can be initialized as individual lines of code as in the previous example, it is often convenient to initialize an array in the same line of code as you declare the array.

You can initialize an array by setting it equal to the values you wish to initialize the array to enclosed within curly braces and separated by commas.

Observe the code initializing the strSixersNames array to the same values, but with one line of code:

```
Dim strSixersNames() As String = {"Allen Iverson", "Aaron McKie", _
                                  "Eric Snow", "Matt Harpring", _
                                  "Derrick Coleman"}
```

Similarly, you can initialize the sngSixersSalaries with the following code:

```
Dim sngSixersSalaries() As Single = {7, 5.5, 4, 2.7, 8}
```

DRILL 8.5

Declare and initialize an array of five prices—19.95, 12.95, 10.95, 99.99, 10.00—called sngPrices of data type Single.

DRILL 8.6

Declare and initialize an array called strMovies of the data type String. The array should be initialized at the time it is declared to these five movie titles: "The Princess Bride", "Space Balls", "Clerks", "Shrek", and "Fletch".

8.2 Two-Dimensional Arrays

Sometimes a problem does not map itself to an array of only one dimension. The arrays that have been introduced so far all have one dimension and are referred to as **single-dimensional arrays**. These arrays simplified your handling of multiple variables, you can also simplify your handling of multiple arrays by using a **two-dimensional array**.

Revisit your rating system application. However, instead of storing the votes for one television show, now store the results for five television shows, as in Figure 8.2.

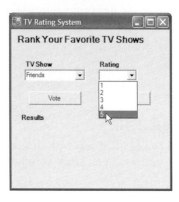

Figure 8.2
TV Ratings application

Now you have the same dilemma that you had before you were introduced to arrays. With five TV shows to track ratings for, you would need five sets of five ratings. You could just repeat the code for each show. NOT! Visual Basic .NET provides two-dimensional arrays, which will efficiently solve this problem.

A two-dimensional array is declared using the following template:

COACH'S TIP

The upper bound of one dimension does not have to be the same as the upper bound for the other dimension.

```
Dim ArrayName(UpperBound1,UpperBound2) As Datatype
```

Now, writing the application to track five TV shows is not significantly more complicated than to track one TV show. First, you must create the interface to a rating for each of five TV shows. You can create the interface in Figure 8.2 by using two combo boxes, a series of labels, and a single button.

Declaring the Array

You must declare a two-dimensional array of ratings in the `Declarations` section of the application. The two-dimensional array of `Integers` can be thought of as a grid with the ratings for each TV show contained within a single row of the grid. Each column of the grid can be thought of as containing the number of votes for each rating. Therefore, the first column would contain the number of votes for a rating of `1` for all shows. However, since an array starts at `0`, the votes for a rating of `1` will be stored in column `0`. This is shown in the following:

	Rating 1 Column 0	Rating 2 Column 1	Rating 3 Column 2	Rating 4 Column 3	Rating 5 Column 4
Show 1 Row 0	(0,0)	(0,1)	(0,2)	(0,3)	(0,4)
Show 2 Row 1	(1,0)	(1,1)	(1,2)	(1,3)	(1,4)
Show 3 Row 2	(2,0)	(2,1)	(2,2)	(2,3)	(2,4)
Show 4 Row 3	(3,0)	(3,1)	(3,2)	(3,3)	(3,4)
Show 5 Row 4	(4,0)	(4,1)	(4,2)	(4,3)	(4,4)

The code follows:

```
'Code to be placed in the Declarations Section
Dim shtRatings(5, 5) As Integer
```

Processing a Vote

The first step in processing a vote is to ensure that both the TV show and rating combo boxes have a valid value. While the choices have been predetermined by placing them in the combo box, it is possible for a user not to specify either a TV show or a rating. If this occurs, you should not process the vote and display a message to the user indicating an error has occurred.

Once you have determined that the selections in the combo boxes are valid, you can use the `SelectedIndex` of each combo box as an index into the two-dimensional array. (If you do not remember how to do this, look back at the Oscar Nomination application in Chapter 6.) The `cboTVShow` combo box will select the row, while the `cboRating` combo box will select the column. The actual vote will be recorded by adding 1 to the value stored at the location specified by the two combo boxes.

The code follows:

```
Private Sub btnVote_Click(...
    'Check for valid input
    If (cboTVShow.Text = "" Or cboRating.Text = "") Then
        MsgBox("A vote will only count if you enter a valid show and rating")

    Else 'Process Vote
        'Record Vote
        shtRatings(cboTVShow.SelectedIndex, cboRating.SelectedIndex) += 1

        cboTVShow.Text = "" 'Clear choice
        cboRating.Text = "" 'Clear choice
    End If
End Sub
```

Outputting the Results

To output the results of five ratings for each of five shows, you must loop through the two-dimensional array one row at a time. Since each row contains the results of one show, you can set up a nested `For` with the outer loop stepping through the TV shows and the inner loop stepping through the votes.

Each TV show will have its name output and then the number of times each ranking was recorded. The results for each show will be output in a separate message box. The code follows:

```
Private Sub btnResults_Click(...
    'Declare variables
    Dim shtTVShow As Integer
    Dim shtVote As Integer
    Dim strOutputString As String

    'Loop through the TV Shows
    For shtTVShow = 0 To 4
        'Store the name of the show in the results
        strOutputString &= cboTVShow.Items(shtTVShow) & " "
```

(continues)

(continued)

```
        'Loop through the possible ratings
        For shtVote = 0 To 4
            'Store results of a vote in a String
            strOutputString &= (shtVote + 1).ToString & "] " & _
                            (shtRatings(shtTVShow, shtVote).ToString) & " "
        Next shtVote

        'Start a new line after each show
        strOutputString &= vbNewLine

    Next shtTVShow

    'Copy results from String to label.
    lblResults.Text = strOutputString
End Sub
```

COACH'S TIP

Instead of a loop from 0 to 4, you could also have used the `Count` method of the `Items` property of the `cboTVShow` combo box to determine the total number of items. Therefore, the `For` loop could have been written as

```
For shtTVShow = 0 To cboTVShow.Items.Count() -1
```

DRILL 8.7

What's wrong with the following code, which declares a two-dimensional array to store the number and name of each of the players for the Sixers?

```
Dim intPlayers(5, 2) As Integer
intPlayers(0,0) = 3
intPlayers(0,1) = "Allen Iverson"
intPlayers(1,0) = 20
intPlayers(1,1) = "Eric Snow"
intPlayers(2,0) = 42
intPlayers(2,1) = "Matt Harpring"
intPlayers(3,0) = 8
intPlayers(3,1) = "Aaron McKie"
intPlayers(4,0) = 40
intPlayers(4,1) = "Derrick Coleman"
```

DRILL 8.8

What's wrong with the following code, which declares a two-dimensional array of integers and initializes each value to 2?

```
Dim intDrillValues(5, 5) As Integer
Dim intRow As Integer
Dim intCol As Integer

For intRow = 5 To 1 Step -1
    For intCol = 5 To 1 Step -1
        intDrillValues(intRow, intCol) = 2
    Next intCol
Next intRow
```

DRILL 8.9

Will the following two sets of code accomplish the same result? If not, explain why not.

```
Dim intDrillValues(2, 2) As Integer
Dim intRow As Integer
Dim intCol As Integer

For intRow = 0 To 2
    For intCol = 0 To 2
        intDrillValues(intRow, intCol) = 2
    Next intCol
Next intRow
```

and

```
Dim intDrillValues(2, 2) As Integer
Dim intRow As Integer
Dim intCol As Integer

For intCol = 0 To 2
    For intRow = 0 To 2
        intDrillValues(intCol, intRow) = 2
    Next intRow
Next intCol
```

DRILL 8.10

Will the following two sets of code accomplish the same result? If not, explain why not.

```
Dim intDrillValues(4, 2) As Integer
Dim intRow As Integer
Dim intCol As Integer

For intRow = 0 To 4
```

(continues)

DRILL 8.10 (continued)

```
        For intCol = 0 To 2
            intDrillValues(intRow, intCol) = 2
        Next intCol
Next intRow
```

and

```
Dim intDrillValues(4, 2) As Integer
Dim intRow As Integer
Dim intCol As Integer

For intCol = 0 To 4
    For intRow = 0 To 2
        intDrillValues(intRow, intCol) = 2
    Next intRow
Next intCol
```

8.3   Collections

Arrays are a good solution to storing some of your data. However, often your needs to store objects will exceed the limitations of arrays. A **collection** picks up where an array leaves off.

There are a few major limitations to an array. An array can only store values of the same data type; an array makes it difficult to look up values; and an array makes it difficult to delete values. A collection gives you the functionality to accomplish all of these tasks effortlessly.

A collection is a class that comes with Visual Basic .NET. You have already used collections when you added items to a combo or list box. The `Items` property of a combo or list box was actually a collection object.

Collections can also be declared in code. To declare a collection, you would follow the same syntax as any other reference variable or object. Observe the following syntax:

```
Dim CollectionName As New Collection()
```

So to declare a collection called `Students`, you would use the following code:

```
Dim Students As New Collection()
```

Once a collection is declared, it can be manipulated using the `Add`, `Item`, and `Remove` methods.

Adding Items to a Collection

Adding an item to a collection is easy because you neither have to worry about what types of objects or variables you add to a collection nor how many items you have in the collection. To add an item to a collection, you simply call the `Add` method with two parameters. Observe the following syntax for adding an item to a method:

```
CollectionName.Add(ItemToAdd, KeyValue)
```

The `ItemToAdd` can be anything. It can be an object, an `Integer`, a `String`, or any value you wish to store in the collection. The `KeyValue` is either a numeric value or `String` that uniquely identifies the value you are adding to the collection.

Imagine if you wanted to create a collection of students that were in a Visual Basic .NET class. You would need to declare a class called `Students`. It should have properties for first name, last name, student number, major, and GPA. Then you could declare a collection called `VBClass` to store the students. See the following code, which shows the class `Students` and declares the collection and places two students within it:

 COACH'S TIP

Pick your `KeyValues` carefully. If you used a last name as a `KeyValue`, the odds are after a while you would have a duplicate last name. This will cause an error to occur.

```
Public Class Student
    'Private attributes
    Private mstrFirstName As String
    Private mstrLastName As String
    Private mstrMajor As String
    Private mlngStudentNumber As Long
    Private msngGPA As Single

    'FirstName Property Statements
    Public Property FirstName() As String
        Get
            Return mstrFirstName
        End Get
        Set(ByVal Value As String)
            mstrFirstName = Value
        End Set
    End Property

    'LastName Property Statements
    Public Property LastName() As String
        Get
            Return mstrLastName
        End Get
        Set(ByVal Value As String)
            mstrLastName = Value
        End Set
    End Property

    'Major Property Statements
    Public Property Major() As String
        Get
            Return mstrMajor
        End Get
        Set(ByVal Value As String)
            mstrMajor = Value
        End Set
    End Property
```

(continues)

(continued)

```
    'StudentNumber Property Statements
    Public Property StudentNumber() As Long
        Get
            Return mlngStudentNumber
        End Get
        Set(ByVal Value As Long)
            mlngStudentNumber = Value
        End Set
    End Property

    'GPA Property Statements
    Public Property GPA() As Single
        Get
            Return msngGPA
        End Get
        Set(ByVal Value As Single)
            msngGPA = Value
        End Set
    End Property

    'Constructor
    Sub New(ByVal strFirstName As String, ByVal strLastName As String, _
            ByVal strMajor As String, ByVal lngStudentNumber As Long, _
            ByVal sngGPA As Single)
        mstrFirstName = strFirstName
        mstrLastName = strLastName
        mstrMajor = strMajor
        mlngStudentNumber = lngStudentNumber
        msngGPA = sngGPA
    End Sub
End Class

    'Declare and instantiate collection called VBClass
    Dim VBClass As New Collection()

    'Declare and instantiate an object of the student class
    Dim clsStudent As New Student("Jeff", "Salvage", _
                        "Computer Science", 123456789, 3.9)

    'Add the student object to the collection
    VBClass.Add(clsStudent, "Jeff Salvage")

    'instantiate another object of the student class
    clsStudent = New Student("John", "Nunn", _
                        "Pre Med", 987654321, 4.0)

    'Add the 2nd student to the collection
    VBClass.Add(clsStudent, "John Nunn")
```

Retrieving Values from a Collection

Retrieving a value from a collection returns a reference to the item you request. It allows you to easily access a value stored in the collection without removing the value from the collection.

There are two ways you can retrieve values that you have stored in a collection. Both use the `Item` method.

The most intuitive way to retrieve items is to look it up using the `KeyValue` you added it to the collection with. See the following syntax:

VariableName = *CollectionName*`.Item(`*KeyValue*`)`

Therefore, if you wanted to retrieve the student with the `KeyValue` `"John Nunn"` from the `VBClass` collection, you would use the following code:

```
Dim clsRetrievedStudent As Student
clsRetrievedStudent = VBClass.Item("John Nunn")
```

> ## COACH'S TIP
>
> The variable you assign to the return value from the `Item` method must be the same data type as the value being returned.

The other way you can retrieve items from a collection is by using the items index. As each item is added to a collection, it is given an index. In the previous example, the first student added to the collection is given the index 1, and the second student is given the index 2. Therefore, if you want to access the object containing Jeff Salvage's information, you would use an index of 1, while if you wanted to access the object containing John Nunn's information, you would use an index of 2.

See the following code, which displays the names of the students in the collection at indexes 1 and 2.

```
'Declare object to hold a student
Dim clsRetrievedStudent As Student

'Assign a student from the collection at index 1 to the object
clsRetrievedStudent = VBClass.Item(1)

'Output information from the retrieved object
MsgBox(clsRetrievedStudent.FirstName & " " & clsRetrievedStudent.LastName)

'Assign another student from the collection at index 2 to the object
clsRetrievedStudent = VBClass.Item(2)

'Output information from the 2nd student
MsgBox(clsRetrievedStudent.FirstName & " " & clsRetrievedStudent.LastName)
```

COACH'S WARNING

You must be careful when retrieving values from a collection. If you retrieve a value and modify it, you will modify it within the collection as well. Observe the following code:

```
'Declare an object to hold a student
Dim clsRetrievedStudent As Student
Dim clsRetrievedStudent2ndTime As Student

'Assign a student from the collection at index 1 to the object
clsRetrievedStudent = VBClass.Item(1)

'Output information retrieved from the object
MsgBox(clsRetrievedStudent.FirstName & " " & clsRetrievedStudent.LastName)
```

(continues)

COACH'S WARNING (continued)

```
'Change the first name of the student stored in the object
clsRetrievedStudent.FirstName = "Bob"

'Assign the student from the collection at index 1 to another object
clsRetrievedStudent2ndTime = VBClass.Item(1)

'Output information retrieved from the object
MsgBox(clsRetrievedStudent2ndTime.FirstName & " " & _
      clsRetrievedStudent2ndTime.LastName)
```

The output in the message boxes would be `"Jeff Salvage"` and then `"Bob Salvage"`. This is because when the object retrieved from the collection was modified, so was the object in the collection.

Deleting Values from a Collection

An item can be deleted from a collection just as easily as it is added. To delete a value from a collection without returning it, use the `Remove` method.

The `Remove` method can be used in two ways, just like the `Item` method. Either you can delete a value by using the `KeyValue` that you added it to the collection with or you can use the index of the item.

The syntax to delete an object from a collection using the `KeyValue` is as follows:

CollectionName.`Remove`(*KeyValue*)

Therefore, if you wanted to delete the student with the `KeyValue` `"Jeff Salvage"`, you would use the following code:

```
VBClass.Remove("Jeff Salvage")
```

The syntax to delete an object from a collection using the index is as follows:

CollectionName.`Remove`(*Index*)

Therefore, if you wanted to delete the first student in the collection, you would use the following code:

```
VBClass.Remove(1)
```

COACH'S WARNING

It is preferable to use `KeyValues` instead of indexes. By using indexes, it is easy to get confused when objects are added or deleted from the collection.

```
'Declare and instantiate collection called VBClass
Dim VBClass As New Collection()

'Declare and instantiate an object of the student class
Dim clsStudent As New Student("Jeff", "Salvage", _
                       "Computer Science", 123456789, 3.9)
```

(continues)

```
'Add the student object to the collection using the key "Jeff Salvage"
VBClass.Add(clsStudent, "Jeff Salvage")

'Instantiate another object of the student class
clsStudent = New Student("John", "Nunn", _
                         "Pre Med", 987654321, 4.0)

'Add the 2nd student to the collection using the key "John Nunn"
VBClass.Add(clsStudent, "John Nunn")

'Removes first student
VBClass.Remove(1)

'Removes remaining student
VBClass.Remove(2)
```

You might think this code deletes the two students. However, when the first student is deleted, the second student becomes the one at index 1. Therefore, the correct remove code should be as follows:

```
'Declare and instantiate collection called VBClass
Dim VBClass As New Collection()

'Declare and instantiate an object of the student class
Dim clsStudent As New Student("Jeff", "Salvage", _
                         "Computer Science", 123456789, 3.9)

'Add the student object to the collection using the key "Jeff Salvage"
VBClass.Add(clsStudent, "Jeff Salvage")

'Instantiate another object of the student class
clsStudent = New Student("John", "Nunn", _
                         "Pre Med", 987654321, 4.0)

'Add the 2nd student to the collection using the key "John Nunn"
VBClass.Add(clsStudent, "John Nunn")

'Removes first student
VBClass.Remove(1)

'Removes remaining student
VBClass.Remove(1)
```

DRILL 8.11

Does the following code execute without error? If so, is anything left in the collection?

```
Dim VBClass As New Collection()
Dim clsStudent As New Student("Jeff", "Salvage", _
                         "Computer Science", 123456789, 3.9)

VBClass.Add(clsStudent, "Jeff Salvage")
```

(continues)

```
clsStudent = New Student("John", "Nunn", _
                         "Pre Med", 987654321, 4.0)
VBClass.Add(clsStudent, "John Nunn")

VBClass.Remove(2)
VBClass.Remove(1)
```

Example: Student Class with Collections for Grades
Problem Description

Create a Student class that can track a student's first name, last name, student number, major, and any number of class grades (0 to 4). The class should have properties to access each of the values being tracked and a method to return the GPA.

Problem Discussion

The decision for the first four values is straightforward. A property must exist for each value tracked. The first name, last name, and major should all be Strings, while the student number should be a Long. Since you want to be able to store any number of grades, a collection is an ideal choice. This will allow you to add, remove, and look up grades by using the methods that are built into a collection.

By implementing the storage of grades as a collection, no additional information is required to write the GPA method.

Problem Solution

The code for all but the GPA method is very straightforward. The GPA method will calculate the average of the grades contained within the collection. A For loop is used to add each grade to a total. Just as with arrays, you can use the For Each syntax of a For loop to loop through all the values in a collection. Finally, by accessing the Count method of a collection, the GPA method can determine the total number of grades and calculate the average.

The code follows:

```
Public Class Student
    'Property Declarations for Student
    Private mstrFirstName As String
    Private mstrLastName As String
    Private mlngStudentNumber As Long
    Private mstrMajor As String
    Private mintGrades As Collection

    'FirstName Get and Set statements
    Public Property FirstName() As String
        Get
            Return mstrFirstName
        End Get
        Set(ByVal Value As String)
            mstrFirstName = Value
        End Set
    End Property
```

(continues)

(continued)

```
    'LastName Get and Set statements
    Public Property LastName() As String
        Get
            Return mstrLastName
        End Get
        Set(ByVal Value As String)
            mstrLastName = Value
        End Set
    End Property

    'StudentNumber Get and Set statements
    Public Property StudentNumber() As Long
        Get
            Return mlngStudentNumber
        End Get
        Set(ByVal Value As Long)
            mlngStudentNumber = Value
        End Set
    End Property

    'Major Get and Set statements
    Public Property Major() As String
        Get
            Return mstrMajor
        End Get
        Set(ByVal Value As String)
            mstrMajor = Value
        End Set
    End Property

    'Grades Get and Set statements
    Public Property Grades() As Collection
        Get
            Return mintGrades
        End Get
        Set(ByVal Value As Collection)
            mintGrades = Value
        End Set
    End Property

'Constructor for Student Class
    Public Sub New(ByVal strFirstName As String, _
                ByVal strLastName As String, _
                ByVal lngStudentNumber As Long, _
                ByVal strMajor As String)
        mstrFirstName = strFirstName
        mstrLastName = strLastName
        mlngStudentNumber = lngStudentNumber
        mstrMajor = strMajor
    End Sub

    'GPA method
    Public Function GPA() As Single
```

(continues)

(continued)

```
            Dim intSum As Integer
            Dim intGrade As Integer

            intSum = 0

            For Each intGrade In mintGrades
                intSum += intGrade
            Next

            Return intSum / mintGrades.Count()
        End Function
End Class
```

Collections of Different Objects

Once you are comfortable with using collections to store objects in a single variable, it is no more difficult to store different types of objects within a single variable. Observe the following code, which creates a collection called `People` and stores a person that was created from the `Employee` class from Chapter 6 and the `Student` class you just created.

```
'Declare and instantiate a collection of people
Dim People As New Collection()

'Declare and instantiate the student Jeff Salvage
Dim clsStudent As New Student("Jeff", "Salvage", _
                              123456789, "Computer Science")

'Declare and instantiate the employee Nelson Brown
Dim clsEmployee As New Employee("Nelson", "Brown", 8, 8, 7, 7, 9, 50.0)

'Add the student Jeff Salvage to the collection
People.Add(clsStudent, "Jeff Salvage")

'Add the employee Nelson Brown to the collection
People.Add(clsEmployee, "Nelson Brown")
```

COACH'S WARNING

Care must be taken so that when you retrieve an object using the `Item` method you assign it to an object of the correct class definition. In the following, observe the correct and incorrect retrieval of objects given the previous code:

```
clsEmployee = People.Item("Jeff Salvage") 'Incorrect assignment
clsStudent = People.Item("Jeff Salvage") 'Correct assignment
```

8.4 Structures

Visual Basic .NET has another construct, a **structure**. A structure in Visual Basic .NET can be thought of as a class with fewer features. Specifically, a structure cannot be inherited as classes can. Other than that, they are very similar except for the fact that structures are allocated quicker than objects. However, the area of memory in which they are allocated is limited, and therefore, structure use should be limited to constructs that require speed.

Objects are reference type variables and must be allocated with a `New` command. However, structures are value type variables and can be instantiated without the `New` command in the same manner as `Integers`, `Decimals`, and `Booleans`.

Just as classes can have property statements and methods, so can structures. Because so much of the functionality of a class is built into a structure, you might be tempted to use structures all the time. However, structures should be used with caution. Inheritance is a key concept that will allow you to reuse code in an efficient manner. You will learn about inheritance in Chapter 10. Choosing a structure implementation over a class will limit the future expansion of your construct.

Furthermore, by allocating memory for a structure from the stack as opposed to the heap, you could have memory allocation problems. The heap, while slower than the stack, is much larger. If a large number of structures are stored in an application, it could lead to problems.

With this long-winded disclaimer out of the way, here is the syntax for creating a structure. It is extremely similar to the syntax for creating a class.

```
Scope Structure StructureName
    Properties Definitions Go Here

    Property Get/Set Statements Go Here

    Methods Go Here
End Structure
```

There is no difference between a class and a structure for defining the properties, property statements, or methods.

To create a `Student` structure, use the following code:

```
Public Structure Student
    'Property declarations for Student
    Private mstrFirstName As String
    Private mstrLastName As String
    Public mstrMajor As String
    Public msngGPA As Single
    Public msngCredits As Single

    'Property statements for FirstName
    Public Property FirstName() As String
        Get
            Return mstrFirstName
        End Get
        Set(ByVal Value As String)
            mstrFirstName = Value
        End Set
    End Property
```

(continues)

(continued)

```
      'Property statements for LastName
      Public Property LastName() As String
          Get
               Return mstrLastName
          End Get
          Set(ByVal Value As String)
              mstrLastName = Value
          End Set
      End Property

      'Property statements for Major
      Public Property Major() As String
          Get
               Return mstrMajor
          End Get
          Set(ByVal Value As String)
              mstrFirstName = Value
          End Set
      End Property

      'Property statements for GPA
      Public Property GPA() As Single
          Get
               Return msngGPA
          End Get
          Set(ByVal Value As Single)
              msngGPA = Value
          End Set
      End Property

      'Property statements for Credits
      Public Property Credits() As String
          Get
               Return msngCredits
          End Get
          Set(ByVal Value As String)
              msngCredits = Value
          End Set
      End Property

      'Method definition for outputting Student information
      Public Sub OutputStudent()
          MsgBox(mstrFirstName & " " & mstrLastName & _
          " " & mstrMajor & " " & msngGpa.ToString() _
          & " " & msngCredits)
      End Sub
End Structure
```

Once you have created a structure, you can use it to create variables just as you would any other automatic variable type. See the following template:

Dim *VariableName* As *StructureName*

Therefore, to create a structure called `JeffSalvage` from the `Student` structure you just created, use the following code:

```
Dim JeffSalvage As Student
```

COACH'S WARNING

You cannot create a structure and a class of the same name in the same project. Therefore, if you tried to create the `Student` class and `Student` structure that was introduced in this chapter in the same project, you would get an error.

CORNER

Expanding the Concept of Arrays to Include Controls

In older versions of Visual Basic, you were able to create arrays of controls directly on the form. By doing so, your code to process the information for similar controls could be greatly reduced.

Unfortunately, Visual Basic .NET will not directly allow you to place controls in an array on a form. You can, however, create an array of controls in code and then programmatically place the controls on the form.

Imagine you want to create an application that rates 5 shows at once. You want to list all 5 shows on the form and have a combo box for each show. The combo box would contain the possible rating values of 1 to 5.

If you did not use an array of controls, you would be forced to write code that checked each combo box separately. While doing this for 5 controls is not overly tedious, if the number of controls was increased, the tedious nature of coding without arrays would be very evident.

Observe in Figure 8.3 how your application should look when it is executing.

Figure 8.3
Rating application while running

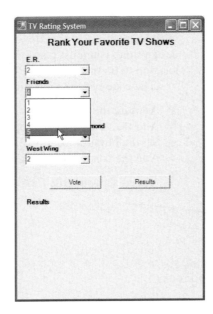

All of the labels and combo boxes are visible. However, when you set up the form, you can only place the labels in the appropriate places, as seen in Figure 8.4.

Figure 8.4
Rating form in development environment

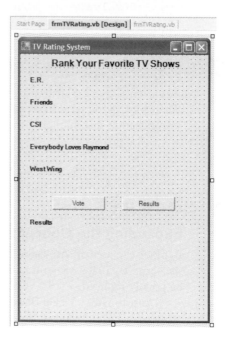

Declaring Variables With your form set up as in Figure 8.4, the code required is not overly complex. First you will need to create a two-dimensional array of Shorts to store the ratings of each of five shows. Additionally, you will have to create an array of combo boxes to store the possible rating of each show. These variables should be coded in the Declarations section of the form.

```
Dim shtRatings(4, 4) As Short
Dim cboRatings(4) As ComboBox
```

Initializing the Combo Boxes Since the combo boxes are not placed on the form at design time, you must place them on the form before the user sees the form. The best location to do this from is the forms constructor.

The code required must do the following for each combo box:

◆ Allocate the combo box
◆ Add the items that will appear in the combo box
◆ Set the physical location on the form for the combo box
◆ Add the combo box to the form's controls object

This is shown in the following code:

```
Public Sub New()
    MyBase.New()

    'This call is required by the Windows Form Designer
    InitializeComponent()

    'Add any initialization after the InitializeComponent() call
    Dim shtShow As Short
```

(continues)

(continued)

```
    'Loop and create 5 combo boxes
    For shtShow = 0 To 4
        'Instantiate and assign a combo box to the array
        cboRatings(shtShow) = New ComboBox()

        'Add individual items to the combo box (1, 2, 3, 4, 5)
        AddItems(cboRatings(shtShow))

        'Set the location of the combo box
        cboRatings(shtShow).Location = New Point(16, 56 + (40 * shtShow))

        'Add combo box to the collection of controls for the form
        Controls.Add(cboRatings(shtShow))
    Next shtShow

End Sub
```

A `For` loop is used so that the code can be written once and applied to all the combo boxes in the array. Each combo box has to be allocated with the `New` command because when the array was declared only a reference to each combo box was allocated.

When the combo box is allocated, its `Items` collection is empty. The collection needs to contain the values 1 to 5. Instead of cluttering the code in the form's constructor, the code calls a subroutine that will populate the collection. This will be shown shortly.

Once the combo box is properly allocated and initialized, it must be placed at the proper location on the form. The `Location` property of a combo box actually is a `Point` object. Therefore, you need to allocate a `Point` with the proper location for the leftmost corner of the combo box. All the combo boxes will be at a horizontal position of 16. The vertical position will be determined in a direct relationship to the combo box's index in the array. The first combo box should be in a vertical position of 56, and each combo box after it should be 40 positions lower.

The final step is to pass the combo box to the `Add` method of the form's `Controls` object.

The subroutine required to add the ratings to the combo box's `Items` property is straightforward.

```
Private Sub AddItems(ByRef cboTVShow As ComboBox)
    'Declare variables
    Dim shtRating As Short

    'Loop and add each rating to the combo box
    For shtRating = 1 To 5
        cboTVShow.Items.Add(shtRating)
    Next
End Sub
```

COACH'S WARNING

It would be more efficient if you could create a single collection for the ratings and assign it in one statement to each of the combo box's `Items` object; however, Microsoft has made the `Items` object read-only, so you cannot do this.

Processing the Vote By your creating the combo boxes as an array, the processing of the votes for all five shows becomes relatively simple. A `For` loop can be used to process each of the combo boxes. With five combo boxes in the array with indexes from 0 to 4, your `For` loop will process from 0 to 4.

As each iteration of the `For` loop is executed, a different combo box and show will be processed. The value of the loop counter, `intTVShow`, will determine the row selected in the two-dimensional array of ratings and the combo box that will be processed.

The process for a combo box is to first check that the combo box has a valid entry. If a combo box has a blank, you will just skip it as a nonvote. Then you must add 1 to the rating selected by the user. Since the ratings indexes map directly to their locations in the array, you can add 1 by selecting the column in the array by using the `SelectedIndex` property of the combo box. The row of the array is selected by using the loop counter, `intTVShow`.

Finally, you will want to reset the `Text` property of the combo box to blank. The code follows:

```
Private Sub btnVote_Click(...
    'Declare variables
    Dim shtTVShow As Short

    'Loop through all 5 TV shows
    For shtTVShow = 0 To 4
        'Check for valid input
        If (cboRatings(shtTVShow).Text <> "") Then
            'Record Vote
            shtRatings(shtTVShow, cboRatings(shtTVShow).SelectedIndex) += 1

            'Clear choice
            cboRatings(shtTVShow).Text = ""
        End If
    Next shtTVShow
End Sub
```

Outputting the Results To output the results of the ratings, you will use a label that will display all the results of all of the ratings.

Again, you will use a `For` loop to process each show. For each show, you will build a `String` that will contain the text to be displayed in the label.

The first item added to the `String` is the TV show's name. Then for each show, the rating and the number of times the rating was selected is appended to the output string. Additionally, a `"]"` and a space are added to the `String` to beautify the output.

When the entire `String` has been built for a TV show, it is output in a message box. Then the outer `For` loop is incremented and the next TV show is processed.

```
Private Sub btnResults_Click(...
    'Declare variables
    Dim shtTVShow As Integer
    Dim shtVote As Integer
    Dim strOutputString As String

    'Loop through all 5 TV shows
    For shtTVShow = 0 To 4
        'Add the name of the TV Show to the output string
        strOutputString &= cboRatings(shtTVShow).Items(shtTVShow) & " "
```

(continues)

(continued)

```
        'Loop through each rating for a TV show
        For shtVote = 0 To 4
            'Add number of votes for each rating to the output string
            strOutputString &= (shtVote + 1).ToString & "] " & _
                (shtRatings(shtTVShow, shtVote).ToString) & " "
        Next shtVote

        'Start a new line for the next TV Show
        strOutputString &= vbNewLine
    Next shtTVShow

    'Copy output to a label
    lblResults.Text = strOutputString
End Sub
```

COACH'S WARNING

Note that the first rating is located at index 0, the second rating is located at index 1, and so on. Therefore, you must add 1 to the index when you display it.

◆ 8.5   Case Study

Problem Description

This case study will be a bit of a departure from the other case studies in the text. Instead of adding functionality to your existing case studies, this case study will show you a method for increasing the efficiency part of your application.

This case study will modify the case study from Chapter 7 so that the selection of the proper pay rate will be more efficient.

Problem Discussion

In the previous chapters, you were shown two methods for selecting the pay rate for an employee. You could have used an `If/ElseIf/EndIf` structure or you could have used a `Select/Case` structure. Both of these methods are perfectly fine when the number of choices is fairly small. However, often the number of choices can grow large. If this is the case, you can optimize your query by placing the most probable choices at the beginning of your structure. This of course will not help the efficiency of those choices listed last.

With the use of arrays, you can solve this problem. By using arrays properly, you can develop a solution that will be equally fast for all choices. Indeed, other than a one-time initialization hit on performance, the speed of execution will not increase at all when the number of choices increases. This is much better than if you used the comparison structures you previously utilized.

All you need to do is declare an array equal in size to the number of items you wish to compare. Then you must initialize the array to store the values you wish to assign if a particular item is selected. Finally, you use the index of the selected item in the list box to be the index in the array. Then you will select the appropriate value without searching all of the choices.

Problem Solution

Step 1: Add the array to the form's declaration section. Since your application has four choices, declare the array to contain four Integers. (See Figure 8.5.)

```
frmPayroll.vb [Design]*  frmPayroll.vb*
frmPayroll                                          (Declarations)
Public Class frmPayroll
    Inherits System.Windows.Forms.Form
    'Constants to define pay rates
    Const intSalesPayRate = 25
    Const intProcessingPayRate = 15
    Const intManagementPayRate = 50
    Const intPhonePayRate = 10

    'Array to store all pay rates
    Dim intPayRates(3) As Integer
```

Figure 8.5   Array added to form's declarations

COACH'S TIP

Remember, if you want four Integers in the array, the upper bound is 3.

Step 2: Add the code to initialize the array. As the list box for the department presents the department choices as Management, Processing, Phone, and Sales, you must initialize the array in the same order. Therefore, at index 0, you should place the intManagementPayRate value; at index 1, you should place the intProcessingPayRate value; at index 2, you should place the intPhonePayRate value; and at index 3, you should place the intSalesPayRate value. (See Figure 8.6.)

```
frmPayroll.vb [Design]*  frmPayroll.vb*
frmPayroll                                          New
    Public Sub New()
        MyBase.New()

        'This call is required by the Windows Form Designer.
        InitializeComponent()

        'Add any initialization after the InitializeComponent() call

        grdEmployees.Rows = 1
        grdEmployees.Cols = 5

        grdEmployees.Row = 0
        grdEmployees.Col = 0
        grdEmployees.Text = "Employee #"

        grdEmployees.Col = 1
        grdEmployees.Text = "Employee Name"

        grdEmployees.Col = 2
        grdEmployees.Text = "Hours Worked"

        grdEmployees.Col = 3
        grdEmployees.Text = "Department"

        grdEmployees.Col = 4
        grdEmployees.Text = "Weekly Pay"

        'Initialize the intPayRate array in the exact order
        'they appear in the combo box
        intPayRates(0) = intManagementPayRate
        intPayRates(1) = intProcessingPayRate
        intPayRates(2) = intPhonePayRate
        intPayRates(3) = intSalesPayRate
    End Sub
```

Figure 8.6   Code added to form's constructor

Step 3: The final step is to remove the previous code that selected the pay rate with a case statement and then replace it with a single statement that uses the array to look up the proper pay rate. By using the SelectedIndex property of the cboDepartment combo box, you have the index for the intPayRates array. Therefore, intPayRates(cboDepartment.SelectedIndex) will return the pay rate of the current employee. (See Figure 8.7.)

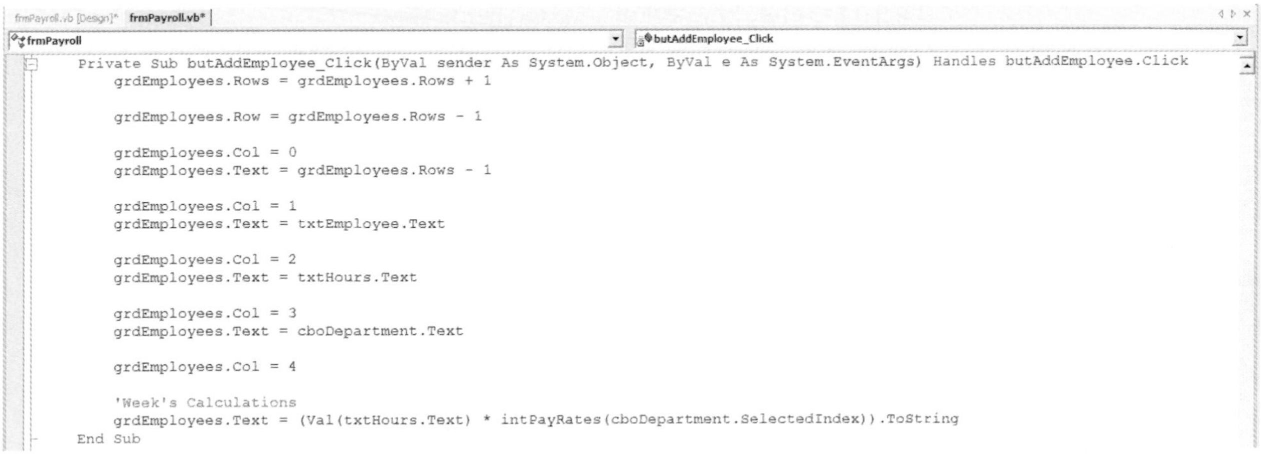

```
frmPayroll.vb [Design]*   frmPayroll.vb*
frmPayroll                                                    butAddEmployee_Click
    Private Sub butAddEmployee_Click(ByVal sender As System.Object, ByVal e As System.EventArgs) Handles butAddEmployee.Click
        grdEmployees.Rows = grdEmployees.Rows + 1

        grdEmployees.Row = grdEmployees.Rows - 1

        grdEmployees.Col = 0
        grdEmployees.Text = grdEmployees.Rows - 1

        grdEmployees.Col = 1
        grdEmployees.Text = txtEmployee.Text

        grdEmployees.Col = 2
        grdEmployees.Text = txtHours.Text

        grdEmployees.Col = 3
        grdEmployees.Text = cboDepartment.Text

        grdEmployees.Col = 4

        'Week's Calculations
        grdEmployees.Text = (Val(txtHours.Text) * intPayRates(cboDepartment.SelectedIndex)).ToString
    End Sub
```

Figure 8.7   Code added to btnAddEmployee's Click event

Key Words and Key Terms

Array
> A construct that allows you to store multiple values of a data type in a single variable.

Collection
> An object that allows the storage of multiple objects of different data types in a single variable.

Single-Dimensional Array
> A construct that allows you to store multiple values in a single row of data.

Structure
> A value type construct that is similar to a class but will not allow inheritance.

Two-Dimensional Array
> A construct that contains rows and columns of the same type of data.

Upper Bound
> The highest valid index of an array

Answers to Chapter's Drills

Drill 8.1
An array's indexes start at 0. Therefore, if there are five elements in the array, the indexes would be from 0 to 4. Thus the upper bound would be 4.

Drill 8.2
An array declared with a 5 between the parentheses has a lower bound of 0 and an upper bound of 5. Therefore, there are six elements in the array.

Drill 8.3

```
Dim strDrillArray(4) As String
strDrillArray(0) = "First Value"
strDrillArray(1) = "Second Value"
strDrillArray(2) = "Third Value"
strDrillArray(3) = "Fourth Value"
strDrillArray(4) = "Fifth Value"
```

Drill 8.4

```
Dim intDrillArray(999) As Integer
Dim intIndex As Integer

For intIndex = 0 To 999
    intDrillArray(intIndex) = intIndex
Next intIndex
```

Drill 8.5
The steps of declaring and initializing can be accomplished in one line:

```
Dim sngPrices(4) As Single = {19.95, 12.95, 10.95 ,99.99, 10.00}
```

Drill 8.6
The steps of declaring and initializing can be accomplished in one line:

```
Dim strMovies(4) As Single = {"The Princess Bride", "Space Balls", _
                        "Clerks", "Shrek", "Fletch"}
```

Drill 8.7
The array is declared as an array of Integers. However, we are trying to store Strings in the second column. You cannot mix data types this way; you will get a run-time error.

Drill 8.8
The code fails to initialize the values in the row and columns with an index of 0. You might have thought that the Step –1 was the problem. However, although it seems odd to initialize the array in this manner, it is correct. If you had written the code to step down to 0, the code would have accomplished the desired results.

Drill 8.9
The two segments of code would accomplish the same results. Although the individual cells of the two-dimensional array are loaded in different orders, the same cells will be initialized to the same values.

Drill 8.10
The two segments of code would not accomplish the same results. The first segment of code would initialize all 15 cells in the two-dimensional array to the value 2. However, the second segment of code would produce a run-time error. Because the number of elements in a row is different than the number of elements in a column, when the row and column values are switched in the For statement, an out of bounds error is generated when intCol equals 3.

Drill 8.11

The code will not produce an error. The first student removed from the collection is the student at index 2. This would leave one student in the collection at index 1. Then that student is removed and nothing remains in the collection.

Additional Exercises

Questions 1–5 are true or false.

1. An array must have a lower bound of 0.

2. An array is used to set the size of a record in a random access file.

3. The first item in a collection has a lower bound of 0.

4. A structure is allocated on the heap.

5. An array of controls can be created interactively in the design mode of the form without using code.

6. Write the code required to declare and initialize an array of `Strings` that contains the name of each month in the year.

7. Write a function that accepts an array of 20 `Integers` and an `Integer` target value to search for. The function should return the number of times the target value is found.

8. Write a function that accepts an array called `decSales` of 20 `Decimal` values and returns the maximum sale value in the array.

9. Write a function that accepts a two-dimensional array called `decSalesAndCost` of 20 sets of `Decimal` values. The first dimension will store the sale price of the merchandise, while the second dimension will store the cost of the merchandise. The function should return the sale that has the largest profit.

10. Write a function that accepts two arrays and a `String`. The first array, `dtePurchaseDates`, should be an array of dates. The second array, `decSaleAmount`, should be an array of `Decimals`. Each array should contain 100 items. The `String strMonth` should represent the month whose total sales will be returned from the function. The function should loop through the arrays and total the sales of the month indicated and return the total.

11. Write an application that uses an array of controls to store students' names and their grades. The application should store 10 sets of student names and grades in two control arrays. The application should contain a button that when clicked outputs the average grade, as well as the name and grade of the student having the highest grade in the class.

12. Write a routine that will output in a message box the name of the student with the highest average in a collection of students. Use the `Student` class that was defined in this chapter.

CHAPTER 9
Files

CHAPTER OBJECTIVES

◆ Introduce file input and output

◆ Discuss sequential files

◆ Discuss random access files

You may have noticed that in the process of developing applications, preloading data into the application was a tedious process. Indeed, if you could only create applications that stored the data you enter during the time it is executing and then lost it when you terminated the application, your applications would not be very useful.

A simple way to store data so that it is accessible the next time you wish to execute the application is to store it in a data file. We will explain two types of data files: sequential and random access. (The third type of file is a binary file. For more information, see the MSDN.)

9.1 Sequential Files

A **sequential file** allows reading or writing the file from the beginning of the file until the end of the file. Files that are read and written sequentially are plain text files commonly known as **ASCII** files. ASCII stands for American Standard Code for Information Interchange. You can view or edit small ASCII files using the Notepad application that comes with Windows, or you can use a word processor and then select the ASCII option when you save the file.

If you wanted to save the information in your Student Search application from Chapter 7, a sequential file of this information might look like one of the following two files:

```
1    Salvage       Jeff      Computer Science        Senior      4.0
2    Cunningham    John      Basket Weaving          Freshman    1.0
3    Pepito        Suzanne   Industrial Engineering  Junior      3.8
4    Burke         Tim       MIS                     Senior      3.92
5    Fletcher      Irwin     Film                    Senior      3.99
```

Fixed-Width File

```
1, "Salvage", "Jeff", "Computer Science", "Senior", 4.0
2, "Cunningham", "John", "Basket Weaving", "Freshman", 1.0
3, "Pepito", "Suzanne", "Industrial Engineering", "Junior", 3.8
4, "Burke" ,"Tim", "MIS", "Senior", 3.92
5, "Fletcher", "Irwin", "Film", "Senior", 3.99
```

Comma-Delimited File

> **COACH'S TIP**
>
> A comma-delimited file does not require quotes around each `String` value in the file. However, when Visual Basic .NET writes a `String` to a file, Visual Basic .NET will add quotes around the entire `String` value.

A **fixed-width file** contains information formatted so that each line stores each data item in a fixed location within the line. In contrast, the **comma-delimited file** stores each data item with a comma separating each item. A comma-delimited file will also place double quotes around `String` fields.

One uses sequential file access when the application reads all the data at once or writes all the data at once. Either a fixed-width or a comma-delimited file can be used. While a fixed-width file is neater to view in a text editor, a comma-delimited file can save space if many of the strings' average sizes are significantly smaller than their maximums. Additionally, a fixed-width file sets size limits on the fields that are not required with comma-delimited files.

9.2 Fixed-Width Files

Visual Basic .NET provides an excellent object interface for accessing fixed-width formatted files. By using a combination of three classes—`FileStream`, `StreamWriter`, and `StreamReader`—you can access a file for both input and output. In order to access these classes, you must include the namespace `System.IO` with an `Imports` statement at the beginning of your file.

General Access of Fixed-Width Files

Step 1: Add the `Imports` statement to the project at the top of your form.

```
Imports System.IO
```

Step 2: When reading fixed-width files it is easiest to read data from a file one line at a time and then divide the data read into individual values. To accomplish this you first must open the text file using the `FileStream` object.

Observe the following syntax for opening a file to read data:

```
Dim FileStreamName As New FileStream("Path and File Name", FileMode.Open, _
                        FileAccess.Read)
```

Observe the following syntax for opening a file to write data:

```
Dim FileStreamName As New FileStream("Path and File Name", FileMode.OpenOrCreate, _
                        FileAccess.Write)
```

FileStreamName is the name of the object that you will use to reference the file from within the application.

The first parameter is the path to the file and the actual file name of the file that you are opening. If you do not include a path to the file, the `FileStream` object will assume that the text file is located in the same directory as the application that is running. By default this is the `bin` directory of your application.

The second parameter specifies the action upon opening the file. This can be either `Append`, `Create`, `CreateNew`, `Open`, `OpenOrCreate`, or `Truncate`. When opening a file for input, you will use the `Open` keyword, whereas when you wish to write to a file, you will use the `OpenOrCreate` keyword.

COACH'S TIP

While you will not use all of these options, here is a brief explanation of what each option is used for:

`Append`: If a file exists, it opens it at the end of the file; otherwise, it creates the file.
`Create`: It will create a new file; if the file exists, it will write over it.
`CreateNew`: It will create a new file if the file does not exist; otherwise, it will cause an error.
`Open`: It will open a file if it exists; otherwise, it will cause an error.
`OpenOrCreate`: It will open a file if it exists; otherwise, it will create it.
`Truncate`: It will open an existing file but reduce its size to zero bytes.

The final parameter indicates the action(s) that will be performed upon the file once it is open. This can be either `Read`, `ReadWrite`, or `Write`. When using a file for input, you will use the `Read` keyword, whereas when you wish to write to a file, you will use the `Write` keyword. When you specify `ReadWrite`, the file can be either read from or written to.

Step 3: While the `FileStream` object will open the file, you need another object if you actually wish to perform an action to the file. The two typical actions you will wish to perform are reading and writing to the file. In order to make the execution of these actions easier, Visual Basic .NET has included two objects, the `StreamReader` and the `StreamWriter`.

A `StreamReader` object will allow you to read data easily from the file you have just opened. Instantiating a `StreamReader` object requires passing it a `FileStream` object. Observe the following syntax to instantiate a `StreamReader`:

```
Dim StreamReaderName As New StreamReader(FileStreamName)
```

Similarly, a `StreamWriter` object will allow you to write data easily from the file you have just opened. Observe the following syntax to instantiate a `StreamWriter`:

```
Dim StreamWriterName As New StreamWriter(FileStreamName)
```

Step 4: Once you have a `StreamReader` or `StreamWriter` object instantiated, you can read or write a line of data using the following syntax:

```
strStringVariable = srStreamReaderVariable.ReadLine()
```

or

```
srStreamWriterVariable.WriteLine(strStringVariable)
```

In the case of the `StreamReader`, a line of input is read from the file and stored in a `String` variable. In the case of the `StreamWriter`, a `String` variable is passed to the object and written to the file.

Step 5a: In order to read data from a fixed-width file, you must divide the single `String` read using the **ReadLine** method of the `StreamReader` object. This can be accomplished using the `Substring` method of the `String` class. For more information about this method, see Chapter 6.

Step 5b: In order to write data to a fixed-width file, you must format the data so that the appropriate number of spaces follow each data element.

The following is what two strings, `"Jeff"` and `"Salvage"`, each padded to 10 characters, would look like if they were concatenated together:

```
"Jeff      Salvage   "
```

In contrast, if the two strings, `"Jeff"` and `"Salvage"`, were not padded, but still concatenated, they would look as follows:

```
"JeffSalvage"
```

The `PadRight` method of the `String` class will be helpful to you. By passing `PadRight` the maximum size of the `String` as a parameter, you can automatically pad the `String` to the right size.

Observe how you might declare a `String`, initialize it to `"Jeff"`, and then pad it to 10 characters:

```
Dim strFirstName As String
strFirstName = "Jeff"
strFirstName.PadRight(10)
```

While this works well, what do you suppose would happen if the initial `String` was initialized as follows?

```
Dim strFirstName As String
strFirstName = "   Jeff"
strFirstName.PadRight(10)
```

The previous code would pad the `String` so that in the end it contained the following:

```
"   Jeff   "
```

While this is not incorrect, it is cleaner to strip the initial spaces from the front of the `String`. This can be done by calling the `Trim` method before you call the `PadRight` method.

```
strFirstName.Trim.PadRight(10)
```

By calling the `Trim` and `PadRight` methods with the size you wish the `String` to be, the `String` will be stripped of any spaces to the left and have the appropriate number of spaces appended to the right. This will simplify your handling of fixed-format files.

Therefore, to build the `String` that you will output, you can use the following syntax:

```
'First data field in the line
strOutputLine = strValue1.Trim.PadRight(intstrValue1Size)

'Second data field in the line as well as any others
strOutputLine &= strValue2.Trim.PadRight(intstrValue2Size)
```

Using the first and last name example, the code would appear as follows:

```
Dim strFirstName As String = "Jeff"
Dim strLastName As String = "Salvage"

'First Name
strOutputLine = strFirstName.Trim.PadRight(10)

'Last Name
strOutputLine &= strLastName.Trim.PadRight(10)
```

COACH'S TIP

`Trim` and `Space` are two functions built into Visual Basic .NET to make working with `Strings` easier. `Trim` will remove any additional spaces from the left or right of the `String`, while `Space` will generate as many spaces as the parameter passed to it indicates.

Step 6: When reading data, you must have a mechanism to check to see if you have reached the end of a file. This can be done by comparing the result of the `Peek` method of the `StreamReader` object to −1. A value of −1 indicates that you are at the end of the file and there is no additional data to be read.

Often you will set up a loop that checks to see if you have reached the end of the file before you read the next line.

Step 7: The last step in accessing files is to close the objects that access the file (and thus the file itself) when you are done. When reading a file, you must close the `StreamReader` and the `FileStream` objects. When writing a file, you must close the `StreamWriter` and `FileStream` objects. All objects can be closed by calling the `Close` methods of each class. Observe the following syntax:

```
StreamReaderName.Close()
FileStreamName.Close()
```

or

```
StreamWriter.Close()
FileStreamName.Close()
```

Example: Fixed-Width Student Grades Application
Problem Description

In Chapter 7, you created an application that allowed the user to enter a student's number, name, GPA, major, and year. However, each time the application was executed, all the information had to be entered again. With the use of files, you can store the information you enter in a fixed-width file and then load it when the application starts.

Problem Discussion

The majority of the application will remain the same. Indeed, the only visible change is that you will add a Save button to the application to allow any changes that have been made to the file.

The new application would look as shown in Figure 9.1.

Figure 9.1
Student Grades application with files

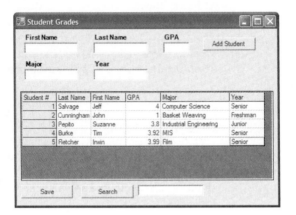

Problem Solution

The solution is really divided into two distinct parts. First, you must load the information stored in the file so that it may be used by the application. Second, you must allow the user to save the changes made to the data.

To load the information stored in the text file, you can require the user of the application to take a manual step, like clicking on a button, or you can have the information stored in the file loaded automatically when the application is executed. Obviously, the latter solution is preferable.

By placing the code to load information from the file in the form's constructor, you can be assured that the information is loaded each time the application is executed. Your application will store its information in the file `Students.txt` located with the application in the `bin` directory so that you do not have to specify a directory for the file.

The code opens the fixed-text file and adds a row to the `grdStudents` MS flex grid for each line in the input file. Since you read a complete line at a time, you need to divide the line into its individual fields by using the `Substring` method. Although not required, you use the `Trim` method with the `Substring` method so that no additional spaces are stored in the grid. This can be seen in the following code:

```
Dim strInputLine As String



Dim fs As New FileStream("Students.txt", FileMode.Open, _
                    FileAccess.Read)
```

(continues)

(continued)

```
Dim srStudents As New StreamReader(fs)


'Loop through the input file
Do While Not (srStudents.Peek = -1)
    strInputLine = srStudents.ReadLine()

    grdStudents.Rows += 1
    grdStudents.Row = grdStudents.Rows -1

    'Student #
    grdStudents.Col = 0
    grdStudents.Text = strInputLine.Substring(0, 5).Trim()

    'Last Name
    grdStudents.Col = 1
    grdStudents.Text = strInputLine.Substring(5, 10).Trim()

    'First Name
    grdStudents.Col = 2
    grdStudents.Text = strInputLine.Substring(15, 10).Trim()

    'GPA
    grdStudents.Col = 3
    grdStudents.Text = strInputLine.Substring(25, 5).Trim()

    'Major
    grdStudents.Col = 4
    grdStudents.Text = strInputLine.Substring(30, 25).Trim()

    'Year
    grdStudents.Col = 5
    grdStudents.Text = strInputLine.Substring(55, 10).Trim()


Loop

'Close file objects
fs.Close()
srStudents.Close()
```

COACH'S WARNING

Notice that at the end of reading the entire input file, you make sure that you close it. Never forget to close your files when you are finished with them, because if you do forget, you may not be able to open them again without rebooting the computer. Also, leaving files open unnecessarily wastes computer resources.

The other code you must add to your application is the code required to save the data in the MS flex grid to the text file. This code will be associated with the btnSave button's Click event.

You need to open the `Students.txt` file so that you can write information to it. This requires changing the parameters when instantiating the `FileStream` object. Instead of opening the file with a `FileMode` of `Open`, you are going to open it with a `FileMode` of `OpenOrCreate`. This ensures that if the file does not exist, it will be created when you open it. Also, the `FileAccess` should be `Write` instead of `Read`.

Instead of using a `StreamReader` object to read a line of data, you will use its counterpart, the `StreamWriter`. You will instantiate the `StreamWriter` in the same manner as the `StreamReader`.

Once your objects are created, you can output the data in your MS flex grid by looping through each row of the grid, excluding the first, and building a `String` containing an entire row's data. When you are working with fixed-width files, each value must be padded with the correct number of spaces so that the data lines up properly in the file. You can do this using the `PadRight` function that you will write. `PadRight` will add the necessary space to the end of each value.

After a row of data from the MS flex grid is contained in a `String`, you need to write it to the file. This can be accomplished with the **WriteLine** method of the `StreamWriter`.

After all of the data is written to the file, you must call the close methods of the `StreamWriter` and `FileStream`.

The code follows:

```
Private Sub btnSave_Click(...
    Dim strOutputLine As String
    Dim intCurrentRow As Integer
    Dim fs As New FileStream("Students.txt", FileMode.OpenOrCreate, _
                        FileAccess.Write)

    Dim swStudents As New StreamWriter(fs)

    intCurrentRow = 1

    Do While (intCurrentRow < grdStudents.Rows)
        'Student #
        grdStudents.Row = intCurrentRow
        grdStudents.Col = 0
        strOutputLine = grdStudents.Text.Trim.PadRight(5)

        'Last Name
        grdStudents.Col = 1
        strOutputLine &= grdStudents.Text.Trim.PadRight(10)

        'First Name
        grdStudents.Col = 2
        strOutputLine &= grdStudents.Text.Trim.PadRight(10)

        'GPA
        grdStudents.Col = 3
        strOutputLine &= grdStudents.Text.Trim.PadRight(5)

        'Major
        grdStudents.Col = 4
        strOutputLine &= grdStudents.Text.Trim.PadRight(25)
```

(continues)

(continued)

```
      'Year
      grdStudents.Col = 5
      strOutputLine &= grdStudents.Text.Trim.PadRight(10)

      swStudents.WriteLine(strOutputLine)
      intCurrentRow += 1
   Loop

   'Close file objects
   swStudents.Close()
   fs.Close()

End Sub
```

DRILL 9.1

Write the code required to read four `String` values from the fixed-formatted data file `DrillFile.txt` into four `String` variables: `strString1`, `strString2`, `strString3`, and `strString4`. The maximum size of the four `Strings` are 10, 20, 15, and 25, respectively.

DRILL 9.2

Write the code required to write four `String` values to a fixed-width data file `DrillFile.txt` from four `String` variables: `strString1`, `strString2`, `strString3`, and `strString4`. The maximum size of the four `Strings` are 10, 20, 15, and 25, respectively.

9.3   Comma-Delimited Files

It would be nice if, to handle comma-delimited files, Visual Basic .NET used objects similar to those used for fixed-width files. However, for some reason, Visual Basic .NET does not use a highly object-oriented approach. Instead, it uses a series of function calls to accomplish the same functionality.

General Access of Comma-Delimited Files

Step 1: Add the `Imports` statement to the project.

```
Imports System.IO
```

Step 2: When reading comma-delimited files, you read data into a series of variables, one for each field in the file. You will require a variable for each field in the record that you are reading. It is best to declare these at the beginning of the code.

Step 3: You are now ready to open the file. The function to accomplish this is the `FileOpen` function.
Observe the following syntax for opening a file to read data:

```
FileOpen(FileNumber, "Path and File Name", OpenMode.Input)
```

Observe the following syntax for opening a file to write data:

```
FileOpen(FileNumber, "Path and File Name", OpenMode.Output)
```

The first parameter, *FileNumber*, is an `Integer` used as a handle to the file once it is opened. The number must be different from any other file numbers of any other simultaneously opened files.

COACH'S TIP

Instead of hard coding the file number, Visual Basic .NET has a function **FreeFile** that will return the next available file number. By using this function instead of hard coding the file number, you can add flexibility as your program grows.

The second parameter is the file path to the file that you are opening. If you do not include a path to the file, the `FileOpen` function will assume that the text file is located in the same directory as the application that is running.

The third parameter specifies the action upon opening the file. This can be either `Append`, `Binary`, `Input`, `Output`, or `Random`. When you wish to read data from a file, you will use `Input`; and when you wish to write data to the file, you will use `Output`.

COACH'S TIP

While you will not use all of these options, here is a brief explanation of what each option is used for:

`Append`: If a file exists, it opens it at the end of the file; otherwise, it creates the file.
`Binary`: It will open a file to be read or written within a raw format. See MSDN for more information.
`Input`: It will open a file so that it may be read from.
`Output`: It will open a file so that it may be written to.
`Random`: It will be opened for input or output in a nonsequential manner. See Section 9.4.

Step 4:   Once the file is opened, you can either read or write data from the file. If you wish to read data from the file, you use the `Input` function. `Input` accepts two parameters. The first is the file number of the file to read from. The second is a variable to store the value that is read from the file. Unfortunately, only one value can be read at a time. See the following syntax for reading data from the file using the **Input** function:

```
Input(FileNumber, Value)
```

COACH'S TIP

Included in the `String` class is a method that can be very useful when dealing with comma-delimited files. The `Split` method will return the `String` divided into substrings based on a delimiter passed to it. It will return an array composed of each substring.

For example:

```
Dim strDelimited As String = "One Two Three"
Dim strDelimitedArray(3) As String
strDelimitedArray = strDelimited.Split(",")
```

Will place the `Strings` `"One"`, `"Two"`, and `"Three"` in the first three elements of the array `strDelimitedArray`.

If instead you wish to write values to a file, you can use the `WriteLine` function. The first parameter is the file number of the file to write to. However, unlike the `Input` function, the `WriteLine` function will allow you to write as many variables as you wish with one function call.

```
WriteLine(FileNumber, Value1, Value2, Value3, Value4 ...)
```

Step 5: When reading data, you must have a mechanism to check to see if you have reached the end of a file. This can be done by calling the `EOF` function. `EOF` will return `True` if the file number passed to it is at the end of a file. Otherwise, it will return `False`.

Step 6: The last step in accessing files is to close the file. Whether you opened the file for input or output, the process is the same. Call the **`FileClose`** function with the file number of the file you wish to close. Observe the following syntax:

```
FileClose(FileNumber)
```

Example: Comma-Delimited Student Grades Application
Problem Description

In Section 9.2, you modified the application from Chapter 7 that allowed the user to store a student's number, name, GPA, major, and year. Change the application now so it contains the same functionality and ability to save and load its data, but implement it with a comma-delimited file instead of a fixed-width file.

Problem Discussion

The only two changes required to this application from the one in Section 9.2 are to the constructor of the form and the `butSave` button's `Click` event. The application would look identical to Figure 9.1.

Problem Solution

Again, your solution is really divided into two distinct parts. First, you must load the data stored in the file so when the application starts, you have access to the data. Second, you must provide a way for users to save their changes as they feel it is appropriate.

You will again set the loading of the data contained in the file to occur in the constructor of the form. This way the data is loaded each time the application is executed.

Your application will store its data in the file `Students.txt` located with the application so that you do not have to specify a directory for the file.

The code opens the comma-delimited text file and adds a row to the `grdStudents` MS flex grid for each line in the input file. You continue reading data from the file until the `EOF` function indicates that you have processed the entire file. Unlike with the fixed-width formatted file, you cannot read all of the data elements on a single line of the file in a single command as before. Instead, you will have to call the `Input` function for each field in the file. Once each of the values is gathered into variables, they can be copied to their respective locations in the MS flex grid. This can be seen in the following code:

```
Dim intStudentNumber As Integer
Dim strLastName As String
Dim strFirstName As String
Dim sngGPA As Single
Dim strMajor As String
Dim strYear As String
Dim intStudentFile As Integer

intStudentFile = FreeFile()
FileOpen(intStudentFile, "Students.txt", OpenMode.Input)

Do While Not (EOF(intStudentFile))
    'Read each of the fields from the file
    Input(intStudentFile, intStudentNumber)
    Input(intStudentFile, strLastName)
    Input(intStudentFile, strFirstName)
    Input(intStudentFile, sngGPA)
    Input(intStudentFile, strMajor)
    Input(intStudentFile, strYear)

    grdStudents.Rows += 1
    grdStudents.Row -= grdStudents.Rows - 1

    'Student #
    grdStudents.Col = 0
    grdStudents.Text = intStudentNumber.ToString

    'Last Name
    grdStudents.Col = 1
    grdStudents.Text = strLastName

    'First Name
    grdStudents.Col = 2
    grdStudents.Text = strFirstName

    'GPA
    grdStudents.Col = 3
    grdStudents.Text = sngGPA.ToString

    'Major
    grdStudents.Col = 4
    grdStudents.Text = strMajor
```

(continues)

(continued)

```
    'Year
    grdStudents.Col = 5
    grdStudents.Text = strYear

Loop

FileClose(intStudentFile)
```

As in the previous application, the other code you must add to your application is the code required to save the data in the MS flex grid to the text file. This code will be associated with the `btnSave` button's `Click` event.

You need to open the `Students.txt` file so that you can write your data to it. You still use the `FileOpen` function as you did when opening a file for input, but instead of passing it `OpenMode.Input` as the third parameter, you pass it `OpenMode.Output`.

Once your file is open, you can output the data in your MS flex grid by looping through each row of the grid, excluding the first, and copy each row's data to individual variables. Since the `WriteLine` function will accept many values as additional parameters, you can call `WriteLine` once and pass it all the variables that need to be saved to the comma-delimited file.

After all of the data is written to the file, you must close the file using the `FileClose` function.

The code follows:

```
Private Sub btnSave_Click(...
    Dim strOutputLine As String
    Dim intCurrentRow As Integer
    Dim intStudentFile As Integer
    Dim intStudentNumber As Integer
    Dim strLastName As String
    Dim strFirstName As String
    Dim sngGPA As Single
    Dim strMajor As String
    Dim strYear As String

    intStudentFile = FreeFile()
    FileOpen(intStudentFile, "Students.txt", OpenMode.Output)

    intCurrentRow = 1

    Do While (intCurrentRow < grdStudents.Rows)
        'Student #
        grdStudents.Row = intCurrentRow
        grdStudents.Col = 0
        intStudentNumber = Val(grdStudents.Text)

        'Last Name
        grdStudents.Col = 1
        strLastName = grdStudents.Text

        'First Name
        grdStudents.Col = 2
        strFirstName = grdStudents.Text
```

(continues)

(continued)

```
        'GPA
        grdStudents.Col = 3
        sngGPA = Val(grdStudents.Text)

        'Major
        grdStudents.Col = 4
        strMajor = grdStudents.Text

        'Year
        grdStudents.Col = 5
        strYear = grdStudents.Text

        'Output the data to the file
        WriteLine(intStudentFile, intStudentNumber, strLastName, _
                strFirstName, sngGPA, strMajor, strYear)

        intCurrentRow += 1
    Loop

    FileClose(intStudentFile)
End Sub
```

COACH'S WARNING

If a file already exists and it is opened for output, it will be overwritten.

To append data to the end of an existing file from the application, use the following code:

```
Open FileName For Append as #Number
```

COACH'S TIP

It's always a good idea to give the users feedback as to the progress of their actions. Previously, you were able to determine that the action was performed, because you saw the results on the form. However, when saving a file, you do not know if the action has actually occurred without physically checking for the existence of the file. In the future, we will show you how to create a progress bar, but for now, it's a good idea to include a message box indicating the completion of the save. You can add this to the end of the butSave button.

DRILL 9.3

Write the code required to read four `String` values from the comma-delimited data file `DrillFile.txt` into four `String` variables: `strString1`, `strString2`, `strString3`, and `strString4`.

DRILL 9.4

Write the code required to write four `String` values to the comma-delimited data file `DrillFile.txt` from four `String` variables: `strString1`, `strString2`, `strString3`, and `strString4`.

9.4 Random Access Files

While sequential files give you the ability to store data permanently, their ability to arbitrarily access different values within the file is limited by their sequential access method. **Random access files** allow you to access data in a file with much more flexibility. You can move forward and back throughout the file reading or writing records as you go. However, in order to accomplish this, you must have each record formatted to a single size.

General Access of Random Access Files

Step 1: Add the `Imports` statement to the project.

```
Imports System.IO
```

Step 2: The nature of a random access file means that you do not have to choose between opening a file for either input or output. Instead, when you open a file for random access, you can read or write data one record at a time. Therefore, you have only one syntax to present for opening a file.

```
FileOpen(FileNumber, "Path and File Name", OpenMode.Random, , , Len(CurrentStructure))
```

The first three parameters should be self-explanatory at this point. The next two parameters are intentionally left empty. They are used for other purposes. For more information, see the MSDN.

The final parameter is the size of the record containing the data to be stored in the file. The easiest way to determine this is to call the **Len** function and pass it a variable defined as a structure defining the record in the file.

Although the next step is listed as Step 3, Steps 3 to 5 could occur in any order.

Step 3: To retrieve a specific record from a file, you must first declare a structure (see Chapter 8), `CurrentStructure`, and a variable from that type, `RecordStructure`. Then you can read a record specified by an `Integer` `RecordNumber` to read a record into the structure `CurrentStructure`:

```
FileGet(FileNumber, CurrentStructure, RecordNumber)
```

Step 4: To write a structure to the end of the file, you must first declare a structure, `CurrentStructure`, and a variable from that type, `RecordStructure`. The values you wish to write to the file must be copied to that structure. Then you can write the end of the file by specifying a record number one more than the total number of records currently in the file.

```
FilePut(FileNumber, CurrentStructure, OneMoreThanTotalNumberOfRecords)
```

COACH'S TIP

To compute the total number of records in a file, divide the length of the file by the length of the record. The length of a structure can be determined using the **LOF** function:

```
LOF(intStudentFile) / Len(Student)
```

Step 5: Updating a record in a random access file is accomplished using the same code as writing a record initially. The only difference is that you must make sure that the record number is the same as the one you wish to update.

Step 6: As always, when you are finished accessing the file, you must close it. You do this the same way as you did with comma-delimited files—you call the `FileClose` function.

```
FileClose(FileNumber)
```

Example: Random Access File Student Grades Application
Problem Description

Your random access Student Grades application will look a little different from the previous Student Grades applications. This application will allow the user to enter a student number, and that student's information will be displayed in a series of text boxes. The user can change the information while the application points to the student's information.

At any time the user can add a student by entering the new information and then clicking on the Add Student button. At any point the user can enter a new student number and retrieve that student's information. However, if the information displayed has been changed and not saved, the changes will be lost.

The application would look as shown in Figure 9.2.

Figure 9.2
Random access file application

No error checking will be implemented at this time.

Problem Discussion

The application will require you to change quite a bit from the previous solutions. You will have to declare a structure to store the record of data in a file. Additionally, you will have to use completely different routines to process the input and output from the file. However, taken step by step, it is not very difficult.

Problem Solution

You need a few declarations in the `Declarations` section of the form. First, you need a variable that will store the total number of records within the file. Second, you need a variable to store the file identification number of the file you are opening. This could be hard coded, but it is better programming practice to allow Visual Basic .NET to pick it for you. Finally, you need a user-defined type that will provide the details for the format of your record within the file. This is shown in the following code:

```
Dim intTotalRecords As Integer
Dim intStudentFile As Integer
Dim Student As StudentRecord
```

(continues)

(continued)

```
Structure StudentRecord
    Public intStudentNumber As Integer
    <VBFixedString(10)> Public strLastName As String
    <VBFixedString(10)> Public strFirstName As String
    Public sngGPA As Single
    <VBFixedString(20)> Public strMajor As String
    <VBFixedString(10)> Public strYear As String
End Structure
```

COACH'S TIP

The length of a file can be calculated by using the LOF function, which accepts a file number and returns the length of the file.

When the form is loaded, you need to first get the file identification number that will refer to your data file from within the application. This will be stored in the variable `intStudentFile`. Then you must open the actual data file as a random access file. Additionally, you need to calculate the total number of records. This can be accomplished by dividing the length of the file by the length of an individual record in the file.

The code to add to the form's constructor is as follows:

```
intStudentFile = FreeFile()

' Open the new file with the FileOpen statement.
FileOpen(intStudentFile, "Students.txt", OpenMode.Random, , , Len(Student))
intTotalRecords = LOF(intStudentFile) / Len(Student)
```

To ensure that the file is closed properly, you will place the code to close the file in the destructor of the form as shown in the following code:

```
FileClose(intStudentFile)
```

When the `btnSearch` button is clicked, you need to find the record indicated by the `txtSearch` text box. Once the information is gathered into the record, you can copy the contents to each corresponding `TextBox`. This is shown in the following code:

```
Private Sub btnSearch_Click(...
Dim Student As StudentRecord

    'Get the record from the file
    FileGet(intStudentFile, Student, CInt(txtSearch.Text))

    'Copy the information from the student structure
    'to the text boxes for display
    txtLast.Text = Student.strLastName
    txtFirst.Text = Student.strFirstName
    txtGPA.Text = Student.sngGPA
    txtMajor.Text = Student.strMajor
    txtYear.Text = Student.strYear
End Sub
```

Writing the individual records to the file is a matter of copying the values in the text boxes to their corresponding fields within the record, incrementing the record counter, and then placing the actual record in the file. Finally, it's a good practice to clear the form of the previously entered values. This is all shown in the following code:

```
Private Sub btnAddStudent_Click(...
Dim Student As StudentRecord
    'Copy values from text boxes to student structure
    Student.strLastName = txtLast.Text
    Student.strFirstName = txtFirst.Text
    Student.sngGPA = txtGPA.Text
    Student.strMajor = txtMajor.Text
    Student.strYear = txtYear.Text

    'increase the total number of records and
    'determine the record number for the new record
    intTotalRecords += 1

    'Place the new record in the file
    FilePut(intStudentFile, Student, intTotalRecords)

    'Clear the text boxes for the next entry
    txtLast.Text = ""
    txtFirst.Text = ""
    txtMajor.Text = ""
    txtYear.Text = ""
    txtGPA.Text = ""
End Sub
```

The code required to update a record does not vary much from the code to add a record. In both cases you must copy the values from the individual text boxes to a StudentRecord variable. The main difference is that when you write the record to the file, you write it to the record number indicated by the txtSearch text box instead of 1 more than the total number of records currently in the file. Finally, as before, you clear the text boxes of their previous values. This is shown in the following code:

```
Private Sub btnUpdateStudent_Click(...
Dim Student As StudentRecord

    'Copy values from text boxes to student structure
    Student.strLastName = txtLast.Text
    Student.strFirstName = txtFirst.Text
    Student.sngGPA = txtGPA.Text
    Student.strMajor = txtMajor.Text
    Student.strYear = txtYear.Text

    'Update the current record in the file
    FilePut(intStudentFile, Student, CInt(txtSearch.Text))

    'Clear the text boxes for the next entry
    txtLast.Text = ""
    txtFirst.Text = ""
    txtMajor.Text = ""
    txtYear.Text = ""
    txtGPA.Text = ""
End Sub
```

The code for `btnUpdateStudent_Click` and `btnAddStudent_Click` can be shared by creating a separate function that contains the repeated code.

While random access files have their place, with the advent of database applications, their use is limited to applications that have minimum data requirements that cannot use a database due to overhead or additional cost of implementation.

◆ 9.5   Case Study

Problem Description

Until now, the payroll system that you developed needed the information to be entered every time the application was executed. Clearly, an efficient payroll system cannot operate in this manner. You need to add the ability to save data and then automatically reload it when the application starts up.

The application looks identical to Chapter 7's because you will perform the load and save operations in the form's constructor and destructor, respectively.

Problem Discussion

The problem description doesn't indicate the type of data file for the application. Indeed, the user of the application would not know what type of data file was used simply by operating the application.

While the decision is mostly one of personal choice, using a random access file would be the poorest choice. If you changed the problem description so that data was saved as it was changed, then a random access file format would be the best choice. However, with the stipulation that you will only save data upon exiting the application, there is no need for a random access file format.

Therefore, the choice is either to use a fixed-format file or a comma-delimited format. Personally, if size isn't an issue, I prefer the fixed-format file, because when you open it in Notepad, it's easier to read. Therefore, your implementation will follow this format.

Problem Solution

The only changes to the application are in the constructor and destructor of the form. The constructor code starts as it did before; however, once the `MSFlexGrid` is formatted, you must then load the data in the CaseStudy.txt data file. You read in each line of data, divide the line into separate data values, and then copy those values to their appropriate place in the `MSFlexGrid`. The code follows:

```
Dim fs As New FileStream("CaseStudy.txt", FileMode.Open, FileAccess.Read)
Dim srPayroll As New StreamReader(fs)
Dim strInputLine As String

Do While (srPayroll.Peek <> -1)
    strInputLine = srPayroll.ReadLine()
    grdEmployees.Rows += 1
    grdEmployees.Row = grdEmployees.Rows - 1
```

(continues)

(continued)

```
            'Employee Number
            grdEmployees.Col = 0
            grdEmployees.Text = grdEmployees.Row.ToString

            'Employee Name
            grdEmployees.Col = 1
            grdEmployees.Text = strInputLine.Substring(0, 20)

            'Hours Worked
            grdEmployees.Col = 2
            grdEmployees.Text = strInputLine.Substring(20, 10)

            'Department
            grdEmployees.Col = 3
            grdEmployees.Text = strInputLine.Substring(30, 15)

            'Weekly Pay
            grdEmployees.Col = 4
            grdEmployees.Text = strInputLine.Substring(45, 10)
        Loop

        'Close file objects
        srPayroll.Close()
        fs.Close()
```

The destructor code needs to open a file for output, loop through all of the rows in the `MSFlexGrid`, format each value to its proper size, and then output the values as a single line to the data file. This is done in the following code:

```
Dim fs As New FileStream("CaseStudy.txt", FileMode.OpenOrCreate, FileAccess.Write)
Dim swPayroll As New StreamWriter(fs)
Dim strOutputLine As String
Dim intCurrentRow As Integer

'Loop through all rows of the grid and output the contents to the file
For intCurrentRow = 1 To grdEmployees.Rows - 1
    grdEmployees.Row = intCurrentRow

    'Employee Name
    grdEmployees.Col = 1
    strOutputLine = PadRight(grdEmployees.Text, 20)

    'Hours Worked
    grdEmployees.Col = 2
    strOutputLine &= PadRight(grdEmployees.Text, 10)

    'Department
    grdEmployees.Col = 3
    strOutputLine &= PadRight(grdEmployees.Text, 15)

    'Weekly Pay
    grdEmployees.Col = 4
    strOutputLine &= PadRight(grdEmployees.Text, 10)
```

(continues)

(continued)

```
      swPayroll.WriteLine(strOutputLine)
Next intCurrentRow


'Close file objects
swPayroll.Close()
fs.Close()
```

CORNER

Common Dialog Box

So far, all of the programs you have used with data files were written assuming the file name and its path was the same as the directory the application was located within. This can be very inconvenient. Fortunately, you can use a built-in dialog box that will prompt the user to select a file from any accessible drive. It returns a string containing the path and the file name that can be used in your application to open the file.

Two of the most useful common dialog boxes are the Open File dialog box (Figure 9.3) and the Save File As dialog box (Figure 9.4).

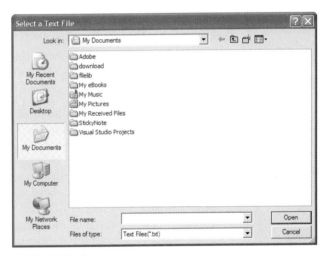

Figure 9.3   Open File dialog box

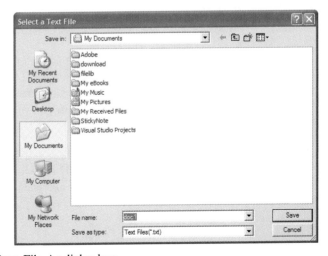

Figure 9.4   Save File As dialog box

While you will place an Open File or Save File As dialog box control on the form, just like any other control, it will not be visible when you run your application. Instead, it will appear below the form (Figure 9.5).

Figure 9.5
Dialog box placed on control

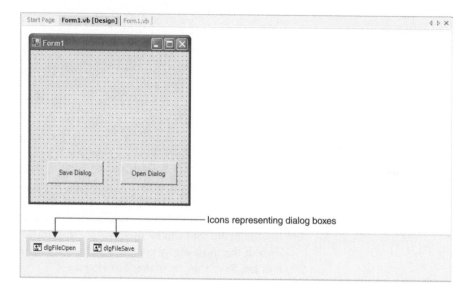

Setting Attributes for a Common Dialog Box

Once a control is placed on the form, you can specify attributes so that your dialog box behaves exactly the way you desire. While there are many attributes, here are the most important ones:

◆ **Title:** Good application development provides users with directions to help clarify what they are trying to accomplish. Therefore, in most cases this attribute should be used to indicate what file is being opened or saved.

◆ **Filter:** Often the user wishes to limit the type of file visible in the dialog box to a specific type. By specifying the `Filter` attribute, you can limit the types of files displayed using standard file name wildcard patterns. In order to indicate a filter, you must first specify a description of the limitation as in `"Text Files(*.txt)"` and then the actual wildcard pattern to limit the files displayed as in `"*.txt"`. These two specifications must be separated by the pipe symbol `"|"`.

Therefore, to set the filter of the dialog box `dlgExample` to show only text files, use the following code:

```
dlgExample.Filter = "Text Files(*.txt)|*.txt"
```

◆ **InitialDirectory:** If this attribute is left unspecified, then the dialog box will be opened using the current directory. However, if you wish the dialog box to open in another directory, then you can specify it by assigning the `InitialDirectory` property to the directory path you wish to open.

Open File Example

Observe the following code, which will present the user with a dialog box to show an Open File dialog box. It will only show text files and have a title of `"Select a Text File"`. Additionally, if you do not select a file, you will display a message to the user and exit the subroutine.

```
Private Sub btnOpenFile_Click(...
    Dim strTextFileName As String 'Variable to store filename

    'Set file open dialog properties
    DlgFileOpen.Filter = "Text Files(*.txt)|*.txt"
    DlgFileOpen.Title = "Select a Text File"

    'Display dialog box
    DlgFileOpen.ShowDialog()

    'Check if file was selected
    If (Len(DlgFileOpen.FileName) > 0) Then
        strTextFileName = DlgFileOpen.FileName  'Set variable to filename
    Else
        MsgBox("No File Selected")
    End If

End Sub
```

File Save Example

Observe the following code, which will present the user with a dialog box to show a File Save dialog box. It will only show text files and have a title of "Save Text File As". Additionally, if you do not select a file, you will display a message to the user and exit the subroutine.

```
Private Sub btnSaveDialog_Click(...
    Dim strTextFileName As String 'Variable to store filename

    'Set file save dialog properties
    DlgFileSave.Filter = "Text Files(*.txt)|*.txt"
    DlgFileSave.Title = "Select a Text File"

    'Display dialog box
    dlgFileSave.ShowDialog()

    'Check if file was selected
    If (Len(dlgFileSave.FileName) > 0) Then
        strTextFileName = dlgFileSave.FileName  'Set variable to filename
    Else
        MsgBox("No File Selected")
    End If

End Sub
```

COACH'S TIP

The keyword `With` allows you to specify attributes in a shorthand notation. Without it, you would be forced to write out the `dlgFileSave` name for each property.

Example Using `With`

```
With dlgFileSave
    .Filter = "Text Files(*.txt)|*.txt"
    .Title = "Select a Text File"
End With
```

Example Not Using `With`

```
dlgFileSave.Filter = "Text Files(*.txt)|*.txt"
dlgFileSave.Title = "Select a Text File"
```

Key Words and Key Terms

ASCII

A standard file format. ASCII stands for American Standard Code for Information Interchange.

Comma-Delimited File

A file format that contains information organized so that data items are stored with a comma separating each item.

FileClose

A function that closes files opened as either comma-delimited or random access.

FileGet

A function that retrieves a record from a random access file.

FilePut

A function that writes a record to a random access file.

Fixed-Width File

A file format that contains information organized so that each line stores each data item in a fixed location within the line.

FreeFile

A function that returns the number of the next available file.

Input

A function that reads a value from a comma-delimited file.

Len

A function that returns the size of the structure passed to it.

LOF

Returns the length of a file passed to it.

Random Access File

A file format that contains information organized in records. Each record is stored in a fixed format, so that the developer can access records easily and nonsequentially.

ReadLine

A method to read a line of data from a fixed-width file.

Save File As Dialog Box

A control that allows the developer to display a dialog box allowing the user to select a file. The control returns the file name including its complete path.

Sequential File
A file that allows reading or writing the file from the beginning of the file until the end of the file in a linear order.

WriteLine
A function or method to output values to a comma-delimited or fixed-format file.

Answers to Chapter's Drills

Drill 9.1

```
'Declare file objects
Dim fs As New FileStream("DrillFile.txt", FileMode.Open, FileAccess.Read)
Dim srDrill As New StreamReader(fs)

'Declare variables to store individual fields
Dim strString1 As String
Dim strString2 As String
Dim strString3 As String
Dim strString4 As String

'Declare variable to store input line
Dim strInputLine As String

'Read line from file
strInputLine = srDrill.ReadLine()

'Copy values from input line to individual variables
strString1 = Trim(strInputLine.Substring(0, 10))
strString2 = Trim(strInputLine.Substring(10, 20))
strString3 = Trim(strInputLine.Substring(1, 15))
strString4 = Trim(strInputLine.Substring(1, 25))

'Close file objects
srDrill.Close()
fs.Close()
```

Drill 9.2

```
'Declare file objects
Dim fs As New FileStream("DrillFile.txt", FileMode.Create, FileAccess.Write)
Dim srDrill As New StreamWriter(fs)

'Declare variables to store individual fields
Dim strString1 As String
Dim strString2 As String
Dim strString3 As String
Dim strString4 As String

'Copy values to individual fields
strString1 = "Some Value 1"
strString2 = "Some Value 2"
strString3 = "Some Value 3"
strString4 = "Some Value 4"
```

(continues)

(continued)

```
'Write values to file
srDrill.WriteLine(PadRight(strString1, 10) & PadRight(strString2, 20) & _
                PadRight(strString3, 15) & PadRight(strString4, 25))

'Close file objects
srDrill.Close()
fs.Close()
```

Drill 9.3

```
'Declare variable to store file #
Dim intDrillFile As Integer

'Declare variables to store individual fields
Dim strString1 As String
Dim strString2 As String
Dim strString3 As String
Dim strString4 As String

'Select an available file #
intDrillFile = FreeFile()

'Open file
FileOpen(intDrillFile, "DrillFile.txt", OpenMode.Input)

'Read individual fields
Input(intDrillFile, strString1)
Input(intDrillFile, strString2)
Input(intDrillFile, strString3)
Input(intDrillFile, strString4)

'Close file
FileClose(intDrillFile)
```

Drill 9.4

```
'Declare variable to store file #
Dim intDrillFile As Integer

'Declare variables to store individual fields
Dim strString1 As String
Dim strString2 As String
Dim strString3 As String
Dim strString4 As String

'Select an available file #
intDrillFile = FreeFile()

'Open file
FileOpen(intDrillFile, "DrillFile.txt", OpenMode.Output)
```

(continues)

```
(continued)
'Copy values to variables
strString1 = "Some Value 1"
strString2 = "Some Value 2"
strString3 = "Some Value 3"
strString4 = "Some Value 4"

'Write values to file
WriteLine(intDrillFile, strString1, strString2, strString3, strString4)

'Close file
FileClose(intDrillFile)
```

Additional Exercises

Questions 1–3 are true or false.

1. You can tell the difference between a file that is in a fixed-width format and a comma-delimited format by the statement that opens it.

2. A comma-delimited file can be opened for input and output simultaneously.

3. A random access file separates each field with a comma.

4. Write an application that outputs the numbers 1 to 100, each on a separate line, in the file Numbers.txt.

5. Write an application that inputs a hundred numbers, each on a separate line, from the file Numbers.txt into an array called intValues.

6. Write an application that outputs the numbers 1 to 100, each delimited by a comma, in the file Numbers.txt.

7. Write an application that inputs a hundred numbers, each delimited by a comma, from the file Numbers.txt into an array called intValues.

8. Write an application that will open a fixed width file, Values.txt, and display the first line of the file in a label. Place a button on the application that will display the next value in the file in the label. Make sure that the application doesn't read past the end of the file.

9. Write an application that will open a fixed width file, Values.txt. Place a button on the application that will write the current value in the text box to the file. Place a button on the application that will close the file when the user is done adding values to the file.

For questions 10–15, use the following information:

Comma-Delimited File

```
Student #, Last Name, First Name, Major, Year, GPA
```

Fixed-Width Format

```
Student Number 1-5
Last Name 6-15
First Name 16-25
Major 26-50
Year 51-60
GPA 61-65
```

Random Access File Format

```
Structure StudentRecord
    <VBFixedString(10)> Public strLastName As String
    <VBFixedString(10)> Public strFirstName As String
    Public sngGPA As Single
    <VBFixedString(20)> Public strMajor As String
    <VBFixedString(10)> Public strYear As String
End Structure
```

10. Write a program that opens a fixed-width format file and saves it to a random access file.

11. Write a program the opens a comma-delimited file and saves it to a random access file.

12. Write a program that opens a random access file and saves it to a fixed-width format file.

13. Write a program that opens a random access file and saves it to a comma-delimited file.

14. Write a program that opens a comma-delimited file and saves it to a fixed-width format file.

15. Write a program that opens a fixed-width format file and saves it as a comma-delimited file.

16. Modify the case study so the user can click on a button so that any changes made to the data are not saved automatically as in the current implementation.

INTERVIEW

An Interview with Michael Iem

Michael Iem is currently a Visual Basic Product Manager for the .NET Developer
Solutions Group at Microsoft Corporation headquarters. Michael graduated from
Purdue University where he received a Bachelor of Science in Engineering. Prior to
joining Microsoft, Michael spent nine years at Tandem Computers as a Senior
Consultant specializing in Client Server. In April of 1996, Michael joined Microsoft
Consulting Services Advanced Technology Group (MCSAT), where he project man-
aged Microsoft's Internet banking server, then moved to product manager of
BackOffice Server and authored its Performance Characterization and Reliability white
papers. A Microsoft Certified Systems Engineer, Michael is a regular speaker at industry events such as Microsoft TechEd and the Professional Developers Conference.

What makes VB.NET better than its predecessor and other programming languages?

Microsoft Visual Basic® .NET is the
newest, most productive version of the
Visual Basic tool set that enables developers to address today's pressing application development issues effectively and
efficiently. Visual Basic .NET enables you
to create rich applications for Microsoft
Windows® in less time, incorporate data
access from a wider range of database
scenarios, create components with minimal code, and build Web-based applications using the skills you already have.

    With new Windows Forms, develop-
ers using Visual Basic .NET can build
Windows-based applications that leverage
the rich user interface features available
in the Windows operating system. All the
rapid application development (RAD)
tools that developers have come to expect
from Microsoft are found in Visual Basic
.NET, including drag-and-drop design
and code behind forms. In addition, new
features such as automatic control resiz-
ing eliminate the need for complex resize
code. New controls such as the in-place
menu editor deliver visual authoring of
menus directly within the Windows
Forms Designer. Combined with greater
application responsiveness, as well as simplified localization and accessibility, these
new features in Windows Forms make
Visual Basic .NET the choice for today's
Visual Basic developers.

Visual Basic .NET opens the door for
Visual Basic developers and offers a
smooth transition to building next-gener-
ation applications today. First, Visual
Basic .NET supports full object-oriented
constructs to enable more componen-
tized, reusable code. Language features
include full implementation inheritance,
encapsulation, and polymorphism.
Second, Visual Basic .NET empowers
Visual Basic developers to consume XML
Web services running on any platform
and build Web services as easily as building any class in Visual Basic 6.0. Finally,
Visual Basic .NET enables developers to
tackle projects of any size. With new mul-
tithreaded applications, developers can
build massively scalable server-side components and Web applications, as well as
more responsive client-side applications
that perform multiple tasks in parallel.

How does VB.NET make your job of software development easier?

With Visual Basic .NET, you can code
faster and more effectively. You can
maintain your existing code without the
need to rewrite. You can also reuse all of
your existing ActiveX Controls. Windows
Forms in Visual Basic .NET provide a
robust container for existing ActiveX
controls. In addition, full support for
existing ADO code and data binding
enable a smooth transition to Visual
Basic .NET.

CHAPTER 10

Advanced Object-Oriented Programming

Although previous versions of Visual Basic contained objects, many of the features commonly associated with object-oriented languages were lacking. Most noticeably absent was the capability to create one class of object and then to be able to create another class from the original class. This form of reuse is a must if a language is going to call itself object-oriented.

Visual Basic .NET's object-oriented capabilities are excellent. Everything in Visual Basic .NET is considered an object. Although this may seem like a purist approach, it gives you great power as a developer. When everything is an object, it allows you to create new objects from the existing objects. Therefore, if the objects that come with Visual Basic .NET do not meet your needs, you do not have to start from scratch. Instead, you can start with an object that contains the majority of the functionality you require and create a new object that inherits the original object's functionality but also contains the additional information.

10.1 Visual Inheritance

As you become more advanced in programming and have developed numerous applications, you will begin to see a pattern in the types of applications you develop. Applications will have common components that you can use from application to application. This is the reason that the toolbox contains so many objects. At one point in time, programmers had to create these objects themselves. As an object became more and more common, it was added to the toolbox.

As you develop applications you will find that your objects are required in more than one application. Sometimes you may be lucky enough to find that the object you developed in the previous application will work unmodified in the new application. However, more often than not, the object will require modifications in order for it to work properly in the new application. While you can just copy the code associated with the object to the new application and then modify it there, this would cause a number of potential problems.

A minor problem is that you are wasting space on your hard drive. Why store an object's definition more than once if you do not have to? More important, what happens when you find a bug in the object's definition? If you have the definition in numerous places, you will have to make the correction in numerous places.

The answer to this problem is to use **inheritance**. Inheritance is the ability to create one object from another. With inheritance you will create a simple class to define an object that will be common to many other objects and then create other classes based on the original class, but with more features.

The original class is known as the **base class**, while the classes created from the base class are known as **derived classes**.

You have already seen some classes that had a number of items in common. You developed an `Employee` class and a `Student` class. Both classes had a first name and a last name, but different additional properties to further define the class. With inheritance it would have been possible to define a `Person` class and then derive a `Student` and an `Employee` class from the `Person` class. While in this very basic example you would not save a significant amount of coding, you can see the potential.

Visual Basic .NET not only allows you to code classes with inheritance, but also you can inherit visually. **Visual inheritance** allows the developer to inherit forms and controls to create new forms and controls. The possibilities are endless.

In its simplest application, imagine a company decides that all of its applications and forms should contain a company copyright and logo. Without inheritance, the company would probably create a form with the logo and copyright message and place it in a central location for developers to copy. This is in essence what has happened for your case studies. Each form had to have the logo added on it separately. While you might not think it was a lot of extra work, imagine if you create hundreds of applications in this manner. Now what happens if the logo changes or the copyright date increments to the next year? You would have to update the logo and any other information that might change on each and every form in each and every application. That's a lot of work and that's just a small example.

Fret not! With visual inheritance you can create the form that all forms are to model and then tell Visual Basic .NET that you wish to create a form based on the original form. With visual inheritance, if you make a change to the original form, all that is required is that you rebuild your applications and the applications will automatically update themselves to reflect any changes to the base form.

To create a form that inherits its properties from a previous existing form, like the one just discussed, you should follow these steps:

Step 1: Create a form, `frmBase`, with a logo in the upper-left corner and a copyright in the lower-left corner, as seen in Figure 10.1.

Figure 10.1
Base form

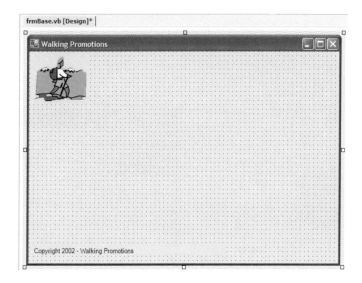

Step 2: Select `Add Inherited Form` from the `Project` menu.
Step 3: Select Open from the dialog box that appears in Figure 10.2.

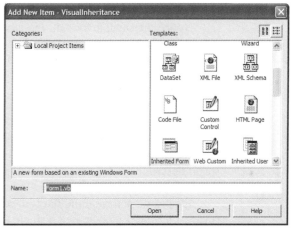

COACH'S WARNING

The only items that will be displayed in the Inheritance Picker will be items that you have already compiled. If you have not compiled the `frmBase` form, it will not show up in the window. You will have to close the window, compile the `frmBase` form, and repeat steps 2 to 4.

Figure 10.2   Add new item Inherited Form

Step 4: Select `InheritedForm` from the Templates. It should be the default. Change the `Name` of the form from `Form1.vb` to the name you wish your new form to be called. You will use `frmDerived.vb` for this example. Click on the Open button. The dialog box shown in Figure 10.3 will appear.

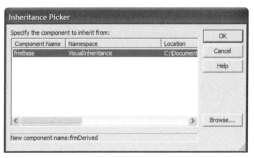

Figure 10.3   Select form to inherit from

Step 5: Select `frmBase` as the form you wish to base your new form on. Click on the OK button and your new form should appear and look similar to the base form that you created it from. (See Figure 10.4.)

Figure 10.4
Derived form

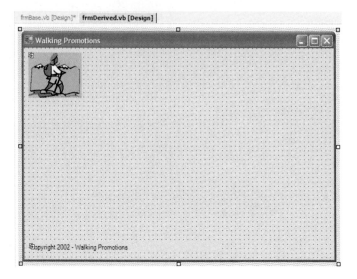

Notice the small arrows on the label and picture box that were inherited from the base form. This is your way of differentiating the objects you have added to the derived form versus the objects you have inherited from the base form.

Visual inheritance does not just apply to inheriting cosmetic changes like logos and copyright information. It applies to any controls or code that you include in a base class or object. Although you won't code this example, it's worth mentioning to show you the power of visual inheritance. Imagine if your company tracked information relating to different types of people. You could have employees, customers, suppliers, and so on. For each group of people you would track some information that would be the same regardless of the group the person belonged to, and some information that would be different.

Ideally, the information that is in common with all groups should be defined in one place. Imagine if you created a single form containing the common demographic data for people. You could create a form with controls to gather the person's first name, middle initial, last name, street address, city, state, ZIP code, email address, and so on. Then additional forms could inherit from this form the basic information and add the information pertinent to the specific group they belonged to. The code associated with the basic information could also be contained in the base form and added to the derived forms.

This allows you to modify the basic demographic information in one place and again have it propagate through all the company's applications with a minimum of effort. It wasn't that long ago that most companies were not tracking email addresses. Then there was a time where some applications would and some would not. Visual inheritance is an excellent way to enforce uniformity across a company.

10.2 Inheritance in Code

Just as visual inheritance is handy to facilitate code reuse, so is utilizing inheritance with code. When you use inheritance through code, you have a great deal of control over what aspects of a class can be modified by the derived classes. In most cases, the base class is defined in the same way any other class in Visual Basic .NET was. However, there are a few exceptions.

Protected Keyword

Previously, you used either the `Private` or `Public` keyword to determine the scope of a property. A property defined with the `Private` keyword allowed only methods and events of the class the property was defined in to have access to it. In contrast, a property defined with a scope of `Public` allowed any routine to have access to it.

With the addition of inheritance, you need another classification for the scope of a property. In most cases, when a base class is going to be inherited, you'll want the properties of the base class to be accessible by methods of the derived class. In these cases, you will need to define a property with a scope of `Protected`.

If you attempt to access an attribute in a base class from a derived class that is defined with a `Private` scope, it will not be accessible from methods in the derived class. Imagine you had `Person` declared as a base class and `Student` declared as a derived class. If you declared the `FirstName` and `LastName` properties with a `Protected` scope, then they would be accessible in the `Student` class. However, if you declared the `FirstName` and `LastName` properties with a `Private` scope, they would not be accessible in the `Student` class.

The syntax for declaring a property with a `Protected` scope is as follows:

```
Protected PropertyName As DataType
```

COACH'S TIP

There is a difference between declaring a property as `Protected` and declaring the property statements as `Protected`. If you declare the properties of a base class as `Protected`, then the derived classes will have access to the property variables. If, however, you only make the property statements for a base class as `Protected`, the derived class will only have access to the `Get` and `Set` statements.

Overriding Methods Defined in a Base Class

When a method is defined in a base class, you can decide whether or not that method can be changed in the derived class. In most cases, you will want to allow the overriding of a method in the derived classes. If you do, you must add the **Overridable** keyword to the base class method definition. Other than that, the syntax for a function or subroutine method is the same. See the following syntax:

```
Public Overridable Function MethodName(ParameterName As Datatype) As Datatype
     'Body of Method
End Function
```

```
Public Overridable Sub MethodName(ParameterName As Datatype)
     'Body of Method
End Sub
```

Defining a Derived Class

When you wish to define a new class that is derived from a base class, you must declare the name and scope of the class as before; however, you must follow the name with the keyword Inherits as well as the name of the base class. Observe the following syntax:

```
Public Class DerivedClassName
     Inherits BaseClassName
```

Clock/Alarm Clock Example

The easiest way to reinforce all of these new ideas is to show a simple class and then show how to create a derived class from that class.

   You will start with a class that you have already defined, the Clock class from the example in Chapter 6. Then you will implement an AlarmClock class. The AlarmClock class will function in a similar manner to the Clock class, except that it will add the functionality of an alarm to the class. This will require storing the time the alarm could be set for and whether the alarm is set or not. It will also require allowing the user to set the alarm.

   As before, your clock will keep military time and should track hours, minutes, and seconds. Therefore, you will need three attributes, each of which will be stored as Integers. Each of these attributes will be Protected in scope because you wish to allow them to be accessible by derived classes.

Class Declaration

When you declare a class that will act as a base class for derived classes, initially there appears to be no difference. Observe how your Clock class is defined with the same syntax you are already familiar with.

```
Public Class Clock
```

Property Declaration

Next you must declare any properties required for your base class. Remember, if you wish the properties to be visible in the derived classes, you must use the Protected keyword to define the scope.

```
Protected mintHour As Integer
Protected mintMinute As Integer
Protected mintSecond As Integer
```

Property Statements

Next you must create property statements to access the new properties. These are identical to the ones created when you were not creating a base class. They are repeated here for your convenience.

```
Public Property Hour() As Integer
    Get
         Return mintHour
    End Get
    Set(ByVal Value As Integer)
         mintHour = Value
```

(continues)

(continued)

```
        End Set
End Property
Public Property Minute() As Integer
    Get
            Return mintMinute
    End Get
    Set(ByVal Value As Integer)
        mintMinute = Value
    End Set
End Property
Public Property Second() As Integer
    Get
            Return mintSecond
    End Get
    Set(ByVal Value As Integer)
        mintSecond = Value
    End Set
End Property
```

Constructors

In your implementation you are going to code two constructors. The first will be the default constructor that will accept no parameters. It will initialize the clock to 12:00.

```
Public Sub New()
    minthour = 12
    mintminute = 0
    mintsecond = 0
End Sub
```

The second constructor will accept parameters for the hour, minute, and second to initialize your clock. All parameters must be present in order for this constructor to be called.

```
Public Sub New(ByVal intH As Integer, ByVal intM As Integer, _
            ByVal intS As Integer)
    minthour = intH
    mintminute = intM
    mintsecond = intS
End Sub
```

Methods

The next method to implement is to display the time. The implementation is nearly identical to the way it was implemented in the original example. However, because this method will be overridden in the derived class, you add the keyword `Overridable` to the method definition. The code follows:

```
Public Overridable Function Time() As String
    Return mintHour.ToString & ":" & mintMinute.ToString & _
            ":" & mintSecond.ToString
End Function
```

The final method, `Increment`, must also be declared as `Overridable`, because you will need to change its implementation in the derived class. However, the implementation other than the addition of the `Overridable` keyword is the same as in the previous example. The code follows:

```
Public Overridable Sub Increment()
    mintSecond += 1
    If (mintSecond = 60) Then
        mintSecond = 0
        mintMinute += 1
        If (mintMinute = 60) Then
            mintMinute = 0
            mintHour = mintHour + 1
            If mintHour = 24 Then
                mintHour = 0
            End If
        End If
    End If
End Sub
```

Once the base class has been defined, most of the work is already done. The goal in creating the `AlarmClock` class is to rewrite the least amount of code possible from the `Clock` class.

When you think about it, the properties for the `Clock` class are all required in the `AlarmClock` class. Although you need additional properties to store the alarm time and whether or not the alarm is set, you can simply add them to the new class.

As far as new methods are concerned, you will have to create a `SetAlarm` method as well as a `ShutAlarm` method to set and shut off the alarm. Where things get tricky is when you wish to modify the behavior of methods that already exist.

A perfect case is the `Time` method. Most alarm clocks will somehow signal that the alarm is set. For your class, when the `Time` method is called, you will display an asterisk next to the time when the alarm is set. Although you could rewrite the entire `Time` method, it would be a waste of code. It would also create a maintenance issue if you ever wished to change the way a time is displayed. As a golden rule, code should only be written once.

Visual Basic .NET gives you complete control of the situation so that you can call the `Time` method in the base class and add the code you require in the derived class.

First you must declare the derived method using the keyword **Overrides**. The syntax for declaring a method that overrides a base class's method is as follows:

```
Public Overrides Function MethodName(Parameter List) As DataType
Public Overrides Sub MethodName(Parameter List)
```

To use the functionality of a base class's method, use the following syntax of code to explicitly call the method wherever you wish it to be called in the new method.

```
MyBase.OriginalMethod
```

With this information, you can now code your derived class. First let's declare `AlarmClock` as a class that inherits the properties and methods of the `Clock` class.

```
Public Class AlarmClock
    Inherits Clock
```

Next you must declare any additional properties required for your derived class.

```
Private mintAlarmHour As Integer
Private mintAlarmMinute As Integer
Private mintAlarmSecond As Integer
Private mintAlarmSet As Boolean
```

Next you must create any Get/Set statements required for the new properties.

```
Public Property AlarmHour() As Integer
    Get
          Return mintAlarmHour
    End Get
    Set(ByVal Value As Integer)
        mintAlarmHour = Value
    End Set
End Property

Public Property AlarmMinute() As Integer
    Get
          Return mintAlarmMinute
    End Get
    Set(ByVal Value As Integer)
        mintAlarmMinute = Value
    End Set
End Property

Public Property AlarmSecond() As Integer
    Get
          Return mintAlarmSecond
    End Get
    Set(ByVal Value As Integer)
        mintAlarmSecond = Value
    End Set
End Property
```

Sometimes when you create a derived class you must create a new constructor. This happens when you need to initialize any of the new properties defined for the derived class or if the derived class behaves differently than the base class.

In this case, you are going to want to initialize the alarm in the clock to be off. Although you could also initialize the time the alarm is set to, you will not because you will set the alarm time when you turn the alarm on.

Because the only new functionality of your constructor is to set mintAlarmSet to False, you should not re-create all of the work done by the base class's constructor; instead, you should call the base class's constructor and pass it all of the parameters it requires. Then you can simply set mintAlarmSet to False and your constructor would look as follows:

```
Public Sub New(ByVal intH As Integer, ByVal intM As Integer, _
            ByVal intS As Integer)
    MyBase.New(intH, intM, intS)
    mintAlarmSet = False
End Sub
```

As with the constructor, your Increment method shared functionality between the base case and the derived class. You wish the Increment method to add a second to the clock, as it did in the base class. However, then you wish it to compare the current clock time to the alarm's time. If they are the same, you will pop up a message box indicating the alarm has rung.

To implement this functionality, explicitly call the base class's `Increment` method and then perform the check comparing the base class's properties to the derived class's properties. Because you declared the base class's properties with a `Protected` scope, they are directly accessible in the derived class.

```
Public Overrides Sub Increment()
    MyBase.Increment()
    If (mintAlarmHour = mintHour) And (mintAlarmMinute = mintAlarmMinute) _
        And (mintAlarmSecond = mintAlarmSecond) Then
        MsgBox("ALARM")
    End If
End Sub
```

The implementation of the `SetAlarm` method is straightforward. This method does not exist in the base class, so it does not contain the `Overrides` keyword. The contents of the method simply set the attributes for the alarm time to the values passed as parameters as well as setting the alarm to on by setting the `mintAlarmSet` attribute to `True`.

```
Public Sub SetAlarm(ByVal intH As Integer, ByVal intM As Integer, _
                ByVal intS As Integer)
    mintAlarmHour = intH
    mintAlarmMinute = intM
    mintAlarmSecond = intS
    mintAlarmSet = True
End Sub
```

The implementation of the `ShutAlarm` method is straightforward. This method does not exist in the base class, so it does not contain the `Overrides` keyword. The contents of the method simply set the attribute `mintAlarmSet` to `False`.

```
Public Sub ShutAlarm()
    mintAlarmSet = False
End Sub
```

The `Time` method shared functionality between the base case and the derived class. Your `Time` method should display the time as it did in the base class; however, if the alarm is set, it should also display an asterisk next to the time.

To implement this functionality, explicitly call the base class's `Time` method and add an asterisk if the alarm is set.

COACH'S TIP

An object that is defined as a derived class can be assigned to an object that was declared as either the derived class or the base class. However, an object defined as a base class cannot be assigned an object declared from the derived class.

```
Public Overrides Function Time() As String
    If (mintAlarmSet = True) Then
        Return MyBase.Time() & " *"
    Else
        Return MyBase.Time()
    End If
End Function
```

10.3 Polymorphism

In Chapter 6, you were introduced to the term polymorphism; however, there was very little that you as the programmer could write to create your own polymorphic constructs.

Polymorphism allows you to develop your classes to contain methods with the same name but different parameter lists. You might wonder why you would want to do such a thing. Sometimes you will have a method that will behave differently if a different type of parameter is passed. Imagine if you created a class from a collection of the `Student` class we developed in Chapter 8. You could develop a GPA method that would search the collection for a student and return the student's GPA. However, how do you wish to search for that student? You could set up the method to search for the student based on student number or you could search for the student based on the first and last name.

A good class would be designed to allow you to search by either name or student number. You could set up two methods. One method could be called `GPAName` and it would accept two `String` parameters. Then you could set up a method called `GPAStudentNumber` and it would accept a `Long` parameter. While this solution will satisfy the requirements, it places an undue burden on the developer.

Why should the developer have to remember two method names when they are really both solving the same problem? This problem would be worse if more than two options existed.

Polymorphism is the answer. We have already seen polymorphism at work when different objects use the same name to produce results. We have already seen operators accept different objects and perform the proper operation. You have created constructors that initialize a class with different numbers of parameters, so why should Visual Basic .NET's polymorphic capabilities end there? Fortunately for you they do not.

Overloading Methods

Just as Visual Basic .NET allowed you to create more than one constructor, as long as the parameter list varied, you can create more than one method with the same name. By modifying the declaration of a method, you can create as many methods with the same name in a single class as long as the parameter list varies in each and every method with the same name.

The following syntax is used for a function or subroutine method that will exist in more than one form. The only difference between this declaration and the original declaration is the addition of the **Overloads** keyword at the beginning of the statement.

```
Public Overloads Sub MethodName(ParameterList)
    Body of Method
End Sub
```

```
Public Overloads Function MethodName(ParameterList) As Datatype
    Body of Method
End Function
```

DRILL 10.1

Do the following method definitions conflict or are they valid definitions for a class?

```
Public Sub DrillMethod(ByVal Param1 As Integer)
    'Body of Method
End Sub
```

```
Public Sub DrillMethod(ByVal Param1 As String)
    'Body of Method
End Sub
```

DRILL 10.2

Do the following method definitions conflict or are they valid definitions for a class?

```
Public Overloads Sub DrillMethod(ByVal Param1 As Integer)
    'Body of Method
End Sub
Public Overloads Sub DrillMethod(ByVal FirstParam As String)
    'Body of Method
End Sub
```

DRILL 10.3

Do the following method definitions conflict or are they valid definitions for a class?

```
Public Overloads Sub DrillMethod(ByVal Param1 As Integer)
    'Body of Method
End Sub
Public Overloads Sub DrillMethod(ByVal Param1 As Integer, _
                                 ByVal Param2 As String)
    'Body of Method
End Sub
```

Example: Adding Polymorphism to Your Clock Class

Let's add a method to the Clock class called SetTime. However, unlike all the other methods that you have added, this method will take on many forms. You might want to set the time and just pass it the hours. However, if you are more specific, you might want to set the time to hours and minutes. Finally, if you were really specific, you might want to set the time to hours, minutes, and seconds.

This can be implemented by creating three versions of the SetTime method. The first implementation will accept only a single Integer to set the current hour. The second implementation will accept two Integers: one for the hour and one for the minute. Finally, the third implementation will accept three Integers: one for the hour, one for the minute, and one for the second.

The code follows:

```
Public Overloads Sub SetTime(ByVal intHour As Integer)
    mintHour = intHour 'Set the Hour to the parameter
    mintMinute = 0 'Reset minutes to 0
    mintSecond = 0 'Reset seconds to 0
End Sub

Public Overloads Sub SetTime(ByVal intHour As Integer, _
                             ByVal intMinute As Integer)
    mintHour = intHour 'Set the Hour to the parameter
    mintMinute = intMinute 'Set the Minutes to the parameter
    mintSecond = 0 'Reset seconds to 0
End Sub
```

(continues)

(continued)
```
Public Overloads Sub SetTime(ByVal intHour As Integer, _
                             ByVal intMinute As Integer, _
                             ByVal intSecond As Integer)
    mintHour = intHour 'Set the Hour to the parameter
    mintMinute = intMinute 'Set the Minutes to the parameter
    mintSecond = intSecond 'Set the Seconds to the parameter
End Sub
```

Now what if you were asked to create a method that allowed only the seconds to be set? Could you do so using the polymorphic nature of methods? Unfortunately, no. If you wanted to create a method that only allowed the setting of seconds, you would need to specify only one parameter, an `Integer`. Since `SetTime` already has a method definition with only one `Integer` parameter, you would get an error when you tried to declare the second `SetTime` method with one `Integer` parameter. If you wanted to have another method that set only the seconds, you would have to name it something different.

COACH'S TIP

As a final thought, if you added the `SetTime` method to the `Clock` class in the same project as the `AlarmClock` class, would you be able to set the time of an `AlarmClock` object in the same way you set an object of the `Clock` class? Absolutely! That's the power of inheritance. As long as you rebuild the classes, when you add functionality to the base class, you automatically get the benefit in the derived classes.

10.4 Destructors

When classes were introduced, a very important type of method was not explained for the sake of simplicity. However, many of your classes definitely should include a method called the **destructor**. A destructor is the last method called when the object's resources are being returned to the operating system. This method is usually used to indicate resources that are not automatically returned. This can include files that an object may have opened, database connections, and so on.

Before implementing destructors is explained, it is a good time to introduce you to how Visual Basic .NET handles returning resources to the operating system. Visual Basic .NET uses a system called garbage collection. When garbage collection is employed, one does not know exactly when resources will be returned to the operating system, but you know that they will definitely be returned. This method is more efficient than returning resources immediately when an object goes out of scope. Garbage collection decides when resources are required and calls the destructor for objects that have gone out of scope automatically. Therefore, if you code your destructor to release resources not automatically released from an object, then you will never experience an issue with leaking resources out of your application. When resources leak out of an application, they are lost and not recovered. Eventually, this will lead to slower execution of your applications and could cause your computer to crash.

Releasing Allocated Memory

Your program knows about objects created at design time and can handle them in memory. When needed, they're created and used. When the program is done with them, they're released from memory. The developer must handle reference type objects. A

developer decides when to create them, when and how to use them, and also when to release them. If these resources aren't released, it can lead to problems ranging from sluggish performance to a system crash. Releasing memory can be accomplished in the code.

When you no longer need to access the reference type object, you must manually return the memory to the heap. To deallocate or dereference an object, set the object name equal to the keyword Nothing, as in the following syntax:

ObjectName = Nothing

Therefore, if you wanted to deallocate the text box txtName from the previous example, you would use the following code:

txtName = Nothing

Coding a Destructor

While coding a destructor is not overly complicated, there are a few important details you must be aware of. A destructor method is called **Finalize**. The Finalize method should never be called directly. The only routine that will call Finalize is the garbage collector itself.

The Finalize method may not be the only Finalize method called for a specific object. When an object is created from another object using inheritance, a Finalize method may be called for each level of inheritance in the object. Therefore, the Finalize method is declared as Protected in scope and it must override the base method. The syntax for the Finalize method is as follows:

```
Protected Overrides Sub Finalize()
'Code to release resources goes here
MyObject = Nothing 'Deallocate an object you created

'Close a file if you had opened it during the execution of the object
StreamReaderName.Close()
FileStreamName.Close()

End Sub
```

A complication in implementing the Finalize method occurs when resources need to be released from a derived class and the base class. If a separate Finalize method is coded for both the base and derived class, then when an object is created from the derived class, the Finalize method of the base class will be skipped.

In order to ensure that the Finalize method of a base class is called, you should code your Finalize methods as follows:

```
Protected Overrides Sub Finalize()
    'Code to release resources goes here
    MyBase.Finalize() 'Calls the base class' Finalize method
End Sub
```

◆ 10.5 Case Study

Problem Description

Often after you have created an application you realize that your users desire more features. Imagine if your users wanted to add another column. Users might want to track a project number that an employee was working on. This would require a change to the grid and an additional text box and label to the form created in the case study of Chapter 7.

You could change the original application or you could create a new form that inherits most of its functionality from the original form. Observe a sketch of the new application, in Figure 10.5.

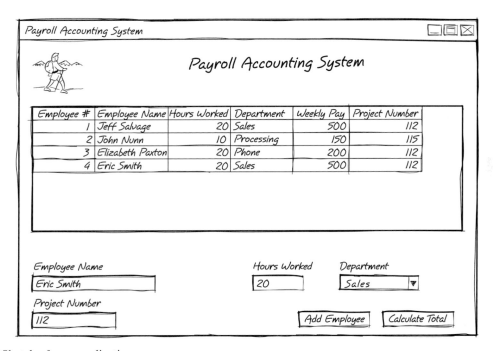

Figure 10.5 Sketch of new application

Problem Discussion

Ideally, you should be able to create the inherited form from the base form, add the text box and label to the form, add a few lines of code, and be done, right? It would be great if real-world applications always worked that way. However, you will find that sometimes solving problems the right way requires a little tweaking.

Depending upon how you go about solving the problem, you may run into a few idiosyncrasies of inheritance. The first changes you will make will be obvious. Placing the label and text box on the form do not require any significant thought. However, changing the grid does. Your new grid must have an additional column. You might think of changing it in the grid's `Col` property from the property window, but you can't. An inherited control cannot be modified in the IDE from the derived form. Therefore, you must change the number of columns programmatically. The best place to accomplish this is in the constructor of the form.

You need to modify the code for the `Click` event of the `frmAddEmployee` button in the base class, but you are not allowed to modify the code of an event in the base class.

The code in the base class adds all of the individual employee's values to the grid. While all that is required is adding the code to copy the project number to the grid, you cannot override events with inheritance. So is everything overstated about the power of inheritance? No, it just means that if you want code in an event to be inherited, you should place it in a subroutine that is overridable. Therefore, you will place the code to initialize the grid in a subroutine called `ProcessAdd`.

As a final note, the code to calculate the total payroll will not change.

Problem Solution

The only changes to the base form are to move the code from the `btnAddEmployee` `Click` event to a subroutine `ProcessAdd`.

```
Private Sub btnAddEmployee_Click(...
    ProcessAdd()
End Sub

Public Overridable Sub ProcessAdd()
    grdEmployees.Rows = grdEmployees.Rows + 1

    grdEmployees.Row = grdEmployees.Rows - 1

    grdEmployees.Col = 0
    grdEmployees.Text = grdEmployees.Rows - 1

    grdEmployees.Col = 1
    grdEmployees.Text = txtEmployee.Text

    grdEmployees.Col = 2
    grdEmployees.Text = txtHours.Text

    grdEmployees.Col = 3
    grdEmployees.Text = cmoDepartment.Text

    grdEmployees.Col = 4
    'First Week's Calculations
    Select Case cmoDepartment.Text
        Case "Sales"
            grdEmployees.Text = (Val(txtHours.Text) * intSalesPayRate).ToString
        Case "Processing"
            grdEmployees.Text = (Val(txtHours.Text) * _
                            intProcessingPayRate).ToString
        Case "Management"
            grdEmployees.Text = (Val(txtHours.Text) * _
                            intManagementPayRate).ToString
        Case "Phone"
            grdEmployees.Text = (Val(txtHours.Text) * intPhonePayRate).ToString
    End Select

End Sub
```

Create a form, `frmCompletePayroll`, as an inherited form from `frmPayroll`. Add the following code to `frmCompletePayroll` constructor:

```
'Add any initialization after the InitializeComponent() call
grdEmployees.Cols = 6
grdEmployees.Row = 0
grdEmployees.Col = 5
grdEmployees.Text = "Project Number"
```

The only other code required is to override the `ProcessAdd` subroutine to call the original `ProcessAdd` of the base form as well as processing the addition of the project number.

```
Public Overrides Sub ProcessAdd()
    MyBase.ProcessAdd()
    grdEmployees.Col = 5
    grdEmployees.Text = txtProjectNumber.Text
End Sub
```

CORNER

COACH'S

Additional Events

Visual Basic .NET's strength lies in the inherent ease of creating interactive applications. An interactive application must have the capability to respond to the user's actions in a robust manner. You have already seen a few ways that Visual Basic .NET accomplishes this. Although it hasn't been stressed until now, Visual Basic .NET responds to a user's actions by processing **events**. Visual Basic .NET has many predefined events that allow the programmer to attach code to be executed when an event occurs.

In your very first application, you coded an event and didn't even know it. When you wanted to add functionality to your Lady or the Tiger application, you attached it to the command button's `Click` event. A `Click` event occurs when the user clicks on the control. The code associated with the event is executed. The `Click` event is usually the most frequently used event; however, there are many more.

While the list of available events is very large, a few of the more popular events will be demonstrated to provide you with a basic understanding of events. The examples given are very simple and in some cases can be accomplished by other methods; however, they will demonstrate the basic concepts and provide you with a springboard to coding with events. You are encouraged to investigate the other events and experiment with them. In addition, although outside the scope of this text, Visual Basic .NET allows you to create your own events. For more information about this, check out the MSDN.

Leave Event and Focus Method

Data validation is a key concept in robust applications. One could wait until all the data has been entered to check to see if the data entered is correct, or one can attach a **Leave** event to the controls for which you wish data validation to occur. `Leave` is an event that is triggered when a control loses the current focus of the application.

Imagine if instead of using a combo box to gather a department you used a text box. You would then be required to verify that the value entered in the text box was valid. Observe the following example that would check the `txtDepartment` text box to see if the value entered is `Management`, `Sales`, `Processing`, or `Phone`.

First you must select the `txtDepartment` text box from the object list box, as shown in Figure 10.6.

Figure 10.6   Selecting `txtDepartment` control

Then, because `Leave` is not the default event, you must select the `Leave` event from the `Procedure` list box, as shown in Figure 10.7.

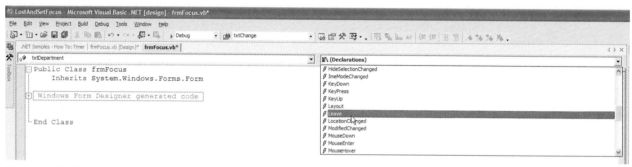

Figure 10.7   Selecting `Leave` event

Now you can add the validation code to the `Leave` event. You need to check if the department entered is not equal to one of the valid ones. If it is not, then a message is displayed warning the user that the value entered was not valid.

```
Private Sub txtDepartment_Leave(ByVal sender As Object, _
                    ByVal e As System.EventArgs) Handles _
                    txtDepartment.Leave
    If (UCase(txtDepartment.Text) <> "MANAGEMENT") And _
       (UCase(txtDepartment.Text) <> "SALES") And _
       (UCase(txtDepartment.Text) <> "PROCESSING") And _
       (UCase(txtDepartment.Text) <> "PHONE") Then
        MsgBox("Invalid Department Entered")
    End If
End Sub
```

So the big question is whether or not displaying a message stating that the user has entered invalid data is enough. In most cases, it is not. Fortunately, you have the capability to force the user to enter a valid value or not allow the user's focus to leave the current control.

Using the **Focus** method, you can shift the focus of the application back to the control that has the invalid data. Observe the rewritten `Leave` code for `txtDepartment`. This code returns the focus of the application to `txtDepartment` when an invalid department is entered.

```
Private Sub txtDepartment_Leave(ByVal sender As Object, _
                                ByVal e As System.EventArgs) Handles _
                                txtDepartment.Leave
    If (UCase(txtDepartment.Text) <> "MANAGEMENT") And _
       (UCase(txtDepartment.Text) <> "SALES") And _
       (UCase(txtDepartment.Text) <> "PROCESSING") And _
       (UCase(txtDepartment.Text) <> "PHONE") Then
       MsgBox("Invalid Department Entered")
       txtDepartment.Focus()
    End If

End Sub
```

MouseHover and MouseMove Events

Visual Basic .NET has many events related to the movement of the mouse over the object the event is coded for. Two simple events are **MouseHover** and **MouseMove**. The MouseHover event will be called when the mouse pauses over an object that has a MouseHover event coded. Similarly, the MouseMove event will be called when the mouse moves over an object that has a MouseMove event coded.

By combining these two events, you can provide feedback to the user about the purpose of certain controls on a form. Imagine you wanted to give the user of your grade giver application additional information about the type of data that could be entered into a text box. You could provide it at the bottom of a form in a label. This label would contain the relevant information about a text box when the mouse hovered over the text box. However, when the mouse moved, the label would be cleared.

Observe Figures 10.8 and 10.9, which demonstrate this behavior.

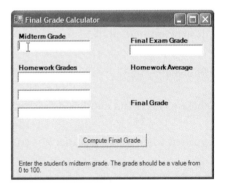

Figure 10.8 After MouseHover event has been called

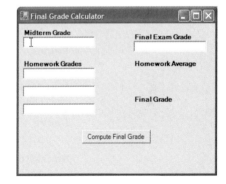

Figure 10.9 After MouseMove event has been called

The code follows:

```
Private Sub txtMidtermGrade_MouseHover(ByVal sender As Object, _
                                 ByVal e As System.EventArgs) _
                                 Handles txtMidtermGrade.MouseHover
    lblHelp.Text = "Enter the student's midterm grade." & _
                "The grade should be a value from 0 to 100."
End Sub
```

(continues)

```
(continued)
Private Sub txtMidtermGrade_MouseMove(ByVal sender As Object, _
                    ByVal e As System.Windows.Forms.MouseEventArgs) _
                    Handles txtMidtermGrade.MouseMove
    lblHelp.Text = ""
End Sub
```

COACH'S TIP

Other similar events for handling the mouse are as follows:

MouseEnter: Occurs when the mouse pointer enters the control.
MouseDown: Occurs when the mouse pointer is over the control and a mouse button is pressed.
MouseUp: Occurs when the mouse pointer is over the control and a mouse button is released.

Key Words and Key Terms

Base Class
A class that other classes are derived from.

Derived Class
A class that is created from other classes using inheritance.

Destructor
A method that is automatically called when an object's resources are reclaimed by the system.

Event
A routine that is called when a specific action occurs.

Finalize
The name of a destructor method in Visual Basic .NET.

Focus
A method that makes the object it is called for the current object.

Inheritance
The ability to create a class from another definition of a class.

Leave
An event that is called when the object that it is coded for loses focus.

MouseHover
An event that is called when the object that it is coded for is hovered over by the mouse.

MouseMove
An event that is called when the object that it is coded for is moved over by the mouse.

Overloads
A keyword used in the definition of a method indicating that the method will have more than one definition with a different set of parameters.

Overridable
A keyword used in the definition of a method defined in a base class indicating the method may be redefined in a derived class.

Overrides
A keyword used in the definition of a method in a derived class indicating the method is redefining a method from the base class.

Visual Inheritance
The ability to create an object from an object within the development environment.

Answers to Chapter's Drills

Drill 10.1
For the same method name to be used to define a method within the same class, the parameter lists must vary. In addition, the `Overloads` keyword must be placed between the scope and the `Sub` keyword. In this case the first method definition for `DrillMethod` contains an `Integer` parameter. The second method definition contains a single `String` parameter. Although the parameter lists differ, the keyword `Overloads` was not used, so the definitions would not be allowed.

Drill 10.2
For the same method name to be used to define a method within the same class, the parameter lists must vary. In addition, the `Overloads` keyword must be placed between the scope and the `Sub` keyword. In this case the first method definition for `DrillMethod` contains an `Integer` parameter. The second method definition contains a single `String` parameter. Since the parameter lists differ and the keyword `Overloads` was used, the definitions would be allowed.

Drill 10.3
For the same method name to be used to define a method within the same class, the parameter lists must vary. In addition, the `Overloads` keyword must be placed between the scope and the `Sub` keyword. In this case the first method definition for `DrillMethod` contains an `Integer` and a `String` parameter. The second method definition contains a single `Integer` parameter. Although the first parameter is the same, the second definition of the method contains an additional parameter. Therefore, the parameter lists differ and the keyword `Overloads` was used, and the definitions would be allowed.

Additional Exercises

1. List the following keywords in order of restrictedness of scope for the constructs defined with them (from most restrictive to least restrictive).

   a. `Public`   b. `Private`   c. `Protected`

   Questions 2–9 are true or false.

2. The `Finalize` method is called immediately when an object goes out of scope.

3. A `Private` attribute of the base class can be accessed from a derived class as long as the method accessing the attribute is defined with the `Overrides` keyword in the derived class.

4. A method can have more than one definition in a class as long as the `Overloads` keyword is used even if the parameter lists have the same variable types in the same order.

5. A method in a base class can be overridden in the derived class using the `Overrides` keyword if the parameter lists are the same.

6. A method in a base class can be overridden in the derived class using the `Overrides` keyword even if the parameter lists differ.

7. You can have more than one destructor for a class.

8. You can have more than one constructor for a class.

9. A base class's method can call the derived class's `Public` and `Protected` methods.

10. Which of the following are events?

    a. Focus   b. MouseMove   c. MouseHover

    d. Leave   e. MouseDown

    Questions 11–13 assume the code defining an `AlarmClock` and `Clock` class have been defined as coded in this chapter.

11. Which of the following code snippets would not cause a compile error?

    a.

    ```
    Dim test As AlarmClock
    test = New Clock()
    test = New AlarmClock(1, 1, 1)
    ```

    b.

    ```
    Dim test As Clock
    test = New Clock()
    test = New AlarmClock(1, 1, 1)
    ```

12. Does the following code compile? If so, what is its output?

    ```
    Dim test As AlarmClock
    Dim intHour As Integer
    test = New AlarmClock(12, 12, 12)

    intHour = test.AlarmHour
    MsgBox(intHour.ToString)
    ```

13. Does the following code compile? If so, what is its output?

    ```
    Dim test As Clock
    Dim intHour As Integer
    test = New Clock(12, 12, 12)

    intHour = test.Hour
    MsgBox(intHour.ToString)
    ```

    Question 14 must be solved to complete questions 15 and 16.

14. Write a class called `Person`. It should have properties of `FirstName`, `LastName`, `Age`, `Height`, and `Weight`. It should have `Property` statements to set and access each of the properties. There should also be a constructor to initialize all of the parameters. Another method should exist to return a `String` containing a complete description of the person using all of the properties.

15. Write a class called `Employee`. It should be a derived class from the `Person` class developed in question 14. It should have all the properties of the `Person` class and a property for `Salary`, `Position`, `Password`, and `YearsOfEmployment`.

It should have Property methods to set and access the `Position` and `YearsOfEmployment` properties. There should also be a constructor to initialize all of the parameters. The constructor should use the base class constructor so only a minimum of work must be repeated. A method should exist to set the `Salary` that requires a password. A method, `GiveRaise`, should exist to give an employee a raise. It should require a password.

16. Write a class called `Student`. It should be a derived class from the `Person` class developed in question 14. It should have all the properties of the `Person` class and a property for `CreditsCompleted`, `GPA`, and `Major`. It should have `Property` statements to set and access the `Major` property. There should be a constructor that accepts `FirstName`, `LastName`, and `Major` and initializes `GPA` to 0 and `CreditsCompleted` to 0. A `RecordGrade` grade method should exist that will accept a grade and the number of credits for the course. `RecordGrade` should calculate the new `GPA` and store that as well. Finally, create an `OutputStudent` method that outputs all of their information in a message box.

17. Define two classes. The first, `Vehicle`, should be the base class. The second, `Car`, should be the derived class. Determine what properties should belong to the base class and what properties should belong to the derived class. Both classes should have property statements defined for all properties and a method called `Description` that returns a `String` containing a complete description of all the properties the class has access to.

18. Improve the case study in this chapter so that a label appears on the bottom of the form with instructions indicating what are acceptable values for each text box. Also, just to add a little pizzazz, when the mouse enters the logo have the picture change to another image and then change back when the mouse moves off the logo.

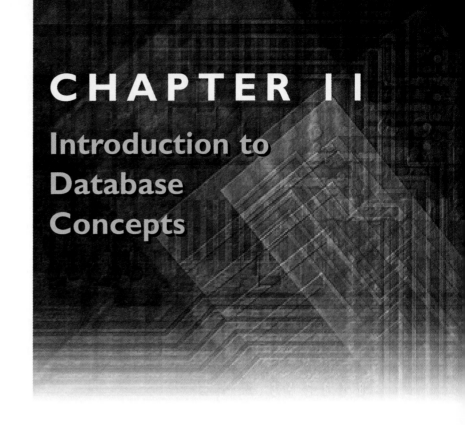

CHAPTER 11

Introduction to Database Concepts

When computers were first invented, their capacity to store **data** was very limited. Their main purpose was to perform calculations faster and more accurately than a human could. As the capability to store more data grew, the need for a way to store, organize, and access this data in a more systematic manner became apparent.

If data is stored on a hard drive in no apparent order, it is just that, data. Data can be thought of as the raw values obtained from a process. However, if that data is organized into a meaningful format so that it becomes valuable in answering questions, it has become **information**.

This is a key issue as you start to explore databases. A database is a collection of tables organized so that the data makes sense. A **table** usually contains data relating to one entity. One table may contain the demographic information for a person, while another table may contain the payroll information related to that person. In relational databases, a common field would link these tables so that a person's payroll information could be easily associated with their demographic data.

Observe the table shown in Figure 11.1, which stores the names of six basketball players and their statistics. It contains a field for each piece of data being stored: LastName, FirstName, Team, GamesPlayed, Points, Rebounds, and Assists.

Figure 11.1
PlayerStats table

You may notice that a table looks very much like the MS flex grid control you used earlier. While the MS flex grid control contains rows (known as **records**) and columns (known as **fields**) and is similar in appearance, tables have an important difference. **Data validation** occurs when values are entered into a table. When data is entered into a table, it is checked to make sure it doesn't violate any rules set forth by the creator of the table. Different software packages, known as **database management systems** (**DBMSs**), allow the user to specify different types of constraints on the data being entered. Universally, all DBMSs verify that the data being entered in each field matches the type of data that was specified. When the table shown in Figure 11.1 was created, the following data types were associated with each field:

Field Name	Data Type	Size
LastName	Text	15
FirstName	Text	10
Team	Text	15
GamesPlayed	Number	Integer
Points	Number	Integer
Rebounds	Number	Integer
Assists	Number	Integer

Other constraints can be placed on data, but the extent to which a programmer can specify rules depends highly on the choice of DBMS used.

11.1 Displaying Data Stored in a Database

One of the single most important features of Visual Basic .NET is the ease with which it allows the programmer to access data stored in a database. By providing objects and controls to interface with the database, Visual Basic .NET removes much of the complexity of database programming. For simplicity's sake, you will initially only access data in one table at a time; however, you can expand the concepts explained to access data across many tables.

The Database Objects

To display data in a form, you will require the use of three objects and a control to display them.

The Database

The database can be any one of many sources that store data. In all of the examples in this text, the database will be a Microsoft Access database stored in a file with an extension of .mdb. You will use a Microsoft Access database because it is the simplest of databases to use. However, in corporate America, Microsoft Access is usually only used for smaller data requirements. Other databases such as SQL Server, Oracle, or IBM's DB2 are examples of more robust systems designed to solve the demanding needs of a corporate environment. Fortunately, the concepts learned using Microsoft Access can be easily transferred to the other databases as well.

COACH'S TIP

All of the databases used in the text will be provided for you on the Addison-Wesley Web site. If you have a copy of Microsoft Access, you may create your own databases. However, a detailed explanation of the creation of databases is outside the scope of this text.

Figure 11.2
OleDbConnection object

The Connection

The first object you will use to access a database is the **OleDbConnection**. (See Figure 11.2.) When you wish to access a database, you will need to communicate to Visual Basic .NET many specifics about the database that you are connecting to.

Visual Basic .NET allows you to connect to almost any data source (including spreadsheets) using a series of special programs called drivers. A driver provides the specific information about the protocol of communication you will use to transfer data to and from the data source.

While many of these drivers exist, you will use the one designed to communicate with Microsoft Access, `Microsoft Jet 4.0 OLE DB Provider`.

COACH'S WARNING

If you are using an older version of Access, Access 97, then you would choose the 3.51 Jet engine.

Once you have specified the provider, you will also be required to specify the physical location of the database. Just as you specified the location of other files in Visual Basic .NET, you will be required to specify the location of the .mdb file that contains your Microsoft Access database.

COACH'S TIP

Although not required for the Microsoft Access databases provided, often databases will be restricted by a user name and password. If a user name and password are required, they can be provided in the connection object as well.

Figure 11.3
OleDbDataAdapter object

The Data Adapter

A data adapter provides the methods to transfer information from the database to the data set using the **OleDbDataAdapter**. (See Figure 11.3.) Different mechanisms exist to specify the data that will be transferred from the database to your application. Most common is the use of an industry standard series of statements defined with a language called **SQL**. Another mechanism is a stored procedure, but this method is beyond the scope of this text. Information is transferred from the database to the data set using the `Fill` method. Information is transferred from the data set back to the database using the `Update` method.

Figure 11.4   `DataSet` object

The Data Set

A `DataSet` object can be thought of as a temporary representation of the data contained in the database that you are connected to. (See Figure 11.4.) While a `DataSet` object has a great deal of functionality, for now, you will focus solely on its ability to cache the contents of a database that you will be accessing. Any changes you wish to make to data in a database is first made to the data set and then the table is updated through the data adapter.

Example: Simple Application with Text Boxes Connected to a Database

The simplest way to show the power and simplicity of connecting an application to a database is to connect controls like text boxes to fields within a table within a database.

Typically, when data is displayed, your application will require a few basic navigational operations. Observe Figure 11.5, which shows how an application that connects to the `PlayerStats` table in the `Basketball.mdb` database might look. It contains button controls to allow the user to move to the first, last, next, or previous record.

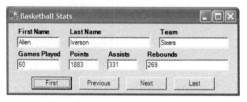

Figure 11.5   Simple database application

When a form loads with the text boxes associated with the database objects, it will display the first record in the table it is associated with. Since Allen Iverson was the first player in the table, his data is shown.

If you wish to move to the next record in the table, click on the Next button. All of the values contained in the text boxes are automatically updated with the data in the next record of the table. In this case, you move to record 2, the data associated with Eric Snow. This is shown in Figure 11.6.

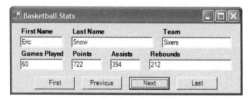

Figure 11.6   Application showing second record of table

Moving one record at a time may be a little slow, especially if there is a large number of records in the table. Therefore, this control allows you to move directly to the last record in the table by clicking on the Last button. This displays the data related to Michael Jordan, as shown in Figure 11.7.

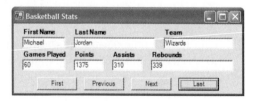

Figure 11.7   Application showing last record in table

COACH'S TIP

You may be wondering why we used text boxes to display the information. You could have used labels, if all you wanted to accomplish was to display the information in the database; however, shortly you will learn how to make changes to the data and have those changes stored in the database.

If you want to move one record back, you can use the Previous button. Moving back from the last record places you at the next-to-last record, belonging to Marcus Camby. This is shown in Figure 11.8.

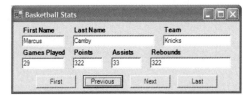

Figure 11.8   Application showing next-to-last record in table

If you wish to return to the first record, you can click on the First button.

Creating the Basketball Stats Project

Create a project called `BasketballTextBoxes`.

Configuring the Controls

The first step in creating a form to access a database is to add and configure the `OleDbConnection`, `OleDbDataAdapter`, and `DataSet` objects.

Adding and Configuring the OleDbConnection Object

The first configuration you must perform is to form a connection with the database. The connection will require you to specify the protocol to communicate with the database and the specific location of the database.

Step 1:   Place an `OleDbConnection` object from the Data tab of the Toolbox.

Step 2:   Click on the `ConnectionString` property in the Properties window. A pull-down icon will appear in the Properties window. If you click on the pull-down icon, a pop-up menu will appear.

Step 3:   Click on the `<New Connection ...>` menu item. The Data Link Properties window will appear. (See Figure 11.9.)

COACH'S TIP

If you mouse over the `ConnectionString` property of the `OleDbConnection` object, you will see all the specifics that are stored in the `ConnectionString`.

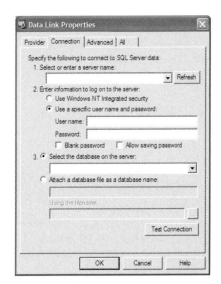

Figure 11.9   Connection tab of the Data Link Properties window

COACH'S TIP

Your list of providers may vary slightly because of other applications you may have loaded on your computer; however, `Microsoft Jet 4.0 OLE DB Provider` should be there.

Step 4: Click on the Provider tab in the Data Link Properties window.

Step 5: Select `Microsoft Jet 4.0 OLE DB Provider`. (See Figure 11.10.)

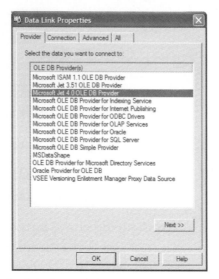

Figure 11.10   Provider tab of the Data Link Properties window

COACH'S TIP

Although not required for this application, notice how you can specify a user name and password for the connection. All databases in this text will allow the default `Admin` user name and no password for making the connection.

Step 6: Click on the Next button. The Connection tab will become active. Notice how the options have changed. Since you selected `Microsoft Jet 4.0 OLE DB Provider`, the Connection Wizard automatically changed the properties you will be required to fill in to match the provider you have selected. (See Figure 11.11.)

Figure 11.11   New Connection properties window

Step 7: You must enter or select the physical location of the Access database file that will be connected to the application. Either type the directory name in the text box or click on the < . . . > button to browse your computer for your `Bastkeball.mdb` file. The path will vary from computer to computer.

Step 8: Once the database is specified, you have completed the specification of the
connection. Click on the OK button to commit the specification. (See Figure
11.12.)

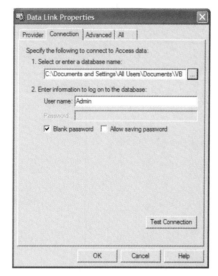

Figure 11.12   New Connection properties window with the database specified

Adding and Configuring the OleDbDataAdapter Object

Once a connection has been established, a data adapter must be configured. This will
allow you to specify the way that you want your application to view, add, edit, and delete
data through the connection. Since you are connecting to a Microsoft Access database,
you will need to create a SQL statement for each action that you wish to perform.
Fortunately, a wizard exists that will create all of the statements for you.

Step 1: Place an `OleDbDataAdapter` object from the Data tab of the Toolbox. The
Data Adapter Configuration Wizard will automatically start.

Step 2: An informational screen will appear, welcoming you to the wizard. Click on
the Next button of the wizard.

Step 3: You will be presented with a window that will allow you to select which data
connection you wish the data adapter to use. (See Figure 11.13.) There will
probably be only one data connection on your form, so it will be automatically
selected. Click on the Next button.

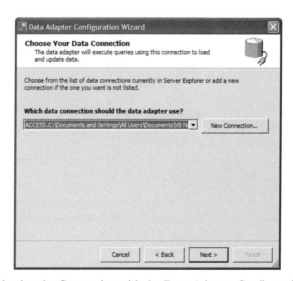

Figure 11.13   Selecting the Connection with the Data Adapter Configuration Wizard

Step 4: The wizard will allow you to select the type of query your data adapter will use. Since you selected a Microsoft Access database, you are limited to SQL statements. Therefore, click on the Next button to select `Use SQL statements`. (See Figure 11.14.)

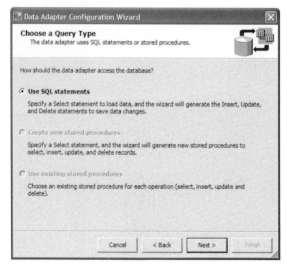

Figure 11.14   Selecting the Query Type using the Data Adapter Configuration Wizard

Step 5: The next window that appears will allow you to generate a SQL statement. (See Figure 11.15.) You have the option of writing a SQL statement from scratch (this is shown in Section 11.3) or having the Query Builder create it for you. For now, it is far simpler to have the Query Builder create the necessary statements.

Figure 11.15
Generate the SQL statements window of the Data Adapter Configuration Wizard

Step 6: Click on the Query Builder button, and the wizard will present you with a list of tables that you can base your query on. (See Figure 11.16.)

Figure 11.16
Add Table window of the
Data Adapter Configuration
Wizard

Step 7: Click on the Add button, and the `PlayerStats` table will be added to the
Query Builder while the Add Table window is still showing. (See Figure
11.17.)

Figure 11.17
Query Builder window of
the Data Adapter
Configuration Wizard

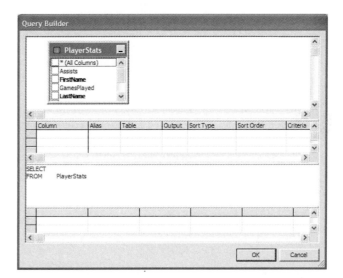

Step 8: Click on the Close button to close the Add Table window.
Step 9: Click on the `* (All Columns)` choice in the PlayerStats window to include
all the columns of the table. (See Figure 11.18.) Notice that the SQL statement
is being created for you. (The syntax of a SQL statement will be covered in
Section 11.3.)

COACH'S TIP

Selecting all the fields
from a table may be
convenient; however, it
can lead to perform-
ance issues if large
amounts of data are
being transferred. If
you only want a few
fields to be selected,
then only click on the
check boxes next to
the fields you want
included.

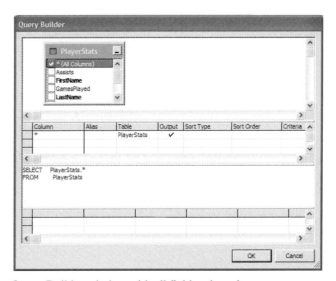

Figure 11.18   Query Builder window with all fields selected

Step 10:   Click on the OK button. You will see the SQL statement you generated in the window. (See Figure 11.19.)

Figure 11.19
Generate the SQL statements window of the Data Adapter Configuration Wizard

COACH'S WARNING

The wizard will only generate all the statements if the table has a primary key defined for it. A primary key uniquely identifies a record in the table. All the tables provided with this text will already have one created for you.

Step 11:   Click on the Next button, and the wizard will create all the statements required for the data adapter. While you interactively created a statement to select data from a table, you will also probably require statements to add, delete, and modify records. If you are only creating a SELECT statement for a query of a single table, the wizard is smart enough to generate the statements required to allow the user of the data adapter to add, delete, and modify records. These can all be generated for you automatically when the data you are accessing is as simple as in your example. (See Figure 11.20.)

Figure 11.20   Results window of the Data Adapter Configuration Wizard

Step 12:   Click on the Finish button, and your data adapter will be completely configured.

Adding and Configuring the DataSet Object

A `DataSet` object must be created to temporarily hold the data from a table in the form. Its creation is quite simple.

Step 1: Click on the form. If the form is not selected, the menu option for Step 2 will not appear.

Step 2: Click on Generate Dataset from the Data Menu.

Step 3: Select the New radio button and type `DsBasketballPlayers` in the text box as shown in Figure 11.21.

Figure 11.21
Generate Dataset window

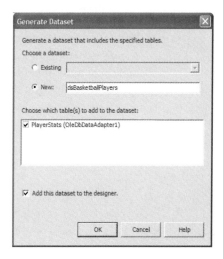

Step 4: Click on the OK button and the data set `DsBasketballPlayers1` will appear on the bottom of the form shown in Figure 11.22.

Figure 11.22
Form with three objects added

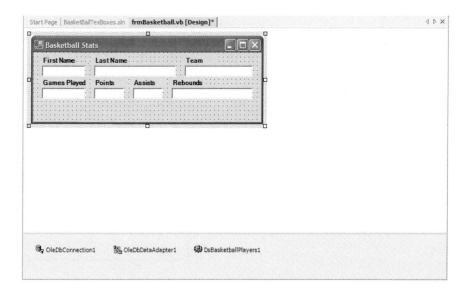

Connecting Other Controls to the Database

In your example, you will connect each text box to an individual field in the table. The procedure is the same for each text box.

Step 1: Place a label on the form to indicate the value stored in the text box.

Step 2: Change the label's Font to be Bold.

Step 3: Change the Text property of the label to reflect the value being stored in the text box.

Step 4: Place a text box below the label.

Step 5: Change the default Name of the text box to a more meaningful name.

Step 6: Remove the default text in the Text property of the text box.

Step 7: Select the field of the database to bind to the text box. Make sure the text box that you want to bind is selected. Then click on the ⊞ to the left of the DataBindings property at the top of the Properties window. The window will expand to show the Text property. Click on the down arrow icon of the Text property. A pop-up window will appear showing the data set DsBasketballPlayers1 with a ⊞ next to it. Click on the ⊞, and the PlayerStats table will appear. Click on the ⊞ next to the PlayerStats table, and a list of fields will appear. Click on the name of the field that you wish to associate with the text box. (See Figure 11.23.)

Figure 11.23
Binding a database field to a text box

After all the text boxes have been added and linked, your application should appear as it does in Figure 11.24.

Figure 11.24
Simple database application

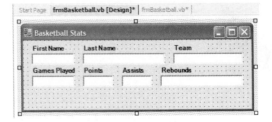

Controlling the Database with Code

Visual Basic .NET allows you to navigate the database programmatically. You will learn to code the loaded and updating of data into the data set as well as moving to the first, previous, next, and last record of the data set.

Coding the Loading of a Data Set

Although you have placed all the required objects and controls on the form, you have not instructed the application to actually load the data from the table into the data set.

Since you most probably would like the information in the table displayed as the form loads, the most logical place to put the code to load the data set is in the constructor of the form.

The syntax required to load data into a data set is as follows:

DataAdapterName.Fill(*DataSetName*)

Therefore, for your application, the following code should be contained in the constructor:

```
Public Sub New()
    MyBase.New()

    'This call is required by the Windows Form Designer
    InitializeComponent()

    'Add any initialization after the InitializeComponent() call
    OleDbDataAdapter1.Fill(DsBasketballPlayers1) 'Load the Data Set
End Sub
```

Moving the Data Set to the First, Previous, Next, or Last Record

In order for the user to control what record is displayed in the text boxes, the user will require a series of buttons. A button should be created to allow the user to move to the first, previous, next, or last record.

Step 1: Add a button to the bottom of the form for each operation. They should be named `btnFirst`, `btnPrevious`, `btnNext`, and `btnLast`. With the buttons added to the form, your form should now appear as in Figure 11.25.

Figure 11.25
Complete application

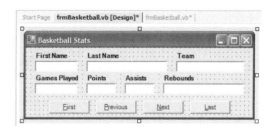

Step 2: Each button control will require coding a change in the current record in the database.

```
Private Sub btnFirst_Click(...
    Me.BindingContext(DsBasketballPlayers1, "PlayerStats").Position = 0
End Sub

Private Sub btnPrevious_Click(...
    Me.BindingContext(DsBasketballPlayers1, "PlayerStats").Position -= 1
End Sub
```

```
Private Sub btnNext_Click(...
    Me.BindingContext(DsBasketballPlayers1, "PlayerStats").Position += 1
End Sub
```

```
Private Sub btnLast_Click(...
    Me.BindingContext(DsBasketballPlayers1, "PlayerStats").Position = _
        Me.BindingContext(DsBasketballPlayers1, "PlayerStats").Count - 1
End Sub
```

11.2 Binding a Data Grid

While setting up access to each of the fields of a table through text boxes will allow a user access to each record in the database, its limited viewing of a single record at a time can become a hindrance to viewing and changing large amounts of data.

A better way is to use the **data grid** control from the Windows Forms Toolbox. A data grid is similar to the MS flex grid introduced in Chapter 7; however, instead of simply displaying data stored in the computer's memory, it allows the display and updating of data stored in databases.

Your previous application could be rewritten and enhanced to exploit the benefits of a data grid. Observe the application shown in Figure 11.26, which contains a data grid linked to the `PlayerStats` table. Notice how more than one record can be viewed at a time.

COACH'S TIP

The look and actions of a data grid should seem very familiar to you. Do you remember where you saw something like this before? A data grid has many similarities to the view of a table in Microsoft Access.

Figure 11.26   Data grid application

If more records exist than can fit in the form, a scroll bar will automatically appear to the right. A user can then scroll up and down through the records to see all the records in the table.

If you choose, you may select at design time to allow the user to resize the form when the application is running and have the data grid resize with the form's change in size.

Functionality of a Data Grid

The data presented in a data grid can be loaded from a table at any time. However, in your case it will make sense to load it from the form's constructor.

Unlike an MS flex grid, a data grid will allow the user to make changes. Users can just click on the field that they wish to change and then type the new value in the place of the old one. The ability to make changes can be shut off if you decide to give the user a read-only view of the data.

If you wish to add a record to the data grid, you can type the new information in the last row. The asterisk to the left indicates this row. If you wish to delete a row, click on the gray rectangle to the left of the row and then click on the <Delete> key of your keyboard.

When a change is made to the data presented in the grid, the actual data in the table is not automatically updated. This must be done with code and may be performed in many ways. The simplest way to accomplish updating the table is to place the update code in a button.

Steps to Create the Basketball Data Grid Application

The steps to create the basketball data grid application are very similar to the steps to create the text box version of the application. Both applications require OleDbConnection, OleDbDataAdapter, and DataSet objects. The objects are configured identically to the way they were for the previous application; therefore, a series of steps with abbreviated explanations will be shown.

Create a New Project

Create a new project called BasketballDataGrid.

Adding and Configuring the OleDbConnection Object

COACH'S TIP

Remember, the OleDbConnection object contains the specifications for the protocol to communicate with a database and any information pertaining to the connection.

Step 1: Place an OleDbConnection object from the Data tab of the Toolbox.
Step 2: Click on the pull-down icon of the OleDbConnection object in the ConnectionString property in the Properties window. A pop-up menu will appear.
Step 3: Click on the <New Connection ...> menu item. The Data Link Properties window will appear.
Step 4: Click on the Provider tab in the Data Link Properties window.
Step 5: Select Microsoft Jet 4.0 OLE DB Provider.
Step 6: Click on the Next button.
Step 7: Select the path to the Basketball.mdb file.
Step 8: Once the database is specified, you have completed the specification of the connection. Click on OK to commit the specification.

Adding and Configuring the OleDbDataAdapter Object

COACH'S TIP

Remember, the OleDbDataAdapter object provides the methods to transfer information from the database to the data set.

Step 1: Place an OleDbDataAdapter object from the Data tab of the Toolbox. The Data Adapter Configuration Wizard will automatically start.
Step 2: An informational screen will appear, welcoming you to the wizard. Click on the Next button of the wizard.
Step 3: Click on the Next button of the wizard.
Step 4: Click on the Next button to select Use SQL statements.
Step 5: The next window that appears will allow you to generate a SQL statement.
Step 6: Click on the Query Builder button, and the wizard will present you with a list of tables that you can base your query on.
Step 7: Click on the Add button, and the PlayerStats table will be added to the Query Builder.
Step 8: Click on the Close button to close the Add Table window.
Step 9: Click on the * (All Columns) choice in the PlayerStats window to select that all the columns of the table will be included.
Step 10: Click on the OK button. You will see the SQL statement you generated in the window.
Step 11: Click on the Next button, and the wizard will create all the statements required for the data adapter.
Step 12: Click on the Finish button, and your data adapter will be completely configured.

Adding and Configuring the DataSet Object

Step 1: Click on the form.

Step 2: Click on Generate Data Set from the Data menu.

Step 3: Click on the OK button.

Adding and Configuring the Data Grid

Once the tree objects have been created and properly configured, the addition of a data grid and its linkage to the database is simple.

Step 1: Add a data grid object to the form from the Toolbox.

Step 2: Rename the data grid to `grdBasketball`.

Step 3: Change the `DataSource` property of the data grid to `DsBasketballPlayers1.PlayerStats`. Notice that columns of the grid are automatically created for the fields in the data set.

Step 4: Set the `Anchor` property of the grid to `Top, Bottom, Left, Right`.

> **COACH'S TIP**
>
> **Remember, the `DataSet` object is a temporary representation of data from a database stored in the computer's memory.**

> **COACH'S TIP**
>
> The **Anchor** property of a control defines a control's placement when the form is resized. By default, controls have the `Anchor` property set to `Top, Left`. However, you will want your data grid to resize when the form resizes. By setting the property to `Top, Bottom, Left, Right`, you are indicating that the control should resize in proportion with the form when it is resized.

Filling the Data Grid

Add the following code to the constructor of the form so that the data grid is filled when the form loads.

```
Public Sub New()
    MyBase.New()

    'This call is required by the Windows Form Designer
    InitializeComponent()

    'Add any initialization after the InitializeComponent() call
    OleDbDataAdapter1.Fill(DsBasketballPlayers1) 'Load the DataSet
End Sub
```

Adding an Update Button

Step 1: Add a button to the form in the lower-left corner.

Step 2: Rename the button to `btnUpdate`.

Step 3: Add the following code to the button's `Click` event.

```
OleDbDataAdapter1.Update(DsBasketballPlayers1)
```

Step 4: Change the `Anchor` property to `Bottom, Right`.

> **COACH'S TIP**
>
> If you set the control's `Anchor` property to `Bottom, Right`, the control will move to the bottom and right of the form in proportion to the form's resizing. This will keep the Update button anchored to the right-left corner of the form.

Accessing Individual Values in a Data Set

While not required for this application, imagine if you wanted to access individual fields within the data set. You might want to add the ability to calculate the total number of points scored by all players or even the total points scored by a single team. While these answers can be obtained by querying the database again using the SQL statements introduced in Section 11.3, they can also be calculated by looping through the data set and inspecting the individual fields.

The syntax for accessing an individual field of a data set is as follows:

DataSetName.`Tables`(*TableNumber*)`.Rows`(*RowNumber*)(*ColumnNumber*)

- ◆ *DataSetName:* The name of a properly configured data set.
- ◆ *TableNumber:* While your data sets have only contained one table, a data set can be made from more than one table. To indicate the first table, you will use a 0 for the *TableNumber*. Subsequent tables would have a higher number.
- ◆ *RowNumber:* Indicates the number of the row containing the field that you wish to access. Row numbers start with 0.
- ◆ *ColumnNumber:* Indicates the number of the column containing the field that you wish to access. Column numbers start with 0.

Therefore, if you were to create the proposed addition to the basketball application, you could do so fairly easily. If you add a text box to allow the user to enter the team whose points are to be totaled and a button to allow the search to be initiated, you would need to loop from the first row in the data set (row 0) to the last row in the data set (the total number of rows minus 1) and check if the team for the current row is equal to the team the user wishes the total points for. If they match, then the points would be added to a variable. When the entire grid has been searched through, a message box can be used to output the results.

The code follows:

```
Private Sub btnTotals_Click(...
    Dim intTotalPoints As Integer 'Stores the total number of points
    Dim intCurrentRow As Integer 'Stores the current row of the grid
    Dim intMaxRow As Integer 'Stores index of the max row of the grid

    'Compute the maximum row of the grid.
    'It's one less than the number of rows in the grid
    intMaxRow = Me.BindingContext(DsBasketballPlayers1, "PlayerStats").Count - 1
    For intCurrentRow = 0 To intMaxRow
        'The points are located in column 4
        'The team is located in column 6
        If (DsBasketballPlayers1.Tables(0).Rows(intCurrentRow)(6) _
                                = txtTeam.Text) Then
            intTotalPoints += _
                    Val(DsBasketballPlayers1.Tables(0).Rows(intCurrentRow)(4))
        End If
    Next intCurrentRow

    'Output the results
    MsgBox("The total points for the " & txtTeam.Text & " is " & _
        intTotalPoints.ToString())

End Sub
```

If you ran the application with the data entered as in Figure 11.26 and entered "Sixers", you would get the message The total points for the Sixers is 2605.

Alternatively, you can also access values with the following syntax:

DataSetName.Tables("*TableName*").Rows(*RowNumber*).Item("*FieldName*")

- ◆ *DataSetName:* The name of a properly configured data set.
- ◆ *TableName:* While your data sets have only contained one table, a data set can be made from more than one table. To indicate the table you wish to access, place the table name in quotes.
- ◆ *RowNumber:* Indicates the number of the row containing the field that you wish to access. Row numbers start with 0.
- ◆ *Item:* Indicates the name of the column containing the field that you wish to access.

DRILL 11.1

Given the data set displayed in Figure 11.26, what value would be returned given the following statements?

```
a DsBasketballPlayers1.Tables(0).Rows(4)(3)
b DsBasketballPlayers1.Tables(0).Rows(1)(2)
c DsBasketballPlayers1.Tables(0).Rows(6)(1)
d DsBasketball.Tables("PlayerStats").Rows(4).Item("Assists")
e DsBasketball.Tables("PlayerStats").Rows(6).Item("Assists")
```

11.3 SQL SELECT Statement

When the database concepts were introduced at the beginning of the chapter, the details of the SQL SELECT statement were skipped over. Visual Basic .NET uses a **S**tructured **Q**uery **L**anguage for manipulating databases. SQL (pronounced either "sequel" or "S-Q-L") is a standard series of statements that allows a programmer to manipulate a database in a concise and efficient manner. Although implementations of SQL can vary slightly from implementation to implementation, the syntax shown here should work in all cases.

The first SQL statement is SELECT. It allows the developer to retrieve data from a table or series of tables. Instead of showing you the complete syntax of the SQL SELECT statement, portions of the statement will be introduced as necessary to aid in your complete understanding of the statement.

Simple Form of the SQL SELECT Statement

The syntax of the SELECT statement has many options. The simplest form of the syntax is as follows:

SELECT *FieldList* FROM *TableName*

- ◆ **SELECT:** A keyword indicating this will be a SELECT SQL statement to retrieve data from a table.
- ◆ *FieldList:* If the developer wishes only some of the fields of a table to be selected, the field list should be a list of the field names desired, with each separated by a comma. If all the fields are to be selected, then an asterisk is used in place of the *FieldList*.

◆ **FROM:** A keyword that indicates the next part of the statement will be the `TableName` from which to retrieve the data.
◆ *TableName:* The name of the table from which the data will be retrieved. The table must exist in the database that you selected when building your SQL statement.

Simple SELECT Statement Examples   For the following examples, assume that the table shown in Figure 11.27 has been created.

Figure 11.27
StudentGrades table
definition

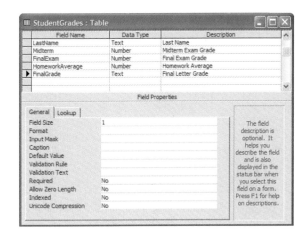

Problem: Retrieve all the student records.

SQL: `SELECT * FROM StudentGrades`

Although the SELECT statement could have been written as SELECT FirstName, LastName, MidTerm, FinalExam, HomeworkAverage, FinalGrade FROM StudentGrades, you employ a shortcut. The asterisk in a SELECT statement acts as a wildcard that will select all the fields in the table. (See Figure 11.28.)

Figure 11.28
StudentGrades records

FirstName	LastName	Midterm	FinalExam	HomeworkAverage	FinalGrade
Jeff	Salvage	99	95	98	A
John	Nunn	85	88	83	B
Elizabeth	Paxton	100	70	82	B
April	Starsinic	62	75	65	D
Anthony	Palumbi	100	98	99	A
Jeffrey	Popyack	53	66	78	D
Michael	Hirsch	70	75	68	C
Elinor	Actipis	77	78	90	B
Susan	Hartman-Sullivan	97	90	94	A
Pat	Mahtani	88	81	77	B
Tim	Souder	12	14	13	F
Lisa	Cho	97	82	85	B
		0	0	0	

Problem: Retrieve only the first and last name of every student.

SQL: `SELECT FirstName, LastName FROM StudentGrades`

Since only two fields are listed in the `SELECT` statement, only two fields are displayed in the results shown in Figure 11.29.

Figure 11.29
StudentGrades records

DRILL 11.2

Write the `SELECT` statement that will retrieve the last name and final grade of every student.

Adding Search Criteria to a SQL SELECT Statement

SQL `SELECT` statements allow the developer to add search conditions to the statement so that only records matching the search conditions are returned when the `SELECT` statement is executed.

The syntax to add a search condition is as follows:

`SELECT FieldList FROM TableName [WHERE SearchConditions]`

- ◆ **WHERE:** A keyword indicating that a search condition will be specified.
- ◆ *SearchConditions:* A search condition for a `SELECT` statement does not vary much from the conditional expressions with which you are already familiar. The main difference is that usually the search condition will contain at least one field from a table. Just as with the earlier conditional expressions, conditional expressions within a `SELECT` statement can be combined using the logical operators `And` and `Or`.

SELECT Statement Examples with Simple Search Criteria

Problem: Retrieve all the records of students who have a final grade of A.

SQL: `SELECT * FROM StudentGrades WHERE FinalGrade = 'A'`

Since an asterisk is used all the fields are returned. The `WHERE` clause limits the results to only those students with a final grade of an A as shown in Figure 11.30.

Figure 11.30
StudentGrades records

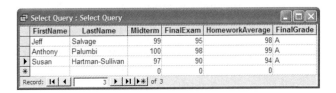

Problem: Retrieve the first and last name of all the students who have a midterm grade greater than or equal to 65.

SQL: `SELECT FirstName, LastName FROM StudentGrades WHERE Midterm >= 65`

The results are shown in Figure 11.31.

Figure 11.31
StudentGrades records

DRILL 11.3

Write the `SELECT` statement that will retrieve the last name and final grade of every student with a final grade of an A or a B.

DRILL 11.4

Write the `SELECT` statement that will retrieve all the records of students who failed the midterm. A failing midterm is a grade lower than 65.

Problem: Retrieve all the records of students who have a final grade of an A, a B, or a C.

SQL: `SELECT * FROM StudentGrades WHERE FinalGrade = "A" OR FinalGrade="B" OR FinalGrade="C"`

The results are shown in Figure 11.32.

Figure 11.32
StudentGrades records

FirstName	LastName	Midterm	FinalExam	HomeworkAverage	FinalGrade
Jeff	Salvage	99	95	98	A
John	Nunn	85	88	83	B
Elizabeth	Paxton	100	70	82	B
Anthony	Palumbi	100	98	99	A
Michael	Hirsch	70	75	68	C
Elinor	Actipis	77	78	90	B
Susan	Hartman-Sullivan	97	90	94	A
Pat	Mahtani	88	81	77	B
Lisa	Cho	97	82	85	B
*		0	0	0	

Record: 9 of 9

Problem: Retrieve all the records of students whose midterm and homework grades are a 90 or higher.

SQL: SELECT * FROM StudentGrades WHERE Midterm >=90 AND HomeworkAverage >= 90

The results are shown in Figure 11.33.

Figure 11.33
StudentGrades records

FirstName	LastName	Midterm	FinalExam	HomeworkAverage	FinalGrade
Jeff	Salvage	99	95	98	A
Anthony	Palumbi	100	98	99	A
Susan	Hartman-Sullivan	97	90	94	A
		0	0	0	

Record: 3 of 3

DRILL 11.5

Write the SELECT statement that will retrieve the first and last names of students who received a B on the midterm. A B on the midterm is a grade of at least 80 and no more than 89.

DRILL 11.6

Write the SELECT statement that will retrieve the records of students who have a failing grade for the midterm, the final exam, or their homework average.

SELECT Statement Examples with Wildcards in the Search Criteria

Problem: Retrieve all the records of students whose last name starts with an S.

SQL: SELECT * FROM StudentGrades WHERE LastName LIKE "S*"

Another wildcard character is an asterisk. By using an asterisk in a string, as in the previous example, you are specifying that the records returned are all the records of students with a last name starting with the letter S. (See Figure 11.34.)

Figure 11.34
StudentGrades records

FirstName	LastName	Midterm	FinalExam	HomeworkAverage	FinalGrade
Jeff	Salvage	99	95	98	A
April	Starsinic	62	75	65	D
Tim	Souder	12	14	13	F
		0	0	0	

Record: 3 of 3

DRILL 11.7

Write the SELECT statement that will retrieve the first and last names of the students whose first name starts with the letter J.

Adding a Search Criterion Using the Query Wizard

If you wanted to add search criteria to your `SELECT` statements with the Query Wizard, it is as simple as adding your criteria to the Criteria column. Figure 11.35 shows how you would specify to return only records with a final grade of an A.

COACH'S TIP

Database fields with a funnel icon next to them indicate that a criterion exists for that field.

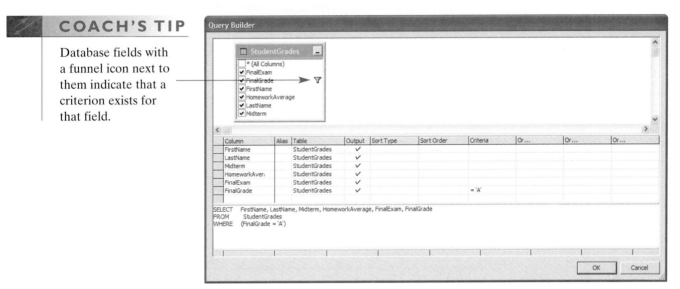

Figure 11.35 Search criteria set to = `'A'`

If you want to list more than one search criterion for a given database column, you can place the additional criteria in the columns to the left of the criterion as long as you wish those columns to be joined by an `Or` operator.

See the query in Figure 11.36, which will return all records with a `FinalGrade` equal to an `'A'`, a `'B'`, or a `'C'`.

Figure 11.36
Search criteria set to = `'A'` or `'B'` or `'C'`

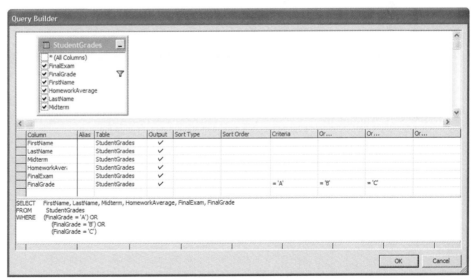

If, however, you want to list more than one field in the search criteria and you wish each criterion to be joined by an AND operator, you can do so by placing the criteria for each database column in its corresponding Criteria column. Observe the Query Builder in Figure 11.37, which is configured to return only the records of students who have an 'A' for a FinalGrade and >= 90 for HomeworkAverage, Midterm, and FinalExam.

Figure 11.37
Search criteria set to = 'A' for FinalGrade and >= 90 for Homework Average, Midterm, and FinalExam

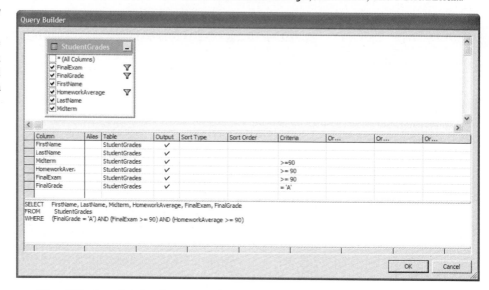

The difficulty with the Query Builder is when you wish to combine conditions of different database columns with an OR operator or you wish to combine conditions of the same database column with an AND operator. Both can be accomplished, but it requires tweaking the Query Builder in an unintuitive way.

For each database field that you wish to have more than one criterion ANDed together with another criterion from the same database field, you must add another reference to the database field in the database field column of the Query Builder. You must also unselect output. You can see this in Figure 11.38 with the FinalGrade field.

For each different database field criteria that you wish to OR together, you must do so by placing the second database field of the criteria in the Or... column. If more than one different database field is ORed together, then each field must be placed in a separate Or... column. You can see this in Figure 11.38 with the FinalExam and FinalGrade fields.

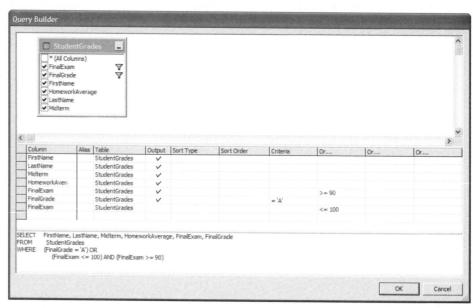

Figure 11.38   Search criteria set to a FinalGrade of 'A' or a FinalExam <=100 and >= 90

Ordering the Records Returned by a SQL SELECT Statement

The SQL SELECT statement also allows you to specify the order in which the records are retrieved. You can order the results based on a list of fields that will sort the results.

SELECT *FieldList* FROM *TableName* [WHERE *SearchConditions*] [ORDER BY *OrderList* ASC *or* DESC]

- ◆ **ORDER BY:** The keywords to indicate that the developer will specify at least one field to sort the results by.
- ◆ *OrderList:* A field or list of fields separated by commas that specify the order that the records will be retrieved.
- ◆ **ASC** *or* **DESC:** The keywords to indicate whether the results should be sorted in ascending (ASC) or descending (DESC) order. If this option is left off, the default order is ascending.

SELECT Statement Examples with an ORDER BY Clause

Problem: Retrieve all the records of students who have a final grade of A, B, or C, in descending order based on their final exam.

SQL: SELECT * FROM StudentGrades WHERE FinalGrade = "A" OR FinalGrade = "B" OR FinalGrade = "C" ORDER BY FinalExam DESC

The results are shown in Figure 11.39.

Figure 11.39
StudentGrades records

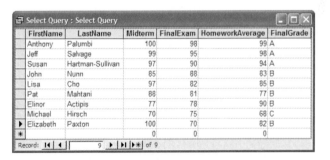

	FirstName	LastName	Midterm	FinalExam	HomeworkAverage	FinalGrade
	Anthony	Palumbi	100	98	99	A
	Jeff	Salvage	99	95	98	A
	Susan	Hartman-Sullivan	97	90	94	A
	John	Nunn	85	88	83	B
	Lisa	Cho	97	82	85	B
	Pat	Mahtani	88	81	77	B
	Elinor	Actipis	77	78	90	B
	Michael	Hirsch	70	75	68	C
▶	Elizabeth	Paxton	100	70	82	B
*			0	0	0	

Problem: Retrieve all the records of students who failed the final exam but passed the midterm, in ascending order based on their midterm. A passing grade is a grade of 65 or more.

SQL: SELECT * FROM StudentGrades WHERE FinalExam < 65 AND Midterm >= 65 ORDER BY Midterm ASC

No records are returned!

DRILL I I . 8

Write the SELECT statement that will retrieve all the final exams greater than 90 and list the records in alphabetical order. Alphabetical order should be ascending by last name and then first name.

COACH'S TIP

When comparing date values, date constants are coded with a pound sign (#) on either side of the date, as in the following example:

```
SELECT * FROM Payroll WHERE Day > #3/10/2001#
```

Using the Query Builder to Order Your SQL Statement

Ordering the results of your query is very easy to do with the Query Builder. If you want to specify an order, you must place a number in the database field's Sort Order column. The query will then order the results by the fields with numbers entered. The lowest number field will be the first field that will be sorted. The remaining fields containing a Sort Order will be sorted from the lowest number entered to the highest.

You can also select either Ascending or Descending for the Sort Type.

Figure 11.40 shows how the Query Builder can be configured to return all the records in the `StudentGrades` table sorted by `LastName` and then `FirstName`, in ascending order.

Figure 11.40
Using the ordering features of the Query Builder

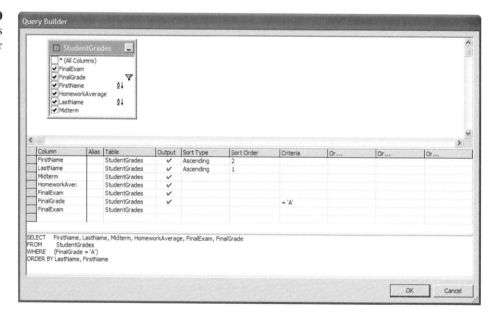

Advanced Features of the SELECT Statement

When you write SQL statements, you must be careful about the amount of data that you return. Wherever possible, you should return the minimum amount of data required.

Consider the problem of totaling the payroll costs in your case study. Imagine you wished to display the total payroll cost for each department in the company.

This could be accomplished by writing a SQL statement to retrieve the daily pay and department for every record in the database. Once the data is retrieved, you could loop through all of the records and add the daily pay associated with each record to a variable tracking the total pay for that department. When the last record is accounted for, you could display the value in each variable.

This method is extremely inefficient. If a database exists on a different computer than the one running the application, all of the data will have to travel over a computer network in order for it to be processed. A better approach would be to calculate the totals within the SQL statement. This will cause the data to be processed on the machine containing the data, and only the total would be passed to the application.

Fortunately, SQL provides you with a mechanism to accomplish this. By using the GROUP BY clause, it allows you to compress records together into a single record where the records have a column or columns in common.

Records can be grouped in many ways. Each field returned in the rows being grouped should have a function that specifies the method for grouping the individual fields of a record together. SQL provides you with a few functions that help you accomplish this.

In this example, you would want to total the daily pay of the grouped records, so you would use the SUM function.

The syntax for a SQL statement that uses the GROUP BY clause is as follows:

SELECT *FieldList with Grouping Functions* FROM *TableName* [WHERE *SearchConditions*]
    [ORDER BY *OrderList* ASC *or* DESC] [GROUP BY *FieldList*]

The SQL statement to total the payroll expenditures would then be

SELECT SUM([Daily Pay]), Department FROM Payroll GROUP BY Department
    ORDER BY Department

COACH'S TIP

Tables can be created with spaces in the field names. But if spaces are used, you must enclose the field name in square brackets [ ] as in the previous SELECT statement. Notice how Daily Pay is enclosed as follows: [Daily Pay].

There is one problem with using the previous SQL statement. What is the name of the calculated value? It is better to use the As keyword and rename the field to a meaningful name.

To rename a field, all that is required is to type As and then the new name after the function call in the SQL statement.

Therefore, if you wished to rename the results of the summing of the Daily Pay column as TotalDailyPay, you could do so with the following SQL statement:

SELECT SUM([Daily Pay]) AS TotalDailyPay, Department FROM payroll GROUP BY
    Department ORDER BY Department

For example, the $900.00 associated with Management in Figure 11.42 is the sum of $500.00 (Record 1) and $400.00 (Record 2) in Figure 11.41.

Figure 11.41 Payroll records

Figure 11.42 Payroll query

Just as you used the Sum function to calculate the total payroll for each department, you can also use other functions with SQL statements. They include:

AVG(*Select_Item*)	Averages a column of numeric data.
COUNT(*Select_Item*)	Counts the number of select items in a column.
COUNT(*)	Counts the number of rows in the query output.
MIN(*Select_Item*)	Determines the smallest value of *Select_Item* in a column.
MAX(*Select_Item*)	Determines the largest value of *Select_Item* in a column.
SUM(*Select_Item*)	Totals a column of numeric data.

DRILL 11.9

Write the SELECT statement that will retrieve the average hours worked for each department.

◆ 11.4 Case Study

Problem Description

With the addition of the databases, you can now store the information about your Payroll Accounting System in a table. Data can be added, modified, or deleted easily with the use of a data grid control bound to your database. Since you can store many records efficiently, you will now track work by the day instead of by the week.

Figure 11.43 will demonstrate what your application will look like.

Figure 11.43
Case study with grid control and database connectivity

Daily Pay	Day	Department	Employee Name	Hours Worked
500	11/11/2002	Management	Jeff Salvage	10
400	11/12/2002	Management	Jeff Salvage	8
120	11/11/2002	Processing	John Nunn	8
150	11/11/2002	Sales	Eric Smith	6
500	1/1/2002	Management	Elizabeth Paxton	10

Payroll Database — Totals — Update

Problem Discussion

Thanks to the robust nature of a data grid, just about the entire gathering and presenting of data for your application can be accomplished with a single control. The only additional control is a button to control the updating of the database with your changes.

Problem Solution

The steps for solving this problem are very similar to the two basketball statistics applications developed in this chapter. You need to link to the data source and connect it to a data grid. The first step is placing and configuring the three database connectivity objects you have been using.

Adding and Configuring the OleDbConnection Object

Step 1: Place an `OleDbConnection` object on the form.

Step 2: Click on the pull-down icon of the `OleDbConnection` object in the `ConnectionString` property in the Properties window. A pop-up menu will appear.

Step 3: Click on the `<New Connection ...>` menu item. The Data Link Properties window will appear.

Step 4: Click on the Provider tab in the Data Link Properties window.

Step 5: Select `Microsoft Jet 4.0 OLE DB Provider`.

Step 6: Click on the Next button. The Connection tab will become active.

Step 7: You must enter or select the physical location of the Access database file that will be connected to the application. My path is `C:\VB Net Coach\ Chapter 11\Code\CaseStudy\Payroll.mdb` file; however, the path may vary from computer to computer.

Step 8: Once the database is specified, you have completed the specification of the connection. Click on OK to commit the specification.

Adding and Configuring the OleDbDataAdapter Object

Step 1: Place an `OleDbDataAdpater` object from the Data tab of the Toolbox. The Data Adapter Configuration Wizard will automatically start, and you will be presented with an informational screen.

Step 2: Click on the Next button.

Step 3: You will be presented with a window that will allow you to select the data connection you want the data adapter to use. There is only one data connection on your form, so it will be automatically selected. Click on the Next button.

Step 4: Click on the Next button to select `Use SQL statements`.

Step 5: The next window that appears will allow you to generate a SQL statement. Click on the Query Builder button, and the wizard will present you with a list of tables that you can base your query on.

Step 6: Click on the Add button, and the `Payroll` table will be added to the Query Builder.

Step 7: Click on the Close button to close the Add Table window.

Step 8: Click on the `*` (`All Columns`) choice in the Payroll window to select that all the columns of the table will be included.

Step 9: Click on the OK button.

Step 10: Click on the Next button.

Step 11: Click on the Finish button.

Adding and Configuring the DataSet Object

Step 1: Click on the form. If the form is not selected, the menu option for Step 2 will not appear.

Step 2: Click on Generate Data Set from the Data menu. The Generate Data Set window appears.

Step 3: Select the New radio button.

Step 4: Change the `Name` property to `DsPayroll`.

Step 5: Click on the OK button. The data set is created.

Add a Data Grid to the Form

Step 1: Add a data grid from the Toolbox.

Step 2: Rename the data grid to `grdPayroll`.

Step 3: Change the `DataSource` property of the data grid to `DsPayroll.Payroll`. The data grid column headers will automatically populate with the columns in your data set.

Step 4: Set the `Anchor` property to all four corners.

Add Code to Load Data to the Data Grid

Add the following code to the form's constructor so that the data loads when the form loads.

```
'Add any initialization after the InitializeComponent() call
 OleDbDataAdapter1.Fill(DsPayroll1) 'Load the DataSet
```

Add Button and Code to Update Database with Changes in the Data Grid

Step 1: Add a button to the bottom of the form.

Step 2: Rename the button to `btnUpdate`.

Step 3: Change the `Text` property of the button to `Update`.

Step 4: Add the following code so that when the user clicks on the button the changes made to the grid are updated to the table.

```
Private Sub btnUpdate_Click(...
      OleDbDataAdapter1.Update(DsPayroll1)
End Sub
```

Step 5: Set the `Anchor` property of the button to `Bottom, Right`.

Add Button and Code to Compute the Total Pay

Step 1: Add a button to the bottom of the form.

Step 2: Rename the button to `btnTotals`.

Step 3: Change the `Text` property of the button to `Totals`.

Step 4: Add the following code so that the user can click on the button and compute the total of all the daily pays. The code loops through each record of the data set and adds the daily pay field to a total. The daily pay field is located at column 0. When the loop terminates, the total is output.

```
Private Sub btnTotals_Click(ByVal sender As System.Object, _
                    ByVal e As System.EventArgs) Handles btnTotals.Click
    Dim sngTotalPay As Single 'Store the Total Pay
    Dim intCurrentRow As Integer
    Dim intMaxRow As Integer

    'Compute the maximum row of the grid.
    'It's one less than the number of rows in the grid
    intMaxRow = Me.BindingContext(DsPayroll1, "Payroll").Count - 1

    'Loop through each row of the data set
    For intCurrentRow = 0 To intMaxRow
         'The Daily Pay is located in column 0
        sngTotalPay += Val(DsPayroll1.Tables(0).Rows(intCurrentRow)(0))
    Next intCurrentRow
```

(continues)

(continued)
```
    'Output the result
    MsgBox("The total pay is " & Format(sngTotalPay.ToString(), "Currency"))
End Sub
```

Your final application will look as shown in Figure 11.44.

Figure 11.44
Final application

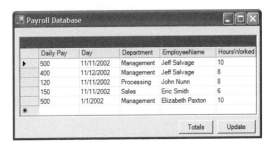

CORNER

Setting up an Access Database

Your system may or may not have Access. Talk to your instructor or lab assistant to make sure your system has Access.

While there are many different databases that Visual Basic .NET can connect with, the most common is Microsoft Access. The following is a very brief explanation of how to create a new database with Microsoft Access.

Create a new database by starting Microsoft Access and selecting the new database option. You will be presented with the window shown in Figure 11.45.

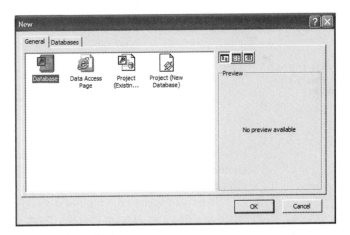

Figure 11.45   New database window

By clicking on `Database`, you will be presented with a File New Database dialog box, where you will select the file name and location of the new database. In Figure 11.46 you have selected the `Chapter 11` directory and have set the name to `NewDatabase`.

Figure 11.46
File New Database dialog
box

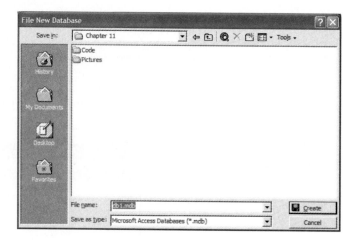

Once the name of the database has been chosen, you are presented with the Database form. It contains many options, but you will focus on the `Tables` object and creating a table in Design view. Currently, there are no tables in your database.

You have several choices for the method you may use to create the table; however, for now you will pick the Design view. By clicking on the `Create table in Design view`, you can add a table to the database. (See Figure 11.47.)

Figure 11.47
Database form

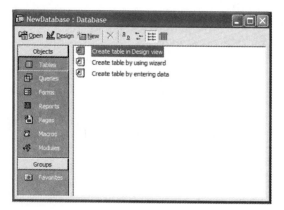

When `Create table in Design view` is selected, the window shown in Figure 11.48 appears, allowing you to specify the fields for your table. You can type the field name in the first box of the form. (Unlike variable names, field names can contain spaces.)

Next you specify the type of data. Unlike Visual Basic .NET, which stores textual data in a `String`, Access uses the `Text` data type. `Text` is the default type.

Although optional, it is a good idea to fill out the Description field to add a comment to the field.

Finally, you can specify more details about the field in the General tab located at the bottom of the form. Highlighted in Figure 11.48 is the most used property, `Field Size`. Here it indicates a `Text` size of 50; however, this is wasteful if your `Strings` won't be larger than 10. Set it to the maximum size of the `Text` field you are declaring.

Figure 11.48
Table creation method

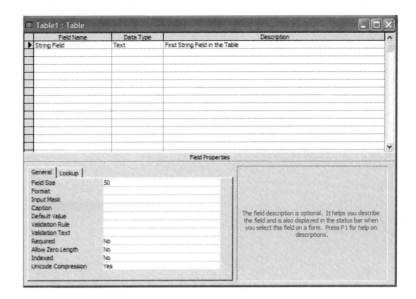

You can continue to add more fields in a similar manner. The choice of data types are shown in Figure 11.49.

Figure 11.49
Different data types

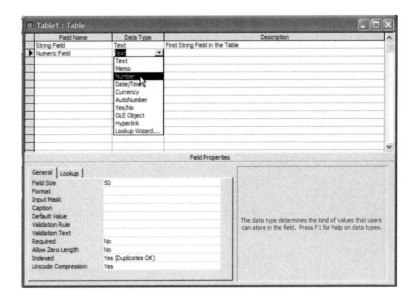

By selecting `Number` from the Data Type pull-down menu, you are presented with different size options within the `Field Size` property. (See Figure 11.50.)

Figure 11.50
Numeric field added

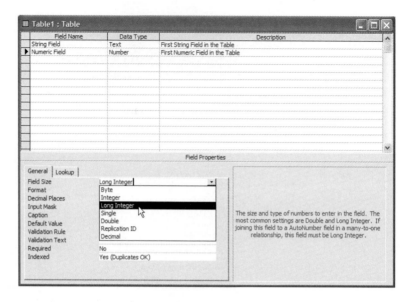

When you are finished adding all the fields, close the Design view. You will be asked if you wish to save changes to the new table you have created. Click on the Yes button, and you will be asked for a name for the table. Enter `"Net Table"` and click on the OK button.

Because you didn't add a primary key (a unique index to improve efficiency), you will be presented with the dialog box shown in Figure 11.51.

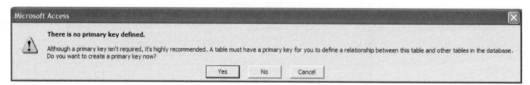

Figure 11.51 Dialog box

For now, do not create one. Simply click on the No button, and the table will be created, as in Figure 11.52.

Figure 11.52
Database form

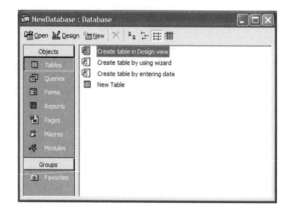

Key Words and Key Terms

Anchor
A property for a control that indicates how the control should be positioned on the form if the form is resized.

Data
Values stored in no particular way.

Data Grid
A control allowing the display, editing, addition, and deletion of data stored in a data set.

Database Management System
A system that relates data together allowing structure and constraints, thus organizing the data into a more meaningful form.

DataSet
A temporary representation of data from a database stored in the computer's memory.

Data Validation
The act of checking data to ensure that it is in the correct form.

Field
A single value in a record of data.

Information
Data that has been organized so that it is meaningful.

OleDbConnection
An object that contains the specifications for the protocol to communicate with a database and any information pertaining to the connection.

OleDbDataAdapter
An object that provides the methods to transfer data from the database to the data set.

Record
A single unit of data composed of fields and stored in a table.

SQL
A standard Structured Query Language used to access and manipulate data stored in databases.

Table
A structure to store a collection of data, usually pertaining to a single entity.

Answers to Chapter's Drills

Drill 11.1
a. Since the indexing of rows and columns starts at 0, indicating values of (4)(3) selects the field at row 5 and field 4 (LastName) of the data set. Therefore, the answer is Camby.
b. Since the indexing of rows and columns starts at 0, indicating values of (1)(2) selects the field at row 2 and field 3 (GamesPlayed) of the data set. Therefore, the answer is 60.
c. Since the indexing of rows and columns starts at 0, indicating values of (6)(1) selects the field at row 6. However, there is no row 6 in the data set, so an error occurs.
d. Selecting row 4 of the PlayerStats table returns the fifth row of the data set. The Assists field of that row contains the value 100.
e. Selecting row 6 of the PlayerStats table returns the seventh row of the data set. There are only six rows, so an error occurs.

Drill 11.2

To select all the last names and the final grades of all the students, you will need to specify each field you desire in the results. The field name for a student's last name is `LastName`. The field name for a student's final grade is `FinalGrade`; therefore, the SQL statement required is

```
SELECT LastName, FinalGrade FROM StudentGrades
```

Drill 11.3

To select only the last names and the final grades of the students with a final grade of an A or a B, you will need to specify each field you desire in the results. The field name for a student's last name is `LastName`. The field name for a student's final grade is `FinalGrade`. Additionally, because you are limiting the students who are returned by the query to only those with A's or B's in the final grade, you will require a `WHERE` clause that compares the final grade to an A or a B. The SQL statement required is

```
SELECT LastName, FinalGrade FROM StudentGrades WHERE FinalGrade = "A" OR
    FinalGrade = "B"
```

Drill 11.4

Because you were not asked to limit the fields, you can use the Asterisk operator to select all of the fields. However, you will need a `WHERE` clause to limit the records returned to those who failed the midterm. The SQL statement required is

```
SELECT * FROM StudentGrades WHERE MidtermGrade < 65
```

Drill 11.5

To select only the first and last names of students with a midterm grade from 80 to 89, you will need to specify each field you desire in the results. The field name for a student's first name is `FirstName`. The field name for a student's last name is `LastName`. Additionally, because you are limiting the students who are returned by the query to only those with a B for their midterm, you will require a `WHERE` clause that compares the midterm grade to >=80 and <=89. The SQL statement required is

```
SELECT FirstName, LastName FROM StudentGrades WHERE MidtermGrade >= 80 AND
    MidtermGrade <=89
```

Drill 11.6

Because you were not asked to limit the fields, you can use the Asterisk operator to select all the fields. However, you will need a `WHERE` clause because you wish to limit the records returned to those students who failed either the midterm or final exam or who have a failing homework average. The SQL statement required is

```
SELECT * FROM StudentGrades WHERE MidtermGrade < 65 OR FinalExam <65 OR
    HomeworkAverage <65
```

Drill 11.7

To select only the first and last names of students whose first name starts with the letter J, you will need to specify each field you desire in the results. The field name for a student's first name is `FirstName`. The field name for a student's last name is `LastName`.

Additionally, because you are limiting the students who are returned by the query to only those whose first name starts with the letter J, you will need a WHERE clause using the LIKE operator. Depending on whether you use Microsoft Access or another database, the SQL statement required is

```
SELECT FirstName, LastName FROM StudentGrades WHERE FirstName LIKE "J*"
or
SELECT FirstName, LastName FROM StudentGrades WHERE FirstName LIKE "J%"
```

Drill 11.8

Because you were not asked to limit the fields, you can use the Asterisk operator to select all of the fields. However, you will need a WHERE clause because you wish to limit the records returned to those who had a final exam grade of greater than 90. Additionally, because you were asked to sort the results, you need an ORDER BY clause to be added to the SQL statement. The SQL statement required is

```
SELECT * FROM StudentGrades WHERE FinalExam > 90 ORDER BY LastName, FirstName
```

Drill 11.9

Because you were asked to average the hours worked in each department, you must group the results by the Department field. Averaging the hours is as simple as using the Avg function on the HoursWorked field.

```
SELECT AVG([HoursWorked]) AS AverageHours, Department FROM Payroll GROUP BY
    Department ORDER BY Department
```

Additional Exercises

Questions 1–3 are true or false.

1. Only one connection can exist on a computer system at a time.
2. A connection can only be made to database management systems.
3. A data grid cannot resize when the form is resized.
4. What three objects are required to communicate with a database?
5. Organize these terms from the smallest entity to the largest entity, the largest being the one that contains the others.

   Field

   Database

   Record

   Table
6. Which term implies that the values stored in a database are organized in a meaningful manner: data or information?
7. What value goes in a data source?

   a. OleDbConnection   b. OleDbDataAdapter

   c. DataSet   d. a database file name
8. What happens if you attempt to move past the first record in a table?
9. What happens if you set the binding of the data set to the first record when you are already on the first record in a table?

10. What happens if you set the binding of the data set to the first record when you are at the last record in a table?

11. What happens to the data in a data set that is not updated when the form closes?

12. Modify the basketball application so that it uses an order by team clause in the SQL statement. This can be accomplished by either changing the SQL manually or using the Query Builder.

13. Write an application that connects to the `PlayerStats` table in the `Basketball.mdb` database. Output all of the fields in the `PlayerStats` table into a fixed format file.

14. Write an application that connects to the `PlayerStats` table in the `Basketball.mdb` database. The application should output in a `MessageBox` the number of players who have played in 60 games or more.

15. Write an application that connects to the `PlayerStats` table in the `Basketball.mdb` database. The application should output to a file, HighScoringSixers.txt, the players who are members of the Sixers and who have scored at least 1,500 points.

16. Write an application that connects to the `PlayerStats` table in the `Basketball.mdb` database. The application should accept a player's name in a text box and output whether the user wishes to have either Points, Assists, or Rebounds displayed. The application should then search the database for that person and, if found, display the statistic in a message box. Otherwise, a message stating the player was not found should be displayed.

INTERVIEW

Interview with Tim Burke

Tim Burke is a Senior Programmer/Analyst at Pep Boys. His job consists of designing and developing client/server applications. In doing this, the process may start with meeting with users to gather requirements for developing the design of an application. Or, Tim may take a completed design and begin by developing an application or modifying vendor packages though VB and DB2. Tim is responsible for supporting end users in various departments, whether it is with the applications his team writes, vendor software packages, or answering requests for other data needs.

What brought you to Pep Boys?

I had been an independent consultant for the past 5 years. With the instability of the economy, I was looking for a more stable job in an established company. I was offered a challenging position at Pep Boys. I accepted this offer and am working with former colleagues and great people.

What kinds of projects are you currently working on?

Pep Boys is an automotive parts retail chain. From merchandising to pricing, my work entails applications that assist in the daily operation of our stores. One project deals with how automotive parts are stored, set up, and displayed in our stores. My current project is a new Point of Customer System. This will enhance how all Pep Boys stores operate. Employees will be better equipped to assist customers through enhancements such as making sure items are stocked correctly and checking out customers at the register efficiently.

How do you like working with VB?

I really enjoy working in Visual Basic. From its easy learning curve to its ability to integrate other software packages, it simplifies the application development process. I've been working with VB since version 3. What I've found is that while Visual Basic has evolved to incorporate Microsoft's new technologies and has required me to have a better understanding of the language, it continues to make

my job simpler and make the applications I develop more powerful.

How will VB .NET make your job of developing software easier?

Since .NET brings VB into the true OOP arena, reusing and deploying applications has become much simpler. The application development process will now expand to everyone's favorite platform, the Web. Since VB.NET integrates the Web with the Desktop, the process of developing solutions for the workplace has become endless!

What advice do you have for students entering the computer field using VB .NET?

Grasp the language! What I mean by this is that .NET will bring about a new generation of application development. When I began programming, one had to learn a development tool for client/server applications, another for building web pages (HTML), and yet another for Web applications (ASP). VB.NET has it all, so enjoy!

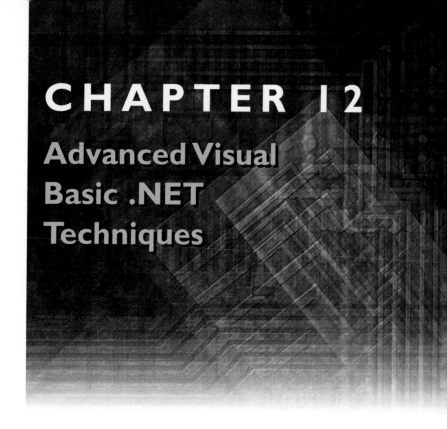

CHAPTER 12

Advanced Visual Basic .NET Techniques

12.1 Improved Error Handling

By now you have definitely written applications that have not executed the intended way and produced a rather unfriendly error message. While the message may not have intimidated you, it will intimidate the user of the application. As a developer, you should program defensively. You should try to prevent errors from occurring by validating input and not allowing situations to arise in code where the system does not know how to react. An example of this is if you present the user with a text box to enter a purchase amount. If the user enters characters instead of numbers, when you try to perform a calculation, an error will occur. This situation could be handled with proper data validation.

However, predicting all possible errors cannot always be accomplished. Users will use your application in ways you never anticipated. Therefore, Visual Basic .NET provides the **Try**, **Catch**, **Finally** block structure, allowing you to code error handling in your applications. It is a structured way of handling errors that is very similar to the way other modern programming languages handle errors.

COACH'S WARNING

There is another method of error handling called the `On Error` statement. Avoid this method. It is a leftover from Version 6.0 of Visual Basic. Its use leads to very unstructured programs.

The syntax of the new structure is as follows:

```
Try
     'Code to check for error
Catch When Err.Number = ErrorNumber
     'Code to handle specific error
Catch When Err.Number = Another ErrorNumber
     'Code to handle other specific error
Catch
     'Code to handle all the other errors
Finally
     'Code to execute directly after
End Try
```

Code placed in a `Try-Catch` structure can be checked for individual errors with specific code written to handle each error, or all errors can be handled by one set of code, or you can check for some specific errors and then allow all remaining errors to be handled by one set of code.

You can think of a `Try-Catch` structure as similar to a `Select-Case` structure. A `Select-Case` statement allowed you to test a value against a series of possible values and execute code if the condition matched. If none of the conditions matched, then the statements associated with the `Case Else` statement are executed.

With a `Try-Catch`, the code that you wish to trap errors for is placed between the `Try` keyword and the first `Catch` statement. Then each `Catch When` statement can be set up to check for specific errors by checking the exact number of the error that occurred. If the error occurs, then the code associated with the specific `Catch When` statement is executed.

If you create a `Catch` statement without a `When` condition, then the code associated with the `Catch` statement will execute whenever none of the previous `Catch When` statements match the error.

After `Catch` statements have been evaluated and possibly executed, the `Finally` statement allows you to specify code that will always execute. This code will execute whether or not an error has occurred in the code you are testing.

Arithmetic Error Example

Imagine if you had to perform a calculation between a series of `Short` variables to output the average commission, to the nearest dollar, for a salesperson over the summer. The calculation might be coded as follows:

```
shtAverageCommission = (shtJuneSales +  shtJulySales + _
                          shtAugustSales) \ shtPeriod
```

The calculation adds the sales of the months June, July, and August and then divides them by the variable storing the number of months in the period.

There are two very obvious possible sources of error. First, remember that a `Short` variable can have a maximum value of 32,767. If the addition of all three months is greater than 32,767, you could get an overflow error.

You also have to worry that the variable `shtPeriod` is not equal to zero, because if it is, you will get a divide by zero error when performing the calculation.

The answer to these problems is to place the code inside a `Try` block as follows:

```
Try
    'Code to check for error
    shtAverageCommission = (shtJuneSales + shtJulySales + _
                            shtAugustSales) \ shtPeriod
    Catch When Err.Number = 6
        'Code to handle arithmetic overflow
        MsgBox("Computing the average commission produced a mathematical error")
        'set the average commission to a valid value
        shtAverageCommission = 0
    Catch 'Code to handle all other errors
        MsgBox(" An " & Err.Description & _
               " error occurred when computing the average summer commission")
        'set the average commission to a valid value
        shtAverageCommission = 0
    Finally
        'Code to execute directly after
End Try
```

COACH'S TIP

Often when an error occurs, you might want to log the error in a file. This way you can see what errors occurred even after the application is no longer running.

Open File Error

Errors can often occur when a resource is unavailable. A very common resource that may be unavailable is a file. Often a file path could be wrong or another user may lock the file and your application is restricted from gaining access. Therefore, when you are opening a file, you should always trap for an error.

```
Try
    Dim FileStreamName As New FileStream("C:\Log.txt", FileMode.Open, _
                                         FileAccess.Read)
    Catch When Err.Number = 53
        MsgBox(" An error occurred when opening the log file")
End Try
```

COACH'S TIP

Remember that to use files, you must include the `System.IO` namespace. See Chapter 9 for more information on files.

12.2 Graphics

You are already familiar with displaying some graphics in your applications. The picture box control allows you to display only images that were previously created. With the additional built-in objects provided in Visual Basic .NET, you have the ability to draw figures in many creative ways.

Although the initial method of using the `Graphics` class may seem a little cumbersome, you will see that once you understand the basics you will be able to explore and master a vast number of objects and methods with your intuition and Visual Basic .NET's type ahead feature.

Using graphics starts by including the **System.Drawing namespace**, which will give you access to numerous classes that, when used together, allow you to draw directly on a form. Any drawing that you will accomplish will require the use of at least the **Graphics** and **Pen** objects as well as **Color**, **Point**, **Rectangle**, and **Size** objects to help specify exactly how you wish to draw. The Graphics object represents the surface you will be drawing on as well as being the object that creates graphical images. The Pen object will determine how you draw on the Graphics object.

We'll introduce these features by showing you how to create a drawing of a man. To create it, you will first need to create a couple objects to allow you to draw the types of figures you desire. (See Figure 12.1.)

Figure 12.1
Completed drawing of
Adam

Step 1:   Before you can draw anything on an object, you must create a Graphics object and then instantiate it. This is done by declaring a Graphics object and then calling a CreateGraphics method of the form. You can declare the Graphics object using the following code:

```
Dim grfGraphics As Graphics
```

Because you will include the statement Imports System.Drawing, you do not need to preface Graphics with System.Drawing. each time you refer to it.

To instantiate the object, you have to call the CreateGraphics method of the form. The easiest way to do this is to refer to the form using the Me keyword.

```
grfGraphics = Me.CreateGraphics
```

Step 2:   Once the Graphics object is created, you need to declare and instantiate a Pen object. A Pen object will be used to draw with the Graphics object. There are four ways to declare a Pen object. The simplest is just to select a color. However, if you want to get fancy, you can also select a **Brush** object to draw with a little more style. This will be shown later. While the default width of a Pen object is 1, you can also specify how wide you wish your pen to draw. For simplicity, you will ignore the Brush object for now. To declare a Pen object, you can use the following syntax:

```
Dim PenName As New Pen(Color.ColorName, PenWidth)
```

- *PenName:* The name of the pen you are declaring and instantiating.
- *ColorName:* One of the predefined colors you can select.
- *PenWidth:* A single value indicating the width of the pen as it draws.

When you instantiate a `Pen` object, you will first select the color of the pen. Selecting a color is accomplished by using the `Color` object. The `Color` object gives you access to all the predefined colors in Visual Basic .NET. Type `"Color."` and a list of predefined colors will pop up. When you select one of these, your color use is greatly simplified.

To create your `Pen` object to draw a red line with a width of 2, use the following code:

```
Dim penOurPen As New Pen(Color.Red, 2)
```

With the `Pen` object created, you can now draw with the `Graphics` object. Let's start by drawing the circular head. The easiest way to do this is to use the `Ellipse` method of the `Graphics` object. It takes a `Pen` as the first parameter and then the X and Y locations of the upper-left corner of a rectangle that bounds the circle or ellipse that you are drawing. The syntax is as follows:

```
GraphicsObjectName.DrawEllipse(PenName, XLocation, YLocation, Width, Height)
```

The final two parameters are the length and width of the bounding rectangle.

Therefore, the code to draw the head would be as follows:

```
grfGraphics.DrawEllipse(penOurPen, 50, 50, 40, 40)
```

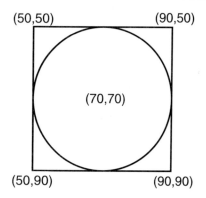

Step 3: To draw the body, you need to draw a straight line. The `Graphics` object contains a method `DrawLine` that will allow you to do this. Notice that the body in Figure 12.1 is blue. Fortunately, you can easily switch the color of the pen by changing the `Color` property of your pen.

```
penOurPen.Color = Color.Blue
```

Step 4: Now you must draw the line. It takes a `Pen` as the first parameter and then the X and Y locations of the starting point of the line and the X and Y locations of the ending point of the line.

```
GraphicsObjectName.DrawLine(PenName, StartingXLocation, StartingYLocation, _
                EndingXLocation, EndingYLocation)
```

The code required to draw your body can then be drawn with the following code:

```
grfGraphics.DrawLine(penOurPen, 70, 90, 70, 150)
```

Step 5: You can follow the same procedure to draw the arms and legs. In the original drawing, Adam's arms and legs were yellow, so you must change the color of the pen to yellow. This is accomplished with the following code:

```
penOurPen.Color = Color.Yellow
```

Step 6: Now you can draw the left and right arms with the following code:

```
grfGraphics.DrawLine(penOurPen, 70, 150, 55, 105)
grfGraphics.DrawLine(penOurPen, 70, 150, 85, 105)
```

Step 7: To add legs, since they are the same color, you do not have to change the Pen object. You can simply use the following code to draw the two lines representing the legs:

```
grfGraphics.DrawLine(penOurPen, 70, 150, 45, 170)
grfGraphics.DrawLine(penOurPen, 70, 150, 95, 170)
```

Step 8: To draw the feet you could use a series of four lines; instead, you will use the **DrawRectangle** method so that you can have practice with a few other objects. The DrawRectangle method takes two parameters: a Pen and a Rectangle. You already have a Pen object created, so you only need to create a Rectangle object. However, to create a Rectangle object you need a Point object and a Size object. Observe the following code, which shows how it all works together:

```
'Draw Feet
Dim rctFoot As Rectangle
Dim pntFoot As Point
Dim szeFoot As Size

szeFoot = New Size(20, 10)

'Left Foot
pntFoot = New Point(25, 160)
rctFoot = New Rectangle(pntFoot, szeFoot)
grfGraphics.DrawRectangle(penOurPen, rctFoot)

'Right Foot
pntFoot = New Point(95, 160)
rctFoot = New Rectangle(pntFoot, szeFoot)
grfGraphics.DrawRectangle(penOurPen, rctFoot)
```

Step 8 : (Alternative)   If instead of drawing an outline of the rectangle to represent the feet of Adam you wanted to fill in the rectangle, you could use the **FillRectangle** method. However, the FillRectangle method requires a Brush object instead of a Pen object. There are many different types of brushes. You can create brushes that paint a solid color, a pattern, or even a texture using a bitmap file. For simplicity, you will create a brush with a solid color.

```
'Draw Feet
Dim rctFoot As Rectangle
Dim pntFoot As Point
Dim szeFoot As Size
Dim bshAdam As SolidBrush

bshAdam = New SolidBrush(Color.Yellow)

szeFoot = New Size(20, 10)

'Left Foot
pntFoot = New Point(25, 160)
rctFoot = New Rectangle(pntFoot, szeFoot)
grfGraphics.FillRectangle(bshAdam, rctFoot)

'Right Foot
pntFoot = New Point(95, 160)
rctFoot = New Rectangle(pntFoot, szeFoot)
grfGraphics.FillRectangle(bshAdam, rctFoot)
```

COACH'S TIP

Other types of brushes are available and function similarly to a `SolidBrush`. Here's a list of brush types and their purposes. By using Intellisense or MSDN you should be able to figure out how to implement them.

`HatchBrush`	Paints using a pattern selected from a large number of preset patterns.
`TextureBrush`	Paints using a texture defined by an image file such as a .bmp.
`LinearGradientBrush`	Paints two colors blended along a gradient.
`PathGradientBrush`	Paints using a complex gradient of blended colors, based on a unique path defined by the developer.

Step 9: The last step is to add text to the drawing. You can control the font and the brush that you draw with. The `Font` object can be created by specifying some or all of the parameters in the following syntax:

FontObject = `New Font(`*FontName*`, `*FontSize*`, `*FontStyle*`)`

- ◆ *FontName:* Specifies the name of the font to display. The font must exist on the machine running the application.
- ◆ *FontSize:* Specifies the size of the font.
- ◆ *FontStyle:* Specifies the style of the font (bold, italics, etc.). The *FontStyle* options can be specified by using the `FontStyle` object.

To create a `Font` object to display the text `"Adam"` in a bold Times 20-point font using the previously created `SolidBrush`, use the following code:

```
Dim fntAdam As Font

bshAdam = New SolidBrush(Color.Black)
fntAdam = New Font("Times", 20, FontStyle.Bold)
grfGraphics.DrawString("Adam", fntAdam, bshAdam, 32, 180)
```

12.3 Creating Menus Using the Menu Editor

By now, you are more than familiar with menus. Menus are present in almost every application, making commonly used options available to the user.

Observe Figure 12.2, showing the menu for Visual Basic .NET and the **submenu** and separator lines.

Figure 12.2
Visual Basic .NET menu and submenu

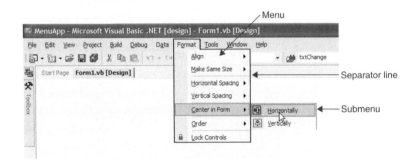

To produce a menu, Visual Basic .NET provides the **MainMenu** object. When the `MainMenu` object is placed on the form, it will not appear on the actual form itself, but rather below it as did the objects associated with connecting to a database.

When the `Menu` object is placed on the form, you can design your menu simply by clicking on the `Menu` object and then typing your menu in the Type Here boxes that appear. See Figure 12.3, which shows the menu editor just after the `MainMenu` object is placed on the form.

Figure 12.3
Menu editor

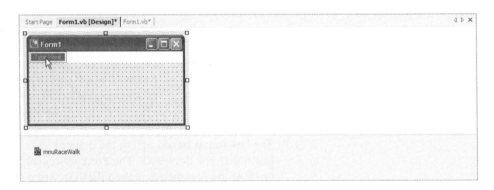

Once the menu name is entered, menu placeholders appear. Menu items can be placed in these placeholders, with additional placeholders appearing as each menu item is added. (See Figure 12.4.)

For each menu item, you will want to attach code to execute whenever the user selects it. The interface Visual Basic .NET provides is as straightforward as it gets. To attach code, just double-click on the menu item and place the code in the `Click` event code that appears, in the same way you would for a button object.

COACH'S TIP

Since the creation of menu items is so simple, it is easy to forget to name the menu and each menu item. Menus and menu items should begin with the prefix mnu. It is also helpful to contain an abbreviated name of the menu in the menu item's name.

Figure 12.4
Menu editor with additional
placeholders

Example: Simple Menu Application

Menus can be used to provide an easy way to access an application's commonly used functions. To focus on your understanding of the operation of a menu, you will create an application that is as simple as possible.

Your application will display a label and a picture that show a race walking competition. The application will contain two menus, one to modify the picture and one to modify the label.

The application should have a menu to modify the border of the picture. It will contain menu items to add a border to the picture and another menu item to remove it.

The Label menu will contain a menu item that will increase the size of the font in the label and another menu item to reduce the size of the font in the label. Additionally, the menu items will be created to set the color of the text to black, blue, or red.

Your menus for the application would look like that shown in Figure 12.5.

Figure 12.5
Sketch of the menu system

Picture	Label
Add Border	Grow
Remove Border	Shrink
	Black
	Blue
	Red

Look ahead at Figures 12.15 and 12.16 to see what this will look like when your application is complete.

Creating the Race Walking Application

Create a project called `RaceWalking`.

Rename Form and Text

Building an Application with a Menu

Step 1: Add a `MainMenu` object to the form.

Step 2: Rename the `MainMenu` object to `mnuRaceWalk`.

Step 3: Click on the `MainMenu` object so the window with `Type Here` appears.

Step 4: Type `"&Picture"` as the title of the first menu. Notice that you use an ampersand in front of the word `Picture`. Just as you used the ampersand as a keyboard shortcut with the button object, you can use it here to indicate that the Picture menu can be accessed by pressing the <ALT> key and then the <P> key to allow a keystroke access of the menu item.

COACH'S
WARNING

Access keys can only be
set up for each letter
once per menu.

Step 5: Just as all controls in Visual Basic .NET have a name, so should menus. Name your Picture menu `mnuPicture` by typing "`mnuPicture`" in the `Name` property of the Properties window. (See Figure 12.6.)

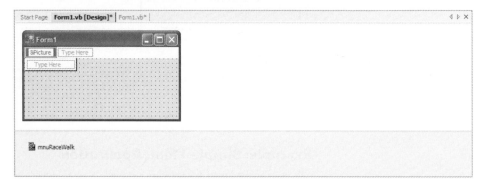

Figure 12.6 Menu editor with Picture menu specified

Step 6: You need to add the menu items that belong to the Picture menu. To associate menu items with a menu, you need to first click on the Type Here box below the Picture menu so that the menu editor moves from the current menu to a space to create the menu item. It will actually create space to the bottom and to the right; however, ignore the space to the right for now.

Step 7: Once you have clicked on the Type Here box, you can enter the new menu item. Type "`&Add Border`". (See Figure 12.7.)

Figure 12.7
First item of Picture menu specified

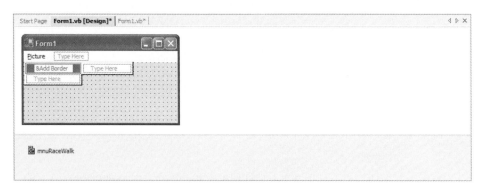

Step 8: Rename the menu item to `mnuPictureAdd`.

Step 9: You can add the second menu item in the same manner. Click on the Type Here box below the `mnuPictureAdd` menu item and fill in `&Remove Border` and rename it `mnuRemoveBorder`. (See Figure 12.8.)

Figure 12.8
Specification of the second menu item of the Picture menu

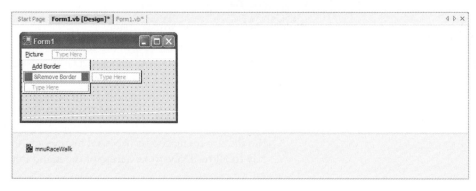

Step 10: Click to the right of the Picture menu on the `MainMenu` object so that you can type in the Type Here box. When you click, additional Type Here boxes will appear and the previous ones along with the Picture menu's menu items will disappear.
Step 11: Type `"&Label"` for the second menu.
Step 12: Rename the menu to `mnuLabel`. (See Figure 12.9.)

Figure 12.9
Specification of the second
menu

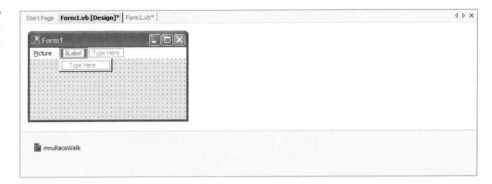

Step 13: You can now specify the first menu item of the Label menu. First, you click on the Type Here box below the Label menu. Then you need to specify `Text` and `Name` properties for the menu item. In this case, the names will be `&Grow` and `mnuLabelGrow`, respectively. (See Figure 12.10.)

Figure 12.10
Specification of the first
menu item of the Label
menu

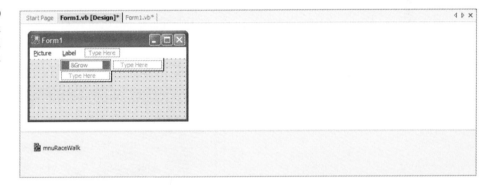

Step 14: You can add the remaining menu items in the same manner. Click on the Type Here box and fill in `"&Shrink"` and `"mnuLabelShrink"` for the `Text` and `Name` properties of this menu item. Repeat this process for `&Black` and `mnuLabelBlack`, `&Blue` and `mnuLabelBlue`, and `&Red` and `mnuLabelRed`. (See Figure 12.11.)

Figure 12.11
Specification of the second
menu item of the Label
menu

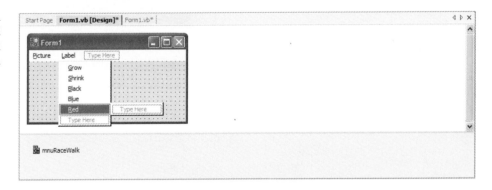

You are now complete with creating the "shell" of your menu; however, you still must specify the code that will execute when the individual menu items are selected.

Adding the Label and Picture Box

This application would really be about nothing if you didn't add a few controls to manipulate the menu items. Add a label and picture box control titling and showing a race walking event.

Step 1:   Add a label control drawn as wide as the form.
Step 2:   Change the `Name` of the label control to `lblTitle`.
Step 3:   Change the `Text` of the label control to `Race Walking Competition`.
Step 4:   Change the `TextAlign` to `MiddleCenter`.
Step 5:   Change the `FontStyle` to `Bold`.
Step 6:   Resize the form to fit an image 400 x 400 pixels wide.
Step 7:   Add a picture box control to the form and size it so that it can fit an image.
Step 8:   Change the `Name` of the picture box to `picRaceWalk`.
Step 9:   Click on the `Image` property and select the `RaceWalk.jpg` file in the bin directory.

Specifying Code to Execute

Each menu item has a `Click` event for which you can specify code to accomplish whatever the purpose of the menu item is.

Step 1:   By clicking on the menu and then the menu item you desire, you will call up the `Click` event code for that menu item. Observe how in Figure 12.12 you click on the Picture menu and then Add Border, and then the code in Figure 12.13 appears.

Figure 12.12
Preparing to enter menu item `Click` event code

```
Private Sub mnuPictureAdd_Click(...

End Sub
```

Figure 12.13   Menu item `Click` event code

Step 2:   Now you can just add your code to set a border around your picture:

```
Private Sub mnuPictureAdd_Click(...
     'Change the border style to a fixed 3D border
     picRacewalk.BorderStyle = BorderStyle.Fixed3D
End Sub
```

Step 3:   To add the code to the menu item `mnuRemoveBorder`, you just repeat the
         process.

```
Private Sub mnuPictureRemove_Click(...
     'Remove the border style by setting it to None
     picRacewalk.BorderStyle = BorderStyle.None
End Sub
```

Step 4:   Repeat this process for the remaining menu items: `mnuLabelGrow`,
         `mnuLabelShrink`, `mnuLabelBlack`, `mnuLabelBlue`, and `mnuLabelRed`.

```
Private Sub mnuLabelGrow_Click(...
    'Increase the Font by creating a new Font from the current Font
    'with a font size of 1 greater than the font
    lblTitle.Font = New Font("Microsoft Sans Serif", lblTitle.Font.Size + 1, _
                    FontStyle.Bold)
End Sub

Private Sub mnuLabelShrink_Click(...
    'Increase the Font by creating a new Font from the current Font
    'with a font size of 1 less than the font
    lblTitle.Font = New Font("Microsoft Sans Serif", lblTitle.Font.Size - 1, _
                    FontStyle.Bold)
End Sub

Private Sub mnuLabelBlack_Click(...
    'Change the font to the color black
    lblTitle.ForeColor = Color.Black
End Sub

Private Sub mnuLabelBlue_Click(...
    'Change the font to the color blue
    lblTitle.ForeColor = Color.Blue
End Sub

Private Sub mnuLabelRed_Click(...
    'Change the font to the color red
    lblTitle.ForeColor = Color.Red
End Sub
```

When you are done, the application will look like Figure 12.14.

Figure 12.14
Simple menu application

Adding a Separator Line

As menu controls grow in size, it is often helpful to divide them into groups of common functionality by separator lines. In the previous example the Label menu already contains five items. Imagine if you added additional colors like yellow and magenta. A separator line would be helpful to divide the menu items to change the size of the font from those that change the color of the font.

Figure 12.15 shows the use of a separator line and the additional menu items.

Figure 12.15
Menu with separator line

COACH'S TIP

If you have more than one separator, remember that all names must be unique. Additional separators should be named `mnuSeparator2`, `mnuSeparator3`, and so on.

To add a separator line, just place a hyphen in the Type Here box of the menu editor.

Adding a Submenu

Although a separator line is a good way of breaking up a large menu, at some point too many menu items under one menu becomes cumbersome. A submenu is an excellent way to combat this.

Observe the Label menu in Figures 12.16 and 12.17. It shows two submenus. The first shows the menu items related to changing the size of the font, and the second shows the menu items related to changing the color of the font.

Figure 12.16   Change Size submenu

The triangle ▶ on each of the Label menu items indicates a submenu exists. This triangle is placed automatically when the submenus are created.

Notice that the S in Change Size and the S in Shrink are both shortcuts. This will work, even though they use the same letter, because one is a menu item and the other is a submenu item.

Figure 12.17 Change Color submenu

Creating a Submenu

Previously, you were told to ignore the Type Here box to the right of menu items. By typing in them, you can create a submenu.

Step 1:   Change the first Label menu item's `Name` and `Text` properties to `mnuLabelSize` and `Change Size`, respectively.

Step 2:   Click on the Type Here box to the right of the `mnuLabelSize` menu item.

Step 3:   Set the `Name` and `Text` properties to `mnuLabelSizeGrow` and `&Grow`.

Step 4:   Click on the Type Here box below the `mnuLabelSizeGrow` menu item.

Step 5:   Set the `Name` and `Text` properties to `mnuLabelSizeShrink` and `&Shrink`.

Step 6:   To create the second submenu, click below the `mnuLabelSize` menu item in the Type Here box.

Step 7:   Set the `Name` and `Text` properties to `mnuLabelColor` and `Change &Color`.

Step 8:   Click on the Type Here box to the right of the `mnuLabelColor` menu item.

Step 9:   Set the `Name` and `Text` properties to `mnuLabelColorBlack` and `&Black`.

Step 10: Repeat the process for the remaining submenu items. (See Figure 12.18.)

While it may seem trivial, you should always use the proper naming conventions. Doing so will greatly reduce the effort required to maintain your applications.

Figure 12.18 Complete submenu specification

12.4 **Multiple Form Applications**

All of the applications you have developed so far have been limited to a single form or an **SDI** (Single Document Interface). This limits the functionality of your applications. As you begin to explore the possibilities of multiple form applications, you will first start with a simple application that does not consider the many issues that arise when you use applications with more than one form. Then, after you are comfortable with the new functionality, you will address the concerns that arise from the use of multiple forms.

Showing Another Form

To open another form from the current form is a simple matter of using the **Show** method of a form. The syntax is as simple as

```
FormName.Show
```

Hiding or Unloading a Form

Once a form has been loaded, you can make the form disappear two ways. If you want the form to merely disappear from the screen but still remain in memory, use the **Hide** event. The syntax for hiding a form is as follows:

```
FormName.Hide
```

COACH'S TIP

Visual Basic .NET provides a shortcut that allows you a great deal of flexibility. Instead of having to type the name of the form you wish to hide, you can use the Me object. Me refers to the form the user has focus upon. Using Me instead of the form name simplifies the code. Therefore, you could use the code Me.Hide to hide the active form regardless of the name of the form.

COACH'S TIP

When we say that we remove the form from the computer's memory, we are referring to the computer's RAM. The form is not actually removed from the computer's hard drive.

The other option for making a form disappear is to remove it both from the screen and the computer's memory. This is accomplished with the Unload command. When a form is unloaded, unless the information that was entered into it is saved elsewhere, it will be lost. The syntax for unloading a form is as follows:

```
Me.Close()
```

Example: Personnel Information

Now that you can create an application with more than one form, you can increase the amount of information you can gather in a single application. For simplicity, you will create an application that gathers personnel information, but it will not save the information anywhere. The case study at the end of the chapter will demonstrate that.

Your application will contain three forms: frmPersonnel, frmDemographics, and frmFinancial. Each will contain different information about a person working for a company. The first form that the user will be presented with is frmPersonnel. (See Figure 12.19.)

Figure 12.19
Personnel information

The Personnel form is the main form of your application. It is the form that will be presented to the user when the application starts. From it, you will be able to call both the Demographics and Financial forms. These forms will be displayed when the `btnDemographics` or `btnFinancial` buttons are clicked. The `btnProfit` button will display a message box containing information from the additional forms of the application. We will explain the code for this at the end of the example.

The Demographics form, shown in Figure 12.20, will contain an individual's demographic information.

Figure 12.20   Demographic information

In addition to the demographic information that the user will enter on this form, notice that we have displayed information from the `frmPersonnel` form (my name) and added the `btnHide` button.

The `btnHide` button will allow the user to remove the form from the computer screen without removing it from the computer's memory. However, if the window Close button (X in the upper right) is clicked, the form will not only be removed from the computer screen, but it will also be unloaded from the computer's memory.

The Financial form, shown in Figure 12.21, will contain an individual's financial information.

Figure 12.21
Financial information

Your Financial form contains text boxes to enter the number of hours and the rate at which an individual billed and worked. Typically, consultants may work more hours than they can bill. Additionally, consultants will be billed out at a higher rate than they are getting paid.

Sharing Data Across Multiple Forms

While the code to instantiate and open the additional forms is rather trivial, a bit more thought is required in coding your application to share data across forms. If you try to access an object on one form from another form, you will get a scoping error. Remember, objects created on one form are scoped to `Private` by default. While theoretically you could modify the code and change the scope of an object, this is not desirable. You shouldn't give complete access to an object if only a specific value from the object is required.

For your application, you will require the `frmDemographics` form's `lblTitle`'s `Text` value to be accessible from the Personnel form. Additionally, you will wish to make the `txtHomePhone`'s `Text` value accessible. The easiest way to accomplish this is to add a series of `Property` statements to the `frmDemographics` form giving access to the required properties.

```
Public Property Title() As String
    Get
        Return lblTitle.Text
    End Get
    Set(ByVal Value As String)
        lblTitle.Text = Value
    End Set
End Property

Public Property HomePhone() As String
    Get
        Return txtHome.Text
    End Get
    Set(ByVal Value As String)
        txtHome.Text = Value
    End Set
End Property
```

Similarly, on the `frmFinancials` form, you will require access to the `lblTitle`'s `Text` value as well as the profit amount. While you could make each text box's values involved in the profit calculation accessible, it is far better to create a property called `Profit` that is automatically calculated when accessed.

```
Public Property Title() As String
    Get
        Return lblTitle.Text
    End Get
    Set(ByVal Value As String)
        lblTitle.Text = Value
    End Set
End Property

Public Property Profit() As String
    Get
        'Profit = Billables - Payables
        Return (FormatCurrency((Val(txtBHours.Text) * Val(txtBRate.Text)) - _
                (Val(txtPHours.Text) * Val(txtPRate.Text))))
    End Get
    Set(ByVal Value As String)
        'Nothing happens, can't set the profit directly
    End Set
End Property
```

Calling and Hiding Forms

The frmPersonnel form is the driver of the application. It will instantiate and call an instantiation of the frmDemographics and frmFinancials forms. Since the instances of the form will be accessed from more than one place in the frmPersonnel form, it is necessary to create a property for each to prevent the developer from making them visible to the entire form. Therefore, add the following code in the form's declaration section:

```
Private frmDemo As frmDemographics
Private frmFinance As frmFinancials
```

While the previous code declares the objects of each form, it does not instantiate them. Each form will be instantiated when the user clicks on the button associated with each form. In addition to instantiating them, the code will also set the Title property you created for the form so that it is personalized with the name of the person specified on the frmPersonnel form. The final step is to display the newly instantiated and initialized form. The code for both buttons follows:

```
Private Sub btnDemographics_Click(...
    frmDemo = New frmDemographics()
    frmDemo.Title = "Demographics for " & txtFirstName.Text & _
                " " & txtLastName.Text
    frmDemo.Show()
End Sub
```

```
Private Sub btnFinancial_Click(...
    frmFinance = New frmFinancials()
    frmFinance.Title = "Financials for " & txtFirstName.Text & " " & _
                    txtLastName.Text
    frmFinance.Show()
End Sub
```

The last code required on the frmPersonnel form is to display the profitability message when the btnProfit button is clicked. The code is merely a concatenation of

Strings that are accessible from the `frmPersonnel` form and the property statements of the `frmDemographics` and `frmFinancials` forms.

```
Private Sub btnProfit_Click(...
    MsgBox(txtFirstName.Text & " " & txtLastName.Text & " Net Profit is " & _
        frmFinance.Profit & ". He can be reached at " & _
        frmDemo.HomePhone, MsgBoxStyle.OKOnly, "Profit")
End Sub
```

What to Do When the First Form Created Isn't the First Form to Be Displayed

When you created your applications, you made sure that you first created the form that you wanted displayed as the default form of the application.

However, this is not always a practical solution. Therefore, Visual Basic .NET allows you to manually set the form to be displayed.

Step 1: Right-click on the MultiFormApp icon in the Solution Explorer.

Step 2: Click on the menu item Properties. Figure 12.22 will appear.

Step 3: Select the form that you wish to be the first form executed. Figure 12.22 shows the pull-down menu where you can select any of the forms in the project as the startup form (found in the Startup object drop-down box).

Figure 12.22
Startup object

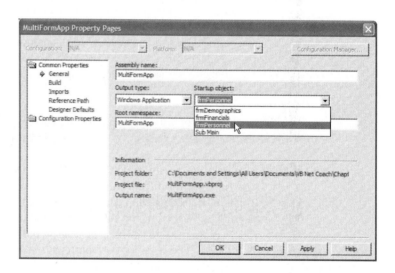

Global Variables

Way back toward the beginning of the text a brief mention was made of global variables. A **global variable** is one that is visible to the entire application. However, until this chapter, all your applications were created with a single form. Therefore, there was no need for a real global variable.

However, you have just seen how forms need to access data from each other. In some cases, it is easier to have a global variable that every form in the application can access without having to create the property statements that you did.

With the warning out of the way, when you do require a global variable, Visual Basic .NET provides an elegant solution. You can create a **Shared** variable in a `Public` class. When you add a single class to your application with only `Public` `Shared` properties declared within, all forms in the application will have access to it.

You may wonder what the difference is between a class defined in this manner versus using property statements. First, the syntax is less cumbersome. Second, and more important, an object of this class does not need to be declared or instantiated within your application. If you create a class as follows, it exists once for the entire application without the need to declare it.

```
Public Class ClassName
    Public Shared VariableName As VariableType
End Class
```

12.5 Multiple Document Interface (MDI)

Although the multiform application you just developed is an improvement over the single-formed applications you previously developed, it does not behave in the same manner as some multiform Windows applications with which you are familiar.

Applications like Microsoft Word are enclosed in a single parent form having child forms contained within it. Observe Figure 12.23, which shows your previous application developed as an **MDI** (Multiple Document Interface) application. Notice how the MDI form contains the three other forms that you created.

The choice of using MDI over the previous multiform implementation is mainly one of style and is easy to implement.

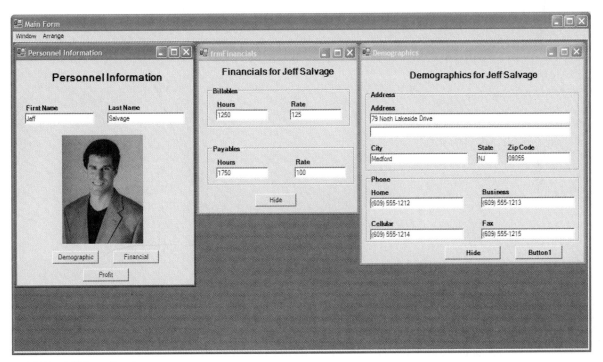

Figure 12.23   MDI application

Creating MDI Documents

The creation and operation of an MDI application does not vary much from other multiform applications. It requires designating one form as the parent form and attaching the other forms as children.

To define a form as the MDI parent, you must set the `IsMDIContainer` property of the form to `True`. To define a form as the MDI child, you must set the `MdiParent` property of the child form to the parent form.

Add the following code to the child window menu options:

```
Private Sub mnuWindowDemographics_Click(...
    frmDemo = New frmDemographics()
    frmDemo.MdiParent = Me
    frmDemo.Title = "Demographics for " & frmPerson.FullName
    frmDemo.Show()
End Sub

Private Sub mnuWindowFinancial_Click(...
    frmFinance = New frmFinancials()
    frmFinance.MdiParent = Me
    frmFinance.Title = "Financials for " & frmPerson.FullName
    frmFinance.Show()
End Sub

Private Sub mnuWindowPersonnel_Click(...
    frmPerson = New frmPersonnel()
    frmPerson.MdiParent = Me
    frmPerson.Show()
End Sub
```

COACH'S WARNING

The way the code is written, the user can receive an error if the Personnel form is not instantiated before the Demographics and Financial forms.

In each case, the code instantiates an object of the child window. The code then assigns the child window's `MdiParent` property to the parent form. Finally, it sets the `Title` property of the child window so that it displays the person's full name from the Personnel form.

There is really no difference between an MDI application's menu (see Figure 11.24) and an SDI application's menu. However, usually an MDI application's menu will include the options to arrange the windows either by cascading them, arranging them horizontally, or arranging them vertically. (See Figures 12.25 through 12.27.)

Window	Arrange
Demographics	Cascade
Financial	Tile Horizontally
Personnel	Tile Vertically
Profit	

Figure 12.24   Menu for your MDI application

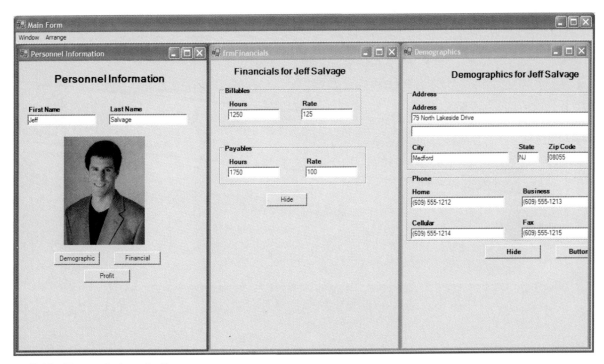

Figure 12.25   Forms tiled vertically

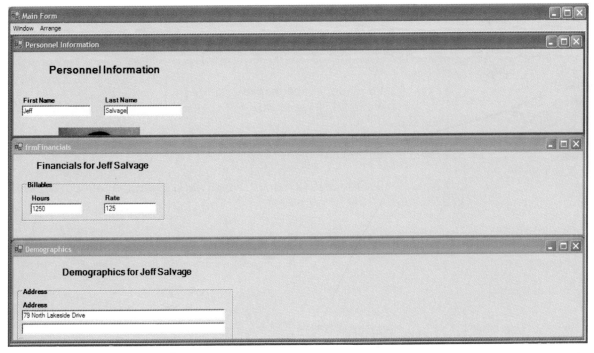

Figure 12.26   Forms tiled horizontally

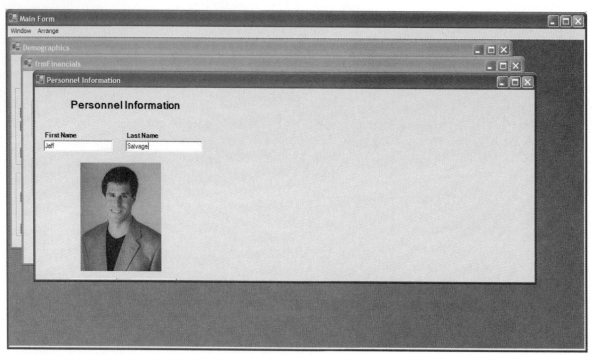

Figure 12.27   Forms cascaded

To arrange the child windows as in Figures 12.25 through 12.27, you must call the `LayoutMdi` method of the parent form as in the following syntax:

`MDIFormName.LayoutMDI(`*LayoutConstant*`)`

The layout constant is defined in the `System.Windows.Forms.MdiLayout` object. Therefore, the code for the menu events is as follows:

```
Private Sub mnuArrangeCascade_Click(...
    Me.LayoutMdi(System.Windows.Forms.MdiLayout.Cascade)
End Sub

Private Sub mnuArrangeHoriz_Click(...

Me.LayoutMdi(System.Windows.Forms.MdiLayout.TileHorizontal)
End Sub

Private Sub mnuArrangeVert_Click(...
    Me.LayoutMdi(System.Windows.Forms.MdiLayout.TileVertical)
End Sub
```

◆ 12.6 Case Study

Problem Description

Your final case study will combine many of the concepts you have learned throughout the text. By combining databases, menus, and multiform applications, you are now ready to develop a fairly usable application.

Observe the sketches of the three forms seen in Figures 12.28 through 12.30.

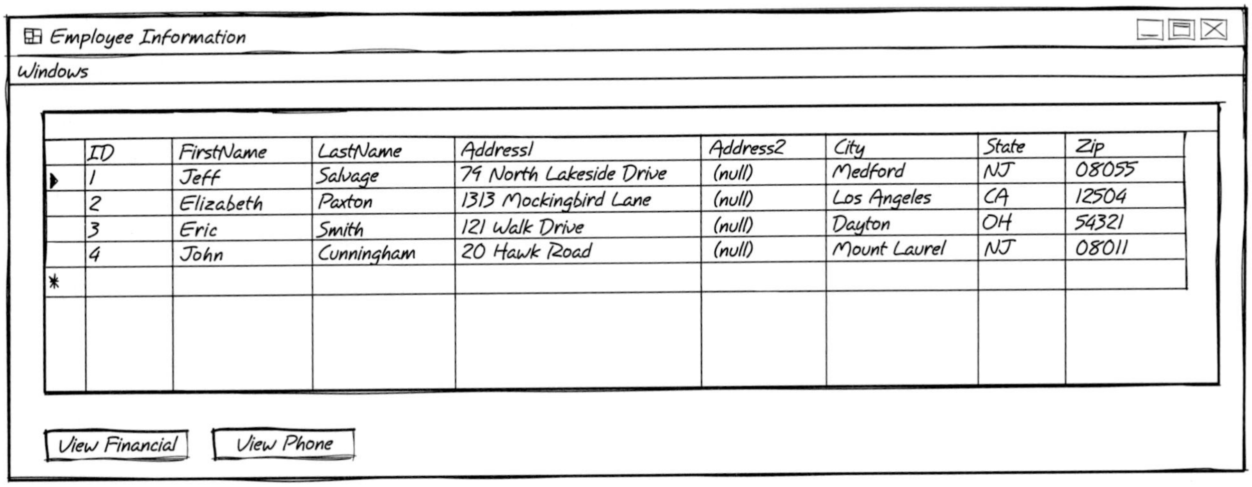

Figure 12.28 Employee form

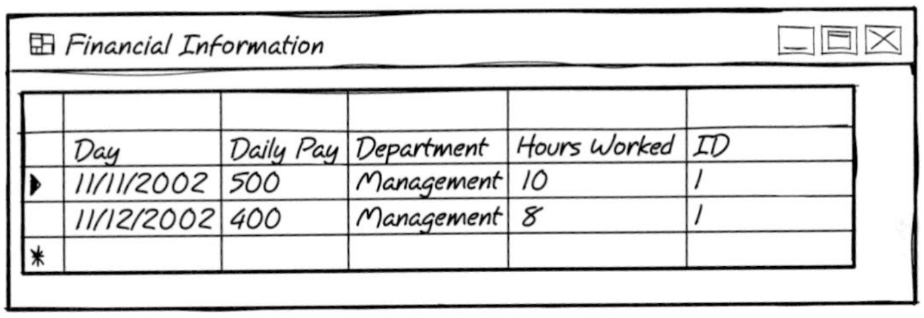

Figure 12.29
Financial form

Figure 12.30
Phone Number form

The three forms will display information in three tables from a new payroll database. The database stores employee information, financial data, and phone numbers for a group of people. Often more information is maintained about a single person than you may wish to display in a single form. Therefore, it is important to be able to link information contained in more than one table and display it in more than one form.

This application will display financial and contact information for the employee currently selected in the data grid of the Employee Information form.

Problem Discussion

The Access database containing the three tables is provided for you in the Chapter 12 directory of the code on the Addison-Wesley web site. Observe the structure of the three tables:

Employee Table

Field Name	Data Type	Size
ID	AutoNumber	N/A
LastName	Text	20
FirstName	Text	15
Address1	Text	50
Address2	Text	50
City	Text	20
State	Text	2
Zip	Text	5

Payroll Table

Field Name	Data Type	Size
ID	Long Integer	N/A
HoursWorked	Single	N/A
Department	Text	30
Day	Date/Time	N/A
DailyPay	Currency	N/A

Phone Number Table

Field Name	Data Type	Size
ID	Long Integer	N/A
HomePhone	Text	14
WorkPhone	Text	14
MobilePhone	Text	14

The ID field is used to link the records of one table to the other. An employee is automatically given an ID number when the record is created. When records are entered in the other tables, the person's ID field must be used.

By using this ID, you can preload the Financial and Contact Information forms with the appropriate employee's data.

While you can use an MDI solution, your solution here will use an SDI interface for simplicity. You will create the Employee form with a menu and call the other forms from there from either a menu item or button.

Problem Solution

Create a project called `Employee`.

Setting Up the Employee Information Form

Step 1: Rename the default form to `frmEmployee`.

Step 2: Change the `Text` property of the form to `Employee Information`.

Step 3: Create a data connection to the payroll database in Chapter 12's case study's code directory (located in the bin directory).

Step 4: Create a data adapter with a query that selects all the fields in the `Employee` table.

Step 5:   Generate a data set called `DsEmployee`.
Step 6:   Add a data grid called `grdEmployees` to the form.
Step 7:   Set the data grid's `DataSource` property to `DsEmployee1`.
Step 8:   Set the data grid's `Anchor` property to `Top, Bottom, Left, Right`.
Step 9:   Add a button called `btnFinancial` with a `Text` property of `View &Financial` to the `frmEmployee` form.
Step 10: Add a button called `btnPhone` with a `Text` property of `View &Phone` to the `frmEmployee` form.
Step 11: Add a main menu called `mnuWindow` with a `Text` property of `&Window` to the `frmEmployee` form.
Step 12: Add a menu item called `mnuWindowFinancial` with a `Text` property of `View &Financial` to the `mnuWindow` menu.
Step 13: Add a menu item called `mnuWindowPhone` with a `Text` property of `View &Phone` to the `mnuWindow` menu.

Code must be added to the form, but you'll add it after the other forms have been created.

Setting Up the Financial Information Form

COACH'S TIP

To place a parameter in the `WHERE` clause, you must place an `= ?` in the Criteria window of the ID column of the Query Builder.

Step 1:   Create a new window's form and name it `frmFinancials`.
Step 2:   Change the `Text` property of the form to `Financial Information`.
Step 3:   Create a data adapter, using the data connector you previously created, with a query that selects all the fields in the `Payroll` table with a parameter on the ID field in the `WHERE` clause.
Step 4:   Generate a data set called `DsPayroll1`.
Step 5:   Add a data grid called `grdFinancial` to the form.
Step 6:   Set the data grid's `DataSource` property to `DsPayroll1.Payroll`.
Step 7:   Set the data grid's `Anchor` property to `Top, Bottom, Left, Right`.
Step 8:   When the Financial Information form is called, you must query the database and load the data grid with only the financial records of the employee indicated by the row selected in the data grid of the Employee form. The easiest way to pass this information from the Employee form to the Financial form is to create a property on the Financial form that stores the current employee. The Employee form can set it when the Financial form is called. All the coding required can be written in the `Set` statement of the property. First the parameter in the data adapter's select query is set, and then the data adapter's `Fill` method is called.

```
Private intEmployee As Integer
Public Property EmployeeID()
    Get
        'Nothing goes here, no need
    End Get
    Set(ByVal Value)
        intEmployee = Value
        OleDbDataAdapter1.SelectCommand.Parameters(0).Value = Employee
        OleDbDataAdapter1.Fill(DsPayroll1)
    End Set
End Property
```

Setting Up the Contact Information Form

Step 1: Create a new form and name it `frmContact`.
Step 2: Change the `Text` property of the form to `Contact Information`.

Step 3: Create a data adapter, using the data connector you previously created, with a query that selects all the fields in the `PhoneNumbers` table with a parameter on the ID field in the `WHERE` clause.

Step 4: Generate a data set called `DsPhone1`.

Step 5: Add three labels, with a bold font, called `lblHome`, `lblWork`, and `lblMobile`, with their `Text` properties set to `Home`, `Work`, and `Mobile`, respectively.

Step 6: Add three text boxes, below the labels, with a blank `Text` field named `txtHome`, `txtWork`, and `txtMobile`.

Step 7: Set the `DataBindings Text` property to `DsPhone1 - PhoneNumbers.HomePhone`, `DsPhone1 - PhoneNumbers.WorkPhone`, and `DsPhone1 - PhoneNumbers.MobilePhone` for the text boxes `txtHome`, `txtWork`, and `txtMobile`, respectively.

Step 8: The code for linking the Contact form to the Employee form is nearly identical to the code you used for the Financial form:

```
Private Employee As Integer
Public Property EmployeeID()
    Get
        'Nothing goes here, no need
    End Get
    Set(ByVal Value)
        Employee = Value
        OleDbDataAdapter1.SelectCommand.Parameters(0).Value = Employee
        OleDbDataAdapter1.Fill(DsContact1)
    End Set
End Property
```

Adding the Final Code to the Employee Information Form

Step 1: Add the following two properties to the form so the forms you create that are referenced from this form can be accessed by the entire form.

```
Private Financial As frmFinancial
Private Contact As frmContact
```

Step 2: While the code for calling the additional forms can be coded in the button and menu items' `Click` events, it is better to create a separate subroutine for calling each additional form. This way the code does not have to be repeated, and if you had to go back and modify it, the code would only require changing in one place.

```
Private Sub FinancialForm()
    Financial = Nothing
    Financial = New frmFinancial()
    Financial.EmployeeID =
DsEmployee1.Tables(0).Rows(grdEmployees.CurrentRowIndex)(0)
    Financial.Show()
End Sub

Private Sub ContactForm()
    Contact = New frmContact()
    Contact.EmployeeID = _
            DsEmployee1.Tables(0).Rows(grdEmployees.CurrentRowIndex)(0)
```

(continues)

(continued)

```
    Contact.Show()
End Sub
```

Step 3: Now the code for both the button and menu objects' `Click` events calling the form are just a call to the subroutine created in Step 2.

```
Private Sub btnPayroll_Click(...
    FinancialForm()
End Sub

Private Sub btnPhone_Click(...
    ContactForm()
End Sub

Private Sub mnuWindowFinancial_Click(...
    FinancialForm()
End Sub

Private Sub mnuWindowPhone_Click(...
    ContactForm()
End Sub
```

The final application will look as shown in Figures 12.31 through 12.33.

Figure 12.31
Employee form

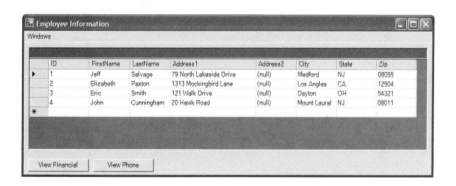

Figure 12.32
Financial form

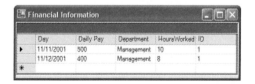

Figure 12.33
Phone Number form

Key Words and Key Terms

Brush

An object used to draw patterns on a `Graphics` object.

Cascade

One of the options for laying out forms in an MDI application that arranges the child windows within each window slightly overlapping the others.

Catch

A keyword used to check error conditions.

Color

An object that stores all the predefined colors available.

DrawRectangle

A method of the `Graphics` object that will draw an outline of a rectangle.

Err

An object that stores the number and description of the last error that occurred.

FillRectangle

A method of the `Graphics` object that will draw a filled-in rectangle.

Finally

A keyword indicating what code should execute after a `Try-Catch` statement is executed.

Global Variables

A variable that is visible to the entire application.

Graphics

An object used to draw on other objects.

Hide

A method that causes a form to no longer to display, although it will not unload the form from the computer's memory.

MainMenu

An object that allows frequently used operations to be accessed in a user-friendly manner.

MDI

Multiple Document Interface, an application that can have more than one form open at a time.

Pen

An object used to draw a line on a `Graphics` object.

Point

An object representing a point on a `Graphics` object.

Rectangle

An object representing a rectangle on a `Graphics` object.

SDI

Single Document Interface, an application that has only one form open at a time.

Shared

A keyword indicating that a variable is accessible by the entire application.

Show

A method that loads and displays a form.

Size

An object that represents a length and a width.

Submenu

A menu that pops up from an existing menu.

System.Drawing Namespace

The namespace required to access the functionality of many graphics.

Tile Horizontally

One of the options for laying out forms in an MDI application that arranges the child windows within each window from top to bottom.

Tile Vertically

One of the options for laying out forms in an MDI application that arranges the child windows within each window from left to right.

Try

A keyword indicating which code to execute while being protected by an error handler.

Additional Exercises

Questions 1–10 are true or false.

1. More than one menu can be associated with a single form.

2. In an MDI application, the first form created will be the first form to be displayed. This cannot be changed.

3. The only way to draw a rectangle is to issue four draw line commands.

4. A `Finally` statement executes only if all the `Catch` statements fail.

5. You can access the `Graphics` object with the default namespace.

6. In an MDI application, the `Private` properties of a parent form can be directly accessed by the child form.

7. There is no difference between the functionality of a `Brush` and a `Pen` object.

8. Hiding a form does not close it.

9. A hidden form's `Public` properties cannot be accessed by other forms.

10. An object with all of its properties declared as `Public` and `Shared` must be instantiated once in order to be accessible by all forms in a project.

11. Identify a menu, a menu item, and a submenu item in the Visual Basic .NET IDE.

12. Are all multiple form applications considered MDI applications? Explain why or why not.

13. Assuming code is placed after the `Try-Catch` statements, what type of error could the following code trap for the protected code?

```
Try
    'Code to check for error
    Protected Code goes here
Catch When Err.Number = 6
    'Code to process this Catch
Catch When Err.Number = 53
    'Code to process this Catch
Catch
    'Code to process this Catch
End Try
```

14. Write a `Try-Catch` statement that checks for an overflow when performing the following calculation: `intSum = intValue1 + intValue2`. If an overflow occurs, set `intSum` equal to `-1`.

15. Write an application that draws a truck using the line and circle commands. (See Figure 12.34.)

Figure 12.34
Drawing of truck

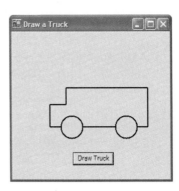

16. Create an application that will draw a square, a circle, or a line on the form in either red, blue, green, black, or yellow. The application should have two menus. The first, Draw Figure, should have the items Draw Square, Draw Circle, and Draw Line. The second, Pen Color, should have the items Red, Blue, Green, Black, and Yellow. When a Draw Figure item is picked, the associated figure should be drawn in the last color picked from the Pen Color menu. If no pen color has been selected, default the color to Black.

17. Convert the case study to an MDI application.

18. The manner in which the case study MDI application was coded allows a form to be opened more than once. Change the application you created in question 17 so that this cannot happen.

19. The manner in which the Personnel application was coded in the Personnel Information example in this chapter allows a form to be opened with a reference to a form that has not been instantiated yet. Change the code to prevent this from happening.

BIBLIOGRAPHY

HOLLIS, BILLY AND ROCKFORD LHOTKA. *VB.NET Programming with the Public Beta.* Wrox Press, 2001.

MSDN Magazine. February 2001, Vol. 16, No. 2. Microsoft, 2001.

MSDN Magazine. July 2001, Vol. 16, No. 7. Microsoft, 2001.

ROMAN, STEVEN. *VB .NET Language in a Nutshell.* O'Reilly, 2001.

SALVAGE, JEFF. *The Visual Basic Coach.* Addison-Wesley, 2001.

Visual Basic Programmer's Journal. February 2001, Vol. 11, No. 2.

INDEX

Notes

Notes

Notes

Notes